PENGUIN BOOKS

THE CHANGE

Germaine Greer was born in 1939 and educated at the universities of Melbourne, Sydney and Cambridge. Her first book, *The Female Eunuch* (1969), was an international bestseller. Her subsequent books include *The Obstacle Race*, *Sex and Destiny*, *The Madwoman's Underclothes*, *Kissing the Rod* (ed.) and *Daddy, We Hardly Knew You*. She lives on three acres near a roundabout in Essex and teaches at Newnham College, Cambridge.

GERMAINE GREER

THE CHANGE

WOMEN, AGEING
AND THE MENOPAUSE

PENGUIN BOOKS

For Ann and Julia

PENGUIN BOOKS

Published by the Penguin Group
Penguin Books Ltd, 27 Wrights Lane, London W8 5TZ, England
Penguin Books USA Inc., 375 Hudson Street, New York, New York 10014, USA
Penguin Books Australia Ltd, Ringwood, Victoria, Australia
Penguin Books Canada Ltd, 10 Alcorn Avenue, Toronto, Ontario, Canada M4V 3B2
Penguin Books (NZ) Ltd, 182–190 Wairau Road, Auckland 10, New Zealand

Penguin Books Ltd, Registered Offices: Harmondsworth, Middlesex, England

First published by Hamish Hamilton 1991
Published in Penguin Books 1992
3 5 7 9 10 8 6 4

Printed in England by Clays Ltd, St Ives plc

Contents

Acknowledgements

The author and publishers would like to thank the following publishers and literary representatives for permission to quote copyright material:

Doreen Asso: to John Wiley & Sons Ltd for extracts from *The Real Menstrual Cycle* (1983)

Elizabeth Bishop: to Farrar, Straus & Giroux, Inc., for the poem 'One Art' from *Complete Poems 1927–1979* (The Hogarth Press, 1984)

Simone de Beauvoir: to André Deutsch Ltd for extracts from *Force of Circumstance* (1965)

Helene Deutsch: to W. W. Norton & Co. for extracts from *Confrontations with Myself: An Epilogue* (1973); to the Institute of Psychoanalysis, London, for extracts from 'The Menopause' published in the *International Journal of Psycho-Analysis, 65* (1984).

Emily Dickinson: to Harvard University Press for poems from *The Collected Poems*, ed. T. H. Johnson (Faber & Faber, 1970). Reprinted by permission of the publishers and the Trustees of Amherst College from *The Poems of Emily Dickinson*, Thomas H. Johnson, ed., Cambridge, Mass.: The Belknap Press of Harvard University Press, copyright 1951, © 1955, 1979, 1983 by the President and Fellows of Harvard College

Rosemary Dobson: to Collins/Angus & Robertson Publishers for an extract from 'Amy Caroline' from *Collected Poems*, © Rosemary Dobson, 1991

B. Evans: to Pan Books for extracts from *Life Change: A Guide to the Menopause, Its Effects and Treatment*, 4th Edition (1988)

Doris Lessing: to Random Century Group for extracts from *The Summer Before the Dark* (Jonathan Cape, 1973)

Patrick McGrady: to Weidenfeld & Nicolson, Ltd, for extracts from *The Youth Doctors* (Arthur Barker, 1969)

Ann Mankowitz: to Inner City Books, Toronto, for extracts from *Change of Life: A Psychological Study of Dreams and the Menopause* (1984)

Gabriel García Márquez: to Random Century Group for extracts from *Love in the Time of Cholera* (1989)

Willa Muir: to Enitharmon Press for the poem 'Where is my love, my Dear?' from *Laconics, Jingles & Other Verses* (1969)

Iris Murdoch: to Random Century Group for extracts from *Bruno's Dream* (Penguin Books, 1987)

Linda Pastan: to W. W. Norton & Co. for poems from *The Five Stages of Grief* (1978)

Margaret Powell: to William Heinemann Ltd for extracts from *The Treasure Upstairs* (Pan Books, 1972). Reprinted by permission of William Heinemann Ltd

Vita Sackville-West: to Random Century Group for extracts from *All Passion Spent* (L. and V. Woolf, 1931). Reprinted by permission of Curtis Brown Ltd, © Nigel Nicolson, 1931

Stevie Smith: to James MacGibbon for extracts from *The Collected Poems of Stevie Smith* (Penguin Books, 1985)

Elizabeth Jennings: to David Higham Associates Ltd for 'Let Things Alone', 'Growing' and 'Accepted' from *Collected Poems* (Carcanet Press, 1986)

While every effort has been made to trace copyright holders, this has not been possible in all cases; any omissions brought to our attention will of course be remedied in future editions.

Introduction

It is not quite forty years since eliminating menopause was first mooted. The idea did not come from women but from men who thought that the cessation of ovulation was a premature death, a tragedy. To be sure there were women who asked for help from male professionals during the climacteric, as the years of the change are not easy to traverse. The help that was given was, at first, the only treatment doctors had for anything, namely bleeding and purging, accompanied by an array of ineffectual medications, some of which continued to be marketed at high prices for hundreds of years as Dr So-and-so's 'female pills', setting a pattern for the exploitation of the 'little health of ladies' that persists to this day. Next the learned gentlemen tried to reactivate menstruation from another site, by opening issues of blood; from this they proceeded to hysterectomy and castration, often for the mental derangements that were thought to accompany the decline of the catamenia, as the menstrual losses were called. No sooner had they discovered electricity than they began thrusting electrified rods into the uterus; one of the first uses for X-rays was to bombard the ovary so as to kill it; Marie Curie had not long discovered radium before radium rods were being inserted in the vagina. Physicians had to content themselves with dosing women with parts of the reproductive systems of other species or with juices derived from their ductless glands.

There was always another school of thought that held that the climacteric was in truth less stressful than other periods in the travailed female life course. As long as childbirth was unavoidable and dangerous, this was clearly true. Partly because there was a disproportionate number of virgins over the age of fifty, climacteric problems became associated with old maids, adding greatly to the prejudice against them and against menopause. By the mid nineteenth century, when the climacteric was first given the name 'menopause', public awareness of a menopausal syndrome was greatly complicating the problems that the middle-aged woman had no option but to face. The irrational certainty that the womb was the real cause of the ageing woman's anger or melancholy effectively obscured the inconvenient possibility that she may have had genuine grounds for protest; women on the other hand obligingly internalized their own rage and produced a bewildering array of symptoms, many of which responded to hideous invasive procedures that can have had no genuine therapeutic function at all. Obstacles to negotiation of what is in fact a stressful stage in female life began to pile up, and menopausal distress accumulated around them.

In the guise of immense chivalrous sympathy for women destroyed by the tragedy of menopause, a group of male professionals permitted themselves to give full vent to an irrational fear of old women, which I have called, from the Latin *anus*, meaning old woman, anophobia. These are the men whose names appear on hundreds of learned papers every year, elaborating the possibilities of eliminating menopause and keeping all women both appetizing and responsive to male demand from puberty to the grave, driving the dreaded old woman off the face of the earth for ever.

There are positive aspects to being a frightening old woman. Though the old woman is both feared and reviled, she need not take the intolerance of others to heart, for women over fifty already form one of the largest groups in the population structure of the western world. As long as they like themselves, they will not be an oppressed minority. In order to like themselves they must reject trivialization by others of who and what they are. A grown woman should not have to masquerade as a girl in order to remain in the land of the living. The result of capitulation to pressure to do just that has resulted in a gallery of grotesques whose pathetic attempts to start all over again are the staple of our gossip magazines. There have always been women who ignored the eternal youth bandwagon and agreed to grow up, who negotiated the climacteric with a degree of independence and dignity and changed their lives to give their new adulthood space to function and flower. In a childish world this behaviour is seen as threatening. Nobody knows what to do with a woman who is not perpetually smiling and fawning. Calm, grave, quiet women drive anophobes to desperation. Women who refuse even to try to empower the penis are old bats and old bags, crones, mothers-in-law, castrating women and so forth. Though female culture cannot afford to give such attitudes even token respectability, we could see our way to exploit male panic if we dared. As women are the arbiters of birth, they are also the managers of death, within the womb and out of it. They have the spiritual resources to confront and deal with both, but men are terrified to leave such matters in their hands.

This is one book that seeks neither to trivialize nor to medicalize the menopause. The climacteric is a mysterious time about which sinister myths continue to cling. It is not illuminated by the proliferation of pronouncements defining it by the Masters in Menopause, those male professionals who with the willing assistance of the pharmaceutical multinationals have made a lucrative career out of an experience they will never undergo. It is a continuing aspect of the menopause industry that the few women practitioners who allow themselves to become involved seldom corroborate either the evidence for massive derangement of female faculties during the climacteric or the miraculous results of the administration of extracts of mares' urine.

Though there is no public rite of passage for the woman approaching the end of her reproductive years, there is evidence that women devise their own private ways of marking the ir-revocability of the change. Part of the mythology is that there are women who experience nothing significant at this time, which if it were true would be lamentable, for the goal of life is not to feel nothing. The climacteric is a time of stock-taking, of spiritual as well as physical change, and it would be a pity to be unconscious of it. Certainly many women do not seek medical help for climacteric distress, but this has more to do with their attitude to doctors and their coping style than with the extent to which they experience symptoms. It is probable, however, that menopausal symptoms are becoming objectively more serious as a result of pre-menopausal medical intervention, especially sterilization and hysterectomy, and of the pressure to keep young, fit and beautiful if you want to be loved, and of addiction and of environmental poisons. There is a proportion of women who suffer unbearable symptoms during the climacteric but the unluckiest ones are the ones who undergo destructive procedures, sometimes a series of destructive procedures, to eliminate disorders that time and patience would have dealt with unaided.

In most medical literature addressed to women there is a tendency to exaggerate the extent to which women have brought their difficulties upon themselves. Arguments based upon the assumption that women are in control of their own lives and get the menopause they deserve simply absolve the practitioner of any obligation or responsibility. Many women only realize during the climacteric the extent to which their lives have been a matter of capitulation and how little of what has happened to them has actually been in their interest. Women discovering for the first time that they are actually poor, dependent, insecure and lonely don't need to be burdened with a weight of guilt as well. They do need, on the other hand, to take the control of their own lives that is now available by default. To be unwanted is also to be free.

The fifth climacteric is the time when a woman plans the rest of her life; if she has not the financial resources, the education or the energy, it is not too late to acquire them. If she approaches this challenge in apologetic mode, haunted by guilt or by fears of psychological inadequacy, she cannot make the decisions upon which her future happiness depends. She must reject any argument that holds that she has brought her present distress upon herself.

On the other hand, if she persists in imagining that control of her life is exercised from outside herself, she will not achieve well-being. She will go down into darkness as a complaining, querulous, naughty, old *girl*.

Whatever her temporary discomforts, the menopausal woman has eventually to confront the problem of ageing. Again medical science can give her very little help. Ageing is the most idiosyncratic of all human processes and predictions cannot be made about any individual's ageing career. Still, the wise woman can decide to age no faster than she absolutely must. This may involve her in drastic alterations of life-style and complete reordering of priorities. Some of the crutches she has been using will have to be kicked away. Bad habits will have to be given up. The role of menopause in her ageing is not easy to evaluate; some women produce significant amounts of oestrogen after cessation of ovulation, others do not. Replacement oestrogen may protect against the effects of ageing on the cardiovascular system and the skeleton, or it may not.

The enormous proliferation of menopause literature belies the utter lack of understanding of what is really going on. No one knows why ovulation ceases or even when it ceases, or what symptoms are caused by it and not by ageing, or even whether younger menopauses are more easily lived through than older ones. Nothing about menopause can be predicted, no risk factors can be isolated, no preventive measures suggested. Every year adds new symptoms to climacteric syndrome and every year takes some off. We have lost involutional melancholy and gained autogenic dysregulation. At all levels and in all therapies placebo response is high, sometimes dominant. All experimental results are compromised by the multiplicity of symptoms and by the self-limiting nature of the phenomenon.

Officially the medical establishment has one treatment for the climacteric, and that is hormone replacement therapy; in fact this is a multiplicity of regimes using a multiplicity of products in various combinations and strengths. No single individual can find his way around the whole gamut, and patients certainly will not be given the option. Selection of patients suitable for treatment is governed by the subjective impressions of the practitioner, and selection of the treatment regimen is a matter of serendipity. Investigations of counter-indications ignore important and common ailments such as varicose veins and give far too much attention to the negligible risk of cancer. Opposing oestrogen with progestogens probably undoes its most important protective effect. The administration of oestrogen by the oral route makes no sense at all. Apart from these considerations, HRT is a valuable contribution to the pharmaceutical armamentarium, particularly for the multinationals who have patented the oestrogen preparations.

Traditionally women have not made a great fuss about menopause. When older women were in charge of the birthplace they witnessed frequent agony and death among the childbearing women, and had reason to congratulate themselves on having survived. They medicated themselves when necessary with simple preparations of plant material according to the season. There is no agreement in this vast pharmacopoeia because it is entirely reliant upon microclimates and cannot be duplicated in different circumstances. When male professionals took over medical practice they too developed nostrums of their own, but the principle of useless standardization was early set. The least destructive ladies' doctors prescribed a cooling diet or adding a little wine to their regimen to keep their spirits up, and recommended a change of air, a long stay in one of the many spas where the middle-aged woman could not only take the waters but rest, walk, fast or diet, and recover from the multiplicity of childbed accidents she was likely to have undergone. Recourse to spas, which was part of traditional medical practice since the iron age, fades into hydrotherapy and alternative medicine, which offers an array of treatments for climacteric distress, most of which have the advantage of being relatively non-invasive and harmless.

No matter how good or effective the treatment of physical symptoms at the climacteric may be, there are some aspects of being a fifty-year-old woman that cannot be cured and must be endured. Sooner or later the middle-aged woman becomes aware of a change in the attitude of other people towards her. She can no longer trade on her appearance, something which she has done unconsciously all her life. There is no defined role for her in modern society; before she can devise one for herself she experiences a period of free fall, which brings with it panic. Her physical symptoms may be such that she is always tired and cannot summon up the energy to haul herself through to the next phase. There are two aspects of her emotional condition at this time; one I have called misery, which has no useful function and should be avoided, and the other grief, which is wholesome, though painful, and must be recognized. The misery of the middle-aged woman is a grey and hopeless thing, born of having nothing to live for, of disappointment and resentment at having been gypped by consumer society, and surviving merely to be the butt of its unthinking scorn. Grief at the death of the womb is, in Iris Murdoch's phrase, an 'august and terrible pain' unlike anything a woman can have experienced before, but she comes through it stronger and calmer, aware that death having brushed her with its wing has retreated to its accustomed place, and all will be well.

Most books about women and ageing devote a significant proportion of their pages to the discussion of sexual activity, regardless of whether the middle-aged reader has the prospect of sexual activity or not. Rather than reassuring the sexually inactive woman that she will become neither mad nor ill as a result of her failure to exercise her genitals regularly or at all, such books address themselves to the wife who is losing interest, encouraging her to use medications and any other resources she can find to fan her waning flame. Rather less is said about what she might do to stimulate her 'partner's' flagging interest, or what she might do to repel his advances if they were unwelcome. If the sexuality of older women were allowed to define itself, it is possible that we would discover that older women are not overwhelmed with desire for even older men. There may be something more to be said for the bar on the Piccola Marina where love came to Mrs Wentworth-Brewster than has hitherto been admitted. The secret lusts of old ladies are not the important point here, however; what is important is to debunk the reverence that hushes the voices of all other writers on the topic, who present sexual congress with one's spouse as a duty from the altar to the grave, rather like cleaning one's teeth and keeping one's bowels open. It is a variant on the author's well-known if misunderstood position that 'no sex is better than bad sex'.

There are of course women in history who have inspired love in middle age and kept it till death intervened, without the aid of cosmetic surgery or oestrogen replacement. The stories of Diane de Poitiers and Madame de Maintenon, both of whom in middle age won and kept the love of a king of France who might have had as concubine any of the most beautiful women in the country any time he wanted, are encouraging, if only because they imply that there is more to a woman than two taut breasts and ankles that she can cross behind her head. Neither of them would have looked good in shorts. The hardy perennials of our own time are less encouraging, because their charms depend upon expensive imitations of the girlish charm of much younger women. They are allowed to be nothing but body; they must take up hours every day preparing the imitation body that is all their stock-in-trade. When transsexuals have stopped stuffing their chests with silastic implants because they have realized that they feel cold, look odd, and have an unpleasant habit of wandering about or working themselves through the skin, beautiful women are unashamed to tell their fans that their nubile bosoms are fake. They would be ashamed, on the other hand, to admit that they were on HRT.

This book suggests other role models for the ageing woman, role models who are not simply glittering threads, some bones, some silastic and hanks of hand-knotted bought hair. If the world has dubbed you crone, you might as well be one. There is no point in growing old unless you can be a witch, and accumulate spiritual power in place of the political and economic power that

has been denied you as a woman. Witches are descended from the
sibyls and female saints; their lineage is noble and no woman need
be ashamed to call herself a witch. This does not mean that she has
to dress up and babble meaningless formulae in cellars and crypts.
The wild white witches live outdoors and hobnob with the lower
orders.

The object of facing up squarely to the fact of the climacteric is
to acquire serenity and power. If women on the youthful side of
the climacteric could glimpse what this state of peaceful potency
might be, the difficulties of making the transition would be less. It
is the nature of the case that life beyond the menopause is as
invisible to the woman who has yet to struggle through the
change as the top of any mountain is invisible from the valley
below. Calm and poise do not simply happen to the post-
menopausal woman; she has to fight for them. When the fight is
over her altered state might look to a younger woman rather like
exhaustion, when in reality it is anything but. The dependent
woman is obliged to believe that only her turmoil of passion, fear,
rage, expectancy and disappointment is living and that when she is
no longer tormented by desire, insecurity, jealousy and the rest of
the paraphernalia of romance she will be as dead as a spent match.
The difference between her clamorous feelings and the feelings of
the silent, apparently withdrawn older woman is the difference
between the perception of the sea of someone tossing upon the
surface, and of one who has plunged so deep that she has felt
death in her throat. The older woman's love is not love of herself,
nor of herself mirrored in a lover's eyes, nor is it corrupted by
need. It is a feeling of tenderness so still and deep and warm that it
gilds every grassblade and blesses every fly. It includes the ones
who have a claim on it, and a great deal else besides. I wouldn't
have missed it for the world.

I

The Undescribed Experience

A few months after my fiftieth birthday, my friend Julia and I
were sitting in Beaubourg, in yellow spring sunshine. Around the
corner we could buy wonderful things to eat with the dew of the
country still on them, wild mushrooms and bitter salads, and
armfuls of cornflowers to look at while we ate them. Our coffee
had been delicious and the croissants light and buttery.

'I won't live like that,' said Julia. Her eyes were fixed on a little
grey lady with a plastic shopping basket apologetically threading
her way through the gaudy prostitutes and lounging boys on the
pavement opposite. 'I won't live in some bedsit with a plate and a
knife and a fork and creep out to the market each day for a slice of
cheese and a baguette. I won't become grey and invisible. I think
what happened to my mother, those years of not knowing where
or who she was. I'm not taking that road. I've thought about it. It
won't be an unconsidered decision. I don't see the point of the
next twenty, thirty years. To get so's your own body makes you
sick, no matter how hard you struggle to keep your looks, and
keep fit. I can't see the point of battling against it, when you
know the outcome can only be defeat. It's so unfair.'

Julia's anxiety, with its telescoping of the next thirty years into a
single grim tomorrow, is typical of the climacterium. We had
both sailed through our forties with very little awareness of
growing older. We had each buried a parent; she had shed a
husband, but we had both remained at the centre of the life we
had built. Suddenly something was slipping away so fast that we

had not had time quite to register what it might be. All we knew was that it was irreplaceable. The way ahead seemed dark. Somewhere along the line optimism seemed to have perished. Neither of us could identify this feeling of apprehensive melancholy; since then I have learned to recognize it in the writings of other women:

Far away behind her, far below the horizon, she knew the sun still shone. But it never rose, it had not risen in her sleep now for days, for weeks. She was still travelling north, away from the sun. Ahead of her lay winter, ice, an interminable dark. (Lessing, 218)

'Those men are our age, probably older than we are.' Julia was looking towards a table where two grey-haired men were being listened to by two sleek, expensive and very much younger women, who appeared to be utterly enthralled by their every utterance. 'It's bloody unfair. Those men can have their pick of women of any age. They can go on for years, and here we are, finished. They wouldn't even look at us.' The unkind sunlight showed every sag, every pucker, every bluish shadow, every mole, every freckle in our fifty-year-old faces. When we beckoned to the waiter he seemed not to see us, and when he had taken our order he seemed to forget it and we had been obliged to remind him.

'Now what do I do?' Julia asked. 'Am I supposed to haunt the singles bars and try to pick up younger men? Am I supposed to descend lower and lower into squalor because I won't live without love? Or am I supposed to just work, and come home and eat and watch telly and go to bed day after day, until I get too old to work? Am I supposed to become that?' Her eyes followed the anonymous lady delicately picking her way home, the end of her baguette poking out of the plastic shopping bag. 'Just thinking about it fills me with terror. I lie awake at night, worrying. What will become of me?'

I would have rattled off some names of other fifty-year-old women who had overcome the climacteric and been reborn into a different kind of life, but they were not names that sprang readily to mind. I needed role models for a woman learning to shift the focus of her attention away from her body ego towards her soul, but for the life of me then and there I could not summon to mind a single one. The journey inwards towards wisdom and serenity is as long, if not longer, than the headlong rush of our social and sexual career, but there are no signposts to show the way. If there are leaders beckoning, most of us have no idea who they might be.

Though the literature on menopause is vast, almost none of it has been written by women. Most of it has been written by men for the eyes of other men; thousands of middle-aged women troop meekly through the pages of hundreds of studies assessing their health, their well-being, their status, their needs, their opportunities, and their problems and we hear hardly one word in their own voices. The Masters in Menopause (by analogy with Masters in Lunacy and Masters in Bankruptcy) are men, men like Wulf H. Utian, who discovered menopause in 1967. His own account is unintentionally revealing (1978, 9):

In 1967 I happened to be in West Berlin and was invited to visit a major international pharmaceutical firm. A new female hormone was mentioned and thereby started my interest in the subject. Upon my return to Cape Town . . . I approached the Chairman of the Department of Gynaecology of the University of Cape Town . . . and spelled out my plans for a menopause clinic.

Utian's menopause clinic, the first in the world, was set up at Groote Schuur, where Christiaan Barnard had performed the first heart transplant two years earlier. Its name was changed to the Femininity Clinic, and then as the notion caught on that menopause could be 'eliminated', it was renamed the Mature Woman Clinic. Utian moved on from Cape Town to the Mount Sinai Medical Centre in Ohio and continues to be the acknowledged doyen of menopause experts, the Grand Master in Menopause.

The multinational pharmaceutical company that has its head office in Berlin is Schering; Schering manufacture and distribute worldwide a formidable array of steroidal preparations for the dosing of women under the names Anovlar, Controvlar, Cycloprogynova, Eugynon, Gynovlar, Logynon, Microgynon, Minovlar, Neogest, Norgeston, Noristerat, Primolut N, Progynova and Proluton. The new hormone was oestradiol valerate, nowadays marketed as Progynova and with a progestogen as Cycloprogynova. Utian's egregious account of a progress from the manufacture of a remedy to the definition of a disease is included in *The Menopause Manual: A Woman's Guide to the Menopause*, published in England in 1978, by which time menopause was big business.

While Wulf Utian was preparing the ground for Schering, the huge Dutch multinational AKZO group was preparing its own onslaught on the replacement steroid market. In 1969 they endowed the magniloquently titled International Health Foundation with headquarters in Geneva and 600,000 Swiss francs a year to spend on furthering 'the health of mankind by identifying and contributing to the solution of human physical, mental and social problems through programmes of research and education and by providing information in medical and all related sciences'. The immediate beneficiary was their wholly owned subsidiary, Organon International BV, manufacturers of ethinyloestradiol in tablet form and as implants, and of Ovestin vaginal cream. Extending the pharmaceuticals operation saved the AKZO group in the early seventies; nowadays pharmaceuticals account for 14 per cent or more of their total operation, which turned over more than 16 billion Dutch guilders in 1986. The International Health Foundation seems to have come into existence to publish three studies on menopause; its director-general was the Dutch Master in Menopause, Pieter van Keep, MD, second only to Wulf Utian in generating learned articles, all based at first on the same AKZO-funded studies. Nowadays the IHF operates from Brussels rather than from Geneva.

The next step in opening up an international market for a new systemic medication is to organize interested professionals into a prestigious body and to publish the proceedings of their meetings. In 1976 the International Menopause Society held its inaugural meeting at La Grande Motte in France and set up its own journal, *Maturitas*, principally to publish the results of further studies and trials of replacement hormones. The ultimate aim was and is to get government funding to spread the gospel of HRT into every hovel on the planet. The arithmetic is simple. Post-menopausal health problems, notably osteoporosis, tie up expensive hospital facilities for hundreds of thousands of woman-hours a year and they will tie up hundreds of thousands more, as life expectancy improves around the globe. Educating women to accept HRT makes sense. God forbid that I should imply that Schering and Organon, Utian and Van Keep are motivated by any but the highest motives.

The official view of the International Menopause Society is that menopause is a social construct, that illness is not the only response, that women need to know what a normal menopause is, whether their own is abnormal, and what doctors can do about alleviating their symptoms, that the approach to menopause is polarized between dismissing the menopausal woman and telling her to get on with it, and treating menopause itself as a deficiency disease, and finally that 'new life-styles' that stress youth, fitness and active sexuality are leading to a new consciousness of the ageing body. Now that menopause has achieved a high profile, other professional bodies have held, are holding and will hold further conferences on menopause management. The pharmaceutical multinationals are only too happy to finance international junkets all over the world in order to publicize their products so that they can be administered to women on a daily basis for billions of woman-years. Given the freebies and the junkets, we are not surprised to find Third World professionals joining in the discussion and gleefully contemplating the scope for marketing steroids to a huge new population of post-menopausal peasant labourers.

Menopause is a dream speciality for the mediocre medic. Dealing with it requires no surgical or diagnostic skill. It is not itself a life-threatening condition, so a patient's death is always somebody else's fault. There is no scope for malpractice suits. Patients must return again and again for a battery of tests and check-ups, all of which earn money for the medic, whether from public or private funds. Robert Wilson, who blurted out the fantastic possibilities of oestrogen replacement from puberty to the grave as early as 1963, greatly embarrassing the profession which prefers to conduct its empire-building with more discretion, has now been reinstated (Keep, 1990). Meanwhile ladies in the provinces are holding bring-and-buy sales in order to finance the setting up of menopause clinics, i.e. outlets for the distribution of replacement hormones, working without reward, as women always have done, for the further enrichment of the richest institutions in the world. In the summer of 1988 the Amarant Trust was officially promulgated as a charity, its function to 'usher in a new lease of life for mature women', i.e. to increase the pressure on doctors to prescribe and on women to accept HRT. In the Trust's first newsletter (March 1988), which was a four-page advertisement that made misleading claims for the proven effects of HRT, women were told that they could pay a monthly levy to support the good work.

Women who work can now give to the Amarant Trust directly, through their pay packets. With your permission your employer can send us up to £10 a month from which he will deduct about £7 from your pay packet; the rest is made up by saving the tax. But if you wish to give less, 'give as you earn' is still a good way to support the Amarant Trust because the government gives us back the tax you would otherwise have paid.

A small announcement at the bottom of the back page imparted the interesting information that the costs of producing the news-letter had been defrayed by 'an educational grant from Ciba-Geigy Plc, and Novo Laboratories'. As an embittered observer once remarked, women are the perfect guinea-pigs; in this case they not only feed themselves and keep their cages clean, pay for the medications both through taxes and directly, administer the drugs themselves, and recruit further experimental subjects, they are also willing to subsidize the promotion of the products. The history of the medication of women in the climacterium is peopled with patients who have said, 'Thank you, doctor, I feel so much better,' whether they have been irradiated, electrocauterized, electroconvulsed, dosed with animal extracts, hysterectomized, dunked in cold water or given placebos. Nevertheless the effrontery of the multinationals producing conjugated equine oestrogens for administration on a daily basis over thirty or forty years of the lives of all women is staggering.

In the ten years to 1978 Wulf Utian 'authored' or 'co-authored' twenty-six publications on the menopause. He had virtually commandeered the field of research into the usefulness of replacement hormones, which is characterized by poorly designed studies reflecting an unacceptable degree of bias. In 1984 John Gerald Greene, who had been working in a menopause clinic in Glasgow, attempted to 'construct a cohesive sociopsychological model of the climacteric' using the existing 'substantial body of empiric research'. Though he paid tribute to Utian's grasp of the biology of menopause, he was obliged to point out that there is no evidence of the deficiency disease that Utian and his cohorts assume to be the cause of climacteric distress, that no one knows how to disentangle the climacteric itself from ageing, and that in properly designed double-blind cross-over trials, the placebo effect is so great as to weaken or even to invalidate the claims made for the medication of choice. Although he makes no direct attack on Utian, and a practitioner in the menopause field would be ill-advised to do so, he does manage to imply that Utian's enthusiasm for the 'mental tonic' effect of HRT is not justified by his own scientific research. The effect of Greene's rigorous review of the literature on climacteric syndrome is greatly to weaken our certainty that there is such a thing, let alone whether there is a cure for it.

One of the basic tenets of feminism is that women must define their own experience. Medical students are expected to rattle off the details of climacteric syndrome, as defined by Utian and Serr in 1976, but women themselves should not. One of the tasks that needs to be done is that the climacteric needs to be rescued from the fog of prejudice that surrounds it. The menopausal woman is the prisoner of a stereotype and will not be rescued from it until she has begun to tell her own story. Besides, anxiety about menopause can only complicate the event itself. Negative attitudes to menopause result in menopause being blamed for events and situations that have nothing to do with it. Interestingly, women themselves do not have, or will not admit to having, negative attitudes towards menopause.

Kayana, Kiyak and Lang (1980) have reviewed, and provided, evidence that in response to various kinds of survey women consider menopause as requiring little readjustment when compared with other life events ... it appeared also that menopause is not viewed with trepidation by younger women, nor remembered as a stressful period of change by the elderly. In fact negative stereotypes of the menopause are less prevalent among women than among men. The climacteric is viewed by men as a major life change. (Asso, 113)

Certainly the campaign to eliminate menopause has been initiated and is run by men. Since menopause became big business there has been a vast explosion of propaganda disseminating male views of menopause. Karen Horney's description of the process whereby men define women's experience is still germane.

Like all sciences and all valuations, the psychology of women has hitherto been considered only from the point of view of men. It is inevitable that a man's position of advantage should cause objective validity to be attributed to his subjective, affective relations to the woman and according to Delius [Vom Erwachen der Frau] the psychology of women hitherto does actually represent a deposit of the desires and disappointments of men. (56)

18

Horney would approve, I think, if I were to point out here that the fact that male researchers remain attached to a view of menopause as catastrophe despite the necessary conclusions from their own research indicates an emotional loading that they themselves are unable to let go. The authors of the 1975 IHF (AKZO) survey make repeated references to 'menopausal crisis' and even conclude that

it is clear that for many women the menopause is a period of disorientation, physical problems and psychological imbalance (49)

when their own evidence proves that ageing is far more problematic. Such skewing of the argument represents something more than researcher bias. However, we must not expect much more rationality from the few women who choose to be connected with the subject. As Horney explains:

An additional and very important factor in the situation is that women have adapted themselves to the wishes of men and felt as if their adaptation were their true nature. That is, they see or saw themselves in the way that their men's wishes demanded of them; unconsciously they yielded to the suggestion of masculine thought. (56–7)

Women who have graduated in a scientific discipline at a university have had to adapt in a very obvious way to the demands of a masculinist discipline, but even so they tend to resist the irrational certainties of the Masters in Menopause. Horney's observation suggests an important corollary, namely, that women who have made the adaptation to male requirements will share the pessimistic view that men take of menopause and suffer more as a result. Men see menopause as the cancellation of the only important female functions, namely attracting, stimulating, gratifying and nurturing men and/or children and, given that they believe that carrying out these functions constitutes women's happiness, it makes sense that they should seek to keep women unchanged. Women who have not internalized this view will not fear the cessation of ovulation like the plague, but they will not escape calumny.

The Masters in Menopause bask in the certainty that they are motivated not by greed or the lust for power, but by the purest chivalry. They offer replacement oestrogen not for their own convenience, but to relieve the anguish of good women. What is at work here has been described by Horney as the profound desire men have to depreciate women; it is in fact a need to show that women cannot manage their own lives without the aid of men, a delusion that women themselves have gone some way to foster. The post-menopausal woman is not allowed to have no further need of men. She is not permitted to transcend her biology once for all. She is defined as suffering from a deficiency disease, and men will once again demonstrate their superiority by supplying the remedy for her defect. Some of the inquiries into menopause demonstrate this mechanism more clearly than others, by including, for example, the question whether or not women become more 'self-centred' at menopause. (If only they did!)

Women have remained relatively silent on the matter. When female researchers test the male hypotheses about menopause, they tend to find them unsubstantiated; when they assess the performance and rationale of hormone replacement therapy, they remain sceptical. The woman who rejects the male construction of menopause and turns to other women will find it difficult even to broach the subject. Women are not given spontaneously to describing their own menopause experiences; women writers, memoirists, bellettristes, diarists, novelists, poets, rarely so much as hint at menopause as an event. In the vast majority of cases women do not see the climacteric as a factor in their development. It seems unlikely that what we are up against is lack of awareness or lack of insight, and only slightly more likely that we are contemplating the more sinister phenomenon of denial. If the denial is simply denial of a male construction of a female event, it is only proper; if it is denial of the event itself, it is neurotic. If HRT is the behavioural expression of that kind of denial it cannot be justified.

If fifty-year-old women were visible in our culture we would know that every climacteric is different; it is only our ignorance that implies that all menopausal women are enduring the same trials and responding in the same way. What happens during what one nineteenth-century gynaecologist called 'this interesting process of the human uterus' summarizes a woman's life and career and provides the impetus for the rest of her life. It is a time of taking stock and making decisions; as such it is stressful. The stress may be complicated by physical symptoms or not; in this discussion the physical syndrome and its sequelae are not the point.

Since I have been fascinated by fifty-year-old women I have turned to biography after biography, memoir after memoir, seeking out the moment of change, the turning of the corner, the beginning of the third age, but have found very little. This is partly, but only partly, because many of my heroines did not make it to fifty. Some, like Mary Wollstonecraft and Charlotte Brontë, died in childbed or of the consequences of miscarriage or giving birth, others of infectious disease or epidemic. The ones who survived to menopause choose not to discuss the matter in literature, even in the most densely encoded fashion. To appear in print is to expose oneself in mixed company. The cessation of the menses is no more likely to be discussed than any other female bodily function. Even so, the utter invisibility of middle-aged women in English literary culture is baffling. The years of the climacteric are, even for the most vociferous of women, silent years, and this phenomenon adds not a little to our anxiety regarding them.

As I have become accustomed to this reticence, I have learned to interpret the signs not only of the climacteric itself, but of the lunatic procedures menopausal women were subjected to by doctors (for which see Chapter 7). We read, for example, that in 1818 Maria Edgeworth was severely depressed and suffered 'alarming weakness' of her eyes. Both are usually explained as a result of family troubles and the worry of serious illness among the Irish peasantry, but they may mean more to us when we realize that in

1818 Maria Edgeworth was fifty-one. She gave up reading, writing and needlework for two years, and recovered. Disturbances of vision are sometimes reported in the climacteric; the person who was alarmed was probably her doctor who, if he was anything like his male contemporaries, almost certainly over-interpreted the symptom. Edgeworth's depression cannot have been materially assisted by the enforced inactivity he prescribed. Sixteen years later she was hale enough to tour Connemara, and then began, at the age of seventy, to learn Spanish. Jane Austen sent her a copy of *Emma*; 150 barrels of flour were sent to her from Boston to help with her relief work during the Irish famine, and when the porters would accept no pay, she knitted each one a comforter. She was very lively right up until the age of eighty-two, when she died peacefully in the arms of her dearest friend, her father's fourth wife, Frances Anne Beaufort.

In fiction, whether written by men or by women, middle-aged women are virtually invisible. All our heroines are young. Even women writers who are themselves fifty or over write about young women. Barbara Cartland, who is over ninety, has written more than 550 books but I doubt that one of them has a heroine over twenty-five. Older women themselves suffer from youthism, and contribute to the prejudice against themselves; they endure the never-ending jibes against menopausal women, against mothers-in-law, against crones in general, without a word of protest. Even the Women's Liberation movement has consistently identified with young, sexually active women, and treated the older woman as one of her oppressors. Virginia Tiger, discussing Doris Lessing's novel about the rebirth of a woman in the climacterium, *The Summer Before the Dark*, feels that she has to ask:

> Was *Summer's* emotional austerity, its insistence that women must develop an impersonal sense of self, evidence that Lessing is now alienated from the authentic feminist perspective? (Tiger, p. 81)

In fact *The Summer Before the Dark* is not simply about the old theme of the discovery of self, but Tiger does not recognize its exact description of an utterly and solely female experience, possibly because she has not confronted it herself and nothing in the literature has prepared her for it. The 83 per cent of the British population who are not women over fifty are uninterested in women who are over fifty primarily because they are not interested in women. Women tend to be interested in women as men are interested in women, i.e. as they relate to men. History is replete with the documentation of women who heroically or uproariously or problematically served men; their stories end when the relationship with their man ends. History records Lady Christian Acland, for example, for her valiant exploits at her husband's side in the Canadian campaign, but after his death in 1778, when she was only twenty-five, she disappears from the record though she lived until 1815.

It is unlikely, if we read *Emma* by Jane Austen, that we even remember Miss Bates. Emma is rude to Miss Bates, whom she finds so 'silly – so satisfied – so smiling – so prosing – so undistinguished and unfastidious . . .'. Mr Weston describes her as 'a standing lesson in how to be happy' (255), though

her youth had passed without distinction, and her middle of life was devoted to the care of an ailing mother, and the endeavour to make a small income go as far as possible. And yet she was a happy woman, and one whom no one named without good will. (21)

Mr Knightley is severe with Emma for humiliating this poor lady; his reasons for condemning her thoughtlessness must have struck dread into the hearts of Austen's unmarried female readers:

She is poor; she has sunk from the comforts she was born to; and if she live to old age must probably sink more. (375)

All our heroines are young. The implications of this statement are serious. If women themselves are not interested in mature women, if even mature women are not interested in mature women, we are faced with a vast and insidious problem. Women over fifty make up one of the biggest groups in Britain, being 17 per cent of the population. Any view of such a group as marginal must be based upon an inaccurate notion of who or what the typical Briton is. Mary Wollstonecraft (who died at the age of thirty-eight) wrote crossly in 1792 of a 'sprightly male writer' (whose name she had forgotten) who asked what business women over forty had in the world. We can afford to dismiss the sprightly writer, for we neither know him nor care for him, but what if we share his ignorance? What if we, the horde of women of fifty, cannot see what business we have in the world? Most of us are no longer sought as lovers, as wives, as mothers, or even as workers, unless there is a conspicuous dearth in our profession, and then only until we are sixty. We are supposed to mind our own business; if we are to do this we need to find a business of our own.

Elizabeth Gaskell wrote *Cranford* when she had just turned forty. The novel was a wild success. Everybody loved the dotty ladies of Cranford, and especially dear old Miss Matty, with her tremulous motion of head and hands and well-worn furrows in her cheeks, Miss Matty who says, 'I had very pretty hair my dear, and not a bad mouth,' and who also says (a thunder-clap this), 'Martha, I'm not yet fifty-two.' She is already getting dithery and sometimes wears one cap on top of another. A hundred pages later Miss Matty cannot walk very fast; she has a touch of rheumatism and her eyes are failing. In case we should console ourselves with the thought that old people get younger with every generation that passes and fifty-year-olds are younger and spryer now than they were then, we are brought up short by Miss Matty saying, 'We are principally ladies now I know, but we are not so old as ladies used to be when I was a girl,' (76). Unwillingly I have to admit to myself, yes, my hip does twinge, and I need my glasses more and more, and I am getting more absent-minded. I am more like Miss Matty than I am willing to admit.

None of these ladies knew the word 'menopause', though the educated among them did know the more correct expression 'climacteric', taken from the Greek word *klimacter*, meaning 'critical period'. The notion of the climacteric is as old as medicine itself; Aristotle noticed that women cannot bear children after the age of fifty, but until very recently only the truly irreverent, like the poet Byron, would dream of making an explicit reference to 'that leap-year, whose leap/In female dates, strikes Time all of a heap' (*Don Juan*, XIV, 52). Byron dares even to refer to the climacteric of Catherine the Great (X, 47). He is unusual among poets in that he was genuinely interested in women as people and aware of the fundamental gravity of the woman question:

> But as to women, who can penetrate
> The real sufferings of their she-condition?
> Man's very sympathy with their estate
> Has much of selfishness and more suspicion.
>
> (XIV, 24)

The general public did not begin to discuss the climacteric until after it had been captured by the medical profession and defined as a syndrome, by which time it was too late to render it respectable. The medical notion of 'menopause' was the brain-child of C. P. L. de Gardanne, who described a syndrome he called 'la Ménéspausie' in *Avis aux Femmes qui entrent dans l'Age Critique*, published in 1816. 'Menopause' was not defined until 1899, in an article on 'Epochal Insanities' contributed by Dr Clouston to *A System of Medicine by Many Writers* edited by Professor T. C. Allbutt (VIII, 302), under the heading 'Climacteric Insanity'. By describing a set of symptoms, and identifying it as a syndrome with a dramatic name, the medical establishment was empowered to treat the 'critical phase', de Gardanne's '*âge critique*', as a complaint in which their intervention was to be sought, rather than as an important process in female development with which women themselves would have to deal.

To be precise, the word 'menopause' applies to a non-event, the menstrual period that does not happen. It is the invisible Rubicon that a woman cannot know she is crossing until she has crossed it. Insistence on an inappropriate idea of a kind of invisible leap leads to some utterly mystifying data on 'age at menopause'. Women are asked, some many years later, when they 'went through menopause'. It would make more sense to ask them when they had their last bleed, which might with reason be dated to a month and a year.

The climacteric is actually composed of three periods, two that exist and one that does not; the first is the peri-menopause, the time leading up to and the last bleed, the second is the menopause proper, the bleed that does not come, and the third is the post-menopause. The critical time corresponds with the fifth climacter of a woman's life, the fifth of her seven ages. Her first age is infancy and childhood, her second adolescence and nubility, her third wifehood, her fourth motherhood, and her fifth the end of mothering and the beginning of grandmotherhood. Generally speaking, we can assume the climacteric to begin at about age forty-five and end at about fifty-five. Most women will traverse the difficult transition from reproductive animal to reflective animal between those years, which we could call middle age. Almost half a modern woman's life lies beyond the transition, yet nothing in her education or her conditioning has prepared her for this new role.

Though women's life expectancy at the turn of the century was no more than forty-eight years, most of the women who died did so when they were infants or during their childbearing; the mean figure also includes a visible proportion of old crones. Women who survived to menopause might live on indefinitely, in ever worsening health. A disproportionate number of them would have been spinsters, who did not run the risks of childbirth, so that the old maid was a more familiar and therefore less cherished figure than the old matron. In the literary culture of the élite, impatience with the symptoms of menopause thus blended with casual ridicule of marginalized, dependent, unattractive old women. From the turn of the century, when the word 'menopause' began to figure in medical literature, the notion that the climacteric was a time of mental and physical derangement became one of the things that everybody knew. There seemed no need to investigate it.

The prejudice was international. The fortunes of an obscure Danish writer called Karin Michaëlis were transformed when, in 1904, she published a novel called *The Dangerous Age*, which swept German-speaking Europe, then France, then the English-speaking world (see also pp. 101–2). Every character in it was obsessed by the idea of a dangerous age, although none had any clear idea of when it might arrive or what form it might take. Nowadays books on the menopause proliferate. The worst of them begin with a description of the female organs, as if women had not all their lives been treated as a set of female organs, as if they had not ever since their schooldays had to consider their bodies as permanently in the lithotomy position, thighs apart, labia held asunder, jabbed with long lines with labels on the end – 'Glands of Bartholin', 'Vaginal Introitus'. Even at menopause woman is to most medical writers nothing but a reproductive machine on stilts. The laborious description of the machinery that is now obsolete drags on and on; there will be another diagram of the lower half of a female sliced down the middle to show her reproductive organs, more labels – 'Germinal Epithelium', 'Tunica albuginea' – and another sliced along the midline to show how the womb fits in with her bladder and bowels, and another of the breast. The women reading these books are acutely aware of themselves as reproductive animals who can now reproduce no longer, and are panicked to think that they are coming to the end of their useful life. What they need is a new perspective on themselves as *people*, to be able to feel that they are at least as important as hearts and minds as they were as wombs. They open a book called *The Menopause*, and find themselves again confronting the same old diagrams that their doctor has been drawing on his blotter ever since they can remember. They are forced to chart the death of the womb stage by painful stage, a peculiar palliative for grief.

When I complained to another middle-aged woman that there

are no novels written about middle-aged women, she said at once, 'Oh, that's because nothing happens to us.' How can this be, I thought, our hearts break, our lives are overwhelmed, spectres of pain and fear loom at every turn, and this is 'nothing happens'? If there is a belief that nothing happens to middle-aged women, it is only because middle-aged women do not talk about what does happen to them. Take the case of Kathleen Sutcliffe, for example.

Nobody can remember if it was actually on her fiftieth birthday that her husband rang her at work to tell her (probably untruthfully) that he'd be working late.

'Who's that?' she asked.

'Who d'you think it is?' her husband asked. She'd never actually heard his voice on the phone before and he was tickled that she could not recognize it. Her reply floored him.

'Oh, is it Albert?' she said. It had never occurred to John Sutcliffe that the motherly woman who served him his meal before he went off on the night shift might have an admirer. Her big brown eyes and masses of black curls had all the boys running after her when he got engaged to her in 1941, but those days were long gone. Like a good Catholic girl Kathleen got pregnant on her honeymoon. After she'd borne seven kids (and buried one) she had no time to go to Mass, especially as her husband was too busy with his sporting and theatrical activities to give her a hand. She'd become a motherly homebody who moved her old mum into the house in 1952 and looked after her till she died in 1964, when Kathleen went out cleaning every week-night and on Saturday and Sunday morning so that her kids could have decent clothes. Her husband spent a good deal of his money on himself, his entertainments and his other women, but Kathleen did not seem to mind.

'She were used to him being out at cricket do's an' all after; they used to have a booze up till three and four in mornin'. Then there were musical union an' all sorts of stuff. She were right innocent about them things so he could get away with it like that. She never used to ask about owt.' (Burn, 118)

Even when her husband groped her sons' girlfriends Kathleen turned a blind eye. She was famous on the estate where they lived for her warm heart and her sweet manner. Her third son used to say, 'She were a right honest sort of person, me mother. Right gullible. You could tell her owt an' she'd believe you without wanting to delve ... she'd stick up for you, me mother ...' Kathleen's one indulgence was that every other Thursday she went to the hairdresser.

So who was Albert? Albert was a policeman who lived two streets away. His wife was a career-woman and worked long hours. Albert sometimes had time on his hands. When Kathleen was walking her son's terrier by the canal he'd be walking his and they'd got to talking, to like talking to each other, and then to need to talk to each other. They made love rarely, in his house, when his wife was out at work, and in his car. He'd telephone her sometimes when she was at work; her husband never did.

'Is it Albert?' she said, because I dare say she so much wanted it, needed it to be Albert. 'Oh, Albert, when can I see you again?' Cruelly her husband decided to pretend that it was indeed Albert. As Albert he rang her several times and finally persuaded her to spend the night with him at a local hotel. He told her to bring something fetching to change into and had the bitter satisfaction of finding in their bedroom a pretty new nightgown in a Marks and Spencers bag. He commanded three of their older children to meet him at the hotel at the appointed time. Two of them turned up, and were the more mystified to see their mother pacing nervously up and down on the pavement outside. Their father let her pace for a minute or two and then went out, grabbed her arm and marched her in to face her kids. 'She didn't remonstrate with him, or cry, or do anything dramatic; she seemed numb; and all the blood had drained from her.' I cannot tell you what she felt when he leaned over, and took her handbag and pulled out the new nightgown.

29

Kathleen tried to get her husband to believe that the relationship with Albert was innocent, but the evidence of the nightgown damned her. He threatened to go to Albert's house and confront him and his wife, so Kathleen confessed. Instead Albert was summoned to their house and ordered never to see Kathleen again. The lovers disobeyed and met once more, but Kathleen's husband caught them. This time he threatened to denounce Albert to his superior officers in the police force. Albert had his pension to consider. He gave Kathleen up.

Her husband thought he probably ought to show her a bit more affection, so when he was watching television he would reach for her hand or put his arm around her shoulders. At such moments, according to her daughter, Kathleen seemed 'dead embarrassed'. She was not well; she was putting on weight, and kept having pain around her heart and difficulty in breathing. She had every possible test but nothing organic seemed to be wrong. She had to give up her Boxing Days when she had all the old people from her own and her husband's family to dinner. She had to give up work. The council moved her to a more convenient flat; the priest began to bring her fortnightly communion. Her eldest son used always to drop in to see her if he was passing in his lorry and would never leave her until he had coaxed her to smile. He reckoned that the scene in the hotel and its aftermath had broken her heart; it was as if she was slowly dying before his eyes. She died in November 1978, less than ten years after she lost Albert, and three years before the world came to know her loving firstborn son as the Yorkshire Ripper.

This is just one reality behind the 'nothing' that is thought to happen to middle-aged women. Most people who read Gordon Burn's book about the Ripper, *Somebody's Husband, Somebody's Son*, will not be reading it for the story of Kathleen, but for the gruesome story of Peter and his wife, Sonia. All credit must go to Burn for rooting out Kathleen's story as we have it, but he and his readers should be aware that they do not have the flesh of it. What did Albert mean to Kathleen? What did their physical love-making mean to her? Was she so apathetic when her husband humiliated her because the worst pain was simply that Albert was not there and she wanted him so much? Or was the worst grief that Albert did not have the gumption to take her away from her overbearing, unfaithful, neglectful husband for good? Or was it guilt and contrition that menopausal lust had undone a lifetime of fidelity to her role of Catholic wife and mother? Did she will herself to death? The story of Kathleen Sutcliffe could, like any great myth, be written a thousand different ways, if only we could place a middle-aged charlady at the centre of our mind-stage. This is one change that needs to happen if middle-aged women are to succeed in regaining their balance and living the rest of their lives in an unapologetic fashion.

In 1973 Doris Lessing published *The Summer Before the Dark*. In the novel, according to the blurb,

Kate Brown is faced for the first time in twenty years with the prospect of being alone, because her husband, a successful neurologist, is going to work for some months in an American hospital. Urged by him to take a job, she embarks on a summer of exploration, freedom and self-discovery, during which she rejects the stereotypes of femininity – which like her conventional clothes, do not fit her any more ... [Lessing's] treatment of the emotional gulf which opens before a forty-five-year-old woman who is not wanted as a wife and mother is a starting point for so much more – confrontation with the threat of annihilation, the terrors of old age and death.

Because Doris Lessing is an important writer, rather than a 'women's novelist', *The Summer Before the Dark* was reviewed by men, mostly respectfully but not enthusiastically. Lessing had already become interested in Sufism and had begun writing non-realistic stories; she had returned to realistic narration to describe the important processes that unfold in a woman at the time of the climacteric.

We are what we learn.
It often takes a long and painful time.

31

Unfortunately, there was no doubt either, that a lot of time, a lot of
  pain, went into learning very little . . .
She was really feeling that? yes, she was.
Because she was depressed? Was she depressed? Probably. (10)

The cancelling of the heroine's role as consort and mother is
dramatized in the book by her husband's suggestion that they let
her big house while he is away and the children are about their
own affairs. Lessing carefully pares away the usual assumptions
about forty-five-year-old women; this one is well dressed and
well preserved, but

she did not walk inside, like the fine, almost unseeable envelope of a
candle flame, that emanation of attractiveness . . . (39)

Kate changes her image, in order to send a stronger signal, and it
works; she attracts a younger man and goes to Spain with him.
She is troubled, however, by a recurring dream in which she is
trying to help a battered seal find its way to the sea. Lessing coins
an unforgettable image of unnatural life:

She dreamed as soon as she went to sleep. She was sitting in a cinema.
She was looking at a film she had seen before . . . of the poor turtle
who, on the island in the Pacific that had been atom-bombed, had lost
its sense of direction and instead of returning to the sea after it had laid
its eggs, as nature ordinarily directed, is setting its course inwards into a
waterless land where it will die. (71)

Once at home she had taken in a stray cat:

The family had treated Kate like an invalid and the cat a medicine.
'Just the thing for the menopause,' she had heard Tim say to Eileen. She
had not started the menopause, but it would have been no use saying
it . . . oh, that had been an awful spring, to follow a bad winter. She had
feared she was really crazy, she spent so much of her time angry. (99)

Part of the difficulty with *The Summer Before the Dark* is that
the climacteric is never identified as a factor and may not be

intended to be understood as a cause of Kate's spiritual malaise. In fact her sensations, that a cold wind is blowing on her, that the stuffing is running out of her, that she is being flayed alive, are all typical of the climacteric. The affair fizzles out; Kate is feverishly ill for some weeks and comes out of it all bones, with her hair grizzled and frizzy, as if the weeks of illness had devastated her as much as the years of the climacteric. Shabby, scrawny and grey, Kate finds that she is invisible. Lessing's writing of this change is classic.

It seemed a long time before the food came. Kate sat on, invisible, apparently, to the waitress and to the other customers: the place was filling now. She was shaking with impatient hunger, the need to cry. The feeling that no one could see her made her want to shout: 'Look, I'm here, can't you see me?' She was not far off that state that in a small child is called a tantrum. (166)

Kate discovers that by concealing the evidence of age she can become visible again. Eventually, after a good deal of turmoil, she decides that she will accept her new condition.

Lessing's novel is an important text in the self-definition of late twentieth-century woman. However, it inspired few emulators. Rachel Billington's novel *A Woman's Age* is more typical of the mainstream in that it deals with anything but the topic named in the title. As soon as the husband of Violet, the heroine of the first part, dies and she decides to go into politics, Lady Rachel switches her attentions to her nubile daughter. Violet makes only summary appearances for the last 200 pages. After her death in rather quixotic circumstances in India, her daughter summarizes the story that Lady Rachel chose not to tell.

'Her problem was reconciling her emotional life with her intellectual. Her intellectual side had taken over. That saddened her. She wanted to find her emotions again but not the selfish emotions of a young girl. Something better.' (489)

That, now that, would have been a novel worth writing.

If we look about us for role models we may see the prime ministers Margaret Thatcher, Mrs Gandhi, Mrs Bandaranaike, Golda Meir. They are impressive figures, to be sure, and all over fifty, but it is difficult to see how we can profit by their example. They demonstrate that there is no responsibility too great for a fifty-year-old woman to assume, but their careers can hardly be imitated by the mass of women. One thing is obvious, they did not begin their acquisition of political power at fifty. By fifty the long years of committee work and party service were bearing fruit. These women had a compensation for the losses of middle age, a compensation for which they had in a sense bartered the years of their youth. Most fifty-year-old women are simply mocked by these examples. Mrs Thatcher gives us no clue how to deal with the loss of parents, with the growing away of children, with the increasing infirmities of age. We hear that she uses hormone replacement, but do not know whether to be encouraged or disheartened by the result, especially now that she has been tossed out by her male colleagues and condemned to silence. We can see that Mrs Thatcher's image is tailored by professionals; she illustrates a standard of middle-agedness to which most of us cannot aspire. Instead we sit on the bus looking at the faded faces of the other women using off-peak transport and we wonder how old they are. 'Is she older or younger than me?' we ask ourselves. 'Am I ageing better or worse than her?'

There may be positive sides to lack of interest in oneself, but there is nothing positive about having a 'low self-image'. If mature women simply forget themselves, that is one thing, but if they actually dislike or even despise themselves, we can expect all kinds of evils to ensue as a consequence. Despite the advances in recognizing women's rights, women, even educated sophisticated women, prefer not to admit their age, and even lie about it. This would seem to imply that being old, for a woman, is somehow shameful. Simone de Beauvoir said that when she admitted at the end of *Force of Circumstance* to being on the threshold of old age, people were shocked and annoyed with her. ' "You're not old," ' people say to me. ' "Fifty is young." ' Every twenty-year-old knows that fifty is old. Abbie Hoffmann used to say in the sixties, 'Never trust anyone over thirty.' He himself was close to thirty then; it was not thirty but fifty that did him in. Abbie was my friend; I loved him (and failed him), but this book is not about the anxieties of ageing men. This book will not devote any of its limited space to the 'male menopause'. The purpose of this book is to demonstrate that women are at least as interesting as men, and that ageing women are at least as interesting as younger women. The climacteric and women's experiences during it and their strategies for managing it all fascinate me. It is not a stage to hasten through, let alone obscure or deny. On these years depends the rest of your life, a life which may be as long as the life you have already lived.

2

No Rite of Passage

'Sometimes I feel I am twelve years old, sometimes seventy . . . I feel uncertain how to behave, how to relate to people, especially men. How do I seem to them? I just don't know . . . I've never felt like this before.'
(Mankowitz, 43)

The problem is not a new one. In 1820, the fifty-year-old Marquise de La Tour du Pin began her memoirs:

I have never before written anything except letters to those I love. My thoughts ramble. I am not methodical. My memory is already much dimmed . . . At heart I still feel so young that it is only by looking in the mirror that I am able to convince myself I am no longer twenty years of age. Let me take advantage, then, of the warmth that is still in me and which may at any moment be chilled by the infirmities of age . . . (13)

The Marquise's is a typically menopausal state of mind; her acquisition of a notebook and inscribing the first page of her autobiography is a DIY ritual to mark the otherwise unmarked transition from the two functions that according to Rousseau justified a woman's life, those of spouse and mother, to something new and unaccounted for. The male theoreticians of the Marquise's epoch held that it was a woman's duty to please; in embarking upon her memoirs the Marquise was taking a long, invisible step. After a lifetime of pleasing others, she was about to please herself. In fact she did not find time to continue the memoirs for many years; it was the beginning, the inditing of her title page that was her rite of passage.

If the Marquise had not chosen to mark the change herself she might have found herself in the muddle that afflicts most women at some stage during the climacteric. 'What are we supposed to wear?' my friend Vivian asked me one day. 'I find it so difficult to choose clothes. How *do* we dress our age? Everything is either pastel crimplene safari suits or tat for the teens and twenties. There isn't anything that is just grown-up and elegant. Half the things I bring home the girls pinch, and tell me that I'm too old for them.' A. S. Byatt lamented in the *Independent Magazine* (16 June 1990, 18):

> Clothes manufacturers are waking up to the fact that over 50 per cent of women are over size 16, but they are still hooked on the idea that the waistless want to flaunt themselves as though they were nubile children. I don't want to look like a tea-lady and I don't want puce spangles and shiny peplums like something out of *Dynasty*. I want to look quietly elegant. I want to be draped in superior cloth like Italian women. I've got the money, not the teenagers. Where are the designers?

It is not simply a matter of designers. There is a pressure upon the middle-aged woman to make herself inconspicuous. Kitty, Duchess of Queensberry, scandalized everyone in 1771 when at the age of seventy she wore a pink lutestring gown at a wedding. The narrator of *Cranford* refused to allow Miss Matty the turban she longed for but pressured her to content herself with 'a neat, middle-aged cap'. In this case it is a younger woman who constrains the older to forgo bright colours and exciting clothes.

> Young women have an acute sense of what should and should not be done when one is no longer young. 'I don't understand,' they say, 'how a woman of forty can bleach her hair; how she can make an exhibition of herself in a bikini; how she can flirt with men. The day I'm her age ...' That day comes: they bleach their hair; they wear bikinis; they smile at men. (De Beauvoir, 1984, 291)

There is, as we all know, no possibility that the glow of youth could be outshone by the *savoir-faire* of the middle-aged woman, but the young themselves are unaware of their bloom, and deeply insecure about their attractiveness. The middle-aged woman for her part is confused; she knows from her own perception that nothing is so macabre or ridiculous as mutton dressed as lamb, but how is mutton supposed to dress? No fifty-year-old woman actually wants to compete with her daughters for attention, or that they should compete with her, but more and more in our society such competition is forced upon us. There is no accepted style for the older woman; no way of saying through dress and demeanour, 'I am my age. Respect it.'

At no time in our history have the generations been pitted against each other as they are now, when households contain only parents and children and no representatives of intervening age groups, no young aunts and uncles, no older cousins, and very few brothers and sisters. The confrontation is all parent-child and child-parent, so that the group as perceived by both polarizes into their generation and our generation, them and us. Yet outwardly, in dress and manner, there is no distinction. Parents cannot disentangle themselves from their children's affairs or vice versa, nor can they insist on any degree of formality or respect in their relationship with their children. Women who are fifty now called their parents 'mother' and 'father', or names to the same effect. Their own children call them by their Christian names, as if there is no difference between them.

There is no point at which a middle-aged woman can make plain her opting out of certain kinds of social interaction. She has a duty to go on 'being attractive' no matter how fed up she is with the whole business. She is not allowed to say, 'Now I shall let myself go'; letting herself go is a capital offence against the sexist system. Yet if a woman never lets herself go, how will she ever know how far she might have got? If she never takes off her high-heeled shoes, how will she ever know how far she could walk or how fast she could run? The middle-aged women who begin to train for marathons will never run as far or as fast as they might have in their teens and twenties, but the women who study to develop their souls can find their full spiritual and intellectual range on the other side of fifty. Developing the muscles of the soul demands no competitive spirit, no killer instinct, although it may erect pain barriers that the spiritual athlete must crash through.

The fifty-year-old woman has no option but to register the great change that is taking place within her, but at the same time she is forced to keep this upheaval secret. The shame that she felt at the beginning of her periods is as nothing compared to the long-drawn-out embarrassment occasioned by their gradual stop-go ending; no woman would step into a shop or an office or a party and announce in ringing tones that she expected special consideration because she was struggling through menopause. She would not wear a badge that said, 'Beware menopausal mood swings'. There is no rite of passage to surround the middle-aged woman with solemnity, no seclusion ordered for her, no special periods of rest. She cannot withdraw to a menopause hut and sit and talk with other menopausal women. She simply has to tough it out and pretend that nothing is happening.

The social invisibility of the menopause serves no useful purpose. In 1973 a researcher reported:

I was surprised to find that those most interested in the subject were *young* people, of both sexes, who had been affected by their mothers' menopause. One young man told me that his mother's 'change' came when he was fourteen, and she did indeed change toward him – from an affectionate and indulgent parent to a moody and rejecting one. Unable to understand what was happening, he felt confused, miserable, guilty. Naturally he felt that the whole subject needed to be brought out into the open. (Mankowitz, 11)

An alarm bell rings when one reads this kind of thing. There is here no suggestion that the young man may have behaved in such a way as to provoke his mother's rejection, though fourteen-year-olds often do. The possibility that the teenager might have been too demanding is not considered. If the climacteric is considered to be one more pathological manifestation it becomes one more reason why women should not be taken seriously. In the same way that the completely negative construction put on the menstrual cycle acts against women's interest and does not assist them in coping with it in any way, the identification of menopause as the sole cause of changes in women's attitudes strips those attitudes of respectability. What would fulfil the purpose of warning off self-obsessed spouses and children at a time when the woman is preoccupied with an upheaval within herself, without caricaturing the woman as sick and deranged, would be a rite of passage.

According to Mankowitz there is no such thing and there has never been any such thing; 'the menopause was and is virtually a non-event in all societies'. 'Why,' she asks,

are there no rites of passage recorded *anywhere* to mark out the menopause, as there are for other crucial events such as birth, puberty, marriage, childbirth and death?

The function of a rite of passage is to give significance to a crucial change in the life of the individual, to give one the support of society during this change and to attempt by means of the ritual to bring down the blessing of the gods at this time of danger both to the individual and to society. Rites of passage usually take place in three parts: first the stage of isolation, withdrawal of the individual from society and into close contact with, and dependence upon, nature; second, the ordeal of severance, an event sometimes painful, involving physical or symbolic renunciation and confrontation with loss and death; and third, a ceremony of rebirth and renewal – the return of a changed being into society and the world. (20)

Mankowitz makes the obvious point that women seldom lived long enough to ensure that society evolved a ritual to mark the cessation of the menses. Historically the few women who lived for any appreciable time after menopause were an emarginated minority. More important is the fact that menopause involves no one but the individual woman; her birth and her death are both celebrated by others; her arrival at puberty, her marriage and her childbearing all involve the exercise of her most important social function and the rituals to celebrate them all dramatize the fact. The menopause signals the woman's withdrawal from this social context and is therefore ignored.

There is perhaps another reason for the invisibility of menopause, which is rather more difficult to grasp. In a culture where women are obliged to maximize their reproductive opportunities, that is, to become pregnant as often as ever they can, menopause is masked by the last pregnancy. Many human societies have suffered such high rates of child mortality from infectious disease, as well as high rates of miscarriage and stillbirth, that their women were pregnant or lactating throughout their reproductive life. In such societies amenorrhoea is the normal condition and menstruation a relative rarity. The last menstruation is likely to occur before the last pregnancy, at a time not obviously connected with the cessation of ovarian function. In such an instance the woman only slowly realizes, when she does not fall pregnant when she weans her last baby, that her childbearing years are over. Lactational amenorrhoea merges indistinguishably with the amenorrhoea of menopause. So many pregnancies, so much labour and lactation, together with the struggle to produce food and keep the growing children healthy, make hard work. Provided she has enough surviving children, the ageing wife is not likely to regret the fact that she will not have to endure another pregnancy. On the other hand she may not be keen to advertise it either, for a wife's menopause can provide a reason for a husband's taking a second, younger wife (Beyene).

In their three-volume study of woman, Ploss and Bartels list hundreds of rituals involving the birth, puberty, marriage and childbearing of females. Older women merit a single, brief, dismissive chapter. This seems both obvious and explicable, yet, though there is no public celebration of the beginning of the last third of a woman's life, I am not at all sure that it is quite true to say that no rites of passage are celebrated at all. Though the male hierarchy may be unaware of women's rites of passage, and therefore the lore of the elders contains no recognition of them, women themselves may have their own ways of signalling their new status, and their acceptance of it, which have escaped the attention of anthropologists.

One obvious way in which women often choose to alter their external appearance in order to signify an internal alteration is by changing the way they do their hair. In 1924, when Harriet Shaw Weaver, James Joyce's patroness, mentor and champion, was forty-eight, her photograph was taken by Man Ray. This famous portrait shows her in pure and severe profile and, for the only time in her life, with shingled hair. Usually she wore her abundant dark hair in a heavy chignon; few of her old friends can have recognized her in Ray's photograph. Her family objected. Miss Weaver grew her hair long again and wore it in whorls over her ears, as befitted the maiden aunt impeccable who cared for all her ageing and ailing relatives, but for a year, whether in mourning or renunciation or rebellion, 'Aunt Hat' or 'Josephine' (as she called herself) was shorn. The drastic alteration in her appearance externalized an important alteration in her *Gestalt*, but Miss Weaver did not explain it and people did not wonder for too long what had 'come over' her.

In *The Summer Before the Dark*, Kate marks the change within her by deciding that she will never again have her hair coloured and shaped.

Her experiences of the last months – her discoveries, her self-definition, what she hoped were now strengths – were concentrated here: that she would walk into her home with her hair undressed, with her hair tied straight back for utility; rough and streaky, and the widening grey band showing like a statement of intent. It was as if the rest of her, body, feet, even face, which was ageing but amenable, belonged to everyone else. But her hair – no! No one was going to lay hands on that. (Lessing, 237)

Mankowitz finds evidence of the individual's celebration of a rite of passage in her Jungian analysis of her patient's dreams (see

Chapter 12). If we look about we can see signs of less arcane and indecipherable celebrations. Because these rituals do not involve the priestly caste of men and do not enhance getting and spending activities they are often unpopular, and are even seen as subversive, backward or superstitious.

In traditional Mediterranean societies women of a certain age begin to wear black. When parents die, an event which usually occurs at about the same time as menopause, a daughter will don black and never again wear any other colour. This custom is regarded by younger people as morbid behaviour, and is nowadays strenuously discouraged. The women in black are those who register bereavement and carry out the duties of mourning by visiting regularly the graves of dead relatives. These practices too are nowadays discouraged. Very few people would agree that the women's quiet activity among the gravestones has any value; they do not see it as part of a contemplative phase in human development, or as a way of conferring form and dignity upon the serendipitousness of life. There may have been no time to mourn the child who died while its brothers and sisters needed all their mother's attention; those children gone their ways, the ageing mother may bring each day the best flowers from her garden to the small grave. Passers-by can click their tongues. The woman herself does not expect them to understand. Her behaviour is proper to her at her time of life, and that thought suffices her.

In countries where these practices are still alive, the cemeteries are not dreary places. In the small town in Ticino where my mother's ancestors are buried, the cemetery is clean, neat and alight with flowers. On the Feast of All Souls the older women will bring their grandchildren to the cemetery and tell them the story of each relative who is buried there, and pray with them for the repose of those souls. In modern progressive societies graves are untended, unmarked or defaced. Cemeteries are bleak and empty. Most people no longer know, let alone inhabit, the places where their ancestors are buried. We do not value continuity, nor do we value the contemplative life. This indifference creates the meaninglessness and marginality of middle age; it is the cold wind that the fifty-year-old woman feels upon her skin.

The woman who chooses to wear black and live in perpetual *lutto* is eschewing the life of spouse and embracing the role of grandmother. Usually she binds up her hair as well, and covers her head with a shawl or *fazzoletto*. These are all signs that she is not to be flirted with or addressed familiarly by men, although she should walk slowly in the street and even sit on a park bench. She is to be treated with respect. Her black liberates her by allowing her to remain invisible, as a kind of secular nun, who is allowed to indulge in her own thoughts.

In Sicily in 1985 I decided to dress in black as an expression of my mourning for my father. At first men displayed no awareness of my unavailable status and still ogled and came sneaking up behind me as I wandered through the temples at Segesta and Selinunte. It was only when I put up my long hair and covered my head that my mourning was respected. I found the new freedom from men's attentions exhilarating rather than depressing. There was also tremendous liberation in not having to think what to wear. Black goes with black. One has only to think of textures, of the part of one's clothing that matters to oneself.

When the Mediterranean woman takes all her clothes and throws them in the copper to dye them black, she is enacting a rite of passage. She is renouncing one kind of life and taking on another. She may weep bitterly, for the end of her young woman-hood, and she may look to the years ahead with foreboding, but she has also the consolation of fulfilling a prescribed procedure. There will be privileges attached to her new status; she will be allowed to rest more, to spend more time sitting at her house-door talking with other women, or praying in church, and even to go away for weeks at a time, on her own, on pilgrimages, so seeing the outside world through her own eyes for the first time.

To the young all these activities are utterly unattractive; they can see no point or pleasure in reflection. They neither know nor care about the spiritual landscape that opens out before older people. Consumer culture denies that such a landscape exists. In the free market economy the frugality and simplicity of old age is anathema. Yet to many troubled souls the calm austerity of old age is a goal to be striven for 'in life's cool evening, satiate of applause'. Poets since classical times have celebrated an ideal stage of tranquil thoughtfulness to round off a busy life. The woman of fifty has even more reason to long for that time; after menopause, when she may be permitted to give up being someone's daughter, someone's lover, someone's wife and someone's mother, she may also be allowed to turn into herself. In 1933, when she was forty-seven, the poet H. D. embarked on analysis with Freud, because, she said, in her *Tribute to Freud*:

There was something that was beating in my brain; I do not say my heart. My brain. I wanted it to be let out. I wanted to free myself of repetitive thoughts and experiences. (16–17)

As analysis proceeded she felt herself struggling against an oceanic swell of unexamined life that threatened to engulf her:

I must not lose grip, I must not lose the end of the picture and so miss the meaning of the whole, so painfully perceived. I must hold on here or the picture will blur over and the sequence be lost. (80)

Changing into yourself does not mean becoming obsessed by yourself, although doubtless there are those who will think the idea no more than an outgrowth of the concept of the 'me generation'. It means rather that you do not continue living your life mainly through responses to the needs of those in your household and workplace. You no longer suppress your own curiosities, and your own insights and opinions, in order to let other people express theirs. Your mind and heart, which have always been full of concern for others and interest in the pursuits of others, may now begin to develop spaces where your own creativity might begin to extend its range, feel its strength, make its contribution on a wider stage, a different stage. This need not be a public stage; the threshold where you stand may open upon a region of the mind, or of the soul. You may be seeking not to express, but to understand.

There are many books written now for ageing women which argue that there need be no change, that the middle-aged woman can continue being what she always was, an attractive and responsive lover, a dutiful wife, an efficient employee. These books never consider the possibility that a woman could actually be tired of being all these things, or that she might be conscious of having led an unexamined life. Such books assume that what the middle-aged woman is afraid of, that there is no point in a woman's life if she is not functioning as lover, wife and employee, is actually true. You are not reading one of those books. This book argues instead that women are whole people with a right to exist and a contribution to make in and as themselves. Moreover, the climacteric is real; it is a fundamental change, which, like the other fundamental changes in women's lives, needs mental preparation and profound acceptance if it is not to be experienced as unbearable.

Though I have no intention of minimizing the impact of menopause or falsely presenting it as avoidable, I do not argue as Ploss and Bartels do, in the few words that they can be bothered to spare for the ageing woman in *Woman*:

> The climacteric is an indication for woman that the period of her vigour is beginning to disappear forever. With more or less rapid steps but steps which admit of no return, woman now proceeds towards old age. (III, 351)

This 'scientific opinion' is stunning in its banality. Every day that passes takes us closer to our death 'with more or less rapid steps'; as we do not know whether the process will take a day or fifty years, the knowledge cannot avail us much. The clock cannot be turned back for anyone of either sex. In explanation of their premature consignment of the fifty-year-old woman sooner or later to the tomb, Ploss and Bartels quote the utterly non-anatomical opinion of Virchow:

'Woman,' Virchow is reputed to have said, 'is a pair of ovaries with a human being attached; whereas man is a human being furnished with a pair of testes.' (351)

The corollary is that when the ovaries die the woman dies with them, but this is clearly not the case. What is the case is that Virchow, like most men whose interest in women is mostly dictated by the testes, does not consider women as human beings but as the objects of his sexual attention. For Virchow post-menopausal women, being unattractive to him, might as well be dead. For women who justify their existence by the amount of male attention they can command, the truth of Virchow's argument is self-evident, but women with more pride than libido do not see their emancipation from the duty of sexual attraction as death-in-life.

Menopause is a change but it is not a change from life to death, or death-in-life. If that change removes us from the sphere of consciousness of the Virchows of the world, it must be a liberation. It would be easier to grasp this if the ageing woman could point to, as well as all the losses that accompany the climacteric, some gains – gains in seniority, privilege, rank, respect, or privacy. Such gains need to be institutionalized by an outward sign, a change in the form of address, in the style of dress, in the attitude of others. The climacteric is signalled by none of these. Part of the difficulty that women face in dealing with the last great change in lives which have gone through so many fundamental changes already is that the change from mother to grandmother has no outward sign – indeed, women who are being buffeted by this tempestuous passage are supposed to pretend that it isn't happening at all. This is the kind of contradiction that has teased and tormented women all their lives.

There was a time when the beginning of menstruation was marked by the lengthening of skirts and the putting up of hair, which did not necessarily coincide with the biological event, but was an acknowledgement that it had happened, that the girl had become a woman or, as they say in Italy, *si era fatta signorina*. All societies place new restrictions on the fecundable female, but usually there are privileges to accompany them which are thought to compensate in some measure. The 'grown-up' girl can wear scent, make-up and high heels, and pretty underwear, and can stay up late. Glamour is her compensation for the squalor of menstruation. A similar strategy might help us to deal with the upheaval of the climacteric.

Though 'civilized' cultures have given up marking the first great upheaval in women's lives, namely the menarche, the onset of the menses, it is still a huge alteration; the boyish little girl watches herself turning into a womanish individual. Though she might not necessarily groan under puppy fat and pimples, she is aware that her body looks different and smells different, and behaves in a new and not exactly pleasant way. One of the first skills young women have to develop is that of dealing with menstruation in mixed company without anybody guessing what they are about, slipping into the lavatory with a sanitary napkin up a sleeve, washing stained underwear on the sly in co-ed digs. It is arguable that young women would find menstruation less problematic if they did not have to behave as if they were ashamed of it. Seclusion of menstruating women in traditional societies would not have endured in practice for so many centuries if it did not have a positive aspect. The little girl who retires with the menstruating women has conspicuously grown up; she is admitted to women-only conversations, the like of which she has never experienced before, and she is allowed a time of rest from her hitherto incessant duty of waiting on the family. She does not cook, but is fed, washes only her own clothes, and rests.

The almost entirely negative feelings of women in the developed world towards menstruation are as nothing compared to the embarrassment of the climacteric. The women who are most blasée about menstruating, not caring a whit who knows it, are likely to be the most anxious to conceal the fact that their ovarian function is on the blink. A very intelligent fifty-year-old woman told me once that she had slipped and broken her ankle coming out of a chain-store pharmacy. 'Serves me right,' she said, 'I was so proud to be seen buying tampons at my age! Out I swept and boom! down I went!' I could not help wondering if the cashier noticed the age of the woman buying the tampons or if she thought that she was probably buying them for someone else or if she gave a damn. I also wondered if the ankle snapped because bone loss was already taking place; the monthly bleeding of which she was so proud could have been anovulatory, break-through bleeding and not menstruation at all. (If she had been using the contraceptive pill this could well have been the case.)

In the developed world more is made of retirement from paid employment than of menopause. Getting your pensioner's bus pass is a far more significant indicator of changed status than anything we have to mark death of parents, adulthood of children and cessation of ovulation. The state and the employer have constituted themselves the arbiters of life-span events and they issue the markers. A bereaved mother in our society may not wear her dead relative's picture on her bosom, but she must show her bus pass and her pension book to any of the many strangers who has a right to see them. We have tacitly allowed visceral events like birth and bereavement to fade from public recognition, and some of the evidence seems to show that we are therefore finding them harder to deal with. If the woman who accepts hormonal replacement of the kind that causes break-through bleeding imagines that she is holding her menopause at bay she may be complicating the transition and adding to her psychic load in a way that may prove ultimately destructive. We would have a better idea of whether or not this does happen if we had any clear idea of the ideal shape of human life. If neither religion nor psychology nor anthropology nor sociology can offer such a thing, we can only improvise, staggering from expedient to expedient and evasion to evasion.

We may be witnessing a distorted version of a rite of passage when we encounter typically pre-menopausal women who badger their doctors to remove their wombs. Hysterectomy is the most frequently performed surgical procedure in the United States; for every five hysterectomies performed in the US, where 30 per cent of women aged between forty-five and forty-nine in 1988 had had their wombs removed (Riphagen *et al.*, 1988), only two are performed in England and only one in Sweden. These contrasts cannot be justified by differences in the health status of the women in the three countries, nor are they solely explained by the greed of practitioners in America. Extirpation of the uterus is considered justified not only by surgeons but also by women for relatively minor uterine dysfunction. Women themselves seem to share the view expressed in 1969 by R. L. Wright (quoted in the *Lancet*, 26 September 1987, 789):

> After the last planned pregnancy the uterus becomes a useless, bleeding, symptom-producing, potentially cancer-bearing organ and therefore should be removed.

The usual justification for hysterectomy in women approaching menopause is that the operation cures flooding: as recently as 1987, an editorial in the *Lancet* (15 August, 376) announced:

> Hysterectomy does of course stop menorrhagia; for the woman who is not interested in having children, or whose family is complete, this solution is often attractive ... [it promises] relief from her symptoms and other expected benefits – greater reliability at work, availability at all times for sexual intercourse, saving on sanitary protection, freedom from pregnancy and freedom from uterine cancer.

At the same time that the *Lancet* was defining the blisses of womblessness, psychologists were discovering that women who reported depression after hysterectomy very often reported depression before hysterectomy (Gath *et al.*); they had begun to consider the possibility that the womb had been blamed for problems that had nothing to do with it, by both patients and doctors. It was realized that a significant proportion of the women of all ages whose healthy wombs were removed for pelvic pain were possibly suffering from a 'somatization disorder' which caused them to convert stresses and unease of non-corporeal origin into symptoms that demanded self-mutilating treatment. In 1981, at the third international congress on the menopause held under the auspices of the International Menopause Society, a German woman professional asked:

What is it that makes such a large number of women allow the prophylactic removal of a healthy organ in the sexual sphere? A similar surgery boom among men would be unthinkable because men, as we all know, only undergo an operation when it becomes absolutely necessary. It is very difficult to find an answer to this question. Actively courageous decisions rarely form the basis for consent to an operation. On the contrary, the decision is often influenced by passive, partly autoaggressive tendencies. These women view themselves and are viewed by others as sexual objects; they behave in many aspects of life as passive objects and are considered to be physically and psychically inferior. The removal of the uterus from such a woman is comparable to removing the tearducts from a crying person. (Keep *et al.*, 1982, 78–9)

So far no one has distinguished a specific group of pre- or peri-menopausal women who seek to eradicate the uterus rather than allow it to 'die' inside them. Surgeons have not begun to suspect that they are being exploited in a mutilation ritual, and they have so far been quite willing to perform the operation despite their awareness that uterine bleeding is a notoriously idiopathic phenomenon. Indeed, they have accepted 'anxiety' about the uterus and its potential for developing cancer as a justification for the procedure. In an article on menopause in *Vogue*, Professor John Studd was reported as saying that in twenty years

A lot of women will elect to have a hysterectomy when their families are complete at forty or forty-five, in the way women are choosing to become sterilized now. That operation will remove their ovaries, cervix and endometrium, the three major sites of gynaecological cancer. They will then start taking Hormone Replacement Therapy and continue it indefinitely.

In other words, the progressive women of the future will undergo devastating major surgery, to mutilate themselves in order to acquire synthetic sexuality, courtesy of the pharmaceutical multinationals. One of the most disconcerting aspects of hysterectomy is that a disproportionate number are performed upon doctors' wives.

Fibroids are common in women in their forties, but the mere presence of fibroids does not justify hysterectomy. Quite large fibroids can be quite asymptomatic; others will cause some pain and increased blood loss at menstruation. In any event fibroids usually shrink and disappear with the involution of the uterus after the cessation of ovarian function. Many more women die of hysterectomy than die from the effects of fibroids. Hysterectomy is a major operation and has a number of common and serious after-effects; it is not an appropriate treatment for disorders that are milder and less dangerous than the effects of the procedure itself. Both willingness to undergo hysterectomy and the evangelism of hysterectomized women are irrational. To some extent both are the result of abuse of their authority by professionals, but there is also an element of women's own eagerness to mutilitate themselves and in particular to inflict wounds upon the abdomen. Hysterectomy is trivialized where mastectomy is dramatized; the visible mutilation (a comparatively minor operation) is dreaded in the same irrational proportion as the internal mutilation is courted.

No woman traverses the climacteric without experiencing vivid awareness of a change; if the adult can only live out the blueprint provided by pre-verbal experience, as in traditional Freudian views of human development, there can be little optimism about this change. Nowadays even in psychoanalysis Freudian determinism has had to give way before developmental accounts of the human career.

The . . . assumption – that men and women undergo significant changes as they age – has not been a congenial one to social scientists until quite recently, for developmental theory had long assumed that the most important aspects of human development took place during childhood and adolescence. Like wound-up clocks adults were perceived to be relatively stable, acting in conformity to the personalities and values they had internalized in their earlier years. By contrast most social scientists today believe that it is change, not stability along the lifeline, that is the keynote of adult development. (Rossi, 1986, 130)

Life-span theories are now very fashionable, but there is no unanimity in them. In 1950, Erik Erikson defined 'Eight Stages of Man'. Daniel Levinson (1978) elaborated this idea into a staircase model, which shows how the successful negotiation of each phase allows progress to the next, but this psychological model was challenged by sociologists who argued that changes are not triggered by chronology or biology, but by the timing of crucial life events and the individual's response to them. The two schools of thought have agreed to differ.

Evidently some people experience distinct stages of adult development while others do not. It is the degree of social complexity on the job or other aspects of everyday life that appears critical. Those who must learn a great deal and adapt to many different roles seem to be the most concerned with trying to evolve an abstract self, conscience, or life structure that can integrate all these discrete events. By contrast, those with a simple job, limited by meager education and narrow contacts, are less apt to experience ageing as a process that enhances autonomy or elaborates one's mental powers. In this connection it is perhaps significant that the stages of adult development have been worked out by psychiatrists such as Erikson and Levinson whose observations are heavily influenced by a privileged upper-middle class and professional élite. Investigators ... who have observed a wider range of lower-middle class or blue-collar people, simply do not see the same clear patterns emerging among them. Identifiable developmental stages thus appear more likely to occur in some persons and in some social settings than others. Absence of stages is the norm among their opposites. (Giele, 8)

It is difficult to relate this view of the human career to women, whose lives encompass so many changes. The growing up of children, the death of parents and the cessation of menstruation are upheaving for women regardless of social class; some of the evidence goes to show that lower-middle-class or blue-collar women are more aware of the change than more privileged women (e.g. Van Keep and Kellerhals, 1974; Severne, 1979; Greene and Cooke, 1980; Polit and Larocco, 1980; Campagnoli *et al.*, 1981). One might also have thought that most women's work, being dead-end, offers little opportunity for alternative patterns of development.

If the theorists can disagree on the fundamental question of whether or not human life proceeds through passages, we clearly cannot expect the revival of rites of passage. The theorists do not consider, of course, the importance of cultural stereotyping and projection of appropriate models, for their research is predicated on questionnaires of individuals. However, they do raise an important question, which is whether or not menopause has been over-emphasized and has become a scapegoat for other more disorienting changes in occupation and social role experienced by women in mid-life.

Fortunately, a book like this one does not need to enter into the questions of definition and discipline that must be addressed by social scientists; it is the woman's awareness of a fundamental change that is the important factor, whether it occurs with menopause, or divorce, or widowhood, or the departure or mar-riage or sexual activity of her children. The change may come early or late; it may be sudden and catastrophic, or it may be slow and long-drawn-out, or it may be jerky, or it may be divided into strands some of which go fast and are sudden, and others of which are slow and inexorable. One thing is certain; it will come and it will keep on coming.

The women of the Newfoundland fishing village studied by Dona Lee Davis between October 1977 and December 1978 saw the female life-span as 'characterized by a series of seven-year-cycles' (79). Davis had a good deal of difficulty in eliciting from these women, toughened by a hard climate and harder work, any subjective account of their own symptoms at menopause. They often described themselves and other women as 'on their changes', whether referring to the processes of pregnancy, birth, lactation and weaning, or the menstrual cycle, or the menopause. They placed a high value on courage and coping in relative silence, although they had a complicated rhetoric of 'nerves'; if asked about the subjective symptoms they attempted to compare or contrast them with the symptoms of others, in preference to making avowals on their own behalf. They did not give themselves the kind of enthralled introspective attention that could give the researcher answers to her questionnaire. As far as they were concerned, a woman who could not cope with her changes was unlikely to be able to cope with anything else; to admit to having symptoms was to complain and to complain was to admit being unable to cope. Davis was obliged to conclude that the standard questionnaires on menopausal symptoms were useless in the circumstances. She had to let the women express their concept of their own situation using their own vocabulary, which invited no comparison or translation into the language of hot flushing, irritability, joint pains, insomnia and so forth.

Modern concepts of four ages or eight ages or no ages seem to me to have no greater validity and a good deal less cultural importance than the seven-year stages of the Newfoundland women's life-span theory, which is much the same as Shakespeare's, which uses Hippocrates' division of human life into seven ages, each divided by a critical passage or climacteric. Mostly the seven ages thus defined are 'ages of man'. Women's lives are constructed of changes so vivid that they might well be called metamorphoses; often these changes, from child to woman to lover to wife to mother to grandmother, are signalled by contrasting body states from skinny to curvaceous or pregnant or obese and back again. The underlying biological changes are mostly to be hidden or denied. Only the change from single woman to married woman, which paradoxically may involve no fundamental change of life-style or biological status, has an outward, ceremonial sign, exaggerated even, in the change of the woman's name. The fifth climacteric signals the end of all the disruptions and remodellings involved in defloration, conception, pregnancy, childbirth and lactation; it is the change that ends changes. It is the beginning of the long gradual change from body into soul.

My definition of the seven ages of woman does not then correspond to Shakespeare's ages of man in all respects. Women's seven ages begin with the first critical phase or climacteric, which is birth and infancy; the second stormy passage is adolescence, the third defloration, the fourth childbirth, and the fifth, menopause. Between them lie the relative calms of childhood, maidenhood, wifehood, and motherhood. The fifth is exceeded in significance only by the grand climacteric of dying. The climacteric is not a rite of passage, but the passage itself. The menopause, being a non-event, the period that does not come, cannot be turned into a ritual. Nevertheless if we look about us we can find examples of female recognition of a change: Josephine Baker began adopting children, when? When she was fifty. Nina Berberova left the Soviet Union for a new life, when? When she was fifty. When did Helene Deutsch leave Vienna? When she was fifty, with half her life still to live, for she died at the age of ninety-seven. Few women devise as drastic a ceremonial as Helen Thayer who, at fifty-two, 'ski'd to the magnetic North Pole with her dog. She pulled a 160-pound sled for twenty-seven days and 345 miles, surviving seven polar bear confrontations, three blizzards, near starvation and several days of blindness.' Thayer courted annihilation, and several times must have thought she had found it; she emerged reborn.

If women are to celebrate the fifth climacteric by claiming special privileges, they will have to award them to themselves. If we consider the behaviour of fifty-year-old women, we may discover that in fact they do. Among the traces of vanished rites of passage we may include the new attitude of older women to jewellery; sometimes this is precipitated by the inheriting of a mother's jewellery, and the rationalization is that it would be a pity to break up the pieces. Gems have a significance of their own;

they are emblems of unchanging beauty and spiritual power; the ageing woman who wears a diamond necklace on a picnic is pleasing herself. The middle-aged woman may declare a taste for her own tipple, and for the first time a bottle of her own appears on the drinks tray. She may become interested in betting on horses or playing bingo. She might even decide to change her house for a smaller one, or for a house in the country, or for a house that demands less housework and more gardening. She might even decide after years of putting up with him for the children's sake to divorce her husband. Whatever she decides, the younger generation will click its collective tongue. The younger generation is not used to her deciding anything, and has never doubted that the pinnacle of her happiness has been achieved waiting on it hand and foot.

Other women content themselves with subtler changes in their image at a psychological stage that seems to them appropriate. Lots of middle-aged women cut their hair and stop dyeing it, and begin to leave off make-up which long-sighted eyes cannot see to apply very well. They do not shop for clothes with the same indefatigability as younger women, and they want the clothes they buy to last longer. With the gradual erosion of their narcissism, many women become more adventurous in their conversation; they begin to make their own jokes instead of laughing at the jokes of others, and to express their own opinions in the face of the most assured derision. In *La Fin de Chéri* Colette lets us see Léa de Lonval after this change has taken place. The voluptuous *femme d'un certain âge* enveloped in cunningly chosen draperies has become a massive, sexless figure like a jolly old man with a shock of white hair and a vulgar manner, who believes that the solution to all human ills can be found in good food. This figure is regarded by Colette without enthusiasm; she is not interested in how Léa became like this, or why, but we are. Colette herself did not follow the same route; she never stopped making herself up and wearing scent, and never allowed her husband to see her before she was presentable. To the last, we are told, she retained her 'femininity'.

If femininity is real, it should amount to more than a streak of kohl and a squirt of scent. Colette, like many other women, feared the virilization that accompanies old age. In *Chéri* she invented a gallery of grotesque older women who represent her middle-aged heroine's future: the Baronne de Berche, whom age is virilizing to a terrifying extent, so that bushes of hair burst forth from her ears and nostrils and flourish on her lip, or the ancient Lili, with her giggling ways, her round face made up like a doll on top of a neck like a belly, who threatens to marry the adolescent Prince Ceste. Léa is to avoid following in the footsteps of Lili by undergoing the ordeal of giving Chéri up to be married to a woman of his own generation, as the much younger Marschallin does in *Der Rosenkavalier*.

For Léa femininity is a matter of iron self-discipline; she allows no scenes, permits herself no reproaches, never in fact raises her voice. She would never leave off her corset, no matter how it pinched – '*Nue si on veut, mais jamais depoitraillée*'; if her legs are swollen, she wears her little blue boots to hide it. She knows she needs white near her face, and very pale pink for her underwear and her *déshabilles*, if the slackening of her muscles and the loosening of her skin are not to become unattractively apparent, but she tells herself too that as soon as Chéri is married and happily disposed of, she will no longer have to exercise such vigilance. Colette's contempt for old age and fear of it is evident in many small touches:

Sitting with her cheek resting on her hand, she penetrated in a dream into her imminent old age, imagined her days each exactly like the other, saw herself with Chéri's mother, kept alive for a long time by a lively rivalry which shortened the hours, and the degrading carelessness which induces mature women first to leave off their corsets, then dyeing their hair, and at last fine lingerie. She tasted in anticipation the rascally pleasures of the aged which are nothing but secret mourning, murderous wishes, and lively hopes springing eternal for catastrophes that spare no one, and no part of the world, and she woke, astonished, in a twilight rosy like the dawn. (1920, 103)

Colette was obese; she would have been surprised to hear that women nowadays consider obesity a much greater crime against femininity than wearing cotton underwear. 'Feminine' women these days prefer to maintain their flesh in a self-supporting condition. She also suffered from arthritis, almost certainly complicated by osteoporosis, aggravated by a life-style that had always been sedentary. Colette's version of femininity is theatrical, a set of assumed behaviours and an appropriate costume. Older women can afford to agree that femininity is a charade, a matter of coloured hair, écru lace and whalebones, the kind of slap and tat that transvestites are in love with, and no more. What women in the climacteric are afraid of losing is not femininity, which can always be faked and probably is always fake, but femaleness. The people who read Colette now are unaware of her dyed hair, her fine lingerie, and her corsets. They are also unaware of her contempt for age. What remains vivid and unforgettable across page after page is Colette's femaleness, which is not a matter of a rag, a bone and a hank of hair.

After centuries of conditioning of the female into the condition of perpetual girlishness called femininity, we cannot remember what femaleness is. Though feminists have been arguing for years that there is a self-defining female energy, and a female libido that is not expressed merely in response to demands by the male, and a female way of being and of experiencing the world, we are still not close to understanding what it might be. Yet every mother who has held a girl child in her arms has known that she was different from a boy child and that she would approach the reality around her in a different way. The onset and retreat of her reproductive years cannot alter that. She is female and she will die female, and though many centuries should pass, archaeologists would identify her skeleton as the remains of a female creature.

What actually happens to the ageing woman during the climacteric is that men lose interest in manipulating her femaleness; they no longer sniff around her. They do not bother to intimidate her by whistles and cat-calls as she passes the building site. They no longer communicate their confidence that she exists for them by assessing her physical charms or acknowledging them. The kerb-crawling stops. In 1973 Doris Lessing told an interviewer in *Harper's Magazine*:

... you only begin to discover the difference between what you really are, your real self, and your appearance, when you get a bit older ... A whole dimension of life suddenly slides away and you realize that what in fact you've been using to get attention has been what you look like ... It's a biological thing. It's totally and absolutely impersonal. It really is a most salutary and fascinating thing to go through, shedding it all. Growing old is really extraordinarily interesting. (1986)

The change hurts. Like a person newly released from leg-irons, the freed woman staggers at first. Though her excessive visibility was anguish, her present invisibility is disorienting. She had not realized how much she depended upon her physical presence, at shop counters, at the garage, on the bus. For the first time in her life she finds that she has to raise her voice or wait endlessly while other people push in front of her.

She does not remember how bitterly she resented being hunted and harried through the world as a desirable female, does not remember having to take in the most spectacular monuments while walking briskly and keeping her eyes trained purposefully ahead, to avoid being accosted by the men who prowled on either side, does not remember being groped in cathedrals and being frightened out of cinemas. She learns to avoid the heavy swing doors that are no longer held open for her, and to avoid places where her new invisibility means that she will be trampled and jostled.

The woman who retains the viewpoint of the young, to whom older people are not only invisible but uninteresting, will manage this transition badly. Yet if there is no objective correlative outside herself by which a woman may take her bearings, no marker buoys for the channel, the most intelligent and sensitive woman can find herself drifting at the mercy of destructive currents.

Simone de Beauvoir struggled for years with her contempt for her own age group. As a result, though she had every resource that any human being could have, intelligence, prestige, work worth doing that health and opportunity allowed her to continue, and an impressive circle of friends and acquaintances, she aged ungracefully and ungratefully. Every day she told herself, 'I am not what I was' and wasted precious time in bitter regret. Though she was spared for longevity, and an old age unbedevilled by poverty or disease, she felt no gratitude, no sense of her good fortune whatsoever. Many happier people have died younger and unwillingly left a life they loved, but Simone de Beauvoir felt she owed them nothing, certainly not to be happy.

Women will have to devise their own rite of passage, a celebration of what could be regarded as the restoration of a woman to herself. The passionate, idealistic, energetic young individual who existed before menstruation can come on earth again if we let her. In a symposium on 'The timing of psychosocial changes in women's lives', a Californian researcher 'took as a given that women themselves are the experts in understanding their own lives and that they need to take the description and analysis of their own experiences into their own hands' (Hancock, 275).

Only when women confronted what life had laid at their feet and began to question where they themselves stood in the configuration of their lives, did they become aware that they had pictured themselves happily embedded in enduring relationships. With these images shattered, they began to realize that investing in relationships without articulating a sense of self could not ensure against change, damage, or loss. Women who could forge a new framework for living in which the self became the subject of experience and the object of care credited their maturity to this process.

The decisive maneuver in this developmental pivot sprang from a person's ability to seize autonomy and wield initiative on her own behalf. A woman who could respond to the disintegration of old assumptions by threading her way back to childhood and catching hold of a girl she could draw strength from and rely on matured. Women who had no such childhood self to retrieve succumbed to defeat. (278)

Before she herself had traversed the climacteric, Helene Deutsch took a dim view of the post-menopause years as a retreat from genitality to immaturity. In her old age, her view changed:

The biological destiny of old age varies from one individual to another. Like all the developmental periods of life, it depends greatly on the events of adolescence. To our stereotyped way of thinking, the process of growing up is identical with the conquest of the stormy forces of adolescence. Yet I feel that my *Sturm und Drang* period, which continued long into my years of maturity, is still alive within me and refuses to come to an end . . . I find that there are still ecstasies and loves within me, and that these feelings are rooted in my adolescence. They may be reaction formations against the threat of death, but at the same time they represent the generous impulses of the most energetic period of my life. (1973, 215–16)

We might develop better strategies for the management of the difficult transition if we think of what we are doing not as denial of the change or postponement of the change, but as acceleration of the change, the change back into the self you were before you became a tool of your sexual and reproductive destiny. You were strong then, and well, and happy, until adolescence turned you into something more problematical, and you shall be well and strong and happy again.

3

The Lucky Ones

If turning fifty gave us the keys to the city, if turning fifty entitled us to first place in the queue, if turning fifty gave us the right to sit down, the physical discomforts of the climacteric would be a small price to pay. Dr Barbara Evans, in the preface to the fourth edition of her book, *Life Change*, tells us:

> Some societies reward women for their services to the race when they reach the end of their fertility, giving them the freedom and often the status they had lacked during their reproductive years. Women from countries where age is venerated suffer less physically than other women at the change of life, or menopause. Unfortunately, ours is not one of those societies. (11)

There are societies surviving on the planet where the principle of seniority is generally respected and where the seniority of the older woman is not negated by the fact of her sex, but none of them is a society in which any of us would want to live or in which any of us could live if we wanted to. We do not actually know whether venerated women 'suffer less physically' (i.e. have less physical discomfort) at menopause, because no systematic study of their subjectively perceived well-being has ever been undertaken. Against the spectrum of toil and pain which is the life of a Third World woman, the distress of the climacteric could hardly be said to bulk large.

It is true that in hundreds of thousands of village communities in Asia and Africa older women find themselves at the centre of social organization, but every one of those societies is under extreme stress. With every year that passes more and more of those communities succumb to the pressures of urbanization and modernization. In any case it should be clearly understood that, though the extended households of traditional Asia represented something for which most people might aim, they were never the majority of households in any settlement. Poverty, conflict, changes in the system of land tenure, famine, migration, illness and death could all frustrate the family building process and usually did, especially in countries undergoing colonization. The success of the extended family involved not only success in bearing the required number of male children and bringing them up to competent adulthood, neither an easy matter, but also complex social strategies, together with skilful management of the household capital and of the intrapersonal relationships that guaranteed the quality of life, and a modicum of sheer good luck. The bigger the family the better it weathered upheavals, because the loss of one senior male did not leave the family rudderless or fragmented. The richer the family the better able it was to profit by the wreckage of other families. In societies dominated by such families there is not the traditional gulf between public and domestic life that guarantees the subjection of women. Power within the family equals power in the body politic. The contribution of the senior female to the extended family is second in importance only to the role of the patriarch, and in some cases not even to that.

. . . the extended family is practically the only organized economic unit in Afghan rural society, sharing production and consumption. It shares all resources belonging to members; it distributes the total production and income among its members according to need and social position . . . The Afghan extended family is also the primary social unit. Individuals are identified primarily by the family to which they belong. Enculturation and socialization take place primarily within the household; children learn the roles that they will perform as children, adolescents and adults . . . the extended families are the base social units through which

64

individuals interact with the larger socio-cultural environment. (Hanifi, 50–51)

In families like the Afghan families, which can be found in greater or less proportion throughout the sub-continent, a single woman is not given total responsibility for the socialization of her children, which is the duty of her whole family; nor are children taken out of the home to be indoctrinated in child ghettos by a horde of underpaid professionals. In all such families women are subject to men, but the fact of segregation means that in terms of daily interaction the women are not at the mercy of the men. They cannot be terrorized or beaten, for example, unless the other women in the family agree to it; they are less likely to be raped by a husband, because their health and the health of their babies is of paramount importance. Husbands are usually not permitted unlimited access to the bodies of their wives, who often sleep alongside their children. Though the relationship of consort is important, and women often have a vivid and hilarious imagery of their own for matters sexual, it is not the only or even the primary relationship.

Companionship is not valued in the relationship between a man and his wife or wives. A man must never show affection for his wife in front of anyone else, and it is assumed that there are few common grounds for conversation between an Afghan husband and wife. The relationship is confined to economic cooperation and sexual intimacy. Such a relationship does not preclude affection, but the only permitted public manifestations of it are economic cooperation and the procreation of children. (52)

For the Asian woman in a traditional family the affection of her mother-in-law and her sister-wives, and of their children, and even of her younger brothers-in-law, may well be more important to the quality of her everyday life than her husband's degree of partiality to her. In western society, by contrast, it is assumed that an ideal sexual relationship should have expanded to engulf all other relationships. This notion in itself increases the load of anxiety on the menopausal woman who feels her interest in sex declining. No other role within her personal relationships is open to her, her mothering function having withered away to that of short-order cook and bottle-washer for a family that more and more nowadays cannot be bothered even to eat together. The western woman has no option but to regard possible loss of sexual interest as tantamount to utter uselessness or even death. The ageing woman in the Afghan household moves closer and closer to the centre of activity at the same stage in her life that the western woman finds herself pushed to the margins.

A woman is outwardly required to submit to the will of her husband, but she is an indispensable part of the household. Much household activity is outside the concern of husbands and this guarantees a wife autonomy to manage these affairs. The wife, like all women, accepts her overall inferiority as part of the Afghan social order, but her immersion in her own affairs greatly mitigates this sense of inferiority. Beneath the outward submissiveness is a realization and understanding of the indispensability of her own household activities. (52)

Those activities are not merely cooking and cleaning. The Afghan, like any other traditional south Asian household, produces its own foodstuffs or buys them unpackaged and unprocessed in bulk. The amounts needed have to be carefully calculated; the quality of the food must be controlled and maintained. The senior wife is responsible for controlling the release of supplies stored in the household. Mistakes in her calculations, or in buying goods of inferior quality, can be catastrophic. A shortfall before the next harvest, rot or infestation in the storage bins can mean having to acquire further supplies when the price is high. The successful economic management of such a household is at least as demanding as the successful management of a small restaurant. As the wife ages and ascends in the seniority scale, more and more of this responsibility with its accompanying power falls to her. If she is incompetent the whole family suffers and may break up. At least one recent observer has come to the conclusion that the cessation of ovulation has been selected for, so essential is the role of the post-menopausal woman to the survival of her family.

The menopause is nature's original contraceptive that freed women for leadership in the extended family and in the broad community. In many traditional cultures a woman's status increases with age, as one might expect, on this sociobiologic basis. (Parry, 20–21)

The life career of a woman in the traditional family in pre-literate society is both difficult and dangerous; as a young bride she comes into the house of strangers where she is last in the pecking order and has to wait upon everyone else. Her status changes noticeably with the bearing of her first male child, but in all things she is subject to her husband and her husband's mother, or to her appointed surrogate, and has to study to please her. As her sons approach adulthood, the wife's prospect of becoming mistress in her own household draws nearer and nearer. She may initiate the splitting off of her nuclear family from the household of her husband's parents, for example if her husband is a younger son or if she is at a disadvantage in relation to another of the wives, so that she can begin to build up a household of her own to which her own sons will bring wives in their turn. She may on the other hand find herself assuming command of the other women and children as her mother-in-law becomes too frail to do so, or dies. At all points in this development she is required to adjust, and the adjustments are often so difficult that she becomes ill. In pre-capitalist or pre-literate societies pregnancy and childbirth themselves are dangerous; survival is anything but assured. The woman who finally makes it and finds herself assuming authority over new daughters-in-law and running the large household must usually have done so during the climacterium, but we would be surprised to find any significant amount of evidence relating to its discomforts on the part of women who have everything to congratulate themselves upon in having reached it.

The importance of climacteric distress grows as the lives of younger women become more liveable. As most women no longer have to endure the bitter grief of infant death, or dread each childbirth as a time of danger, or spend most of their reproductive years pregnant or lactating, all the negative aspects of the years of fertility have faded from recall. We have only the relatively minor inconveniences of practising contraception and regular menstruation to mar 'the best years of our lives'. As most of our dealings with traditional families have involved us in concerted attempts to control their high fertility, we have always addressed ourselves to the reproducing women, and have always assumed that their mothers-in-law were tyrannical, unsexed figures who treated their daughters-in-law like breeding machines. Because we encountered stress and unhappiness among young wives we assumed that the husband's mother was by definition a hated, repressive figure. If in fact she is, the extended household will soon fission. The successful mother-in-law rules the extended family by love. Her wisdom, based upon her experience, should protect and guide the economic activity of the whole group to the perceived advantage of all its members; in a well-run extended household life should be perceptibly easier than in separate nuclear families. If there is less work for individuals because it is done collectively, if there is more food because it is more efficiently produced or economically bought, stored and prepared, if children are safer and happier, there can be small motivation for splitting up. If on the other hand a younger wife feels herself persecuted or put upon she will stop at nothing until she can escape into a home of her own, even if it is a rented hovel or a slum on the outskirts of a city. The woman who wins the love of her daughters-in-law and extends her household by keeping all her sons and their wives and children with her is vividly aware of her success and good fortune, even if she is not to be spared the heavier household tasks, not to be offered the choicest morsels at each meal or allowed to spend all her time playing with the babies and young children, or allowed to smoke tobacco and drink with the male elders.

It would not bother Balram's wife if anyone should watch her. She is old and her head is always covered . . . Balram's wife is now undisputed mistress of the household . . . Because of her age and greying hair she moves about the neighbourhood with her face only partially covered. She enjoys diversions as much as does Balram. Once when a special fair was held at the temple near Mainpuri, six miles from here, she wanted to go. They do not own an oxcart nor did she have the bus fare. So she went and returned on foot, delighted with all that she had seen and heard, and, except for tired feet, not much the worse for wear.

She spends most of her time sitting in her own courtyard where she can watch all the comings and goings in the lane . . . She is old enough to be free of most restrictions, so when one of the sons of Prakash's family comes into the courtyard and younger *bahus* cover their faces, Balram's wife carries on in her high-pitched voice with whatever tale she is relating . . . Jiha and the *bahus* enjoy her. She is not fussy, nor is she easily offended, and seems able to create laughter at all times. Circulating gossip – amusing gossip – is her chief contribution . . . (Wiser, 81–3)

Balram's wife's good humour fails her only when one of her daughters-in-law goes home to visit her mother, and she must do her chores for the duration:

. . . her taste of freedom as a mother-in-law has made routine work seem heavier than it was before. (83)

What we observe in societies organized upon such lines is a female hierarchy existing alongside the male power structure, with its own sphere of influence and considerable bargaining power. In the community of Ksar-Hellal in the Tunisian Sahel, for example,

Women pass through an expectable series of age roles in which they establish skills and personal relationships in the family and household through which they exert influence and control. (Stamm, 26)

Marriages are arranged, usually by negotiations with neighbouring families initiated and conducted until the final stages by the older women. For many women the most painful aspect of the system is their separation first from their own mothers, and then from their daughters. The painfulness of this separation from the mother, considered to be the source of love, is eased by the allowing of long visits by daughters to their mothers' homes. It is common for wives to return to their mothers' houses for their first and subsequent confinements, and to remain there for weeks and sometimes months after the child is born. With the birth of sons and the cementing of the relationship within the new family the woman gradually acquires influence in this new sphere, but she never forgets her strong attachment to her own mother.

It is in her role as mother of adult children that a woman has the opportunity to exert the greatest degree of social power . . . adult children more frequently turn to their mothers for advice and support . . . with increasing age . . . women in Ksar-Hellal continue to represent a source of affection, assistance and advice for their adult children, and thereby maintain their role of influence within the family. Rather than losing the main orientation of her female role in her older years a woman in Ksar-Hellal extends her influence into the households of her married children. (28–9)

The fact that the Ksar-Hellal love and honour old ladies is not going to popularize their life-style in our own countries nor will it materially aid its survival in Tunisia. In South India these matrifocal values have survived transplantation to the cities.

Many women become grandparents in their early forties and this adds a new dimension to their domestic roles. Daughters come home for their confinement, and stay for long periods. If they live in Madras, they visit very frequently . . . Most women welcome and accept eagerly their role as grandmothers and if they have grandchildren living with them they devote a great deal of time and attention to them . . . the position of a wife is one of subordination, that of a mother is much more powerful. (Caplan, 58–9)

Among the Tamils of Jaffna the situation is analogous; post-menopause is seen as a parallel with pre-puberty, with important differences:

While the young child has little influence except over an adoring father, the middle-aged woman can wield great influence over her family. She retains the auspiciousness of the married state and is less fettered by the social reticence expected of a young bride. She is in the optimal position to influence decisions of significance in her family, especially in the crucial matters of marital alliances for her sons and daughters. (David, 99)

However, we can learn little about this interesting situation because it has failed to intrigue most anthropological researchers, who have tended to be, if not young and male, young and male-dominated.

This stage has not been extensively researched and deserves the greatest consideration for an adequate understanding of the role of women in South Asian society. (99–100)

Few women living in modern society would regard the supremacy of mothers-in-law as a desirable phenomenon, partly because they do not like to think of themselves as doomed to spend thirty years or so playing such a repellent role. Clearly, too, such a system is very hard on childless wives. Moreover, the numbers of single women in societies organized on these principles are insignificant; where marriage is arranged by the imperialist family, marriage is a universal condition. The lucky women for whom the climacterium is associated with positive gains in prestige, freedom, leisure, authority and influence are a minority; they have always been outnumbered by the women who have not yet made it or did not make it. The sufferings of widows in such societies can be terrible: Indian widows are not usually permitted to re-marry and often stripped of their possessions and forced into perpetual mourning and seclusion. In countries like Iran, where men marry women much younger than themselves, 23 per cent of women aged between forty-five and fifty-four are already widowed; among women aged fifty-five to sixty-four the propor-tion rises to 48 per cent (Rudolph-Touba, 233–4). In most Asian communities such women are entirely at the mercy of their relatives. The lucky mother-in-law must keep not only herself and her sons alive long enough for her to come into her own, but her husband as well. Where the middle-aged woman with a husband is powerful and auspicious, the middle-aged widow is an outcast.

In modern nuclear families there is only one relationship of intimacy and importance and that is the relationship between spouses. If that does not work the family must be jettisoned, the feelings of the children being of relatively little account. The modern woman has only two possible sources of satisfaction, her relationship with her husband and her relationship with her employer. Some of the limited studies that have been done seem to indicate that women who have rewarding work to do deal best with menopause; it seems fairly obvious that women with work they enjoy doing will ignore symptoms, if they form them, for as long as they can, so that they can continue effectively with the work they love and will refute any suggestion that the effects of the climacteric may disqualify them from doing it. Though the menopause itself may have no positive aspect, there are positive reinforcements for making light of it.

The women who have satisfying, well-paid work to do are another lucky minority. Many of the studies of their attitudes can hardly be applied to the condition of minority women or working-class women, many of whom have endured the hardships of the life of a junior female only to find when they themselves become senior that the rewards have been cancelled. Nowadays fifty-year-old women who respected their mothers and nursed their grandmothers find themselves without honour and left to the care of strangers. They have been caught in the transition from one kind of system, a system identified perhaps with the self-help networks of the working class or the ghetto, to another generally considered better, more progressive. At worst the woman who grew up in a house with her gran and her mother and her aunts and did her bit to help out for them will eventually find herself imprisoned in an inadequately heated council flat that she is too frightened to leave because old women are easy pickings for the muggers on the streets outside. For a woman in such a situation every marker of advancing age brings real dread. Symptom formation for her is part of a strategy of survival, for only if she is sick will someone look after her.

The loneliness and vulnerability of old women is the ultimate achievement of a centuries-long campaign in the western world to destroy the power of the mother. She has relinquished her sway not to the sire of her children but to the patriarchal bureaucratic state of which each authoritarian family is a microcosm. In order to maintain his authority in our tiny households a husband must continually assert the primacy of his needs over the demands of the children. The mother in such a family must play the consort before all else; she can expect no fulfilment in her mother role. Indeed, she may be required to give the care of her children into the hands of menials and professionals, in order to concentrate all of her attention on her functions as her husband's sexual partner and the principal indicator of his wealth and social standing. Though twentieth-century wives do not have armies of servants to care for their children, they are obliged to commit the children to nursery school, to school, to camp, to bed in their own rooms before daddy gets home, and even to the tender mercies of the baby-sitter. The woman who works outside as well as inside the home has even more difficulty in giving in to the demands of the love affair with her babies. As Estelle Leontief put it in her poem 'Painting in Pompeii':

> We shut the album on the mother
> who's always crying,
> always wild
> with unrequited love.
>
> (Luria and Tiger, 144)

In terms of the individual woman's life, the attack upon her mother-right was mounted as soon as her children were conceived, when professionals took over the management of her pregnancy and the birth. The mother's body was denied her children, who slept apart from her. They were driven about in carts and carriers instead of carried in her arms or on her back, and for some generations at least were even denied the breast. It is not up to a mother to socialize her child or to teach it the family's way of doing things. These functions having been taken over and carried out inefficiently by the state, the mother is denied the honours of maternity.

All that remains to the mother in modern consumer society is the role of scapegoat; psychoanalysis uses huge amounts of money and time to persuade analysands to foist their problems on to the absent mother, who has no opportunity to utter a word in her own defence. Hostility to the mother in our societies is an index of mental health. Mothers whose hearts yearn for their children are told that they have over-identified with their mothering role, that they were possessive or over-protective. Mothers are forced to learn to dissimulate their vulnerability, to harden their hearts, and this often before their children are at all able to cope alone. Whether immature, confused or even disturbed, at eighteen years old our children are no longer our business, though they have no compunction in using us whenever they wish to exploit our vulnerability to them. In societies where this is not the case, where a mother's love and nearness are considered among the sweetest sweets of existence, seeing one's daughters become mothers is a joyous experience.

Organizing relationships so that mothers accumulate prestige, power and autonomy as they grow older requires matrilocality, which simply means that the mother is within physical reach of her grown-up children, who are not being moved about will they nill they at the behest of an employer. Equally essential perhaps is a degree of social stability which allows the development of patterns of interaction and accretion of experience that can only remain relevant in the absence of rapid technological or economic change. In traditional societies, the ageing mother has mothering functions to perform in the families of her grown-up children, caring for the birthing woman, mothering the older children when their mother is involved with a new-born, disciplining and socializing them according to the family's system of values. In such families there is not a single scapegoat mother, but a succession of big mothers and little mothers, some of whom are male.

We can see some such mechanisms surviving in some working-class communities in Britain, or in black communities in the United States.

The patterns of black female role behaviour rarely result in depression in middle age. Often the 'grannie' or 'auntie' lives with the family and cares for the children while the children's mother works; thus the older woman suffers no maternal role loss. (Bart, 215)

The mother-centred household is associated with stagnation, with high fertility and with poverty, all indices of backwardness. Most people in the industrialized world see such systems as situations to escape from, rather than to aim for. Aiming to build an extended family in western society would be futile in any case, for one cannot live in such a system without intensive training from birth. The nuclear family has difficulty lasting until its children are grown up and could only in the most exceptional circumstances turn into a larger and more durable social unit. Having to live with one's in-laws is regarded principally as a penalty for improvidence. Though many couples have to do it, none of them is proud of the fact and nearly all of them experience the situation as all but unbearable. Living with the in-laws is regarded as sufficient explanation for marital break-up.

With every year that passes, the role of the grandmother is further weakened so that there is in it for most women absolutely nothing to be looked forward to. Older women must look for satisfaction where men do, in their relations with their employer, which will end with a crunch at retirement age, usually earlier for women than for men. A recent study of the well-being of women in their middle years found that the principal determinant of women's perception of the two factors studied, 'mastery' and 'pleasure', was employment status; the higher the prestige of the job they held, the higher their well-being rating.

The findings of this study cast doubt on the utility of the constructs often cited as critical for understanding the psychological well-being of women in the middle years. The major correlate of the sense of mastery was employment status, a construct rarely given serious consideration either in theory or in clinical practice, as central to psychological well-being. Occupational prestige, even more neglected as a 'woman's issue', is also an important determinant of well-being. (Barnett and Baruch, 109)

The greatest subjective awareness of pleasure was in the combination of married state (husband present) plus high-prestige employment (cf. Nathanson, 1980). Menstrual status, subjectively assessed as pre-menopausal, menopausal and post-menopausal, was irrelevant. When asked if they would have lived their lives differently the unmarried women said they would not have married, and the childless did not regret their childlessness. The 'empty nest' was of no importance. The results are less surprising when we learn that the sample was composed only of white women living in a small town in the Boston metropolitan area. Less privileged inhabitants of our world might find little to admire in their system of values.

Though most of us would shudder at the thought of being co-opted to the zenana or the harem in the interests of a happy post-menopause, we might feel more attraction to the Tiwi way of organizing sexual relationships. The Tiwi, of Melville Island, Northern Australia, believe that just as menstruation is caused by sexual intercourse, the cessation of intercourse brings about the cessation of the menses:

. . . by the time a woman reaches menopause she is likely to have had extramarital sexual relationships, and, more importantly, she is likely to have had two or more husbands . . . a woman's first husband may be a man much older than herself, and as she grows older and her elderly husband dies, she is married to perhaps a succession of men, each one younger than the preceding one. Her older co-wives may also die off until she becomes the oldest wife of a young man. If this happens, the young man may have several quite young wives whom he prefers as sexual partners. Extramarital love affairs for the older woman also tend to diminish as the young men reach the age of contractual marriage. These three facts: relative age of husband and the aging woman, relative age of wife among co-wives, and the declining possibility of extramarital affairs, may, when taken together, affect the frequency of sexual intercourse and may be the reason for the statement that 'stopping of sexual intercourse causes menopause'. (Goodale, 227)

The older woman has many consolations for the stopping of intercourse:

... as a women approaches menopause, her power and prestige directly increase. (227)

Not only does the woman have a position of particular authority with regard to her son-in-law, she may also be a first wife, who 'can sit all day in a camp and send the other wives out hunting' and instruct the other wives in the manner of rearing their children, for she is the 'supreme mother' of all the co-wives' children.

Her daughters and her co-wives' daughters will in all likelihood remain members of her domestic group until she dies and thus continue to be influenced by her. (227)

Moreover,

Old women are ... treated with a great deal of respect by their sons. They are not only looked after and cared for but their advice is sought and frequently taken. (227)

We can only wonder how much less women might suffer at menopause if they were to acquire power, prestige and responsibility instead of losing all three. We can barely imagine a world in which fifty-year-old women are routinely asked to advise their adult sons, and that advice is taken, or where grandchildren are reared according to grandmothers' ideas of child management. Already, when Jane Goodale was working with the Tiwi in 1954, the system had begun to break down; widows were not remarrying, officialdom was treating husbands as heads of families and ignoring female authority, and young women were demanding modern monogamous marriage.

African women writers are aware that the power and influence of matriliny are being corroded by the effects of modernization and its attendant social disruption. With the mechanization of agriculture women are being driven off the land while their families are menaced by the iniquity of outwork and migration to urban centres. In a short story called 'New Life at Kyerefaso', Efua Sutherland fashions a new myth for dispossessed women in which the matriarch is served and honoured by the new men and enriched by their technology.

'See!' rang the cry of the Asafo leader. 'See how the best in all the land stands. See how she stands waiting, our Queen Mother. Waiting to wash the dust from our brow in the coolness of her peaceful stream. Spread skins of the gentle sheep in her way, gently. Spread the yield of the land before her. Spread the craft of your hands before her, gently gently.

Lightly, lightly walks our Queen Mother, for she is peace.' (22–3)

This tranquil, majestic figure does not exist. Western mythology furnishes many examples of groups of female types that may be no more real. One is the group of women who go mad and commit suicide both at and because of menopause; the other is the group of women who blithely traverse the climacteric years with never a moment of panic or a hot flush. Just how many such women there might be and who they might be is impossible to discover. Everyone who has considered the problem has targeted a different group and questioned them about different sets of symptoms. Some questionnaires muddle up symptoms of ageing with symptoms thought to be caused by cessation of ovarian function, and others make an equally misguided attempt to separate them. Some try to question well women, others women reporting to clinics, others all women between the ages of forty-five and fifty-four, and others the female population of all ages. Questioners discovered that women who had never complained of a symptom would nevertheless admit to suffering from it if questioned. They were not so quick to figure out that, if they asked about symptoms that they associated with menopause, the woman who admitted to experiencing them might have suffered from them for most of her life. The questionnaires were specifically designed to circumvent the women's own definition of menopausal experience; the women were seldom offered the opportunity to distinguish between chronic problems and new ones that they connected with menopause. It was as if the researchers were defining the experience and then challenging the women to admit to it. It is conceivable, for example, that the successful matriarch or prime minister when questioned about climacteric symptoms could admit to having symptoms of considerable severity and because of the design of the questionnaire, or the terms of the interview, would not have the opportunity to add that severe or not, they were *unimportant*. Given women's tendency to underrate their symptoms on one hand and the common prejudice that they overrate them on the other, the outcome of investigations of apparently symptomless women at menopause is completely inconclusive.

Researchers sought to prove one or other of two hypotheses, one that menopause is insignificant, the other that it is catastrophic.

In 1880 A. Arnold, Professor of Clinical Medicine and of the Diseases of the Nervous System in the College of Physicians and Surgeons in Baltimore, contended that all the recent studies of menopause reported no pathology associated with it. In 1897 Andrew Currier called the negative view of menopause a 'hoary' tradition with no basis in fact. In 1900 Dr Mary Dixon Jones writing in the *Medical Record* angrily called the notion of menopause as a 'dangerous period' a libel on the natural formation of one half of the human race. In 1902, writing in the *Transactions of the Tennessee State Medical Association*, M. C. McGannon wrote with regard to menopause that 'it is in no sense a critical period'. (Banner, 6)

In her note to this passage Lois Banner quotes nine more authorities, all of whom argue that there is no pathology connected with menopause, and balances them against the medical propaganda of 'climacteric insanity' and 'involutional melancholy'. Despite the sturdiness of the opposition, however, belief that the climacteric is a problem phase is still unshaken.

Thinking about menopause, then, is rather like thinking about the menstrual cycle: the schools of thought are two. One holds that nothing of any significance is taking place, and the other that the stress and strain of what is taking place are so acute that sensible behaviour is not to be expected of women. Both kinds of arguments conceal crude misogyny. The 'nothing happening' school reserves the right to despise women who are encountering difficulties, and the '*Sturm und Drang*' school allows itself to treat femaleness as a pathological condition. Women's experience of menopause is of a piece with their experience of menstruation; neither is fun but both can be managed. Both would be managed better, of course, if the concerns of women counted for more than the concerns of big business. If technology was at the service of women, we would by now understand what is going on in middle-aged women's bodies and we would take steps to ensure that the natural process was not frustrated or distorted.

It is clearly true that some women simply stop menstruating and that is more or less that, while others undergo as much as ten years of struggle. Some sources claim that two-thirds of the fifty-year-old female population feels as well and happy as ever it did. Mary Anderson, writing at the behest of the Medical and Nursing Editor at Faber & Faber in 1983, recommends the positive approach:

It is important that women should keep the menopause in perspective, and remember that it has been estimated that only one-third of menopausal women will experience symptoms of any degree of importance to them . . . so strongly does the author feel about this point that *no apology will be offered in the next chapter for reiteration of the fact that*

the topic discussed may never be experienced by the individual woman.
(35-6)

The next chapter discussed 'Menopausal symptoms and signs', and again at the top of the list Dr Anderson places in capitals 'NONE'. And at the end of the chapter she reiterates:

There may be many symptoms and signs associated with the menopause but, especially in the well-balanced, educated, contented woman who finds her family, sexual and professional life fulfilling, *there may be no symptoms whatever.* (58)

Researchers at King's College Hospital Medical School, including John Studd, Consultant Obstetrician and Gynaecologist and founder of one of the first menopause clinics in England, put the case rather differently:

Far from being a welcome relief from fertility, these years may be a time of great stress and are currently regarded as being more than a mere manifestation of the normal ageing process, but as a chronic endocrinopathy associated with varied symptomatic and degenerative changes which may be greatly affected by the patient's socio-cultural background. The symptoms are severe enough in 25 per cent of women for specific replacement therapy to be considered. Fifty per cent of women have minimal symptoms which last for up to a year and the remainder seem to be untouched by any characteristic climacteric problems. (Studd *et al.*, 1977, 3)

Studd's method of arriving at these figures is nowhere explained. It seems unlikely that only a quarter of the women attending King's College clinic will be offered hormone replacement therapy, but it is difficult to see what other statistical basis Studd has available to him. The clinic population is already atypical in that it is attending a clinic at all. As Dr Herman noticed in 1898,

Women will not keep under medical care for what they know to be a natural process. (585)

Studd's division of the female population passing through the climacteric into a quarter who feel symptoms grave enough to require treatment, a half who have 'minimal' symptoms, and a quarter who are 'untouched' is probably completely arbitrary.

The people who are pushing oestrogen replacement have a different attitude. As they are peddling a remedy, they have to encourage people to feel the illness. Sir John Peel, who used to be Queen Elizabeth's gynaecologist, introducing Wendy Cooper's *No Change*, a polemic intended to persuade women to demand hormone replacement therapy, describes menopause in terms that make us wonder how every woman traversing it does not capsize:

The changes that affect both the body and the mind at and after the menopause are immensely complicated. Not only are there hormonal changes, but also emotional, social and family changes, and no one really knows why in fact some women, *albeit the minority* [my italics] pass through their fifties and sixties with little physical or emotional disturbance. (7)

What Sir John, Fellow of the Royal College of Physicians, Fellow of the Royal College of Surgeons, means by *immensely* complicated changes is simply that he and his distinguished colleagues do not understand them. They are capable of understanding much more complicated phenomena, but the endocrinology of femaleness has never commanded sufficient attention or sufficient funding to make a tenth of the advances made in, for example, sports medicine. Gynaecology has never really been a prestige area, for reasons too obvious to state.

Raewyn Mackenzie, who set up the first menopause clinics at the Auckland branch of the Family Planning Association in 1981, would not agree with Dr Anderson that the women who traverse this tricky period without noticing anything amiss may be as many as two women out of three:

Some women, and usually those whose hormonal systems have slowed gradually, find that they have few problems at menopause. But others of us experience sudden drops and then accompanying bursts of hormones, and our bodies may act in a confused and deprived way until the transition back to a non-fertile state is achieved. According to surveys about 80 per cent of us will experience some symptoms ... (18)

Mackenzie is using the data from a United States National Health Survey made between 1960 and 1962 in which 16 per cent of respondents said that they had 'experienced no symptoms at all'. There is clearly a difference between this percentage and the 60 per cent of Dr Anderson's English patients who experienced no symptoms 'of any importance to them'. Dr Anderson's two-thirds probably do not realize with complete equanimity that their periods have stopped, throw away their unused sanitary napkins and face the future with optimism and confidence, glad, if anything, that the worries of contraception and the inconvenience of the 'curse' have both gone away, but they do not recognize their difficulties as symptoms requiring treatment. Again the situation parallels attitudes to menstruation as described by Doreen Asso in *The Real Menstrual Cycle*:

It appears that two broad approaches among relatively 'aware' women can be discerned. Some will feel that, because they are being controlled by biological processes, they are helpless to remedy the situation. Others will use their knowledge to attribute adverse responses to the cycle, and will compensate for its effects ... As regards the 'unaware' women, there are also two broad groups. Firstly, those who do experience and report biologically-based variations which they do not relate specifically to the menstrual cycle. Secondly, there are those, apparently a small minority, who state that they do not experience any significant changes. There is some evidence ... that this group do in fact experience changes of the same magnitude as the women who do report changes. (175)

Indeed, some of Asso's evidence seems to show that women who do not attribute their problems to the menstrual cycle find them harder to deal with than the ones who do:

For example there is the finding that women who report no premenstrual symptoms attempt suicide more often premenstrually than women who do report symptoms ... Another example is a study showing that, in response to the same amount of stress, there was a significantly greater (measurable) physiological reaction premenstrually than at other times in the cycle, for all women, including those who reported no change in their subjective state. There is no need to invoke hypothetical mechanisms such as 'denial' to explain this lack of awareness of important menstrual changes on the part of some women. Some of them believe that changes are part of the general course of events and do not know that they are specific manifestations of the menstrual cycle. (175–6)

Asso's conclusion is at least as true for the climacteric as it is for the cycle:

All women have to incorporate and adjust to the changes as best they can, with very little information or support, and some have preferred to see them as an unremarkable matter of course rather than to appear awkward, self-important, neurotic and so forth. We have seen, for example, that in general some individuals label their internal sensations as important, and some do not. The point of interest is that profound changes take place in the cycle in all women, including those who do not report them. (176)

Applying Asso's observation of the menstrual cycle to the climacteric, then, we can agree that the climacteric is a difficult period for every woman; the real difference between the 'lucky' and the 'unlucky' is that some women experience their difficulties as medical problems and others do not. A 1980 study by Fairhurst and Lightup found that the climacteric symptoms experienced by women who did not call upon their doctors were much the same and of the same severity as the symptoms of the ones who did.

When women managed their own bodies, delivered their own children and medicated themselves, the difficulties they encountered in managing their reproductive processes were dealt with within the female community. Women were shy of sharing such matters with strange young men, and such shyness still discourages many older women from seeking treatment for trivial but sometimes humiliating and painful ailments. Women's shyness colludes with men's lack of interest in older women to produce our present ignorance about the avoidability and otherwise of climacteric distress. This is not a tendency that anyone would wish to encourage, but the medicalization of menopause is equally undesirable.

There is much to be said in support of Dr Anderson's attempt to stress the possibility and even likelihood of a symptom-free transition from fertility back to infertility, for anxiety about symptoms can well produce them, but pretending that most women find traversing the climacteric easy is equally counter-productive. Women who find menopause difficult are the more likely, in the presence of a mythology that says it is usually easy, to believe that they are part of an unlucky minority and in need of treatment. As every menopause is different, doctors can hardly be blamed for refusing to tell women what to expect, but it should also be understood that symptoms become more manageable if we have an explanation for them. One of the problems that appears in menopause literature is 'fear of serious disease' or 'worry about health'; the woman whose joints are paining her might fear, for example, that she is rapidly developing a chronic arthritis. To learn that severe and inexplicable joint pain can be connected with menopause is consoling rather than otherwise.

The truth is that the fifth climacteric is hard for every woman, but some are able to deal with it unaided, and others are not. To differences in the kinds and degrees of difficulties encountered must be added the woman's greater or lesser tendency to self-reliance and/or the degree of her acceptance of pain and misery and/or her perception of how much others, and particularly younger women, are suffering. Once women are actually being questioned about their symptoms in the climacteric and they have agreed to talk about them, it is very difficult to assess how much subjective importance those symptoms have. If the questioners have already decided what symptoms constitute the climacteric syndrome and ask about these, we can no longer tell if the woman herself relates them to the climacteric. Headaches are a case in point. Headaches are listed among climacteric symptoms; menopausal women have admitted to having headaches; subsequent researches have tended to show that women who are headachy at menopause have reported headaches at other times, and sometimes more often. It would of course be very strange if a woman who responded to stress by developing a headache did not have headaches at menopause. It would also be odd if these women thought that the headaches they had during menopause were menopausal headaches. On the other hand, many women do not know that joint pains, pins and needles and crawling skin are more often experienced at menopause and may be expressions of vasomotor disturbance.

Many women have discovered, moreover, that complaining does not always make things better. The reactions of others, whether members of the family or health professionals, can make us regret that we ever allowed a groan to pass our lips, for many of us find that we are better able to cope with our own distress than anyone else. Nobody wants to be fussed over at menopause, nor does any woman want to invite callous indifference. Rather than add other people's reactions to her problems she may well decide to button her lip and tough it out.

The increasing tendency of younger women to show an interest in menopause and to begin to ask for information about it is due in part to their growing awareness of their bodies and their understanding of the importance of being in good shape to handle whatever might be demanded of them. They exercised for efficient childbirth and they expect to be able to prepare for the stress of the climacteric. The current concern may be summed up as: 'The climacteric is a period of exceptional somatic stress and we need to be fit to deal with it, but what kind of fit should we be?' What they encounter when they begin to ask for information about the management of their post-reproductive career is utter befuddlement.

Women who have achieved their reproductive aims go on menstruating notwithstanding. This may be a good idea but equally it may not. Modern women menstruate more than any other women in history, and some of the evidence seems to indicate that the repetition of dozens of episodes of frustrated ovulation does constitute a stress upon the female body. Women who have been pregnant for more of their lives tend to cease menstruating later; perhaps by imitating pregnancy and resting the ovaries, as it were, for more of a woman's reproductive career we could delay the final cessation of ovulation. Some women must encounter menopause simply as the non-reappearance of their periods after the birth of a child; it would be interesting to know for certain if these menopauses are symptom-free. The scanty evidence we have seems to indicate that they are. Alternatively, menopausal symptoms in such cases may be masked by the stresses of late childbirth and lactation, exacerbated by the exhaustion caused by the unremitting demands of manual work and a large family. Climacteric distress may be noticeable only to women who are well enough to feel it. This, however, does not constitute a ground for ignoring it in the women who do feel it.

The woman who asks for information because she does not want to make heavy weather of her climacteric will find little understanding of the nature of her request. One thing she is likely to be told is that she will probably have the same kind of menopause as her mother did. This could be encouraging or deeply depressing, depending upon the mother in question. The likelihood is that a daughter's reproductive career has been so different from her mother's that the small degree of probability represented by heredity is counteracted by factors such as their differing marital status, ages at childbearing, different number of children borne, whether they lactated or not, used contraception, smoked, were obese, worked outside the home. Your mother's menopause may give an indication of what yours will be like, but only if all other things are equal, which they are unlikely to be.

While British doctors tend to discourage a younger woman

from trying to prepare for menopause and even to withhold helpful information, some had no sooner observed what they took to be beneficial effects of hormone replacement on the health of post-menopausal women than they began prescribing replacement hormones for women who were still menstruating regularly, as part of a strategy for deferring the ageing process. This is the dippy and dangerous side of menopause medicine which peddles eternal youth. Most women are too sensible to toy with any such notion. It is the more reprehensible then that to the woman who accepts the fact of transition and simply wishes to handle it wisely, the medical profession can say nothing helpful.

Should we wish to be younger at menopause to cope with menopausal stress or is it better to delay it? Should we lose weight or try to put it on? Should we exercise or rest? Can we take a little more wine than usual, or is this more likely to burn up our oestrogen supply? Should we eat more, differently, less? Should we give up red meat, cheese, chocolate? What is it that the women who experience 'no symptoms at all' are doing right?

If our medical practice followed the rules of common sense (or motor mechanics) we might have the answer to that question. We might know enough about well women to understand what is not working for the women who feel unwell. We should by now have identified the mechanism which enables two-thirds or 20 per cent or 16 per cent or indeed *any* women to feel no unmanageable physical symptoms during the climacteric. If one woman on earth can get through the climacteric without missing a beat, then all women should be able to. Many of the women who suffer symptoms during menopause want to know if 'there is anything wrong' with them. They are told either that their suffering is normal, i.e. not the symptom of an illness, and to be borne, or that it is the symptom of a deficiency disease for which they should be treated. What they are not told is why some women do not suffer during this natural process, from which we may infer that though the process be normal suffering is not an intrinsic part of it, or why some women have developed a deficiency and others have not.

While preserving due scepticism about the existence of a group of women who are absolutely 'symptom-free' at menopause, we must not forget that the existence of a proportion of 'lucky ones' provides the justification for the view that menopause is a natural process and not a disease entity.

4

The Unlucky Ones

'I will now show you,' the great Kraepelin used to say in his lectures on clinical psychiatry, 'a widow, aged fifty-four, who has made very serious efforts to take her own life.'

This patient has no insane history. She married at the age of thirty, and has four healthy children. She says that her husband died two years ago, and since then she has slept badly. Being obliged to sell her home at that time, because the inheritance was to be divided, she grew apprehensive, and thought that she would come to want, although, on quiet consideration, she saw that her fears were groundless. She complained of heat in her head and uneasiness at her heart, felt weak and excited, and was tired of life, especially in the morning. She says she could get no sleep at night, even with sleeping powders. Suddenly the thought came to her, 'What are you doing in the world now? Try to get out of it, so as to be at rest. It's no good any longer.' Then she hung herself up behind the house with her handkerchief, and became unconscious, but her son cut her down and brought her to the hospital. (Kraepelin, 6)

In the hospital she began to recover and was allowed to stay with her married daughter. In less than two weeks her condition had deteriorated so much that she had to return to the hospital, where her recovery was slow and she suffered many setbacks.

She has no real delusions, apart from fear that she will never be well again. Indeed, we find that the real meaning of the whole picture of disease is only permanent *apprehensive depression*, with the same accompaniments as we see in mental agitation in the sane – i.e. loss of sleep and appetite, and failure of the general nutrition. The resemblance to anxiety in a sane person is all the greater because the depression has followed a painful external cause. But we can easily see that the severity, and more especially the duration, of the emotional depression have gone beyond the limits of what is normal. The patient herself sees clearly enough that her apprehension is not justified by her real position in life, and that there is absolutely no reason why she should wish to die. (7)

It seems unlikely that Kraepelin and the widow understood the same thing by her 'real position in life' or by being 'well'. We can guess that the widow had never had anything in her life besides her husband and her children, and we may doubt whether an unhappy older woman was really welcome in the households of her children. We may understand too that leaving the house where she had reared her children was a severe and disorienting wrench. At least some of the widow's behaviour could be understood as protest against her own emargination. 'I have nothing to live for' can be translated as 'You have left me nothing to live for', but women are discouraged from attributing blame to any but themselves. In the hospital she was at the centre of Kraepelin's and his pupils' attention at least some of the time; there was no encouragement to show steady improvement and nothing to leave the hospital for. As for not eating or sleeping, hospitals are not noted for appetizing food or surroundings conducive to sleep.

From observing cases like this, Kraepelin arrived in the fifth edition of his *Psychiatrie* at a definition of involutional melancholia.

Melancholia, as we have described it here, sets in principally, or perhaps exclusively, at the beginning of old age in men, and in women from the period of the menopause onwards ... About a third of the patients make a complete recovery. In severe and protracted cases, emotional dullness may remain, with faint traces of the apprehensive tendency. Judgement and memory may also undergo considerable deterioration. The course of the disease is always tedious, and usually continues, with many fluctuations, for from one to two years, or even longer, according to the severity of the case. (1896)

The heat in the head might have been the vasomotor disturbance of menopause, which the widow misinterpreted because she did not know that it was a common and unpleasant but meaningless symptom; likewise the 'uneasiness at her heart' might have been palpitations, unnerving at first, but equally insignificant. The poor woman was truly unlucky to lose her husband and her home during the immediate post-menopause; twenty-four years of marriage with four children are not the best preparation for living on one's own. Running one's own home is not the best preparation for living in someone else's. Struggling to make the new adjustment, to come to terms with a set of circumstances over which she had absolutely no control, the widow broke down. If she really decided to die, those who observed her decided that her decision cannot have been rational. If she was threatening suicide as a form of protest, she was behaving hardly less irrationally. She was sick. Unable to treat her situation, the medical establishment had to treat her.

The treatment of the malady cannot, as a rule, be carried out, except in an asylum, as thoughts of suicide are almost always present. Patients who show such tendencies require the closest watching day and night. They are kept in bed and given plenty of food, though this is often very difficult, on account of their resistance. Care is taken to regulate their digestion, and, as far as possible, to secure them sufficient sleep by means of baths and medicines. Paraldehyde is generally to be recommended, or, under some circumstances, alcohol, or occasional doses of trional. Opium is employed to combat the apprehension, in gradually increasing doses, which are then by degrees reduced ... Visits from near relations have a bad effect up to the very end of the illness ... (Kraepelin, 1904, 9–10)

... when presumably the patient decides that enough is enough, and resumes control of her own life. Kraepelin found in her case evidence for the existence of a specific climacteric syndrome, but by any common-sense assessment the widow was undergoing a series of catastrophic shocks when she was least able to bear them. An uncomfortable menopause complicated by mourning, not in itself a rare phenomenon, together with protest, placed her in a madhouse and in the psychiatry textbooks for the next fifty years.

Popular awareness of menopause as 'the dangerous age', already high at the end of the nineteenth century, was itself a cause of anxiety. Women themselves feared the coming alteration because of the prevailing general impression that they would be transformed into something monstrous, a bristling half-man, beset by lecherous urges and bitter malevolence. Not only did middle-aged women fear that they might be doomed to 'climacteric insanity', they also had to deal with other people's prejudices based on assumptions about their menstrual status. Whether they were actually undergoing the change or not, whether they were register-ing their own symptoms or not, they were treated as if they were. We are not surprised to find in such cases that women become extremely frustrated and irritable as a consequence. If any protest on the part of middle-aged women is to be regarded as the widow's was, as evidence of a pathological condition within her, middle-aged women are under more pressure than ever to suffer and be silent. The only strategies available to them are either to deny menopause to the only persons who will credit its denial, namely themselves, or to develop symptoms that positively demand intervention and treatment. The treatment was likely to be drastic, for not only did the women unconsciously pressure doctors for destructive procedures, conspicuously failing to respond to conservative treatment, the doctors were only too willing to give it to them. Bleeding, cupping, purging, and provoking issues in menopausal women are all ritualistic mutilations that persisted despite the vociferations of a few professional men and rather more women, who could see that there was no rational therapeutic basis for any of these treatments.

In 1798, in the midst of the furore about the introduction of 'man-midwives', S. H. Jackson, a distinguished London physician, took it upon himself to address female patients directly. Unusually he included remarks on the correct understanding of menopause:

> On the principle menstruation commenced, so it ceases . . . With these important changes, the constitution may sympathise, and be discomposed, if improperly treated; but by the laws of nature, the general health, both before and after these local alterations may be better than when under the influence of menstruation, which was solely ordained for one important function in a woman's life . . . (Jackson, 20–21)

In 1833 the American William Potts Dewees also tried to dispel the prevailing impression that the climacteric was attended with special risks.

> The vulgar error, that 'women at this time of life are all in danger' is replete with mischief for the suffering sex. (148)

He argued, moreover, that if forty-five-year-old women are imbued with the notion that the future is

> so replete . . . with horrors to come . . . we may very justly suspect apprehension to be the cause of some of the distressing symptoms which sometimes accompany this interesting process of the human uterus . . . (145)

After a lifetime of delivering babies and treating their mothers, the Widow Boivin declared in the book published in England in 1834 as *A Practical Treatise of Diseases of the Uterus* that

> Derangements of the catamenia, whether as causes or effects, very frequently occur in the early period of life, and it does not appear that the time of their cessation abounds in diseases. (13)

The English translator adds:

> (Note: We merely remark that this influence has been exaggerated. M. Benoiston of Châteauneuf has proved by numerous extracts from

burial registers, that mortality is not more considerable, from the fortieth to the fiftieth year, in women than in men.)

After many years dealing with the truly frightful sufferings of women in childbed, Mme Boivin was unlikely to treat as serious any disorder that did not result in increased morbidity or mortality. Though other practitioners seeking a lucrative practice among older women might write feelingly of the danger of severe mental derangement and permanent invalidism, Mme Boivin dismisses the entire climacteric experience in a few terse words:

Sometimes irregularities occur, indicating approaching cessation. The catamenia may be, for once, insufficient in quantity and fail shortly after; then at some indefinable period a copious and continuous flow may ensue: these evacuations may sometimes occur twice in a month, then several months will pass without any appearance. The persons who have been subjected to these irregularities for three or four years, have grown thin and been alarmed, but have afterwards perfectly recovered their health. (14)

Samuel Ashwell, writing a *Practical Treatise on the Diseases Peculiar to Women* ten years later, includes a whole chapter on the 'Disorders attendant on the Decline of Menstruation'. He begins coolly enough:

It has become too general an opinion that the decline of this function must be attended by illness; but this is surely an error; for there are healthy women who pass over this time without any inconvenience and many whose indisposition is both transient and slight. (196)

He acknowledges that women have their own ideas about the climacteric, but in his version they themselves are responsible for the spread of apprehension about it:

Females themselves anticipate this period as extremely eventful, denominating it 'the critical or dodging time', 'the turn of life' etc. . . . There are women who have never been vigorous and well during the middle period of their lives and some who have suffered from protracted illness or chronic uterine maladies who after this time acquire what they term 'a settling of the constitution' and good health. (196–8)

Though Ashwell's common sense persisted in some quarters, a different view was being disseminated and, for no obvious reason, becoming an unquestionable certainty. In 1851 an anonymous author contributed an essay on 'Woman in her psychological relations' to the *Journal of Psychological Medicine and Mental Pathology*, in which the sinister changes attendant on the cessation of ovarian function were described:

With the shrinking of the ovaria . . . there is a corresponding change in the outer form . . . The form becomes angular, the body lean, the skin wrinkled. The hair changes in colour and loses its luxuriancy; the skin is less transparent and soft, and the chin and upper lip become downy . . . With this change in the person there is an analogous change in the mind, temper and feelings. The woman approximates in fact to a man, or in one word she is a *virago* . . . This unwomanly condition doubtless renders her repulsive to man, while her envious, overbearing temper, renders her offensive to her own sex. (35)

One would imagine to read this that the author had never met a jolly, fat old woman. By 1874 J. M. Fothergill could insist, in *The Maintenance of Health*, that the climacteric is a time of crisis which tests women beyond their endurance.

The records of the Divorce Court, the annals of asylums, the dates on the tombstones in the churchyard, all tell us of the severe strain put upon the system of the woman during the change of life. (112)

If Fothergill had bothered actually to consult the records of the law courts, madhouses and graveyards, he would have seen that his impression was not borne out by them. Perhaps this irrational certainty derived from France, where in 1848 a story called 'La crise' by Octave Feuillet was published in the *Revue des Deux Mondes*, and so captured the public imagination that it was immediately adapted for the stage and eventually played at the Comédie Française. In the story the wife of a magistrate has gradually gone peculiar. From being utterly sweet and biddable, she 'now speaks a language full of sharp, bitter words, harsh and peevish maxims'. Her husband finds 'in her conversation – previously so mild – a banal melancholy, a sharp, poetic flavour, with a socialistic tendency'. As the possibility that this behaviour might signal a justifiable revolt against the dictatorship of the family is quite unthinkable, it is decided that the problem is simply her '*âge critique*' (Cooper, 69–70).

Some commentators have seen in the heightened French awareness of the menopause evidence of a greater interest in scientific matters. The same interest, presumably, encouraged Georges Apostoli in 1856 to begin wiring up a selection of rods and knives to a battery, running an electric current through them and inserting them into the uterus, the cervix having first been dilated by uterine sounds 'to the diameter of a No. 10 bougie', and another electrode being placed on the abdomen (Allbutt, 316). The negative pole was used to disintegrate tissue, the positive where an astringent or condensing action was wanted. There was no lack of eager customers:

A second effect, which one may often observe in cases under treatment, is the production of a sense of improved well-being which is frequently felt from the first. Everyone who has had an experience of any extent in the treatment of pelvic diseases by electricity must have noticed how often the patient expresses herself as greatly benefited by the treatment long before any definite change can be detected in the local condition. (Allbutt, 317)

In 1896, when this was written, electrogynaecology was all the rage and had generated a large body of research, principally relating to the ways and means of setting up the equipment. Higher and higher charges were being used; fibroid tumours were being pierced and electrocuted, pelvic tissue was being burnt; patients were dying of shock, infection and the untreated original condition. Meanwhile in more than fifty years no direct beneficial effect of electricity on uterine tissue had ever been demonstrated. There was no option but to abandon the method. By 1920 it was no more than a bad memory.

In 1858 John Charles Bucknill and Daniel H. Tuke published the first textbook of psychiatry, *A Manual of Psychological Medicine*, which remained the authority for twenty years. They took the trouble to investigate what Fothergill had merely assumed, and found that Dr Webster's review of 1,720 cases admitted to Bethlem Hospital indicated that change of life was the least common physical cause of insanity in women.

The most common physical influence which occasioned insanity among women, was unquestionably puerperal, of which description 70 examples were enumerated. Uterine disturbances, as also prolonged lactation and change of life, were besides often recorded as the apparent physical cause inducing mania in females; but these were by no means so frequent as either puerperal influences or intemperance. (260)

They described a case of 'Suicidal Melancholia, changing to Mania', 'Supposed cause of insanity the climacteric period'.

A gentlewoman aged fifty. Has been a most active, intelligent woman, exemplary in all the social relations, and ruling a large family with much judgment and force of character ... Insane three months. *Mental State.* – Much distressed, full of gloomy forebodings, distressed about pecuniary matters, wondering how things are to be paid for, thinks all her family are ruined, &c.; hears noises which sometimes she wonders at and cannot understand; at others, she recognizes them for the voices of her children, and then holds conversations with them; has great weariness of life; begs to be hung or otherwise destroyed, and makes constant efforts to commit self-destruction; watches every opportunity to secrete articles to tie round her neck, and grasps her throat with her hands until she becomes black in the face: when baffled in this thrusts articles down her throat ... (514)

Her bowels were 'torpid, functions of the uterus suppressed'. Her head was shaved and anointed with a cooling lotion. All her symptoms became more acute when her bowels had not been opened, so opened they were, with calomel and jalap, Seidlitz powders and castor oil in pill form. Two or three times a week six leeches were applied to her temples. Every other night she was given a warm bath, and every night she was given morphia. After six months the poor woman was desperate to be allowed to go home; her altered condition was construed as mania.

... works at her needle; has frontal headaches; eye restless, suspicious and angry ... her melancholy gave place to a continued angry excitement; very obstinate and impatient of interference; full of complaints at being kept from home; it often required several nurses to administer her medicine; sleep sometimes good, sometimes she walks her bed-room all night. (515)

For this they dosed her with tartrate of antimony and warm baths.

She retains her angry, wilful bearing, with strong personal antipathies; while her sarcastic remarks and shrewd observations ... show that the intellectual faculties retain their full vigor ... (515)

She improved in the eleventh month but in the twelfth she began to misbehave again, so they dosed her hard with calomel.

During the twelfth month great fluctuations, – sometimes angry, railing at everyone, and at others conversing rationally and courteously. (515)

By force of regular dosing with violent purges her bowels would not function without daily doses of castor oil, nevertheless, eighteen months after she was admitted to the asylum, she was pronounced recovered and allowed to go home. Though neither Bucknill nor Tuke believed the diagnosis of climacteric melancholia, the certainty of the mass of practitioners that such a thing existed was not shaken. Another case of acute melancholy with delusions, though accompanied by scanty catamenia in a woman of forty-four, was ascribed to moral causes, for the poor woman had expected the man she was living with to marry her when his wife died, but her younger sister made a set at him and the ensuing fracas persuaded him that he did not want either of them. Though the asylum attendants bathed her in tepid baths and sprayed cold water on her hot head and applied leeches to her temples, she showed no sign of recovery. They tried five grains of crude opium five times a day but it made her feel sick and her head continued to be very hot. Then they cupped her from the nape of the neck, six ounces a time, once a week for four weeks, but she made no improvement. As might be imagined, this tender care simply reinforced her desire to die. The prognosis was bad.

Bucknill and Tuke were comparatively merciful; they did not allow the mechanical restraint of patients no matter how violent, still less the beatings and cold-water duckings that were still practised in some institutions. Nor did they allow themselves to fantasize about the kind of woman who was most likely to encounter difficulties during the climacteric. Their work was the beginning of rational care for the mentally disturbed; it is the more to be regretted that their scepticism about the influence of the uterus on the brain was not more widely shared. Women themselves did not share it and produced symptoms of derangement which corresponded to their attendants' expectations, somatizing their psychic distress in ways which are nowadays never seen. By the turn of the century gynaecologists were loudly insisting on a close relationship between the uterus and the brain, which they demonstrated by pointing to women whose insanity had been cured by correcting 'retroversions' and prolapses, and by oophorectomy and hysterectomy. Lunatic asylums began to appoint gynaecologists and carry out spaying and hysterectomy as an integral part of treatment, long before such operations were safe.

In the introduction written for the first French edition of *The Dangerous Age* by Karin Michaëlis which was included in the English translation of 1912, Marcel Prévost claims that

in all the countries of Central Europe the most widely read novel of the present moment is *The Dangerous Age*. Edition succeeds edition, and the fortunes of the book have been increased by the quarrels it has provoked. (8)

Prévost considered that the novel owed much to 'medical science' and saw it as an important contribution to fashionable sexual psychopathology, yet when we put pressure on the novel what emerges is not a description of climacteric syndrome, and may even be a denial of its existence. The heroine is forty-two when she leaves her husband, whom she married for his money, to live in a virginal house where her bedroom has a glass roof through which she can see the stars. She has a young maid whose emotional life is equally stunted by women's inability to follow the dictates of their own idealism and their enforced capitulation to male demand. The heroine's friends, though of differing ages and temperaments, are in difficulties too. One suicides, one runs away with a younger man. The heroine invites the only man she has ever loved to visit her, imagining that at last they will be lovers. He comes, but she is turning grey and has got too heavy for her favourite white dress. She sees at once that he no longer loves her and decides to go back to her husband, only to find that he is to marry a nineteen-year-old. She and her maid decide to take a trip around the world.

From the outset Michaëlis's heroine and her friends are aware of the belief that women are supposed to traverse a 'dangerous age'. Agatha Ussing, the suicide, has bought the whole idea, including the notion of psychopathy consequent upon cessation of ovarian function.

If men suspected what took place in a woman's inner life after forty, they would avoid us like the plague or knock us on the head like mad dogs . . . The worst of it is I know my 'madness' will only be temporary. It is a malady incident to my age . . . (58)

Another friend makes a suggestion with which I have a good deal of sympathy:

Somebody should found a vast and cheerful sisterhood for women between forty and fifty; a kind of refuge for the victims of the years of transition . . . Since all are suffering from the same trouble, they might help each other to make life, not only endurable, but harmonious. We are all more or less mad then, although we struggle to make others think us sane. (90)

Though her friends might be so certain of the source of their distress, the heroine herself is obliged to ask 'a woman's specialist':

When is the 'dangerous age'? He looked seriously at me and answered: 'Really there are no absolute rules as to age. I have had cases at forty; again I have known of them at sixty.' (122)

If the 'woman's specialist's' cases are not connected with the climacteric, they must be connected by something else. The key in all cases seems to be misbehaviour involving the rejection of a woman's lot. We might as well consider Nora's walk-out in *A Doll's House* as a manifestation of the dangerous age. Michaëlis's heroine seized the opportunity to widen the application of the term:

Thereupon we began to discuss the thousands of women who are saved by medical science to linger on and lead a wretched semi-existence. Those women who suffer for years physically and are oppressed by a melancholy for which there seems no special cause. At last they consult a doctor; enter a nursing home and undergo some severe operation. (122–3)

It might seem that Karin Michaëlis shares the general conviction that the vicissitudes of the uterus render women's lives a misery to themselves and others, but there is an undercurrent of scepticism that shows in this extract. Women were indeed having their bodies cut about in an effort to cure vague malaises of all kinds, and the procedures were apparently producing the right result, but Michaëlis leaves open the possibility that they are simply destructive. It seems very unlikely *a priori* that natural menopause produced the same derangements that were treated in younger women by inducing artificial menopause.

One school of thought held that women became amoral at menopause, because their sexuality was liberated from its reproductive function and became like a man's. Michaëlis appears not to hold with the common notion of the virilization of older women.

Hitherto nobody has ever proclaimed this great truth; that as they grow older – when the summer comes and the days lengthen – women become more and more women. Their feminality goes on ripening in the depths of winter. (91)

In fact Michaëlis's heroine has broken out of a cool and passionless marriage, not because of rejection of her sexuality but because of a realization of the injustice that she and women like her must be doing themselves, only to discover that, as far as her male contemporaries are concerned, it is too late. Michaëlis dramatizes her heroine's helplessness by having her educated by a rich old man who is rearing her to be his wife, only to be rejected by him because she cannot hide her disgust when he becomes ardent, then having her fall in love with a penniless artist whom she rejects for the solid loyal husband without whom she cannot survive. Her divorce sets her free. We may be permitted to hope that in her trip around the world she finds sexual and emotional fulfilment – not too tall an order for a well-preserved, well-to-do Danish woman of forty-five or so.

There were many attempts to debunk the notion of the dangerous age. In 1923, Laetitia Fairfield examined the data collected in a survey of the health of elementary schoolteachers in England, nearly three-quarters of whom were women. Her conclusions were published in the *Lancet*: at that stage menopause phobia had reached such levels that, in her words, one 'famous institution' had adopted a practice 'of getting rid of its women employees at forty-five years'. Fairfield protested against the injustice of such a system and the disincentive that it provided for the professional women of the future. She pointed out that ascribing a cluster of ills to menopause could obscure genuine pathology that needed treatment, and that the fear of menopause itself could cause illness. She found that women in the climacteric age group had less absenteeism than women in other groups, probably because most of their absenteeism in other age groups, which was conspicuously higher than men's, had been caused not by their own illnesses but by their children's, and that women's illnesses connected with menopause caused less absenteeism than any other factor. She thought it worth pointing out that she had found 'not a single case of insanity' through such a cause. Hers is the voice of common sense:

No woman can be expected to *like* such a concrete reminder that middle age is upon her, and those of unstable and imperfectly adjusted temperaments will inevitably find adaptation to this new phase of life a difficult matter. Of the 'geyser-like eruption' of the emotions which is said to precede the physical signs I have been unable to discover any traces. As far as my observation goes, the neuroses due to emotional repression seem to be much more common in the middle thirties than in the forties. One finds that cantankerousness and groundless suspicion are not the monopoly of any one period . . .

Even other contributors to the *Lancet* did not take her point. H. Crichton Miller, writing a few months later on 'The Physical basis of emotional disorder', assumes that menopause phobia is completely justified. He begins with an unfunny witticism.

The menopause presents problems in every department of medicine, with the possible exception of orthopaedics. The menopause has necessarily the most profound significance from an emotional point of view for the women whose maternal aspirations are unsatisfied . . . we must not ignore the endocrine side, for the withdrawal of ovarian hormone has a repercussion on both thyroid and adrenals ... A temporary vagotonia ensues which, if it replaces a previous sympathicotonia, determines grave physiological changes. To ascribe the neuroses of menopause to psychic conflict is to express a partial truth ... (*Lancet*, 23 February 1924, 380)

The followers of Dr Miller, having seen the remarkable results of the treatment of thyroid deficiency with thyroid extract, treated all these grave derangements with various endocrine substances, most of which were completely inert. A huge business sprang up; every meat-packing company formed a medical division where the ductless glands of slaughtered animals were processed to provide the life-giving extracts. Professor Langmead, lecturing to students at St Mary's Hospital Medical School in 1922, pointed out to them that the extracts of ductless glands could not possibly be exerting any biochemical action to bring about the effects attributed to them, lamenting the 'pall of reckless assumptions and commercial enterprise in which [endocrine therapeutics] is now befogged' (*Lancet*, 14 October 1922, 820), but the traffic in expressed ovarian juices kept on expanding.

The ovarian extracts given to women may have done no good, except as placebos, but at least they did no harm. The same cannot be said of the treatments offered for the heavy bleeding of the pre-menopause, which were often more dangerous than the bleeding itself. All kinds of symptoms, including giddiness, palpitations, delusions, nervousness, and general debility, were attributed by the learned gentlemen to anaemia resulting from such bleeding. The women themselves were prostrated as much by terror as by lack of red corpuscles, until some were apparently in actual danger of death, though no death from such a cause was ever verified. The doctors, unable to replace the blood or rapidly to correct the anaemia by any other method, resorted to all kinds of techniques to stop the bleeding. The classic technique was curettage, which stops bleeding caused by retained placental matter or overgrowth of endometrium. Much of the uterine bleeding they saw was caused by fibroids; one solution was to stop the bleeding by removing the bleeding organ, by surgical hysterectomy. Many surgeons preferred this method, which is still popular and used on the same slight justification. Others, who noticed that fibroids shrink naturally at menopause, were in favour of castration. Though surgical oophorectomy was practised for other ills such as nymphomania or *furor uterinus* (which if it existed at all was probably a manifestation of thyroid storm), it was not the method of choice for bleeding in the peri-menopause.

In 1905 Halberstadter discovered that bombarding with X-rays caused atrophy in the ovaries of rabbits. Within months doctors began to use massive doses of X-rays on women to kill the ovaries and induce menopause. There was little agreement about the amount or the method, for the mechanism was little understood. The treatment was lengthy and expensive and could be carried out only in a specially equipped hospital. Other doctors favoured castration by the insertion of radium rods into the vagina; this had the disadvantage of causing local burns, and involving other organs, but the method was portable and easier to administer than X-rays. Deaths from ulceration of the bowel and intestinal burns certainly ensued. Though the response of patients seemed highly idiosyncratic, gynaecologists began to entertain the idea of radiating quite young women in order to control heavy bleeding and bring about a normal discharge. We can only wonder now at the flimsy rationale behind such drastic use of novel and mysterious techniques. How much carnage resulted, we shall probably never know. Many of the women who died had not the faintest idea what had brought about their untimely demise.

To complain to a doctor is to demand treatment; to get treatment, of any kind, sometimes persuades the suffering woman that her condition is improving. The more ceremonious, dramatic and expensive a treatment, the greater the placebo effect. Besides, climacteric distress is of short duration; a treatment that takes six months or so may simply coincide with the end of the business, especially as most women have waited for months or even years before asking for help. In the case of the unfortunate widow who attempted suicide during the climacteric, the treatment for her melancholia may well have protracted her suffering. If it worked at all, it may have worked as aversion therapy. The contrast between her life as it was and her life in the madhouse may have been strikingly to the advantage of her life as it was, which seemed utterly bearable by contrast. Women who attempt suicide are clearly experiencing life as unbearable, but we cannot decide therefore that it is the climacteric that makes life seem unbearable. Such distress is always 'multi-factorial'; to emphasize the element of stress due to menopause is to throw the woman back upon her own resources, which are plainly exhausted. Women can bear the unbearable just so long. Women who leave their husbands and/or children during that period do so not because they are finding the climacteric unbearable, but because they are finding their husbands and/or children unbearable. The woman who lashes out at menopause has found the breach in her self-discipline through which she may be able to escape to liberty. Many of the treatments she will be offered are simply ways of walling up her escape hatch and condemning her to quiescence.

There is of course an element of stress in menopause. Ageing is not easy for anyone, but it is easier for some than for others. For some women, some say one in three, others one in four, it is very much more difficult than for others. Studies of menopausal females in general, as distinct from women attending clinics, tell us variously that 95 per cent of menopausal women admit to feeling irritable (Neugarten and Kraines, 1965) or only 35 per cent (Jaszman et al., 1969b) and only 21 per cent to feeling tired (Thompson et al., 1973) or as many as 93 per cent (Sharma and Saxena, 1981); either 78 per cent of all menopausal women experience depression (Neugarten and Kraines, 1965) or only 21 per cent (Thompson et al., 1973); insomnia affects either 67 per cent (Sharma and Saxena, 1981) or 27 per cent (Thompson et al., 1973). If the figures of the principal studies of the occurrence of symptoms in the general population are averaged out, we arrive at something like the percentages collected by Jaszman, who concluded that women who are approaching menopause are likely to exhibit fatigue, irritability and depression, and those coming away from it, insomnia and mental imbalance. The first group of symptoms is taken to be the result of oestrogen deficiency; the second the consequence of ageing.

The symptoms reported by women attending menopause clinics are often divided into three categories: somatic, psychosomatic and psychological. The first group comprises symptoms that are considered purely physical: hot flushes, cold sweats, weight gain, flooding, rheumatic pains, aches in the back of the neck and skull, cold hands and feet, numbness or tingling in extremities or crawling skin, breast pains, backache, swollen ankles, bloatedness, and bowel disorders. The psychosomatic symptoms include fatigue, headache, palpitations, dizzy spells and blind spots before the eyes. The distinction between physical and psychosomatic appears synthetic to say the least; deciding *a priori* that a headache is a psychosomatic symptom seems a suspect diagnostic procedure at best. If fluid retention is present, headache is to be expected as a purely physiologic response to the engorgement of the brain. As researchers have failed to relate hot flushes to oestrogen deficiency, or indeed a deficiency of anything, there seems to be no reason for deciding that it is a purely somatic symptom. Any woman could tell researchers that a hot flush is more likely to occur after frustration or embarrassment than when she is tranquilly proceeding with a task that presents no particular problems. Women often resent hot flushes that are otherwise bearable because they think that other people can observe them. Sometimes hot flushes present as a kind of sensory hallucination; one's clothes seem to have grown burning hot or one's hair seems to be burning one's neck.

The psychological symptoms would be better described as behavioural symptoms: irritability, nervousness, feeling blue or depressed, forgetfulness, excitability, insomnia, inability to concentrate, tearfulness, feelings of suffocation, concern about health, panic attacks, 'mental imbalance', fear of nervous breakdown or insanity have all been reported by women complaining of climacteric distress. Some of these are clearly responses to existing physical symptoms; a woman who feels exhausted will not be able to cope with vasomotor disturbance, and will be kept awake by it at night and so becomes more exhausted, and expresses her exhaustion in whatever way is natural to her, by becoming weepy or irritable or infuriated. Older women react differently to climacteric distress than younger women, well women than sick women, happy women than sad women.

At all points along the climacteric continuum the health practitioner is invited to make judgements. He (much more rarely she) is drawn to decide whether his patient is a good coper, whether she is stable, whether she relates well to others, with only the foggiest notion, if any, of what she might have to cope with, what shocks may have rocked her stability, who the others might be to whom she is relating well or ill. Insomnia is always regarded as a symptom of psychological disorder, when there are clear changes to be observed in sleep patterns as a result of ageing. A symptom is more likely to be psychological if it is typical of the woman's response to other stresses not themselves connected with menopause, in which case it is properly not menopausal at all. If all clinicians were to take the attitude of Bodnar and Catterill that

the emotional changes (during the climacteric) are of multi-factorial etiology, and the climacteric may only accentuate a pre-existing psychic insufficiency. (2)

women would be ill-advised to ask them to help in handling the menopause. The concept of 'psychic insufficiency' is not only unscientific, but intensely moralistic, but many of the Masters in Menopause hold it, or something like it. Even Lauritzen, the German Master in Menopause, can permit himself to observe that

The climacteric uncloaks many of the neurotic and psychogenic symptoms that women have managed to suppress until then. (1973, 5)

He might as well argue that menopause corrodes the ego and

reveals what has been hiding behind character armour for fifty years. Such attitudes lead directly to the implication, an implication that women all too readily pick up, that if you have a bad menopause it must be your own fault (see Chapter 5). Women who sail through, on the other hand, can feel superior to women who don't, thus increasing the pressure upon distressed women to conceal or disguise their suffering. One of the psychogenic factors operating is anophobia (irrational fear of old women) on the part of the clinician, which has more to do with his relations with his mother and wife than with the demeanour of his patient.

Studies of the female population attempting to discover the frequency of symptom development during menopause are few and mostly unsatisfactory. The first was conducted by the Council of the Medical Women's Confederation in 1933; 1,000 women whose ages ranged from twenty-nine to ninety-one, many of them institutionalized, were asked if menopause had incapacitated them. The study concluded that

in view of the general impression acquired from the literature on the subject it was somewhat surprising that approximately 900 of 1,000 unselected women stated that they had carried out their routine tasks without a single interruption due to menopausal symptoms. (*Lancet*, 1933 i, 106)

It was thirty years before another attempt was made to study the occurrence of menopausal symptoms in the middle-aged female population; the number of symptoms that featured in these investigations varied from forty to eight (Greene, 43). Sometimes the point was to find which symptoms were properly menopausal, in which case sometimes younger women were included in the sample, and whether they could be distinguished from general symptoms of ageing, in which case sometimes men were included in the sample. Given the size of the 'constellation of symptoms' reported at menopause, it is not surprising that research-ers have never been able to find sharp peaks in the prevalence of any of them 'at menopause'. No woman could have survived having all the symptoms, nor could she expect to endure them throughout the climacterium. Some of the studies seemed to show that certain symptoms were more likely to show up before menstruation actually ceased and others afterwards. The way that the women questioned interpreted menopause itself clearly has a bearing upon their reporting of the symptoms. If you think, as Mrs Thatcher's biographers did, that menopause is the kind of event that can be over in a month, you may well associate menopausal problems with some unconnected factor and you will be a good deal readier to decide that your efficiency remained totally unaffected. On the other hand, if menopause is presented as the cause of all the ills that afflict middle-aged females, unconnected symptoms may be interpreted as manifestations of menopause.

Agreement on the symptomatology of menopause is far from universal. Very few studies, for example, mention menopausal acne, yet some women who have never ever had any kind of skin eruption get a crop of pimples during the climacterium. Dutch researchers include carpal tunnel syndrome among the symptoms caused by autogenic dysregulation; if I had known that two years ago when I had surgery on both hands for progressive loss of sensation as well as pins and needles and painful numbness, I would have taken oestrogen before undergoing painful surgery which resulted in an infection and permanent weakness in one hand. The symptoms were serious, the muscles in one hand were already wasting, and I might have had to have the surgery in any case. And I might not.

The characteristic symptom of menopause is 'vasomotor instability'; this is understood to be a direct result of the cessation of ovarian function, but no one understands what the connection is.

Of all the troubles that women experience at the time of the menopause they complain most bitterly and most frequently about the hot flush. Flushing occurs when the nervous mechanism which controls the blood vessels is impaired and, in medical terminology, 'vasomotor instability' results. (Evans, 15)

This sounds like an explanation, until we begin to examine its terms. What sort of thing is a 'nervous mechanism'? What does 'control the blood vessels' and why should menopause impair it? Can it be mended? Though everyone knows about hot flushes or 'flashes', as some women call them, a better expression because it conveys the suddenness of the feeling, nobody really knows why they should happen. The process that causes the blood vessels on the surface of the skin to dilate is similar to the mechanism that makes some of us feel hot with embarrassment and go red, but why it should run amok at menopause is a mystery.

Surveys of menopausal women in the general population to see how many of them suffer from symptoms give varying results. Hot flushes, for example, are experienced by anything from 61 per cent to 75 per cent of all women at menopause. This would be depressing information if it were not for the fact that the seriousness of vasomotor symptoms is very variable. Some women feel a sensation as if they had been sprayed with hot oil, which quickly passes and can easily be ignored. Others find that as the sensation of heat fades they are seized by shivering and cold sweats; still others suffer palpitations, panic attacks, or feel their skin crawling. At night the same dysfunction can cause disturbance of sleep and night sweats so copious that the sufferer must change her nightclothes and her bedding. Some women find that a hot flush can be expected after dealing with a crisis or making a concerted physical effort; others find the recurrence of flushing completely unpredictable. Some women will have only a few hot flushes during the climacteric; others will have them several times a day for years on end. A quarter of all the women who experience flushes will experience them for more than five years.

Next in order of inevitability are the problems related to the atrophy of the tissues of the vagina and urethra. These literally do dry up when ovarian function ceases.

In atrophic vaginitis . . . the vagina loses its texture, becomes smoother and thinner and its cells suffer from loss of a carbohydrate substance called glycogen. This, in turn, leads to a reduction of the protective

secretion of acid, so predisposing the thinned vaginal lining to infection
. . . Pruritus, or itching of skin around the vaginal opening, can also be
troublesome, even maddening. In addition, as the vagina becomes less
well lubricated, more sore, and less distensible, sexual intercourse
becomes increasingly difficult and is often painful . . . The urethra is
subject to the same atrophic change as the vagina, and this may affect
the sensitive base of the bladder . . . (Evans, 16)

As far as the individual woman is concerned, the symptoms of
ageing do not need to be separated out from the symptoms of
menopause, for she experiences them together. They are not
simply concurrent, however; they interact. Typically, women
carry out their busy lives without too much reflection about the
rate at which they might be ageing. The first hot flush can come
as a thunderclap. One of the commoner reactions to menopause is
resentment that it has come so soon, when in fact it has come in its
due season. This kind of expression of resentment needs to be
decoded into a protest against the swiftness of the passing of our
own youth, and the childhood of our children. The woman who
feels regret to the point of bitterness is not necessarily exhibiting a
pathological symptom of deep maladjustment. Most of us are
carrying loads of stress too heavy to be borne without hurting; we
may have struggled, through the years when our children were
growing up, to provide all the things that we were given to
understand were necessary, only to find that they are grown and
gone without our having had the joy of them. Consumer society
exists to diddle people; many a woman at menopause comes to
realize that she has been gypped. There may be a period of
turmoil as she comes to terms with this; there should be a period
of turmoil, for coming to terms with disappointment is not easy.
Women, left to their own devices, will handle it as they handle all
the other upheavals that make up women's lives, if they have
room to manoeuvre.

Younger women have been shown to have more negative
attitudes to menopause than older ones (Eisner and Kelly, 1980;
Dege and Gretzinger, 1982); women who regard themselves as

menopausal are less negative. The finding shows women coping; it probably also shows that as menopause fades into the general spectrum of ageing, ageing is perceived and experienced as more difficult. The higher a woman's educational level, the more positive the attitude to menopause:

Family members of women of lower educational status had many more negative attitudes and beliefs about the menopause, thought there was much less communication about these within the family and tended to be less supportive. These families also saw the events occurring around the woman at that time of life as involving mainly loss, and discontinuity, resulting in emotional instability ... The authors regard these negative attitudes as primarily determined by social class, being based on a subcultural stereotype of the role and status of the postreproductive woman. They also add that 'those who had the most life stress and the least control over it were those who had the most negative attitudes to menopause'. (Greene, 140–41)

So much for the common prejudice that labouring women do not carry on about the menopause as much as pampered middle-class ones. It seems obvious that if your life is hard, menopause will make it harder.

Lev Tolstoy married in 1862; he was thirty-four, his wife eighteen. He was mostly uninterested in her and in her children, of whom he gave her thirteen. Though he preached chastity, he used his wife whenever he needed to, despite his own feelings of repugnance, and then rejected her. In 1895, when she was fifty-one, she wrote in her diary:

... his biographies will tell of how he helped the labourers to carry buckets of water, but no one will ever know that he never gave his wife a rest and never – in all these thirty-two years – gave his child a drink of water or spent five minutes by his bedside to give me a chance to rest a little, to sleep, or go out for a walk, or even just recover from all my labours. (Tolstoy, 126)

In 1897 she moved out of their bedroom but Tolstoy continued to have intercourse with her when he wanted, using her as coldly as a rapist. In the last year of his life he did not even want her for that. By this time Countess Tolstoy was virtually demented; she was diagnosed as 'paranoiac and hysterical, with a predominance of the first'.

The woman who relates primarily to her husband, whose husband relates with her primarily through sex without tenderness, is psychologically battered; though her husband has never struck her she has terrible internal bruising. Her ego is already so undermined that cessation of ovarian function removes the last shred of self-esteem that she has. If her husband makes clear that though he uses her for sex her old body (in Sofia Andreyevna's case bearing the marks of thirteen pregnancies) is unattractive, her insecurity will reach the critical stage at which Countess Tolstoy, aged forty-six, wrote desperately in her diary that she feared her husband would cast her out altogether. Countess Tolstoy was married to a great artist, a hero. The demands of his ego, and his guilt about his own sexuality, would have crushed the life out of a stronger woman than Sofia Andreyevna, even if she had not had to make fair copies of all his work, run his estate, his business affairs and his household, bring up his children and educate them herself, and submit to his compulsive sexuality, while he paraded himself before the world as a celibate. The verdict of history is that she was a bad wife.

Countess Tolstoy would have done very badly on the 'Subjective Adaptation' score: 'Satisfaction with daily life, health, physical appearance and daily tasks; view of the future'. Dr Evans would not be at all surprised to find that she had handled menopause badly, and the finding would not have much to do with her social class or her educational level. (For a fuller discussion of Countess Tolstoy's understandable state of mind, see pp. 288–90.)

Many women feel during the climacteric that they are changing personality; these changes occur so spectacularly that it is almost as if one person, the person you know, is being stuffed inside a new one. The most unnerving, even terrifying, change is a sudden horrible propensity to blind rage. The smallest frustration can reduce a woman struggling with the climacteric to gasping fury, so that before she knows what she is saying, she has said the unforgivable. She finds herself calling down horrible vengeance and uttering mad threats, which seem to be throttled out of her, as if she was being squeezed in a giant hand. Sometimes the outburst is accompanied by a feeling of physical anxiety, amounting to pain, or a feeling of unbearable pressure in the head, or behind the eyes. This is the reality behind what doctors refer to rather prissily as 'irritability'. Such an access of choking rage is usually followed by exhaustion, helpless guilt and a futile wishing that whatever it was had not happened, that the victim had not been abused or slapped, that the recalcitrant object had not been thrown or smashed, that the cat had not been kicked or the dishwasher knob torn off.

Very little organized observation of these mood swings has ever been attempted. Until women keep diaries of the climacteric, and chart their own course, we will not be able to form any idea of what causes them. They seem on the face of it to be connected with vasomotor disturbances, for hot flushes very often coincide with stress, and stress is often associated with other people. Consciously trying to keep calm simply adds to the stress. Sometimes the hot flush and the ungovernable feelings come after a prolonged effort, as if some internal monitor had turned off.

There may be another more sinister explanation of personality change at menopause. People in the developed world are exposed to relatively high levels of lead pollution; it had been thought that most of the lead that finds its way into our bodies was safely locked in the bony matrix and could not escape into the bloodstream. In May 1989, researchers at the University Hospital at Lund, in Sweden, found that accelerated bone loss at menopause causes release of lead stored in the long bones into the bloodstream. Childless women, who have not disposed of accumulated lead, are more likely than others at menopause to exhibit significantly elevated levels of lead in their blood, up to 20 per cent higher than the pre-menopausal level. Research with rats at the University of

Rochester has shown that the lead thus released from the long bones accumulates in soft tissues. The brain is one such tissue. Surges of lead into the biochemistry of the brain during the climacteric will cause brain toxicity, affecting intellectual function, memory, and mood control. There are two ways of dealing with this; one is to prevent accelerated bone loss; the other would be to neutralize the effects of the lead release or bring about its rapid elimination – so far, I think, impossible.

Despite the huge body of research into the frequency and the nature of symptoms at menopause, the sum of our ignorance still far outweighs our knowledge. We suspect that the climacteric syndrome is culturally determined, that its severity is mediated by other factors, pathological, environmental, socio-economic and psychological. One thing, however, seems certain: the women who imagine that the solution to the complex of problems they must surmount during the climacteric can be supplied by the medical establishment have historically turned out to be the unluckiest of all.

5

All Your Own Fault

Oppressed women have got rather used to doctors, the only individuals most of them can turn to in time of need, becoming rather testy when faced with problems for which they can find no solution. Many women have given up complaining because of the prevailing response which implies that really they should just get on with it and stop feeling sorry for themselves. Dr Mary Anderson, setting forth 'the plain facts of the menopause' in a 'straight-forward and commonsense way' in her book *The Menopause*, might be thought to express the same attitude as the gym mistress who tore up notes explaining that certain girls had their periods and were to be let off PE.

It is an interesting reflection that before the menopause became 'popular' I used to advise anxious women who might seek a consultation solely for the purpose of knowing 'what to expect at the menopause' not even to learn to spell the word, far less memorize possible problems. Nowadays such a tritely facetious comment is unacceptable, but the basis for it remains. (36)

What can the basis for the 'facetious comment' be if not a poor opinion of women's intellectual abilities? It would be an incurious physician who did not ask, 'Why are you worried about it?' Most women who ask what will happen at menopause suspect that they are already experiencing pre-menopausal symptoms but are reluctant to age themselves by admitting the fact.

The same attitude can be sensed as the basis for Dr Anderson's confident assertion that two out of three women feel nothing of 'any importance to them' during and after the cessation of their periods. Women are only too accustomed to not feeling very well, and are more likely to seek remedies for their children's ailments than their own, which have little 'importance to them', but they should not be encouraged in their self-neglect. Traditionally, the medical establishment has given little weight to women's subjective testimony out of an ill-founded conviction that women over-report their symptoms, whereas the case is directly contrary. Menstruation and contraception both affect the quality of women's lives; to many women menopause is just part of a continuum of not-quite-wellness that they accept. *The Menopause* produces no proof or even evidence for the unscientific statement made on the cover of the book that many women pass through this phase of their life with no effects at all. In their clinics gynaecologists usually see only those who complain, and outside a doctor would be unlikely to hear anything about menopause at all. Women don't usually discuss flooding and flushing at dinner parties and a busy professional like Dr Anderson probably does not have much time to spend gossiping with the girls.

More insidiously Dr Anderson's argument in *The Menopause* appears to associate lack of menopausal symptoms with sanity, virtue and social status:

There may be many symptoms and signs associated with the menopause but, especially in the well-balanced, educated, contented woman who finds her family, sexual and professional life fulfilling, *there may be no symptoms whatever*. (58)

These words must have a regrettable knock-on effect upon the woman who has bought a copy of *The Menopause* because she is experiencing symptoms.

Samuel Ashwell, writing in 1844, made the same point, and went on:

That this does not more constantly happen, arises from the fact, that nature and health are often sacrificed to fashion and luxury . . . habits unwisely begun, and still more unwisely continued. (196)

A hundred years later, though the case had never been proved, the same point was still being made. In 1958 Norton issued a fourth impression of a book by two eminent psychiatrists, O. Spurgeon English, MD, Professor and Chairman, Department of Psychiatry, Temple University School of Medicine, and Gerald H. J. Pearson, MD, Dean of the Philadelphia Association for Psychoanalysis. The distressed woman who turns to *Emotional Problems of Living: Avoiding the Neurotic Pattern* for some insight into her climacteric will read this:

. . . women who have lived unwisely between the ages of twelve and forty-two can build up a great many regrets over which to be irritable, depressed, remorseful and pessimistic when the menopause appears . . . Studies of the personalities of those suffering from severe menopause neurosis or psychosis reveal similarities in personality make-up. Such a woman tends to be sensitive and to live a rather isolated social existence. She has not been warm and gregarious, rather one of those women who proudly declare they never visit around much but stay at home and mind their own business. In other words, she has made a virtue of the fact that she was afraid to associate with people or that she did not like people sufficiently to be friendly. Usually she has been strict and pedantic in training her children, often excessively religious, meticulous about cleanliness, many times the excellent housekeeper in whose home no one can be comfortable. She has been sexually frigid, ungenerous and prone to be critical. Such women take little from and give little to the world, so that by the time menopause is reached they not only have no more activity of the sexual glands, but they likewise have become emotionally and spiritually impoverished. (431–2)

In short, women who suffer at menopause are bad people. In undue fairness, it must be pointed out that this is a picture of the typical sufferer from 'severe menopause neurosis or psychosis', and not the typical menopausal female, whereupon it must also be pointed out that no such syndrome as 'severe menopause neurosis or psychosis' has been identified. *Clinical* depression is no more common at menopause than in any other epoch of female human life, and the *clinical* depression observed at menopause has no features to distinguish it from any other depression. These men, who should be helping the women who trust them, have utterly abandoned their scientific method in order to vilify a kind of woman whom they do not like. They note with satisfaction the high placebo response to the kinds of hormone replacement available in the fifties and go on:

In a problem of the menopausal syndrome the personality factor that has produced this menopausal symptom should be treated and the doctor should not depend upon ductless glandular preparations too much ... Women who are not enjoying bringing up their children, who are working too hard and taking life in deadly seriousness, should have it pointed out to them that if they continue this course they are almost certain to be tired, disillusioned people at fifty. (433–4)

There is no group of women which has not been identified as courting disaster at menopause. Women who have not exercised their reproductive function in due time have been identified as a specially vulnerable group by some, while others have been equally convinced that women who were excessively attached to their mothering role tend to suffer more. According to Maxine Davis,

Often busy mothers or energetic careerists who are unwilling or unprepared to acknowledge the termination of the reproductive phase of their lives and the inception of a new era are thrown into considerable turmoil by this event.

The basic reference on menopause in the Cambridge University Medical Library, published in 1976(!), includes an article on 'emotional response to the menopause' by Margaret Christie Brown, then a hospital psychotherapist in London, who thought that

where overvaluing, undervaluing or imposing of other attributes on the function of reproduction has occurred, difficulty is to be expected with the menopause. (Campbell, 113)

The continuation of her argument involves an unusual twist,

which brings her to the point of blaming symptomless women for their lack of symptoms:

Surveys have shown that the group of women least likely to have menopausal symptoms are single women who have not suffered from dysmenorrhea. The reasons for this must be multi-factorial but one important factor is that these women have come to terms gradually over a number of years with non-fulfilment of a female role. It may have been a deliberate way to avoid the vulnerability of being female or it may have been by force of circumstances, in either case she is likely to have faced many of these issues many times and learned to tolerate them over a number of years. So that rather like living with a seriously ill member of the family, the mourning is done while the patient is alive and often death is welcomed as relief. (114)

Psychiatrists have no option but to blame people for their own suffering; admitting that unhappiness might be justified would undermine the entire rationale of medicating the mind. There can be no suggestion that feeling tired and disillusioned at fifty might be the appropriate response and that convincing yourself that you are happy and fulfilled might be self-deluding to the point of insanity. 'Bringing up' children is not necessarily enjoyable; our children are not necessarily nice people and if they are it is not something we can congratulate ourselves upon. In any event, by the time we are fifty our children are likely to be relatively difficult of access. If English and Pearson had actually studied the epidemiology of menopause, they might have observed that women who have enjoyed mothering most often suffer worst at menopause, in which case it is still their fault, because they have been too attached to the mothering role.

Mary Anderson has not the excuse of being a Freudian psychiatrist of the fifties, nevertheless the crisp statement quoted above from her book, *The Menopause*, implies that if you have managed your life correctly, i.e. you have a husband and children who all love you, and you have always enjoyed and are still enjoying sex with your husband, and have a fulfilling job, you are more likely, most likely, perhaps even certain, to whisk through menopause with your usual efficiency. Mrs Thatcher, according to her goofiest hagiographers, accomplished the climacteric in February 1972; the implication of Anderson's no-nonsense approach is that if you can't do the same, then you're likely to be a moaning Minnie. If you haven't managed to get a husband, let alone keep him alive and by your side until you are fifty, if you haven't borne any children or have been unable to get the ones you have brought up to treat you decently, if you didn't manage to get a decent education, let alone a decent job, then you'll probably make a hash of the menopause as well. Before dealing with medical treatments for the misery of the climacteric, Mary Anderson permits herself the following non-medical observations:

Regrettably it is true to say that in all age groups throughout the Western world there is excessive drug use, leading to actual abuse of these drugs. They have become a household by-word – a music-hall (or TV) joke. Who is to blame? The drug firms certainly, the doctor certainly – but patients themselves must take a large share of responsibility. How often do patients go to the doctor's surgery specifically to seek a tablet to calm them down or to buck them up, because they are either anxious or 'stressed' or 'depressed' and feeling low? Modern life itself must take the main responsibility for all this with its stresses, anxieties and pressures. But do we not create the life we lead, are we not largely responsible for many of the situations in which we find ourselves and should not we be more able to find resources within ourselves to cope rather better without necessarily having recourse to drugs? (71)

While admitting that modern life is not particularly liveable, Dr Anderson chooses to put the words 'stressed' and 'depressed' in inverted commas; 'feeling anxious' is a pretty grudging way of describing an anxiety state. The key to Dr Anderson's attitude is in the rhetorical question 'do we not create the life we lead?' This is one rhetorical question that should not be answered in the affirmative, for the true answer is, 'Probably not, and certainly not if we are women.' From the time women first come to consciousness their lives are strenuously moulded by others; this conditioning has been so often described at length that there is little point in reiterating it here, but as the point is so central a synopsis may be in order.

From the first weeks of life, when mothers feed boys who vociferate but soothe girls, feed boys more often and longer and praise girls for behaviour that they discourage in boys, and when the behaviour of fathers may range from total invisibility and distance to sexual abuse, women learn that their fate is not in their own hands. The pattern of responding rather than initiating is early set. If it is not, the chances of a female's life career following Dr Anderson's ideal are slimmer rather than better. In the co-educational system the girls quickly learn to or decide to let the boys dominate; when sexual activity is initiated it is on the boys' rather than the girls' terms. Though the rhetoric may support equal opportunity, equal opportunity for women in education, professional training and employment does not exist. Women do not understand the systems of self-promotion employed by men; they are not taught the ways in which from their boyhood men establish groups and contacts that will serve them in their professional careers. If women keep up in the professional race, it costs them a great deal more in terms of application and concentration, and yields them a great deal less in terms of human contact. Their male peers, on the other hand, will generally prefer women who do not compete with them.

Nearly a third of western European women will never marry; the higher a woman's educational qualifications and the better her job, the more likely she is not to marry. Unmarried men cluster at the bottom of the social scale; unmarried women at the top. Married men are the least likely to seek treatment for psychological disturbance; next come single women, next married women. The last, most vulnerable population, selected out of the marriage market, are the single males. Any discussion of menopausal women that assumes that all are or should be married and have had children is based upon a mythical paradigm. Of the women aged fifty or over in Great Britain, nearly half a million will be divorced and never remarried, while more than 3 million will be widows, and three-quarters of a million or more will never have been married; in all, nearly half the total number are single. The largest group of households in Britain are the households with a single occupant. Incidence of divorce increases exponentially, while failure to marry is more and more often refusal to marry, not because the woman is immature or suffers from any other psychological blight, but because the institution of marriage is not designed for women's better health or optimal functioning. More divorces are initiated by wives than by husbands. There are rational grounds for eschewing or ending marriage; the women who choose to do so are taking control of their lives. Survival as a single woman is not easy, but the struggle is one's own struggle. Single women are less likely to form symptoms that demand treatment simply because they have assumed responsibility for themselves. Even so, menopause doctors see as one of their chief functions the curing of ailing marriages. Despite all the evidence to show that celibates are no madder and often a good deal healthier than the rest of the population, they persist in the irrational belief that regular psychosexual release is essential for the proper functioning of all individuals.

The most obvious area in which a woman cannot be said to 'make her own life' is in marriage. Though she may choose her husband, she cannot make him choose her. She cannot control the pace at which intimacy progresses; though women nowadays initiate contacts more readily, they are as powerless as ever in pursuing them. Though a young woman may not shrink from telephoning a man she is interested in, there is little she can do if he does not return the call, or does not return it for a week. She can telephone again and complain, and in my experience usually does, but the result is worse than if she had let the matter drop. Eligible men live in a sellers' market, and they know how to exploit the fact. Ineligible men are just that.

Supposing a woman gets the husband of her choice rather than the man who chose her (and the man she gets is the man she thinks he is, though love be blind), she has no way of ensuring that he remains the man of her choice. Though she conceive her babies at the right time and take all precautions to see they come out right, she will have very little to do with their socialization and their enculturation, which has been taken over by an inadequate education system. She knows that she is more vulnerable to her children than they are to her. Chances are that, whether she wants to or not, she will have to work to service the family debt. The work she does outside her home is most likely to be poorly paid drudgery; inside the home, of course, drudgery is unpaid. Men nowadays are supposed to share housework; the extent to which they actually do can be guessed from the activities of advertisers, who long ago gave up any attempt to show a man in the kitchen and never, ever showed a man cleaning the lavatory.

What has been set up in the adult female is a pattern of response. She responds to the needs of her man, her children, her employer, her customers. The happier she feels in responding, the more successful she is likely to be in her roles as lover, wife, mother, secretary, waitress, saleswoman. What happens during the climacteric is that the people she has served all her life stop making demands on her. She becomes a moon without an earth. What she wants is to be wanted, and nobody wants her.

Unless of course she has the perfect husband, the perfect children and the perfect career. The woman who does have all those really cannot congratulate herself on her own good management; the woman who has none of them must not blame herself for what is after all a matter of luck. Luck is another name for privilege. Health, intelligence, beauty, educational and career opportunity are all positively correlated with affluence and social class.

Curiously, in her tiny book *The Menopause* Mary Anderson includes a chapter in which she describes a phenomenon that she admits does not exist, namely, the male menopause. This happens to 'the male in his middle years', between the ages of forty-five and fifty-five when he is in the 'most active phase of his career', when, because of anxieties about ageing and what have you, he may suffer from impotence. Dr Anderson does not enter into the vexed question of how many women have suffered from impotence all their lives or how much their failure to reach orgasm has had to do with the inconsiderateness of their husbands. In the mythology of sexual monogamy in the leafy suburbs women reach orgasm with their husbands twice a week until something goes wrong in the middle years.

What happens then very much depends on the personality of the man, his social and his economic status. (100)

(What has happened ever since a girl was married has depended very much upon the man's social and economic status.)

He may react in a variety of ways.

(Nothing new here either. The man has always had the choice of a variety of ways of reacting and his wife has had very little opportunity to influence his choice.)

He may try to ignore what has happened and throw himself into his work even more. His partner who herself may be undergoing climacteric changes resulting in loss of sexual interest may be quite relieved, and so a state of relative contentment develops but without the fulfilment of sexual enjoyment. Occasional attempts at intercourse may cause vaginal pain to the woman ... Then again his partner may become frustrated and angry and this can only result in greater reduction of his sexual drive and performance. If the man's personality is such that he is unable to work through this time of crisis he may become depressed and develop true psychiatric symptoms – anxiety and what is called reactive depression. He may sleep badly, he may begin to drink too much, he may gamble ... Extra-marital affairs are commonest at this age ... (100)

And on the other hand he may have done some or all of those things from the beginning. Gamblers and alcoholics and philanderers usually have an excuse for their social vice. The symptoms of the misbehaving male are not expressed in inverted commas; the misbehaviour itself is here elevated to the status of a symptom. How different is this deference to symptoms in the male from Anderson's attitude to female people who feel 'stressed' or 'depressed'! Women too may drink during their mid-life crisis, and for them the health consequences of even a small and irregular intake of alcohol can be catastrophic. Anderson does not find space in her book to discuss female alcohol abuse or the ill-health resulting from it. The solution to male gambling, infidelity and even excessive alcohol consumption, as intrinsic a part as it is of male bonding, lies in the model wife's behaviour.

With greater understanding of herself and her bodily changes at this age, with adequate treatment of symptoms if they arise it behoves her to remember her partner also. To remain attractive, caring, interested and interesting must be half the battle surely. (101)

'*Only half!*' the exhausted woman cries. The very notion of *remaining attractive* is replete with the contradictions that break women's hearts. A woman cannot make herself attractive; she can only be *found* attractive. She can only remain attractive if someone remains attracted to her. Do what she will she cannot influence that outcome. Her desperate attempts to do the impossible, to guide the whim of another, are the basis of a billion-dollar beauty industry. All their lives women have never felt attractive enough. They have struggled through their thirties and forties to remain attractively slim, firm-bodied, glossy-haired and bright-eyed. Now in the fifties 'remaining attractive' becomes more than a full-time job. Does Dr Anderson recommend face-lifts, mammoplasty, buttock-lifting, aerobic dancing – what? Jane Fonda's body may look terrific, what there is of it, but has anyone looked at the strain taken up by her face and neck muscles? Does Dr Anderson not know what succulent young bodies are available for the jaded executive's pleasure? Is a middle-aged woman supposed to have the buttocks of a twenty-year-old? Such buttocks are displayed on advertising hoardings all over town. The man who is still making love to the wife of his youth may be thinking of other breasts than his wife's. There is no lack of spectacular publications to furnish such imagery. The middle-aged woman who tries to compete with her husband's fantasy sex partners hasn't a hope.

Dr Anderson was probably not thinking of the kind of attractiveness represented by Joan Collins. No doubt she was meaning trimfigured, neat and tidy, pleasant-looking, rather than obese, whiskery, swollen-ankled and, well, old. Attractive here probably means not totally repulsive. The middle-aged woman whose husband is not turned on by her ought certainly to take care to look good, but not primarily to revive his flagging interest. A man who is depressed and frightened by the signs of his own advancing age is panicked by the thought that he is 'matched with an ageing wife'. The behaviour of the young women around him convinces him that he is younger than his wife in mind and body. His wife can exercise till (like Jane Fonda) she has a heart attack, can spend all day being depilated, massaged, oiled, scented, coiffed and painted, until she beggars herself. Remain attractive indeed. Women might well ask, 'When in this life will I be allowed to let myself go?' Is one never to be set free from the white-slavery of attraction duty?

Dr Anderson's 'well-balanced, educated, contented' female is not supposed to attract at random. Any suggestion that a woman has a duty to attract anyone but the person she is committed to by religious ceremony, public registration or cohabitation would be shocking, after all. We might wonder whether, if a husband preferred his wife with a handlebar moustache, Dr Anderson would not advise her to grow one. Some husbands in order to find their wives attractive do require them to do things rather more unsavoury and peculiar.

A husband's responsibility for his wife's pleasure is nowhere discussed in Mary Anderson's book. Having erected the cliff of remaining attractive and commanded her readers to scale it, she remarks discouragingly:

There is no evidence whatsoever that declining sexual pleasure is inevitable after the menopause. (101)

Something which is not 'inevitable' can still be probable, even overwhelmingly probable. Yet, though Dr Anderson does not deny that lots, perhaps most, perhaps nearly all women, will suffer declining sexual interest after menopause, she nowhere suggests that they can be let off their conjugal duty. They have still got to appear 'interesting and interested'. She has nothing to say whatever about women who have never had a proper partner, and now are less likely than ever to find one. Women, who do not have desirable 'partners', or 'partners' of any kind, who might find pretty disheartening the news that they may be tormented by unfulfilled sexual desire all the way to the grave, are not to be re-assured.

Though Dr Anderson does fleetingly consider the possibility that, by some mismanagement or another, a husband might just conceivably be dead or married to someone else, she does not suggest that a husband might be unattractive. Or even that he might be maladroit as a lover, or coarse, or brutal, or demand peculiar rituals to keep his flagging interest up. The idea that a woman of spirit might reject the kind of sex her husband is offering never enters Dr Anderson's book. To read it you would think that all the fat, beefy, beery, smelly, tobacco-stained men you see about you did not exist or were nobody's 'partners'. Many a man who was attractive and amusing at twenty is a pompous old bore at fifty. Many men married to 'interesting and interested' wives are too dull to be interested in them or by them. Many a fascinating woman is stunned into silence by an overbearing husband who has never really listened to anything she has said. In the world according to Dr Anderson no husband ever says, 'Shut up, dear.' The more extreme defenders of the myth of the thirty-year-long monogamous marriage would argue that a repulsive husband is his wife's fault, which is merely the corollary of the view that people with penises can do no wrong, whatever it is they choose to do. Most of them would be deeply offended to find their writings compared with the Hindu scripture that enjoins women to accept everything a husband does and forgive it.

A more sophisticated version of the argument that seeks to

blame the middle-aged woman for her own menopausal distress is offered by J. G. Greene, in *The Social and Psychological Origins of the Climacteric Syndrome.* After reviewing the evidence for a specific 'climacteric syndrome' and finding that the only symptoms that can be specifically connected with the cessation of ovulation are hot flushes and dry vagina, Greene is obliged to define a vulnerable group whose 'physical, psychological and social distress' will become apparent during this 'critical transitional phase of their lives'.

Many of the characteristics and functions adversely affected during the climacteric are also at the same time declining with age, or may represent the accentuation of an existing problem or the recurrence of an earlier one ... the climacteric does not seem to act as a primary vulnerability factor per se, but tends to *accentuate* an already existing problem, *accelerate* the effects of ageing, or cause previous problems to *recur.* Nor, given the modest magnitude of the increase in, for example, non-specific, in contrast to the large increase in vasomotor symptoms, can these effects act equally on all women to the same extent. This raises the question of whether we can identify those women, or those groups of women, who, during the climacteric, are more vulnerable than others. The answer to this question seems to be a very definite 'yes'. (211)

The accentuation of existing problems, acceleration of problems to come and recurrence of old problems at the same time as one is struggling with vasomotor disturbance, i.e. hot flushes, night sweats, painful intercourse, etc. may not constitute a climacteric syndrome to Dr Greene's satisfaction, but they would loom large in the lives of any woman, whether or not she is heroically trying to deny the existence of problems, whether or not she has any faith in the powers of doctors to solve the problems she has. Dr Greene identifies his vulnerable population as *underprivileged* women.

By this is meant, those of low social class, of low family income, of low educational level, as well as those living in arduous and culturally deprived environments. Women who had no occupation outwith [*sic*] the home were also more vulnerable, but this too was associated with being underprivileged, since being employed had a protective effect only if the woman was of higher social class or pursuing a professional career, and had a detrimental effect if otherwise . . .

Moreover, when more personal and individual circumstances were examined, it was found that it was women with pre-existing problems or long standing difficulties, such as marital dissatisfaction, problems in early development, financial and economic difficulties, who reacted most adversely during the climacteric. (211–12)

This view might be called the 'last straw' view of the climacteric, in which the few symptoms actually caused by the cessation of ovarian function trigger off a string of others which are not. Insistence on separate enumeration of symptoms under three categories, labelled somatic (bodily), psychosomatic (bodily-cum-mental) and psychological, distorts a basic reality, namely that they are all connected. Fatigue, caused by sleeplessness caused by vasomotor instability, will cause many of the other symptoms in its turn, and carrying out hard physical labour in uncomfortable circumstances will make the fatigue much worse. Headache (labelled psychosomatic) and tearfulness (psychological) might well result. Greene's approach is analytic; he must separate out the elements and try to standardize them.

Greene does not quite reverse Anderson's argument that women who are 'well-balanced, educated, contented' are also likely to suffer less at menopause to read that women who have not been at the mercy of an unequal education system, unfair conditions in employment, the whims of men, and the demands of their children, will suffer much less at menopause. Though he is more merciful than she, his analysis too is necessarily patient-oriented, so that rather than discuss the limited control that women have over their lives, he tends to rate them as if they were solo performers. The idea that right attitudes will lead to the right menopause is the inescapable corollary of this kind of concentration on the patient as the treatable entity and the source of all her woes. Women who have 'adverse reactions' to marriage, for example, measured on a 'marital adaptability' score, can be expected to have 'adverse reactions' to menopause as well. They are 'adverse reactors' and hence problematic by nature. Likewise women who identify 'too closely' with their bodily and reproductive functions or are 'too dependent' on their mothering role are seen as asking for trouble at menopause.

Even Pauline Bart, writing in a feminist collection entitled *Women in Sexist Society*, blames the middle-aged woman for her own depression:

Women who have overprotective or overinvolved relationships with their children are more likely to suffer depression in their postparental period . . . Housewives have a greater rate of depression than working women . . . Middle-class housewives have a higher rate of depression than working-class housewives . . . The patterns of black female role behaviour rarely result in depression in middle age. Often the 'grannie' or 'auntie' lives with the family and cares for the children while the children's mother works; thus the older woman suffers no maternal role loss. Second, since black women traditionally work, they are less likely to develop the extreme identification, the vicarious living through their children that is characteristic of Jewish mothers. (109–12)

This could all have been put quite differently, so that it did not appear that depressed women had got it wrong, had overinvested in their children and therefore suffered inevitable rejection. The black woman who continues to fulfil a female role is not dealing better with her empty nest, because her nest is not empty. Her children are probably still living with her not because of tradition so much as poverty. Black women do not do the work they do because of tradition, but because of necessity. Also black families are 'traditionally' fatherless; the black matriarch is likely to be the boss in her own home. Keeping that home on an even keel, and all the children, hers and her daughters', at school or in work and out of trouble, is the most demanding kind of work. The fifty-year-old black woman is anything but unwanted; the fifty-year-old middle-class housewife and mother fiddling about in her empty house has no way of ignoring the fact that she is unwanted.

These contrasting situations cannot be described in terms of choices, mistaken or otherwise.

If both women, black and white, were unmarried and depressed, they would have been told that women who have not fulfilled their reproductive destiny are the most likely to incur depression at menopause. All the arguments that attribute depression at menopause to failures and excesses in the individual woman's life career are essentially circular. This kind of argument says, for example, that a woman who becomes obsessed at menopause by an abortion she once had is not disturbed by menopause but by the abortion; therefore the abortion is responsible for her menopausal difficulties. These pseudo-arguments should be tossed out. Difficult menopause is not a punishment that a woman brings upon herself. It is a time of stock-taking, though, and some grieving that was not done at the appropriate time, usually because of the demands of others and the refusal of others to take the situation sufficiently seriously, might have to be done during the climacteric.

It is of no help to the menopausal woman to hear that her depression is the inevitable result of mistaken strategies and decisions taken long before. It must compound a woman's grief to hear that she has mismanaged her life for the last fifty years. It is not astonishing that a feminist commentator could permit herself such hostility towards her own mother; expression of such hostility is one of the ways women can begin to refashion their own images and roles. What is sinister is that a fundamentally irrational position here masquerades as argument and analysis. Women have not yet grasped the extent to which male authority rejects their protests and trivializes their real complaints; there is little hope that they will when feminist theorists use the same tactics.

If a woman's life does not live up to Dr Anderson's model or Dr Greene's Scandinavian model, it seems only proper that she should be angry about it. Fortunately for society, if unfortunately for them, women's anger usually expresses itself in self-punishment. Obligingly women internalize resentment which then takes the form of guilt. One of the most interesting results of any test made of the effects of replacement oestrogens on personality, most of which were inconclusive, was the conclusion reached by Schiff, Regenstein, Tulchinsky and Ryan in 1979.

Schiff *et al.* included in their assessment three personality scales, the Clyde Mood Adjective Checklist, the Gottschalk-Gleser test and the Minnesota Multiphasic Personality Inventory. These tests assess in all some 26 attributes of personality but in only two of these were any changes observed. Following oestrogen women became less outwardly aggressive but more inwardly hostile. How this is to be interpreted the authors do not say. (Greene, 35)

Such an observation opens the intriguing possibility that women's submissiveness is mediated by oestrogen; deferring to the dominant male is clearly a necessary part of reproductive function. Hens hunker down before the rooster. Receptive she-cats present the nape of the neck to ingratiate themselves with the tom, but unreceptive she-cats turn and fight with as much ferocity as males. It is interesting to consider the famed 'mental tonic' effect of HRT as inducing a 'contented cow syndrome'. The possibility, ever so faintly adumbrated here, that menopause puts women back in touch with their anger after thirty-five years of censorship by oestrogen, is delightful to contemplate. Interestingly, though replacement oestrogen facilitates sexual intercourse, it does not restore lost libido, which demands testosterone; in this at least oestrogen is clearly the biddability hormone.

It would be foolish to expect the male medical establishment, even when represented by those few female members who care to be associated with menopause, to encourage women to act out their anger or hostility or resentment in middle age. In this best of all possible worlds such feelings are never appropriate. We are only dimly coming to a recognition that the anti-social behaviour of demented old women might be an expression of justifiable rage too long stifled and unheard. When we find a frantic old lady in the nursing home cursing foully and soiling herself we are witnessing the end result of long corrosion of the personality. We should not be surprised to find that the most eldritch old hag was once the most self-effacing soul, nor should we assume that her present state has no connection with her earlier condition.

Some of our negative feelings about menopause are the result of our intolerance for the expression of female anger. As little girls and adolescents we feared the anger of our mothers. We sensed that there was a debt of hostility in consequence of all that motherly self-sacrifice and self-effacement, but though we pretend that saying that we had not required either self-sacrifice or self-effacement will stand in lieu of payment, we know better. We are not really surprised when menopausal women spit out bitter home truths to their children, but we pretend that it is the hormonal imbalance that is speaking, turning anger into illness so that we can evade implication in it. Robert A. Wilson embarked on a lifetime career of oestrogen prescription because of happenings that predestined his career, principal among them the decline of his 'gentle, almost angelic mother':

At the time I could not understand it. What was a boy in his teens to make of a phrase like 'change of life'? – especially if it were spoken in that tone of voice that in those days was used to mention any number of things then considered unmentionable. How could anything connected with my mother be spoken of in that tone of voice? Yet something terrible was obviously happening. I was appalled at the transformation of the vital, wonderful woman who had been the dynamic focal point of our family into a pain-wracked, petulant invalid. I could feel the deep wounds her senseless rages inflicted on my father, myself and the younger children. It was this frightful experience that later directed my interest as a physician to the problem of the menopause. (165)

Poor Mrs Wilson. If she was as ill as she seems to have been, it must have been particularly dementing to be denied treatment because everyone had a diagnosis – 'change of life'. She had a teenage child and younger ones; how old could she have been? If she suffered from rheumatoid arthritis or early onset Alzheimer's and was being tormented with nonsense about climacteric symptoms her rages would have been anything but senseless. Robert A. Wilson based a whole career on amateur diagnoses overheard in his youth. His mental anguish at his mother's rejection of him was exacerbated by another trauma, the sight of a woman's bloated body being torn open by a grappling hook as it was fished from a reservoir near his childhood home. Her suicide too was caused by (whisper, whisper) 'change of life'. Robert became a crusader. In fact he suffered from an acute form of anophobia (fear of old women).

Anyone who has ever been employed in a business directed by a menopausal woman executive is familiar with another variant of this [menopausal negativity] syndrome. The work week becomes a futile, inefficient round of violent ups and downs, adult tantrums and pointless chicanery. The woman in a position of authority has a ready-made means of side-stepping the passive kind of menopausal negativism. She is presented with an irresistible and unlimited opportunity to take out her frustrations on her poor employees. (85)

The middle-aged female employer, dealing with a work-force who ignore everything she says because they have decided that she is menopausal, is quite likely to have to think of a number of strategies to get their attention. Criticisms of Margaret Thatcher's way of running her cabinet reflected this mechanism, and doubtless she capitulated to it. Anophobia is an accretive phenomenon; it causes the kind of treatment of middle-aged women that they react to in a way that seems to justify it. A good deal of the anxiety of the middle-aged woman is caused by her awareness that she is turning into some kind of a harridan, a scold, a jade, a drab, a fishwife, a beldame, but if you can't get attention any other way, what are you to do? There is no way out after all; the vituperative woman, the viper, the virago (vagina dentata) will be told that she has only herself to blame for the negativity that surrounds her. Nagging is painful utterance that the more it is repeated, the more inexorably is it ignored.

Railing has a positive value. Railing in literature, called variously satire, tragic or comic, lampoon, burlesque, invective, has been highly valued, first as entertainment and second as a corrective to abuses, yet though we have female poets we do not have female satiric poets. Though there are hundreds of literary attacks on women by men, there are very few attacks on men by women, and the few we have are almost all answers to unprovoked attacks by men. It is almost as if women's rage is, like women's sexuality, too vast and bottomless to be allowed any expression, for fear it would swamp and capsize the male equivalent. Despite the best efforts of feminists to awaken women's anger and to turn their hostility outward so that it becomes a force for social change rather than the procreator of symptoms, we have failed. With one or two magnificent exceptions, no race of hilarious harridans has appeared upon the earth.

The medicalization of menopause is the last phase in the process of turning all the elements of female personality that do not relate to the adult male into pathology. Virginity is pathology; lack of interest in heterosexual intercourse on demand is pathology; 'excessive' involvement in mothering is pathology; middle-aged truculence and recalcitrance are the most pathological of all. Now we have pills for all of them and women are obediently taking them. Doctors cannot change social, cultural, economic or political conditions; they can only try to tailor the patient to fit better into her circumstances. We cannot blame the patient if she asks for help. We cannot blame the doctor if he gives the only help he can. We cannot blame the woman if she experiences the alteration in her responses as an improvement in her health, and chooses to ignore the underlying problems which she cannot solve.

If you are drifting around an empty house that no one wants to spend time in, the children being about their own mysterious affairs and your husband staying late at the office most days, you are oppressed. If you are stagnating in a dead-end job on a miserable rate of pay watching younger people rise past you through the promotion scale, you are oppressed. If you are a widow or a divorced woman struggling to adjust to a new life on your own in one of our unsafe and brutalized cities you are oppressed. If people take no pains to conceal their lack of interest in you, if people refuse to take you seriously because they have decided that you are menopausal, you are oppressed. If you believe that this state of affairs has been brought about by your inadequacy, and you have to add guilt to your emotional burden, you are not only oppressed, you will feel depressed. You will see yourself as dull, dumpy and grey and not blame the people who do not conceal their lack of interest in you. You are not, after all, interested in yourself.

If you are dumpy and dull and grey, how did you get that way? You might look to your family and your employer and ask as the neglected wife asks in *The Comedy of Errors*:

> Are my discourses dull? Barren my wit?
> If voluble and sharp discourse be marred,
> Unkindness blunts it more than marble hard . . .
> What ruins are in me that can be found
> By him not ruined?
>
> (II, ii, 90—96)

The evidence seems to show that the more dissatisfied you are with your life the bumpier the ride through the climacteric is going to be, as if your life is trying to jump the tracks. The only people who offer help, the medicos, can offer treatments that will keep you on the rails. The bumps may smooth out but you need to be sure that you want to go on in the same direction. If you do not, there is no reason to feel guilty. There is no reason to feel guilty if your life has fallen to pieces all around you, either. If until this point your life has not been under your control, as is all too probable, you can now take control. Indeed, you may have no option. Feelings of vertigo and panic are to be expected, and not to be apologized for. The truth behind the research that failed to find a significant increase in stress at the climacteric is that, though the new life may be more strenuous, it will not be more difficult than the old. Anxiety about ageing and worry about health are concomitants of menopausal uproar; when it is over the prospect of illness and decrepitude recedes once more to a manageable distance. Negative feelings are not your fault either. None of it, neither the mood swings, nor the weight gain, nor the loss of interest in sex, nor the insomnia, should incur the added burden of guilt.

6

The Unavoidable Consequences

Everything that is born must die. Death is the only certain outcome of birth. The born may not grow up to maturity, may not produce children of their own, may not grow old, but sooner or later they must die.

When most people witnessed death in the immediate family, nobody would have been shocked by these statements. In the late twentieth century, when death has been driven underground and out of sight, dying is the only human activity that is regarded as obscene. Where once the dying individual occupied centre stage, surrounded by her family and employees, and gave her last energies to making a good end, she is now prevented from dying until she can no longer influence the manner of her death. Though a minority might try to revive the old *ars moriendi*, the art of dying, by forming groups to press the case for giving the terminally ill a choice, most people are content to have death happen out of sight and earshot. The last utterances of the dying used to have immense importance; a deathbed statement, an accusation or confession, had a particular status in law and religion. In a good death the dying would call her children and their children to her one by one, take her farewell, make her peace with God and man; then, composed for death, she would speak no more, except perhaps to pray.

Once, in a hospital tent in Ethiopia, I stood with an English doctor who had taken on death. He would snatch up collapsed children, whose anguish was to all intents over, and begin resuscitating them, searching out the head vein in order to run a hollow needle into it, to rehydrate them and bring them back to a life of the deepest misery. 'What is the solution to all this?' he asked, sweeping his arm along the row of silent, emaciated women and children.

'Death?' I ventured.

'Unacceptable,' he answered.

Mothers with several sick children were handed back the infants they had thought dead, now barely alive, packed into boxes with hot water bottles and attached to intravenous drips, and told to look after them, without a thought of how, if they had no time to look for firewood and tend the fire, they could keep the bottles warm. If the mothers took over the English doctor's battle against death of the youngest child, they could not attend to the needs of those who had so far survived. Some of the babies resuscitated in this way had no living kin. Some were brain-damaged, some were blind and some were mad with grief. In Ethiopia in 1984 I learned to love and respect death rather than to fear it. Blighted life can be far, far worse than death.

At menopause as never before a woman comes face to face with her own mortality. A part of her is dying. If she has been encouraged all her life to think of her reproductive faculty as her most important contribution, the death of her ovaries will afflict her deeply. Nothing she can do will bring her ovaries back to life. The grief of menopause affects every woman consciously or otherwise. The feeling that one's day has passed its noon and the shadows are lengthening, that summer is long gone and the days are growing ever shorter and bleaker, is a just one and should be respected. At the turning point the descent into night is felt as rapid; only when the stress of the climacteric is over can the ageing woman realize that autumn can be long, golden, milder and warmer than summer, and is the most productive season of the year. The elegiac strain never fades quite out of the middle-aged woman's consciousness, but it gives poignancy to the now rather than the bitterness of regret that is felt by some so keenly at menopause. When the fifty-year-old woman says to herself, 'Now is the best time of all,' she means it all the more because she knows it is not for ever.

> This thou perceivest, which makes thy love more strong,
> To love that well, which thou must leave ere long.
>
> (Shakespeare, Sonnet 73)

Simone de Beauvoir noticed with wrath how time speeded up in her middle age, so that just when she wanted things to slow down and let her savour the moment the years sped past her. *Carpe diem.* Awareness of time as flying has some advantages; it precludes boredom, for one thing. It matters little that younger people find older people boring or slow. Older people have a right to resist being rushed, to stand and stare at the fragile world that has become so unspeakably dear to them. For the lucky ones, who will not have to leave while they are still in love with life, there will come a later time when that passion too will fade, but while one is still possessed by that great tenderness, it must be yielded to.

Death is the inevitable outcome of life, but ageing is a privilege. Ageing and dying are different processes but not distinct; the overlap in ageing and dying as fields of research is one of the reasons we cannot understand what ageing necessarily involves and what aspects are avoidable. Subjectively, we do not experience ourselves as old or young. We can only assess our own age relative to other people's and that only vaguely. At fifty-three I am not to say that I am old. I am only as old as I feel, people tell me, and allowing yourself to feel old is wrong. Phooey, say I, for though in my self I *feel* neither young nor old I *know* that I am old. If you are older than most of the people on earth, it seems more than a little silly to persist in claiming to be young. The young know that we are not young. If they murmur in disagreement when we call ourselves old, it is because they feel that we are denigrating ourselves. They certainly do not think it is for us to decide that young is what we are. If our society was based on age sets that knitted us into our own generation we might have objective markers by which to place ourselves on some sort of seniority scale. Then we might actually know what it means to 'be our age'. As it is, most of us simply cannot judge how old we are. In some things we are positively juvenile and in others virtually senile. We feel younger than many younger people and older than some people our parents' age. Many of us feel that we do not belong in the company of our own generation and seek to move in a younger circle, imagining that it keeps us young; it is the company of the thoughtless, graceless, self-obsessed young that makes others feel old.

As the populations of the developed worlds grow older and older, as a result of falling birth rates and death rates, they seem obliged to pretend that they are younger and younger. Patrick McGrady wrote in *The Youth Doctors* in 1969, and it is if anything truer in the post-Reagan years:

The tantalizing but elusive idea of youthfulness at any age is the number one obsession of our people in our time. The old are ashamed of having squandered it. The middle-aged attempt to revive it by gamely plastering over the insults of time. And the young – even they – are conscientiously passing for younger still. (15)

Nobody will admit to 'being old' regardless of her chronological age. In fact one's chronological age is usually obvious. If a woman of fifty or over is particularly vigorous or attractive, others will say that she is 'marvellous for her age' rather than that her age itself is a mystery. Nobody who is asked the question, 'How old do you think I am?' ever answers the question honestly. The question that is answered is, 'How old do you think I think you think I am?'

Nobody wants to be old. Most people don't want to be dead either, but there comes a point when one has to accept one or the other. If we were more aware of death, we would possibly be less resentful of ageing. If we were more familiar with older people we might not be so unprepared for the inconveniences that accompany the winning of extra years of life on earth.

Ageing begins before we are born and continues throughout our lives; the only cure for it is death. It is not a uniform process, however. Human beings age jerkily; not only do we only become aware of gradual changes when forced to take stock of ourselves for some reason or another, the actual degenerative changes of ageing are accelerated by unusual stresses and strains. When someone says that an experience aged her ten years or took ten years off her life, she is actually giving an exaggerated account of objective truth. Though it is never true to say that a trauma turned someone's hair white overnight, it is true that the loss of hair pigmentation can be accelerated by privation, shock or grief. Impaired vision may become obvious only when for some reason we are too tired to make the extra effort to focus; then a first pair of reading glasses may do for ten or twenty years, or not.

There is little that an individual woman in the throes of the climacteric can find out about her likely future career. The study of ageing is itself young, and has come to very few conclusions, but they are important for the menopausal woman who feels that the bottom is falling out of her life. In 1986, Nathan W. Shock of the National Institute on Aging summarized the results of longitudinal studies of ageing, that is, studies that follow the progress of a group of individuals over time, rather than contrasting the performance of older with other younger people.

Although relatively few longitudinal studies of aging adults have been completed, results lead to a number of general conclusions. The first is that relatively few individuals follow the pattern of age changes predicted from averages based on measurements made on different subjects. Aging is so highly individual that average curves give only a rough approximation of the pattern of aging followed by individuals.

There is little evidence for the existence of a single factor that regulates the rate of aging in different functions in a specific individual. Because of the large range in the performance of most physiological variables among subjects of the same chronological age, it appears that age alone is a poor predictor of performance . . . Gerontologists are now beginning to recognize the importance of lifestyles such as diet, exercise, smoking habits etc., in influencing health status and life-span. (739–40)

It is only with the greatest difficulty that doctors can separate the symptoms of the menopause from the symptoms of ageing. This they need to do in order not to be accused of quackery, for the accusation that they offer hormone replacement therapy as the elixir of eternal youth is easily made. In a Dutch study led by Dr L. J. Benedek Jaszman (1969b), it was noticed that some symptoms that made their first appearance in the peri-menopause, including palpitations, joint pains and sleeplessness, persisted more than five years after the last menstrual period. These were taken to be associated not with the cessation of ovarian function but with ageing, and these are the symptoms unlikely to respond to attempts to correct oestrogen deficiency. The same conclusion was reached by Professor Carl Wood (1979) in a study of Melbourne women: complaints of sleeplessness, joint pains, numbness, palpitations, dizziness and weakness were commoner in older menopausal women (Evans, 51).

The changes associated with ageing have been summarized as a continuous decrease at the rate of a per cent or so a year of basal metabolism, vital capacity, maximal breathing capacity, glomerular filtration rate, standard cell water and nerve conduction velocity. These are biologically more precise ways of saying what ordinary people mean when they say that when people age they 'slow down' and 'dry up'. The rate of decrease is affected by genetic and environmental factors; some people will age twice as fast as the mean, others half as fast. The slowing down may manifest itself in a disintegration of bodily function as messages take longer to get around the system; clumsiness, even dizziness and loss of co-ordination result. Organs do not age at the same rate; the heart beats more than two and a half billion times in a life of seventy years; no other muscle in the body can remotely approach this kind of efficiency.

It little avails the menopausal woman to know that the atrophic thyroid gland of the mature individual hypertrophies and increases its secretory activity . . . that the ground substance of connective tissue increases . . . that the collagen content in muscle declines, particularly in the limbs, not so much in the abdomen . . . that of the endocrine glands, the gonads change first, then the pituitary, then the thyroid, or that the adrenal glands take over part of the function of the gonads until they too fail in what has come to be called the 'adrenopause'. A bench-mark study, of 1937, by Henry S. Simms and Abraham Stolman at the Columbia University Medical School found that tissues of people over seventy contained 'more water, chloride, total base, sodium and calcium' and 'less potassium, magnesium, phosphorus, nitrogen and ash' than the younger tissue. Older people sweat less and do not produce the kind of sweat that smells sharp.

Cardiac output declines. Renal function declines 35 per cent between ages twenty and ninety but some studies show that in particular individuals it improves. The liver gets smaller; from 2.5 per cent of body weight at middle age, it declines to 1.6 per cent by the tenth decade and the blood flow to the liver also decreases (Geokas and Haverback, 1969). Therefore it takes longer for drugs, etc. to be excreted. In 1973 researchers reported that they had found a significant fall in rosette-forming T-cells in blood occurring between forty-six and sixty years of age. What this means is that the body's defences against disease, its ability to produce an antibody response, begin to weaken (Hausman and Weksler, 1986). This may in fact be an advantage; the inflammatory response seems to be less violent in older people. They may take longer to recover from infection, but the course of the disease, say a cold, may be less violent. If the declining immune response in older people were to be bolstered or 'rejuvenated' we would expect to see an increase in auto-immune disease and inflammatory conditions like rheumatism and arthritis.

Menopause is a big blip on the ageing curve; the cessation of ovarian function is itself caused by ageing and is a part of ageing. The separation of management of menopause from the management of ageing, therefore, does not make sense. What happens to fifty-year-old eyes, hair, skin, ankles, feet, waistlines is at least as important as what is going on in the genito-urinary tract. The woman who comes hard up at menopause against the fact of her advancing age should have some way of knowing which of her symptoms is an unavoidable concomitant of ageing and which signifies ill-health. She may also have to consider whether or not she is not ageing too fast, and why that might be. If she is overweight, smokes, drinks, and takes little exercise, she is piling on the burdens that the ageing organism has to carry; you are only as young as your most fatigued component, be it heart, lungs, liver, brain, skin or skeleton.

We think of our skeletons as solid, the framework upon which our bodies are built, a set of struts and girders that will endure unless they are twisted by some sort of earthquake or battered by other objects as solid or solider. In fact the human skeleton is alive; it absorbs and it excretes; it heals when it is injured, absorbing damaged bone and regenerating healthy bone. The skeleton constitutes 10–15 per cent of total body weight; calcium not only forms the mineral content of bone but provides the conductivity in nerves, is involved in hormonal activity, inhibits and activates enzymes, plays a role in blood clotting and in immune function. Vitamin D, available only from oily fish, eggs and sunlight, controls the calcium–phosphorus balance. There is a marked decrease in calcium absorption in middle-aged women, which is aggravated by inadequate Vitamin D exposure, impairment of kidney function and – menopause. Bone loss occurs in all vertebrates with age; indeed, changes in calcium behaviour may be the principal mechanism of ageing:

It is a matter of everyday clinical experience that the avidity of various tissues for calcium increases with age. This tendency manifests itself in the formation of gross calcification in the cardiovascular system, cartilaginous structures, tendons, periarticular tissues, and lens of the eye (cataracts) as well as the development of calcareous concretions in such areas as the pineal gland, prostate and urinary passages. In addition . . . there occurs with age a gradual increase in the chemically detectable calcium content of various organs . . . It is generally held that calcinosis is a secondary result of 'decreased tissue vitality' and presents a 'dystrophic' phenomenon; yet a review of the literature shows that several investigators have considered the possibility that an increase in tissue calcium concentration may be the cause of many of the changes characteristic of senility. (Selye *et al.*, 1)

The particular form of rat torture devised by Selye, Strebel and Mikulaj to test the hypothesis need not concern us here. It is now generally agreed that as we age calcium migrates from our bones where it is useful to other areas where it is not. Menopause is thought perhaps to accelerate bone resorption, the minus side of the process that is our skeleton, because the lack of oestrogen allows unopposed action of the parathyroid, the gland responsible for inhibiting growth, so that trabecular bone in particular is rapidly resorbed, leading to the characteristic fractures of the wrist and the head of the femur, and the crush fractures of the vertebrae that produce the collapse and distortion of the spine known as 'dowager's hump'. Bone loss is most rapid within the five to ten years following the last menstrual period. The present state of knowledge is insufficient to show whether administration of replacement oestrogens over this period is sufficient to prevent this kind of bone loss altogether. In fact there are no oestrogen receptors in bone, and nobody knows why HRT should affect osteoporosis (Guinan *et al.*).

There is no distinct group of individuals who can be identified as likely sufferers from severe osteoporosis.

Osteoporosis is not a single disease entity, but it is the end result of a number of processes which become more common with increasing age and lead to the diminution of the amount of bone in the skeleton. (Exton-Smith, 524)

Increasing porosity of bone will manifest itself sooner in people whose skeletons at maturity were at the lower end of the percentile of body weight, whose diet has been deficient in calcium, who have been sedentary or, worse, immobile, and who have been given prolonged treatment with cortico-steroids. Increased protein and phosphorus intake (as for example in a diet rich in red meat) accelerates calcium excretion.

Even vigorous young men will lose bone mass if they are bedridden or if they are weightless in space. The skeleton needs not only to be stimulated by the action of the sinews in order to maintain a healthy balance of accretion and excretion, but also, it seems, to be in contact with the ground. It would be interesting to learn if middle-aged women who habitually sit on the ground rather than in chairs ever display the characteristic fracture of the head of the femur that costs health authorities so many millions each year. When the facts that such women do not eat red meat and do eat yoghurt and green vegetables and walk for tens of miles each day usually carrying loads on their heads are taken into account as well, we would be surprised to find dowagers' humps among them. A hundred million or so such women live in the Indian sub-continent. Osteoporosis does have a genetic component, but it is also a disease of affluence.

Lanyon 1980, 1982 in animal experiments has demonstrated fundamental relationship between bone mass and load-bearing requirements. Bone mass can be increased by exposing bone to strain changes which are well within the limits of normal daily activity. It appears that the frequency with which the strain is applied is a more important oestrogenic stimulus than the magnitude of the peak strain. (Exton-Smith, 529)

The salvation of the skeleton then, is the same as the salvation of the rest of us: work, good, hard work that tires us but does not over-extend or exhaust us. All the other treatments to delay bone loss have long-term consequences of one sort or another.

Though the Indian peasant woman of my example will not suffer from osteoporosis, she will be unmistakably aged, bony and gaunt. There is no escaping ageing, which can be observed all around us, in every living thing and many inanimate things, cars, houses, furniture and clothes, but nobody quite knows what it is or why it happens. The second law of thermodynamics tells us that a self-perpetuating mechanism is impossible, but biologists have so far been unable to enunciate a similar law for their own discipline. Cells, it seems, can go on living and reproducing indefinitely, if the medium is right. Nobody dies of old age; without an illness to knock her off she will stick around indefinitely. So some biologists have come to the conclusion that, though death is inevitable, ageing is always pathological. Death is biologically useful; ageing is not. Most creatures don't hang about as they become gradually more and more decrepit, but conk out smartly once they have passed on their genes. The human female is unique among living organisms on this earth because she can live twice the time of her reproductive span and more. Many a butterfly might like to continue making love to flowers once her eggs were laid but the choice is not hers. The human female, having served the species, is the only one that can build a life of her own; it is too bitter a biological irony to think that she may not have the heart.

One reason she may not want to live out her allotted span is that the extra life is blighted by the consequences of ageing, so that it is not life but half-life or shelf-life. No one seems to know whether human ageing (as distinct from death) is avoidable or not. The best discussion of the mystery of ageing is still Alex Comfort's first and best-written book, *The Biology of Senescence*. Some have thought that we are born with a biological time-clock inside us that counts down a life-span which can only be 'artificially' interrupted or lengthened. Their notion is strengthened by the observable hereditability of longevity and by the fact that most species exhibit a uniform maximum life-span. Though creatures may die of myriad causes before they reach the end of their biological lease, they cannot live beyond it.

Discussions of longevity are difficult to keep out of discussions of human ageing, but they blur it impossibly. The Cumaean sibyl lived for ever, but she was so wasted that she spent all of her unnatural life longing for death. The person who inherits arthritis along with longevity (a fairly unlikely combination) is not likely to be overcome with gratitude. The woman trying to understand what ageing will inevitably involve will find that the people who should be telling her (who are mostly younger than she) will waste her time babbling on about centenarians in Georgia or Kashmir. What they cannot prepare her for is what will happen to her in the fifty years before she turns a hundred. Most studies of ageing are studies of the already aged. The woman who is anxious not to become a member of the nursing home population can learn little from studies of such populations. One of the worst fears of menopause is that bouts of confusion and memory loss are the first signs of Alzheimer's or senile dementia. The questions we all ask when we see the trembling old lady being buttoned into her coat are 'How did she get like that? How do you know when you are getting like that?' And when younger people treat us with pitying condescension we wonder if we have not already got like that.

Those of us who believe that dying is a service we should eventually perform in the interests of the ecosphere and the other people who arrive on the planet every day may be equally sure that ageing benefits nobody. Decrepitude is a source of pain and frustration to the decrepit and a dreadful oppression for those who care for her, in any sense of the word. A woman who desires to remain vigorous for as long as possible, and take her leave quickly when she is too tired to go on, will not find much in gerontology that will help her to devise a strategy. For one thing gerontology is the study of old men; nowadays there is some embarrassment about this. Alex Comfort would like to have replaced the word with geratology, the study of old age, but this would be merely window-dressing. Until relatively recently, women were despaired of. The menopause put them beyond help. The real impetus for the attack on ageing came from the ageing male élite, who wanted to enjoy the fruits of a lifetime's accumulated power, namely the love and adulation of young women.

In case this should be thought to be mere loony feminist nonsense, let me summarize as briefly as possible the history of loony virilist nonsense. In 1889, seventy-two-year-old Professor Brown-Séquard of the University of Paris announced to a learned gathering of his colleagues that he had just been enabled to have congress with young Madame Brown-Séquard because he had injected himself with animal testicular extract. Brown-Séquard was the first of the hundreds of youth doctors whom Patrick McGrady dubbed the Erector Set, led by Eugen Steinach, Serge Voronoff, Julius Romulus Brinkley and Paul Niehans, who treated 'popes, millionaires and potentates' and very few women. After Niehans treated Pope Pius XII, his fresh cell injections, never systematically investigated, were imitated by other doctors.

One apprentice doctor confessed to [McGrady] that he had treated two women simultaneously for menopausal disorders with pituitary cells. His first injections were followed six months later with a second series. The women, who had developed pituitary antigens from the first shots, immediately went into anaphylactic (shock) reactions and died. (103–4)

A middle-aged woman was treated by Niehans for a host of complaints.

Even though eight months later the C[ellular] T[herapy] had failed to relieve her insomnia, the main reason for treatment, her liver attacks, had stopped . . . it was not until six years later that she began to sleep regularly.

'Can you imagine,' said the credulous patient, 'those grafts took six years to take?' (108)

Clayton Wheeler, who 'addressed himself, with flowers and hand-kissing, to a predominantly female clientele' (49), was an out and out fraud. The glandular extract suppositories he supplied were desiccated hamburger. Niehans's therapy was practised in London by Peter M. Stephan, who treated women not for loss of sexual function, but for worry 'about their breasts', in treating

which Stephan claimed to have 'about fifty per cent success'.
McGrady's report of the conversation with Stephan unintentionally reveals how gross their shared assumptions about women and
ageing must have been: Stephan replies to the question, 'Can you
really make something out of a pancake?':

'Let's be logical . . . absolutely logical about it . . . there are drooping
breasts and there are drooping breasts, are there not? I mean, don't give
me an impossible case. Let's have a sensible case. A woman of fifty. All
right, so they're drooping a bit and she has to wear all kinds of supports.
That you can *help*. If they're pancakes, as you call them . . . *no*.'
'Can you get a breast to upturn?'
'I've done it.' (127–8)

The female equivalent of restoring erection in the ageing penis
is understood by both as restoring turgidity in the breast.
Unfortunately the sum of the evidence seems to bear out the
impression that what men wanted from the youth doctors was the
energy of youth while women were content with the appearance
of youth. If men wanted to enjoy, women sought to attract. The
youth doctor who treated women was, until Robert Wilson
began the touting of hormone replacement in 1966, typically a
cosmetician.

Most women first detect, and often remain obsessed by, the
evidence of ageing in their faces, that is, wrinkles. Extraordinarily
enough, nobody knows what a wrinkle is. The anatomy of
wrinkled skin is the same as that of unwrinkled skin. Wrinkles are
not only or even principally evidence of ageing; they are also
evidence of repeated exposure, especially to the sun, but also to
wind and cold. More than is usually realized, premature wrinkling
of the facial skin is brought on by the prolonged use of our
favourite drugs, alcohol, caffeine and nicotine. An Australian
woman who lives in the sun, and smokes and drinks, has a face ten
years or more older than her body. Even in the faces of women
living in seclusion and using no stimulants, age shows its hand
eventually; the facial muscles slacken and the skin loosens as the

collagen layer is depleted. Though the faces of fifty-year-old nuns are pale and smooth by comparison with our weather-beaten Australian forty-year-old's, they are not young. Dry skins wrinkle sooner than oily ones, blond skin before olive, olive before brown, brown before black. Nevertheless black women die before brown women who die before olive women who die before blond women, and not simply because of the differences in their socio-economic circumstances.

The fifty-year-old woman's face tells us not only that she has lived fifty years but where and how she has lived it. It is not in itself unattractive or attractive, beauty being after all in the eye of the beholder, but the woman herself may feel that it gives too much away. Women who have worn make-up all their lives are masked women: what happens as the years pile on is that the wrinkles burst through the mask; too often they are lines of frowning, pouting or tightening the lips. The shining girl-face begins to look serious or anxious, or even to lower. We cannot be surprised that ageing women look perpetually sad or worried or cross or that they will go to some lengths to smooth out a face that invites an instantaneous negative response. The poor use Preparation H which shrinks haemorrhoids to gain a temporary face-lift; the rich go for the real thing. The doctors who make a fortune out of trimming away 'the debris of years' use the same pitch as the oestrogen replacers: 'You should have come to me years ago. Now you can never leave me.' A face lifted once has to be lifted again, and still the neck and the hands and the rheumy old eyes will give it away. A better way of looking serene and glowing for a party is to take half an hour before the guests arrive for a warm bath, with or without invigorating aromatics.

This is not the place to discuss ways of smoothing ageing faces, whether by peeling off layers of skin or cutting out the sag. There are literally hundreds of such procedures, none of which fool anyone but the woman who pays for them. Cosmetic surgery has been found to be of benefit with women who have very low self-esteem, and has been used to advantage on prison inmates, who identified particular features as stigmata, and interpreted the changing of their faces as a changing of themselves. The woman who does not wish to dump or deny a part of herself will not try to junk her used face. During the climacteric she will be painfully aware of the changes in her physical appearance, which may be exacerbated by her mental state, but she will come to like her new face at least as much as she liked the one that, though young and vivid, seemed to need so much make-up to look good. One of the changes a woman ought to make at the climacteric is to change her make-up or perhaps, life being so short, to eliminate it altogether. If one's face is becoming something to look out of, rather than to be looked at, it does not need to be painted.

Why should skin wrinkle? Why should age spots appear on the backs of hands? Why do necks wattle and the skin over the breastbone turn into red chicken skin? Why do toenails grow thick and woody? Why does hair go grey and thin and, worst of all, fall out? Why do some people have bushy white hair and others a few colourless wisps? Why do joints get knobby and feet misshapen and knees and elbows horny? Why do eyes grow dim? These superficial changes are not the ones that biologists concern themselves with; there is no learned paper on relative changes in toenail density over a period of fifty years. Because, as one gerontologist put it, 'no one dies of old skin', most gerontology books do not discuss what happens to the skin as it ages. The truth is that the skin, the largest and most complex organ of the body, does age steadily throughout life, and analysis of the skin may offer the most reliable indicators of biologic age.

The changes are complex and not well understood; at menopause a woman's secretion of sebum declines sharply until it is only half as much as that of a man the same age. Her skin suddenly gets perceptibly drier and thinner, though there is no alteration in its complex structure. As the years pass there is a gradual muting of the histamine response, which may be a blessing, because there is usually a gradual increase in sensitization as the incidences of exposure mount up. Older people show allergic responses to more substances, but the responses are milder. Sensitivity to pain also decreases and the inflammatory response to a potential irritant is slower, so older people show a different pattern of reaction to skin contact with detergents or cosmetics or medication. The symptoms are slower to appear but may cause more damage and be less easily reversible. There are changes in the distribution of subcutaneous fatty tissue and the underlying vascular structure which in turn cause changes in heat retention. These changes are all too gradual for the changer herself to notice them, but at menopause she may become aware of them as sudden reversals. Your menopause summer may be the summer when you realize that you no longer tan nor peel the way you used to and the beach is no longer the place for you.

One of the clearest patterns in the longevity of laboratory rats is that restricting their food intake prolongs their lives (Masoro, 550–51). Hundreds of studies have produced the same result; variation of protein intake both within and without the restriction of diet has produced conflicting results. Human beings are not rats, who may have millions of years of experience of feast and famine behind them; nevertheless it makes sense that people who are not growing or reproducing need less food than people involved in either or both. A slower metabolic rate simply cannot process as much food as fast as a faster one. Both the storage of the surplus and the elimination of the waste products involve effort, using energy which the ageing woman may well want to free up for something else. There is also some evidence that changes in the gut alter digestive processes so that a good deal of the vitamin and protein content is merely excreted. All the evidence seems to indicate that the ageing woman should eat less and better. She should also increase the proportion of bulk and fibre in her diet. As for the changes in the intestinal tract, one of the theories of ageing that held sway at the turn of the century explained ageing as caused by the deleterious action of an unbalanced microbial population in the gut, which could be counteracted by eating yoghurt. Surgeons were only too willing to cut yards of healthy bowel out of patients who swore that the procedure had restored them to youth and vitality (Trimmer, 81–91). For once the womb was not the culprit.

The meaning of studies which have shown that the depression of body temperature in laboratory animals leads to longer survival is not easy to assess. It seems that chilling, as it were, is associated with delaying tumour development and depressing immune responsiveness. If auto-immune reponses are involved in the typical diseases of ageing such as arthritis, it makes sense to depress or retard them, but the drugs that depress human body temperature, which include chlorpromazine, reserpine, L-dopa, and THC, have other effects more spectacular than a mean statistical extension of hypothetical life-span.

Ageing involves gradual mutations in many patterns of behaviour. As menopause is a jolt in this otherwise reasonably continuous process, permanent alterations may be perceived as sudden and aberrant. One of the behaviours that alters with age is sleep. Middle-aged women are not capable of the dormouse sleep of younger creatures. A pattern of eight or more hours sleep may be turning into a pattern of napping. If the menopausal woman insists upon following an inappropriate sleep pattern she may find herself lying wide awake in bed for many potentially useful hours. The adjustment will be made more difficult if she is trying to fit her sleep pattern to someone else's, lying open-eyed in the dark alongside a snoring partner, whose snores never used to disturb her before.

Sleep comes in two basic kinds, REM and Non REM (NREM). REM stands for rapid eye movement, which is not to be observed in the onset of sleep, when the brain goes through various stages of activity that show characteristic patterns on an encephalogram, a mixed stage, a stage showing two patterns called the K complex and the sleep spindle, and a third stage called slow wave or delta sleep. In REM sleep the encephalogram shows a pattern similar to that of the waking brain and the eyes move rapidly in synchrony, while the reflexes that functioned normally during NREM sleep seem to be suspended. After about eighty minutes of NREM sleep, ninety or a hundred minutes of REM sleep ensue and the two continue to alternate during the total sleep time (Williams *et al.*, 1974; Miles and Dement, 1980).

Middle-aged females in REM sleep exhibit the highest arousal threshold, that is, are the most easily wakened and the most sensitive to traffic noise in sleep. In the sixth decade of life a high proportion of people, about a quarter, have no stage 4 sleep at all. It looks as if slow wave sleep can be increased by physical exercise (Baekeland, 1970; Horne and Porter, 1975) and by fasting (Parker *et al.*, 1972; MacFayden *et al.*, 1973; Karacan *et al.*, 1973). In any event, there is no evidence that disturbed sleep is damaging to the organism. Nobody knows what particular function slow wave sleep might perform. More important is the absorption of oxygen during sleep; deprival of oxygen during sleep, either by frequent apnoea or holding of the breath, or obstructed airways, is associated with daytime sleepiness, morning headaches and personality changes. Life-long snoring is related to heart disease and hypertension. One out of every two women in her sixties snores.

Nocturnal wakefulness is not necessarily a disadvantage. Though one might occasionally yearn for the long, deep sleep of yesteryear, there is a sort of aptness in the fact that the older members of the group are on watch at night, when the young are sunk in slumber. The nocturnal sleeplessness of older primates has an obvious function in ensuring the survival of the group and has probably been selected for. The wee small hours belong to older women; this is the time when the leprechauns come and sweep the kitchen hearth and polish the pots; not the leprechauns at all, of course, but their old mistress comes noiselessly to get her kitchen just as she likes it, without guilt-tripping the younger members of her household. The world over, older women are up betimes. What they say is that they don't need much sleep; what they don't say is that they cherish those hours in charge of a houseful of sleeping people and feel a pang of regret when the bathroom door begins to slam and people sticky with the heavier sleep of the young begin to stumble about the house, complaining about having to get up at all. If they do not notice that yesterday's wet shoes have been carefully dried and the creases got out of yesterday's crumpled overcoat, so much the better.

It should not be forgotten, however, that sleeplessness is a feature of depression, and the sleep pattern of the elderly resembles the sleep pattern of depressed people. It is possible that some of the psychiatric disorders associated with ageing are aggravated or even caused by sleep pathology. During the climacteric temporary disturbances merge with, mask, or even exacerbate the gradual long-term change, so that the Circadian rhythm can be prematurely and excessively warped. The middle-aged woman should give some attention to techniques of relaxation, so that she does not continue to wake herself up by holding her breath or by repetitive involuntary movements. She may need quieter circumstances, away from traffic noise; she may need more or fresher air, rest and exercise; she may need a colder bed or a colder room. She does not need a heavy evening meal with lots of alcohol, coffee, and her own or other people's cigarettes. If the climacteric were respectable, she could expect such consideration as a matter of course. It was to find fresh air, rest, exercise and an appropriate diet that for centuries ladies in their late forties made their way to Aix-les-Bains or Buxton, and it is still not a bad idea.

7

Medical Ignorance

Women are born with all the ova they will ever produce. Until the menarche they are dormant. The young woman grows tall and strong, learns both to work and to play, and wonders about the day when she shall start having 'the curse'. When she is approaching physical maturity, but need by no means have arrived at her full growth and strength, hair begins to appear in her armpits and on her pubis, her body shape and complexion change and, sometimes slowly, painfully and messily, she begins to menstruate. The one change among the changes of puberty that is actually welcome to the young woman is the growth of breasts, and this too can be irregular, painful and delayed.

Many a young woman at menarche wonders how she will cope with the rest of her reproductive life, when the beginning of it is so smelly and cramp-laden. The cyclical changes in mood control, the swelling of hands and feet, backache, headaches and depression that many women experience as a regular part of their menstrual cycle, represent a real deterioration in the quality of a teenager's life. Even at this stage she is likely to be given the idea that it is she who is making heavy weather of a natural process and she should look to her attitudes and sort herself out so that she is glad and proud to bleed once a month. The palliatives for cyclical distress are all inadequate, despite the cases their pedlars make for them.

The fourteen-year-old struggling with hormonal chaos is hardly likely to be consoled by the fact that she has only thirty years or so to endure her menstrual cycle. A few women, those for whom contraception has been an ordeal or a failure, or whose reproductive system never seemed to function smoothly, may look forward to 'menopause', and some actively induce it by undergoing hysterectomy long before ovarian function is due to cease. For most women menopause is a word of fear.

In order to understand what happens when the menstrual cycle slows down and ceases we need to understand what it is. Not only is the cycle cyclical in the sense that it passes through a series of phases each leading one into another, what is happening is a cycle of stimulus, secretion, reaction and abreaction. Most explanations interrupt the process rather arbitrarily at the point where a part of the brain called the hypothalamus or 'under-bed' sends a biochemical prompt to the pituitary gland to release chemicals of its own manufacture; the substance carrying the chemical prompt is called by what it does rather than what it is, either follicle stimulating hormone releasing factor (FSHRF) or luteinizing hormone releasing factor (LHRF). Because nobody knows how the prompt for FSH might differ from the prompt for LH, some sources prefer to call it GnRH, gonadotrophin releasing factor. This message sent to the pituitary releases follicle stimulating hormone (FSH for short) or the other, the luteinizing or 'yellow-body-making' hormone, LH.

FSH is what causes some of the follicles in the ovaries to begin to swell and ova to ripen. The stimulated follicles come to the surface and one of them pops, releasing the egg. Nobody knows how the candidate for maturation is selected or why it is that at a certain point in a woman's life, though there are many follicles still on the stalk, no more of them seem capable of swelling and popping, no matter how much FSH is pumping around the body in which the ovaries live. The mechanism by which the ovum is selected for maturation being unknown, we cannot know why it sometimes ceases in young women, let alone why it ever has to cease. When young women's ovaries fail there is no lack of FSH excreted in their urine and it seems to be normal; if they are further dosed with natural FSH their ovaries will not respond.

One possibility is that they are producing antibodies to their own FSH or to their own ovarian substances. Another possibility is that there are intermediate steps in the ovulation process that have never been detected.

As the follicles ripen they release oestrogen, the hormone that women need in order to feel good. The oestrogen in its turn sends the signal back to the brain that it is time to turn off the FSH. As oestrogen levels in the blood rise and rise, the pituitary is stimulated to release more LH, and this is the chemical signal that causes the follicle to burst and shed the ovum. The oestrogen also prompts the uterus to rebuild its lining. However, it is important to remember that ovarian activity is not the sole source of oestrogen in pre-menopausal women.

A most important concept to understand is that the total sex-steroid hormone production in the pre-menopausal female is made up of two components. There is a relatively constant base level of estrogen, principally oestrone produced by peripheral conversion (extraglandular formation) from androstenedione. On this is superimposed the second component, namely, a fluctuating secretion of oestradiol from the developing graafian follicles and the corpus luteum. There is also a constant production of androgens with a small proportion contributed by cyclic activity. (Utian, 1980, 30)

The broken follicle turns into a dot of yellow matter, called the corpus luteum, which in turn secretes progesterone, the gestation hormone that is intended to maintain pregnancy. Progesterone also acts on the lining of the womb, which thickens, accumulates blood vessels and forms glands filled with secretion, to provide the correct cultural conditions for an implanted fertilized ovum, should one drop in. The combination of progesterone and oestrogen is also the chemical signal that tells the brain to throttle back on the production of both FSH and LH.

If no fertilization occurs, the secretion of oestrogen and progesterone ceases, the womb lining is starved and begins to drop away, to be shed and flushed out with blood. In the absence of oestrogen and progesterone, the hypothalamus starts up again sending out FSH and LH, and off we go again. What happens at menopause is that these interlocking processes begin to misfire and slow down. The process is not uniform; the old mechanism often runs on irregularly under its own momentum, so that the default system cannot stay switched on long enough to take over. We simply do not know what is happening to the relationship between the hypothalamus, the pituitary and the ovary during the pre-menopause when menstrual patterns begin to be disrupted.

There have been few studies designed to assess the amounts of circulating gonadotrophins and oestrogens in the bloodstream of untreated pre-menopausal women; examination of urine produced conflicting data (e.g. Pincus *et al.*, 1954; cf. Furuhjelm, 1966). The paucity of hard information and the recurrent disagreements about the significance of what data we have can be explained by difficulties inherent in the subject itself. Nowadays hormonal activity can be measured in various ways, by radioisotopic tracer studies, by taking blood from peripheral veins, or from the gland itself, or by taking urine samples over twenty-four hours, by bioassay of tissue receptors, or by a combination of methods, but as the synthesis and secretion of hormones vary according to all kinds of stimuli and respond to all kinds of factors, the results of these measurements are difficult to quantify. When hormones are bound to their carriers they behave in a completely different way from the free hormone.

Understandably, new techniques of radioimmunassay have been exploited mainly to assess the efficiency of various delivery systems of replacement hormones, for such expensive procedures can be undertaken only as part of a drug-testing scheme. There is simply no one to pay the enormous cost of long-term investigation of the healthy middle-aged woman. Justification for mass studies involving expensive and time-consuming techniques of sampling can hardly be found, for they cannot be shown to save lives or directly to influence the incidence of life-threatening disease.

The belief that it is oestrogen deficiency that causes climacteric symptoms has never been substantiated by empirical proof, despite the best efforts of an army of clinicians and biochemists supported by the vast resources of the pharmaceutical multinationals. The usual account makes it seem as if only ovulation and menstruation can keep women feeling well. This is not what the young woman herself perceived, when after fourteen years or so of feeling as well as well can be, menstruation suddenly made her feel sick. It is a poor lookout indeed if mid-cycle pain, pre- and post-menstrual tension, cramps, bloating, backache, headache, and all the palaver of the cycle are the purest well-being compared to the physical condition of the female after menopause. The obstacle to understanding here is the defect that disfigures all gynaecological investigation; we do not know enough about the well woman to understand what has gone wrong with the sick one. Gynaecologists are like motor mechanics who have never worked on a car that actually went.

In order to understand the role played by oestrogen in keeping women healthy, energetic and optimistic, we need to know a great deal more about the systems of secretion of oestrogen, and the variability in the levels of circulating oestrogen in women of all ages. If oestrogen secretion knocks out another hormone which makes little girls feel well, perhaps we ought to be investigating replacing the little girl hormone rather than oestrogen in older women. If this is impossible or inappropriate, then perhaps we should be considering stimulating oestrogen production from androstenedione instead of simply 'replacing' natural oestrogens with synthetic steroids in women suffering menopausal distress or post-menopausal deficiency. Unfortunately we do not know enough about the whole woman, whose anatomy is generally studied as if it were simply a man's body with a reproductive system installed in it, to have any clear idea of how the endocrine balance of well women differs from that of ill women, or, indeed, what degree of variability there is in endocrine function in both well women and sick women. One substance whose role is not understood is prolactin, which governs lactation and, some say, nest-building and migration in other species, and is secreted in elevated quantities during extreme stress. Some infertility in older, high-achieving women is thought to be caused by elevated prolactin levels. We know that secretion of prolactin parallels secretion of oestrogen, is stepped up at puberty and declines at menopause. Administration of oestrogen seems to trigger increased secretion of prolactin, which may not prove ultimately to be a net health benefit.

After menopause the ovary changes in structure; the cells that excrete oestrogens and progesterone are gradually lost, and the cells in between, the stromal cells, become more abundant and active. It is thought that these interstitial cells might secrete androgens, but nobody knows whether they do or not. An important study by Procope in 1968 identified two distinct groups of post-menopausal women; in one group the ovaries were completely atrophic and their removal made no difference to the women's levels of circulating oestrogens and androgens; in the other the ovaries were not completely inert, but showed 'ovarian cortical stromal hyperplasia' and were producing sex steroids. No subsequent studies were able to develop the revolutionary notion that 'all women are not the same' or to relate the difference in the ovaries to an overall difference in health status. One possibility is that the women of the second group do not lose interest in sex and the women of the first group do. Some such difference between post-menopausal individuals has been observed and recorded but no systematic examination of the phenomenon has ever been undertaken. Researchers simply argue about it, rather in the way that medieval natural philosophers sought to prove or disprove the existence of other worlds by debate rather than developing a telescope.

One thing we do know is that we cannot duplicate the intricate patterns of secretion in the pre-menopausal female in the post-menopausal female. We know that to get free hormone circulating we have to give at least a proportion of expensive animal hormones. Giving oestradiol by mouth, or transdermally, will apparently get women to feel well, but we cannot claim to be replacing the missing hormone cocktail. We do not actually understand why menopausal women should feel better when given oestradiol, but we do know that we are not obliged to administer oestradiol in quantities far greater than those produced by natural secretion. If we give oestrogens by mouth most of the active substance will be degraded and excreted; we do not know by what biological pathway the active agent reaches the target organs. It is at least possible, if not likely, that treatment with replacement oestrogen to ablate the fluctuations in menopausal levels may effect the switch-over to a new pattern of secretion relying upon the stromal cells and the adrenals. The battering of this delicate mechanism with large amounts of exogenous steroids may prevent its establishment, so that the long-term outcome of the kind of haphazard dosing of women during the climacterium is to compromise their health and accelerate their ageing. This possibility is never discussed. By contrast, any suggestion that men displaying signs of testosterone deficiency should be routinely dosed with 'replacement' testosterone is swiftly refuted on precisely those grounds.

It is misleading to talk of the reproductive years as if they consisted of four hundred and fifty or so uniform cycles. The Menstrual and Reproductive History Research Program of the University of Minnesota, which began observing and testing a cohort of women in 1934, showed that during the ten years following the first menstruation cycles were often variable, and the variability decreased with age. Over the next two decades a steady decrease in cycle length was observed; women of twenty-five tended to have a thirty-day cycle, women of thirty-five a twenty-eight-day cycle. During the years immediately preceding menopause, marked variability was noticed again (Treloar *et al.*, 1967). This transitional phase varied greatly in length and showed both unusually short and unusually long cycles.

It took twelve years for some of the same researchers to set up a preliminary study to determine whether they could establish a pattern in the variations of menstrual cycle preceding menopause; the job was made harder because although women could correctly recall the year of their menopause, they could not recall the details of the menstrual uproar that preceded it. A hypothesis appeared that late menopause was associated with greater variability of cycle patterns and therefore, as late menopause was also associated with a greater risk of breast cancer, greater variability in cycle patterns was thought possibly to be the crucial factor (Wallace *et al.*, 1978). What was found was that women 'with a later age at menopause had a transitional phase characterized by longer intermenstrual intervals and greater cycle variability. Women who ceased menstruating before they were forty-four had an average cycle length of fifty-seven days in the two years before the last period; women who did not cease menstruating till they were fifty-five or older had a mean cycle length of eighty days' (Bean *et al.*, 1979). The standard deviations in these figures were all fairly high, from forty-six and a half to sixty-four.

By taking the basal body temperatures during these cycles it could be seen that it was the follicular phase, i.e. the period after menstruation and before ovulation, when FSH is circulating at a high level, that was prolonged. By the same evidence, in women whose cycles had reached their shortest duration, just before the transitional phase had set in, it could be seen that it was the follicular phase that was more quickly completed. The luteal phase remained constant throughout the reproductive years. However, during both the first and the last years of menstruation, cycles with no temperature blip signalling ovulation could be observed. Women aged between forty and forty-five by gynaecological computation (i.e. when age at first menstruation had been standardized) exhibited 34 per cent of anovulatory cycles (Sherman *et al.*, 1979).

Several studies revealed, in the early phase of the cycle, in women aged forty-six to fifty-six, levels of FSH up to 25 per cent higher than in women aged between forty and forty-five. It seemed as if, as the follicles were proving less and less sensitive to

FSH, the hypothalamus was stepping up the instruction to the pituitary, which was flooding the system with FSH which eventually succeeded in stimulating a follicle to push the process on to the next stage, until after the last menstruation, when finally no follicle would respond. This by its nature was something that could not be known until it had happened. The process by which increased levels of FSH are secreted begins much earlier than anyone had suspected and is well established by the time a woman reaches her early forties; it is followed by an increase in secretion of LH in the late forties. All kinds of explanation for these changes in hormone profiles have been suggested. The favourite is that the woman suffers some depletion of her oestradiol secretion, but no such depletion has been demonstrated. The next possibility was that there might be in women something like the substance called 'inhibin' in males, a follicle stimulating release inhibiting substance, FRIS (Van Look *et al.*, 1977; Chari *et al.*, 1979), which was secreted in diminishing amounts as women grew older. Perhaps the unknown circulating body chemical acts directly on the follicle. Others wondered whether it might be age-related changes in the hypothalamus and/or pituitary that produced the changes in the pattern of secretion. All observers knew that the older a woman who entered an *in vitro* fertilization programme, the more FSH was needed to get her to produce enough eggs for fertilization.

Why follicles should become less responsive is not known. The degree and causes of variation in menstrual pattern were summed up in 1979 by Barry M. Sherman and Robert B. Wallace of the University of Iowa College of Medicine and Alan E. Treloar of the University of North Carolina in this fashion:

The irregular episodes of vaginal bleeding in perimenopausal women can be interpreted as the irregular maturation of residual ovarian follicles. The potential for hormone secretion by the remaining follicles was diminished and variable. Menses were sometimes preceded by maturation of a follicle with limited secretion of both oestradiol and progesterone, but vaginal bleeding also occurred after a rise and fall in oestradiol without measurable increases in progesterone, compatible with an anovulatory cycle. (Sherman *et al.*, 26)

So as women approach menopause they may experience normal cycles, longer cycles, and episodes of anovulatory bleeding. Moreover,

Because episodes of abortive follicular maturation and vaginal bleeding are often widely spaced, perimenopausal women may be exposed to persistent oestrogen stimulation that may be related to the dysfunctional uterine bleeding common at this time. (28)

Ironically perhaps, the spur to this research was a concern to know what contraception was appropriate for women in the perimenopause, and in discussing this, the researchers revealed that they could not actually know when menopause had occurred, although they had no scruple in asking women themselves to name a day. Most of the studies of age at menopause rely upon the recollection of the women in their sample, and seem to encounter no vagueness in their answers. This has surprised at least one researcher. Dr Helen Ware of the Department of Demography at the Australian National University, in response to a statistical paper on 'Factors affecting the age at menopause' in a sample of Dutch women, exclaimed:

I am amazed that there were not many who replied to Dr Van Keep's postal questionnaire that they either did not know the date of menopause, or were not sure. In our experience of face-to-face interviewing in Australia only 24% of women knew both the year and the month of menopause, and even after probing only 26% could estimate either the month or the year although the oldest women in the sample were only 59. (Parkes *et al.*, 52)

It is likely that women who have no periods for six months or more are certain that they have passed menopause. If a bleed happens after this time, they have to revise this impression, but the position is still the same; the woman simply repeats the same thought. Given the anatomical confusion and the genuine vagueness of the phenomenon, what the woman probably recalls is her recognition of her menopause, her acceptance of it. In the absence of any other definition, she has to define it herself. Dr Ware was told that Australian women were probably less aware of the menopause than Dutch women, a suggestion to which she made no reply. The Dutch women probably filled in their postal questionnaire with assistance from family members, who may have more cause to identify a day and an hour for menopause than the woman herself. In the face to face interview no such collusion was possible.

The family planners had no joy from any of the papers attempting to establish firm statistical parameters for menopause and to declare a *terminus ad quem* after which ovulation could never occur.

The hormonal studies confirm that the potential for ovulation during the perimenopausal period, while much reduced, is present. To prevent conception contraceptive practices, if desired, should be maintained until the onset of permanent menopausal amenorrhea. No basis was known, other than clinical experience, for judging whether a given interval without menses was likely to represent permanent amenorrhea. (Sherman et al., 30)

All that the statisticians could calculate was a set of unsurprising probabilities; the older you are the more likely it is that after six months without a period you will not have another, 52 per cent if you were aged forty-five to forty-nine and 70 per cent if you were over fifty-three. Ten per cent of the women in this sample, more than a year after the last bleed, had had another bleed which was not associated with illness or with taking hormones of any kind (Sherman *et al.*, 30). This was a surprise. The received medical wisdom is that

post-menopausal bleeding (i.e. bleeding occurring a year or more after your periods have stopped) is never normal. Thorough investigation of this important symptom involves a D and C (dilatation and curettage, or womb scrape), and you should never be persuaded to agree to less than this. (Shreeve, 4)

This medical opinion comes from Dr Caroline Shreeve, who is an alternative practitioner of herbalism and hypnotherapy. Dr Mary Anderson agrees that 'post-menopausal bleeding', i.e. bleeding a year or more after the cessation of menstruation, 'must be investigated by a specialist'.

One of the commoner causes is an early cancer of the endometrium of the uterus and if it is found it can be treated very successfully. *Such an episode of post-menopausal bleeding should never be ignored by doctor or patient alike, whatever the patient's age.* (32)

The analysts of the data from the Menstrual and Reproductive History Research Program of the University of Minnesota did not find a single case of the 'commoner cause' in their sample of post-menopausal bleeders, although it would be hoping too much to assume that they bothered to look. What they said was:

Moreover, even after one year (360 days) of amenorrhea, over 10% of subjects recorded an episode of vaginal bleeding, apparently not associated with significant illness or exogenous hormone consumption. (Sherman *et al.*, 32)

The word 'apparently' apparently indicates that D and Cs were not routinely performed in these cases. The researchers decided therefore that they could not be certain that follicular activity had actually ceased, and menopause could not reliably be said to have occurred.

It would thus appear prudent to maintain contraception, if desired, for a minimum of twelve months of amenorrhea.

The possibilities are therefore two; if you bleed more than a year after your last bleed, you may have gone through menopause a year ago, or, conversely, you may not. Either following Dr

Shreeve's instructions would involve you in an unnecessary D and C or it would not. As a result of such 'studies',

> Most doctors now advise women over 50 to continue with contraception for a year after their last period and women under 50 to use contraception for two years after their last period. (Mackenzie, 46)

Provided of course they know which period is their last.

The greatest irony is that if you are on a contraceptive pill and in the peri-menopause, you can go on having regular break-through bleeds long after you have ceased ovulating. Then nobody knows if or when you have passed the menopause.

> It is difficult to know when a woman on combined oral contraceptives has reached menopause, and this necessitates her using another method while waiting to see if she is still menstruating. (Mackenzie, 48)

This process could of course go on for ten years or more. This advice comes after Mackenzie has advised women to continue using whatever contraception they have always used, provided it 'has always been acceptable and problem-free'. Advice of this kind leads one to wonder what kind of world family planners live in. I know no one who has used only one kind of contraception in her life and no one who has found any kind of contraception both acceptable and problem-free. No woman over forty-five should be using oral contraceptives in any case, because of the elevated risk of stroke, thrombosis and heart attack. An IUD would seem to be a better option for a middle-aged woman, unless she is not in a stable relationship, in which case she should reconcile herself to the use of condoms, 'acceptable' or not. At a workshop on oral contraception for women over thirty-five organized by the International Health Foundation in Lausanne in March 1988, R. K. E. Kirkman of the Manchester Family Planning Centre asked:

> What about the IUD in the pre-menopause? Should we leave it in place until one year after the menopause?

He was answered by J. R. Newton of the Obstetrics and Gynaecology Department of Birmingham Maternity Hospital:

In my view there seems to be no reason for leaving an IUD in place beyond the age at which the failure rate of the IUD is greater than the risk of unprotected intercourse. I prefer to remove the IUD before it becomes embedded after the menopause and would certainly not let an IUD remain there longer than six months after the last menstruation.

Wulf Utian interpolated:

The presence of an IUD at this age often complicates the interpretation of clinical signs and this may be reason to remove the IUD.

Dr Newton answered:

I could not agree more. I do believe in the value of the IUD as a contraceptive method after the age of 35. But even though the users may be enthusiastic to retain the IUD we should know when to remove the device.

How they might go about deciding which menstruation is the last, given the frequent return of bleeding after more than six months, the learned gentlemen do not say. How long it takes the device to become embedded they do not say either (*Maturitas*, Suppl. 1, 97).

(It does not do to suggest that mature people might find alternatives to intromission, i.e. penetration, which were less challenging to the male, more pleasurable for both, and less compromising to the woman's health. Imagination in sex is one contraceptive that is never suggested.) Despite the contradictoriness of her own argument, Mackenzie includes as a caption to a cartoon of a smiling woman throwing caps, pills, pessaries and condoms out of a window:

Being free of the worry of contraception and conception is one of the pluses of the menopause. (Mackenzie, 51)

Curiouser and curiouser, for she has just spent a whole chapter telling us how the menopausal woman should continue to use contraception.

It is small consolation to a woman who is flooding one week, and sees no periods for six months, and then has what seems a normal period, and then again nothing or a flood, that the medical establishment is nearly as muddled as her system appears to be. To the one question to which she really desires answer, 'When will it be over?', there are only other questions: 'When did it begin? Has it begun? How long can it last? How short could it be?' Generally speaking the climacteric, or the peri-menopause, is taken to be ten years, from age forty-five to age fifty-five. Hormonal uproar will begin some time after forty-five, but it will not necessarily end before fifty-five. All the more reason then to cease talking about 'the menopause' as if it were a single event, and to resume referring to the period of change as 'the climacteric'.

The conclusion of the paper which Barry Sherman presented to the Eighth IPPF Biomedical Workshop admitted that

... knowledge remains very incomplete. The importance of events that occur during the perimenopausal and early menopausal years cannot be overestimated. In addition to the immediate problems of contraception during the perimenopausal years, and treatment of menopausal symptoms, the age-related problems of osteoporosis, hypertension, atherosclerosis, and carcinoma of the breast and endometrium are intimately related to the changes in the hormonal environment consequent to menopause. (Sherman *et al.*, 32)

Dr Sherman was then bombarded with questions. A professor of endocrinology from Bombay wanted to know whether there was any correlation between oestradiol levels and menopausal symptoms. Dr Sherman answered:

There are not many studies on the correlation between hormone levels and symptoms. Our studies show that individual women may have high menopausal levels of gonadotrophins and irregular cycles preceding any symptoms by many months. During continuous blood sampling over 24-hr periods we detected no change between changes in oestrogens or gonadotrophins and the individual episodes of hot flushes. The mediation of these symptoms is unknown. (Parkes *et al.*, 54)

Dr Sherman could have cited Hunter *et al.*, 1973; Stone *et al.*, 1975; Aksel *et al.*, 1976; Studd *et al.*, 1977; Chakravarti *et al.*, 1977; Dennerstein, 1987; and Hutton *et al.*, 1978, all of which did test plasma levels of ovarian hormones and failed to find a correlation, but for some reason he prefers to pretend that the matter has not been investigated. He should have cited the example of Mulley and Mitchell writing in the *Lancet* in 1976:

. . . no correlation has so far been established between hormonal changes and menopausal flushing . . . we contend there is no clear-cut relation between hot flushes and oestrogen deficiency. (1397)

Even Utian has had to register the complexity of the case:

The mechanism of flushing has not been elucidated. The long popular theory that flushes are due to increased gonadotrophins is no longer acceptable. Nor does flushing appear to be related to particular concentrations of plasma oestrone, oestradiol, or andrestenedione levels. This does not exclude the likelihood of a declining level of oestrogen being responsible for the flushing response; that is a changing state, rather than an absolute state. (Utian, 1980, 110)

(At this point, we must stifle a shout of 'Bravo!' for it seems as if Utian is about to emerge from blind adherence to the deficiency theory; however, this flash of insight does not prompt him to desist throughout his 1980 monograph in referring to symptoms as caused by oestrogen deficiency.) Utian continues:

Sturdee and co-workers [1978] have reported the onset of the hot flush to be associated with a sudden and transient increase in sympathetic drive. This finding has been disputed [Ginsburg and Swinhoe, 1978]. Hutton *et al.* [1978] have suggested that catecholoestrogens may be involved, but this too is unproven. Flushing is associated with endogenous adrenergic discharge and exogenous catecholamines [Metz et al., 1978]. Further research along this line will hopefully solve this puzzle in the near future and perhaps result in suitable alternatives to oestrogen for treatment.

Further research has not elucidated the matter one bit. In 1988 David Sturdee and Mark Brincat, staunch supporters of HRT, are obliged to admit:

The hot flush remains the enigma of menopause. Discovery of the origin and mechanism may provide an insight into the aetiology of the menopause and a rationale for specific therapy. (39)

The Indian professor asked again:

What about sexual responsiveness and its relation to oestradiol levels?

Again Sherman could only reply:

I do not know of any data about the relationship between the hormone levels in individual women and their sexual activity.

The head of research at the National Institute of Demographic Studies in Paris asked how 'one can recognize a cycle in which there is fertilization but no implantation and in which the blastocyst dies after a few days'. His question was prompted by the consideration that among the erratic cycles of the middle-aged sexually active woman would be some which looked as if they were anovulatory and were not. He may have been wondering about the causes of very sudden and heavy bleeding in the peri-menopause. Dr Sherman could only reply:

I do not know of any method.

A woman teacher of physical anthropology from Montclair State College in New Jersey quoted a 1975 study that showed 'that postmenopausal women still have a few remaining primary and secondary follicles although they are not in good condition. Is there any information on how long a woman can maintain primary follicles?'

Again Dr Sherman replied:

The studies are few and I cannot say how long primary follicles can remain.

Dr John Studd, who set up one of the first menopause clinics in England, tells us in 'Management of the Menopause' (Campbell, 1976) that

The ovary contains the maximum number of oocytes (egg-cells) during the fifth month of foetal life. Thereafter the numbers decline and only one million are present at birth and as few as twenty-five thousand remain at menopause. . .

To most of us 25,000 egg cells would seem more than enough. These numbers are not such that they explain anything. We are left wondering why fertility begins to decline before birth, and what the excess oocytes are for and what is different about the ones that stay behind, and whether anything could be done to slow the ageing of the ovary by, for example, lengthening menstrual cycles. Dr Studd did not indicate any distinction between primary and secondary follicles, so his statement cannot answer the anthropologist's question.

Dr Sherman had then to contend with the Professor Emeritus of Population Studies at Harvard Medical School, who wanted to know if there was any way a doctor could determine whether or not a female patient was past the menopause.

It used to be thought that a few days' treatment with human menopausal gonadotrophin would indicate whether or not a woman was past the menopause, depending on whether or not such treatment induced a rise in the level of oestrogen.

Dr Sherman could not justify this procedure.

I have not used such treatment. Some of these women already have high levels of endogenous gonadotrophin. They can be followed for many months and suddenly they will have an oestradiol surge followed by menses, but we do not understand why it happens at a particular time. . .

The problem seemed to be the basic one, as phrased by the Professor Emeritus of Obstetrics and Gynaecology from the University of Aberdeen:

What normally selects the population of primordial follicles to be recruited is not known.

Ten years ago, then, medical researchers did not know why the menopause happened or when it happened, let alone why it causes a variety of symptoms from trivial to unbearable, or whether it causes these symptoms in a few, some, many or most women. As demographers the learned men and women gathered under the auspices of the Galton Foundation and the Ciba Foundation in 1979 had to determine how to devise family planning strategies for the middle-aged, so they were understandably anxious to arrive at a basis for a statistical model, but no parameters were forthcoming. If the statistics worked one way they would not work another. In order to tell a patient whether she was likely to have passed the menopause, according to one contributor, a doctor would have to break down her life-table according to half a dozen variables and even then he could only state a probability, a probability the woman had already postulated.

Business and professional women tend to have an earlier menopause, according to some rather old studies, but then working women tended to be single and married women not, so other researchers considered that 'a physiological amount of sexual intercourse' fended off menopause (Kisch, 599). Others thought that marriage selected women less likely to suffer early menopause or 'dry up' like old maids. A woman's age at the birth of her last child and the number of children she has are both associated with a later menopause; the use of oral contraceptives at any stage in the reproductive career delays menopause according to some studies and not according to others. Late onset of menses is associated with early cessation, but the data is not reliable. Smoking accelerates all the ageing processes including the ageing of ovarian follicles, and smokers tend to have an earlier menopause; obese women have a later menopause.

The middle-aged woman who opts for sterilization as terminal contraception, because she has already achieved her completed family size, presumably carries out her own cost-benefit analysis and should be encouraged to do so. Sterilization is now the most popular form of family limitation. Far too many women are being sterilized when their fertility is already decreasing, and far too many women will undergo hysterectomy after sterilization, some within months of the operation. If we were to tot up the number of times a woman in the developed world, especially an American woman, undergoes some form of invasive pelvic surgery, caesarian, laparoscopy, laparotomy, curettage, abortion, tubal cautery, cutting or ligation, oophorectomy, salpingectomy, surgery of the cervix, amniocentesis, hysterectomy and hysterotomy, we would notice a regular pattern of abdomen piercing and cutting that should be listed among the techniques of psychotic self-mutilation, with the chilling distinction that these are forms of self-mutilation in which doctors have been only too happy to cooperate. A man who demands that his penis and/or his testicles be cut off will be immediately understood to be deranged; a woman who for no good reason wishes to extirpate her uterus will be given every assistance. Female castration has always been a popular procedure, carried out in a multiplicity of ways, some of which were widely practised even when they carried with them a high risk of subsequent illness and death. When we have understood the psychopathology behind both the practitioner's enthusiasm for destroying the female organs of generation and the patient's conviction that they are what is making her sick, we shall have taken one step on the road to restoring the female eunuch to her full vigour and potential.

No human organ has been so often operated on as the uterus and yet doctors do not agree if and when to perform hysterectomy.

'When in doubt cut it out' is the policy generally followed, but even then surgeons and gynaecologists cannot agree whether to leave the ovaries or take them out. The removers say that retained ovaries can turn cancerous, that retained ovaries hardly work or do not work at all, and hysterectomized women too often present for further pelvic surgery. The preservers maintain that patients feel better after the operation if their ovaries are still in, that they will not suffer hot flushes and other symptoms associated with menopause, such as osteoporosis, and that continued oestrogen secretion protects against coronary heart disease. The removers say that exogenous sex steroids protect better against these undesirable sequelae. The patients themselves often proselytize for the particular form of devastation that they have undergone, convinced that after it they feel better than ever they did before.

One in four women will develop uterine myomas or fibromas, 'fibroids' as they are popularly known. Nobody knows why they form or how to treat them. Enormous ones can be asymptomatic, tiny ones symptomatic. They, or something else, may cause heavy bleeding in peri-menopausal women, especially if we include women in their early forties under this definition. At menopause myomas usually subside; in some women they continue to give trouble. Nobody knows why they should. Nobody has any idea whether there might not be a systemic medication that would shrink fibromas. There is after all no need to look for one, because a hysterectomy will finish them once for all, and take with it any prospect of cancer of the cervix or endometrial carcinoma. The fact that hysterectomy is a major operation, with an inbuilt risk of fever, infection and other complications, is neither here nor there. Fibromas should not be a justification for destructive surgery, but they are a counter-indication for HRT. Fibromas are oestrogen-dependent, and post-menopausal hormone replacement therapy could interfere with their involution, but most menopause manuals make no mention of them at all. Wendy Cooper's book-long advertisement for HRT, *No Change*, mentions no counter-indications for HRT, as if none of her readers was likely to have suffered from either endometriosis or fibromas. This kind of omission encourages the woman who has fibroids to think that she has something grave and rare and to accept major surgery for a minor problem.

What we have failed to find out about the menopause, a condition which every GP now considers himself qualified to treat, is really quite extraordinary.

We do not know what is happening.

We do not know why it happens.

We cannot tell in a particular case if it is about to happen, happening or over.

We do not know why some women form some symptoms, others different symptoms and sets of symptoms, or if it is true that some experience none at all.

We do not know which symptoms are related to menopause, and which to ageing, and which to neither.

We do not know what a hot flush is, beyond the fact that it is the one symptom that everyone associates with menopause.

We do not know why some women sweat profusely during flushing, some after flushing, some not at all, or why some have feelings of panic and others do not.

Nobody knows why some women suffer intense joint pain at menopause.

Nobody knows why women have disturbed sleeping patterns during the climacteric; sometimes these are described simply as a consequence of vasomotor disturbance, but there are many cases where women who are unable to sleep are not suffering from hot flushes or dripping with sweat. They are simply awake. This symptom is sometimes described as a 'psychological symptom'.

We do not know which menopausal symptoms are primarily physical, which psychosomatic and which psychological.

We have no idea which symptoms might indicate distortion of a natural function.

We do not know in what measure ageing complicates menopause or indeed *if* ageing complicates menopause. Some studies show that early menopause, including surgical or radiation menopause, is the hardest to deal with, others do not.

The menopause muddle is part of the general fog of incomprehension about the health status of the middle-aged woman. It is complicated by the availability of an expensive panacea which seems to obviate the necessity for further expensive, mass, long-term studies. Indeed it looks very much as if researchers will run out of untreated women to study long before they will have reached any firm conclusions. Already studies are complicated by the presence in the study population of a large proportion of hysterectomized women, women who have used or are using oral contraceptives and women who have undergone surgical sterilization with and without sequelae.

The practitioners who deny that there is too much that they don't know are the most dangerous; a wise doctor knows the extent of his/her ignorance. If your (young male) doctor is doctrinaire, change him, preferably for an older (woman) doctor who knows what you are talking about. Taking responsibility for your own health is the first step towards 'coping with menopause'.

8

The Treatments – Allopathic

The conventional doctor faced with an ageing female patient who complains of all kinds of distress needs to identify an illness, so that he can treat it. Dr Barbara Evans, whose book *Life Change: A Guide to the Menopause, its Effects and Treatment* is one of the most grown-up and intelligent discussions of HRT easily available, having listed all the complaints of women questioned by the International Health Foundation survey (AKZO), has to enter a caveat.

It must not be assumed that all these symptoms were necessarily due to the menopause. A psychiatrist would put many of them down to depression. A rheumatologist would see in the list many symptoms of rheumatoid arthritis. The menopause coincides with a period of life when stresses and domestic problems mount, and cause problems which are unrelated to the menopause. (17)

Matters are not made easier for the whole woman if her gynaecologist treats her as a pair of dead ovaries, her rheumatologist as a collection of joints, her bone specialist as a skeleton, her psychiatrist as a set of traumas, her gerontologist as an unsuitable candidate for treatment and her GP as a nuisance. The cessation of ovarian function may not be a direct cause of depression, tiredness, irritability and sleeplessness; nevertheless the effects of oestrogen deficiency may be felt more acutely in the presence of these other factors and are even perhaps aggravated by them. The climacteric syndrome is a case for holistic medicine, for treating the whole person, and for asking the patient not simply to cooperate in her treatment, but to make her own analysis of cost-benefits and accept responsibility for her own health strategy. The most significant obstacle to her doing this with any degree of confidence is the lamentable state of medical understanding of what is going on in her body.

Historically, doctors asked to prescribe palliatives for climacteric distress have done their best. They have let blood, prescribed violent purgatives, sent women to spas and mountain resorts, dosed them with bromide, mercury, sulphuric acid, belladonna, and acetate of lead. Suspecting that the problems women encountered were directly caused by the cessation of ovarian function, they turned to glandular extracts, plant hormones, and bits and pieces of the reproductive equipment of other species, dried corpus luteum from pigs, grilled ovaries from cows and sheep, but nothing worked.

When natural oestrogens were first isolated in 1923, their potential usefulness in treating menopausal distress was recognized but no feasible mode of administration was established. Robert A. Wilson dosed his patients with 'a crude extract made from dried sheep's ovaries' but the allergic reactions outweighed any improvement. In the 1930s stilboestrol was prescribed for menopausal distress, but the side-effects, nausea, headaches and skin reactions, were worse than the condition. In the late 1930s German chemists managed to synthesize oestradiol benzoate, which was effective in cases of climacteric distress but had to be given by injection. It was not until the 1960s, after the contraceptive problem had been solved to the satisfaction of the birth controllers if not that of the users, that the steroid manufacturers turned their research departments on to the problems of the peri-menopause.

The popularization of oestrogen replacement in the 1960s was so successful that between 1963 and 1973 sales of oestrogen preparations quadrupled; half the post-menopausal female population was using HRT or, as the Americans call it, ERT, 'estrogen replacement therapy'. Then came the bombshell; incidence of endometrial cancer was up 10 per cent. The increase in incidence was much less than the increase in use of the hormones, and endometrial cancer was still rare, but the news media made nothing of that. The actual presence of cancer was not always confirmed. What rose by 10 per cent in ten years was the number of diagnoses of endometrial cancer. Though between the two national surveys, the one in 1948-9 and the other in 1969-71, the incidence of endometrial cancer had doubled, the death rate had halved. Given the extraordinary alacrity with which American doctors perform hysterectomies, nobody can know what the 10 per cent rise in diagnoses of endometrial cancer in twenty years actually represents, especially when the widely varying dosage patterns followed during the early years of HRT are taken into account. All genital cancers have become more common over the last fifty years; the causes may well be found to lie in environmental changes and behavioural changes as well as in the use of hormones. American doctors could not afford to examine the data and investigate the case further. Out of terror of malpractice litigation they became overnight as reluctant to prescribe HRT as before they had been enthusiastic.

To ask for more rational approaches to women's health is to cry for the moon. The proponents of HRT were trapped by the logical weaknesses in their own position. They had never proved that there was an oestrogen deficiency, nor had they explained the mechanism by which the therapy of choice effected its miracles. They had taken the improper course of defining a disease from the therapy, and though the hysteria about the rise in incidence of endometrial cancer was no more logical than the case for oestrogen replacement, the whole shaky edifice collapsed. Sales of oestrogen preparations in the United States halved; and over the next two years diagnoses of endometrial cancer fell by a quarter. QED. Oestrogen replacement was too dangerous to use. To the women who said that they didn't care about the risk of cancer, their doctors, well aware of the legal implications, said that they could not allow them to run it.

Enter the British. In 1976, Stuart Campbell, then Senior Lecturer at Queen Charlotte's Hospital in London, summarized the HRT experience:

The American experience has been none too reassuring and an apparent alliance between feminist movements and certain gynaecological interests has produced the 'feminine forever' cult which implies that oestrogens should be prescribed from the cradle to the grave. This specious therapeutic approach to therapy has unfortunately not been accompanied by adequate epidemiological and follow-up studies and now from the USA there is evidence of a major reappraisal of hormone therapy due to the findings of two poorly documented retrospective studies (*NEJM*, 1975) that there may be an association between postmenopausal oestrogens and endometrial cancer. This syndrome of therapeutic overkill followed by overreaction can only be avoided by a deep understanding of the psychological, hormonal and other pathophysiological changes of the perimenopause . . . we are at the moment a long way from this . . .

If Campbell knew more about feminists, he would have been aware that feminist movements have from the outset been deeply suspicious of steroids. In 1969 Barbara Seaman published *The Doctors' Case Against the Pill* and led the campaign to force the Nelson hearings on the safety of the contraceptive pill to take evidence from women; for the next eight years she studied the effects of exogenous steroid use on women's health and then published *Women and the Crisis in Sex Hormones*, a seminal text of the feminist health movement. The National Women's Health Network lobbied successfully to force the drug companies to include a list of all side-effects and contra-indications in every package of steroids and replacement oestrogens that is sold.

The feminist position on oestrogen replacement is vigorously summarized in an article by Rosetta Reitz, 'What doctors won't tell you about menopause':

They didn't tell me my estrogen supply continues even though I'm not producing eggs. They imply it stops cold in order to sell me their estrogen-replacement therapy. But I'm not buying that . . . I know if I don't put any foreign estrogen into my body, my endocrine glands will regulate my hormonal activity and my adrenals will step up their estrogen production. The doctors don't know how this works or which unidentified glands also rally into this activity, but they admit it is so when they speak among themselves. (If some of the medical research money that went into studying the men on the moon could have been used to learn about the women on earth during the menopause, I would consider the money better spent). . . Experiment with my body, which could produce sore breasts, nausea, vomiting, bloating, cramps, or nervous tension? While they are guessing and charging me besides? Never. (Dreifus, 209–10)

Campbell's extraordinary misunderstanding of the feminist position is less forgivable than his diplomatic vagueness about 'gynaecological interests'. The international conference at which he was speaking was sponsored by some of the most important marketers of steroids for the dosing of women, namely Ayerst Laboratories, manufacturers of Premarin, the US market leader, Schering Chemicals Ltd, Syntex Pharmaceuticals and Abbott Laboratories.

Campbell must have known that the 'forever feminine' cult was not the product of an unholy alliance between feminists and gynaecological interests but of Robert A. Wilson MD (FICS, FACS and FACOG), Consultant in Obstetrics and Gynaecology at three New York hospitals, Diplomate of both the American Board of Obstetrics and Gynaecology and the 'International College of Surgeons', fellow of four more learned societies, member of seven more, and President of the Wilson Research Foundation, New York. Wilson administered oestrogen therapy over forty years to 5,000 patients before he began his public preaching in 1962. In 1963 he and his wife Thelma together worked on articles pleading for 'adequate estrogen from puberty to the grave', offering to 'eliminate the menopause'. By 1965, when he wrote the seminal text *Feminine Forever*, Wilson had authored or co-authored thirteen publications on oestrogen therapy and accumulated the twenty-one titles listed on p. 177 of the English edition of 1966. *Feminine Forever* is intended to impress the common sense out of the laywoman. A ringing preface by another of the Masters in Menopause, Robert Greenblatt, declared:

Woman will be emancipated only when the shackles of hormone deprivation are loosed. Then she will be capable of obtaining fulfilment without interrupting her quest for a continuum of physical and mental health. (15)

Whatever that may mean. Most of us would be surprised to discover that we were involved in any such quest; Greenblatt's rhetoric seems to imply that sanity and well-being are for most women as far-off and mysterious as the Holy Grail.

Dr Wilson, too, recaptures the poetic prophecies of a distant day when he endows woman with her right to be forever feminine. (15)

It is most gratifying to find that learned medical gentlemen have at last come round to the idea that women should have rights; it is rather less gratifying to discover that the Masters in Menopause see those rights as within their gift. By that time the recipients of oestrogen replacement therapy numbered 'between six and twelve thousand'. Wilson is not troubled by his own vagueness in the matter, which seems to indicate some inadequacies in follow-up. Instead he tells us that we can recognize these women just by looking at them.

The outward signs of this age-defying youthfulness are a straight-backed posture, supple breast contours, taut, smooth skin on face and neck, firm muscles, and that particular vigour and grace typical of a healthy female. At fifty such women still look attractive in tennis shorts or sleeveless dresses. (17–18)

What woman could ask for more? Wilson was certain that the menopause was 'a serious, painful, and often crippling disease' (29). He had 'known cases where the resulting physical and mental anguish was so unbearable that the patient committed suicide' (39).

I have seen untreated women who had shrivelled into caricatures of their former selves. Some had lost as much as six inches in height due to pathological bone changes caused by lack of estrogen. Others suffered sweeping metabolic disturbances that literally put them in mortal danger.

Though the physical symptoms can be truly dreadful, what impresses me most tragically is the destruction of personality. Some women, when they realize that they are no longer women, subside into a stupor of indifference. Even so, they are relatively lucky. The most heart-breaking cases, I feel, are those sensitive women who witness their own decline with agonizing self-awareness. (39–40)

We can only hope that Dr Wilson's utter faith that the dread disease menopause was the sole cause of every physical and mental symptom in the middle-aged women he saw did not involve him in too many misdiagnoses. In his enthusiasm to eliminate menopause Wilson was soon prescribing replacement sex steroids for women before menopausal symptoms made their appearance, in some cases long before. He invented for himself a stereotype of the 'estrogen-rich' woman who was a perfect companion for man, taut-breasted, sexually responsive, free of menstrual tension. Wilson saw as his enemies 'old wives' who whispered that his wonder-drug caused immorality and cancer; his first publications addressed themselves to the second of these irrational fears. The discovery of increased incidence of endometrial cancer in women on HRT brought the whole bonanza to a halt.

In 1978 Professor Campbell and Dr Malcolm Whitehead published the results of their own study. Of 167 women attending their clinic at King's College Hospital they found that three already had endometrial cancer, and no fewer than eleven already exhibited uterine hyperplasia. When these eleven were given progesterone the womb lining returned to normal. Campbell and Whitehead then devised sequential dosing systems for forty-six patients, in which they were given oestrogen opposed by a progestogen in the second half of a monthly cycle; in other words they decided to imitate the secretory rhythm of menstruation and induce break-through bleeding. Out of the forty-six there was only one case of hyperplasia instead of the three to nine that would have been expected on an unopposed oestrogen regimen. This improvement was considered to justify the imposition of break-through bleeding and the other side-effects of progestogens on all forty-six (Whitehead, Campbell *et al.*, 1978; Whitehead, McQueen *et al.*, 1978; Campbell, McQueen *et al.*, 1978).

In 1980 John Studd reported on a series of 745 patients at Dulwich Hospital and the Birmingham and Midlands Hospital for Women. Almost 10 per cent, seventy-two of the 745, at some time developed uterine hyperplasia. This condition comes in three kinds, cystic hyperplasia, adenomatous hyperplasia and atypical hyperplasia. The last one is the most worrying, for about half the women who show this kind of overgrowth of the endometrium will develop uterine cancer. Only four of Studd's cases were of this kind; sixty were of the least worrying kind, cystic hyperplasia, and all of these cases returned to normal after taking progestogens; six of the eight women with adenomatous hyperplasia also returned to normal after taking progestogens and even two with the atypical type. However, the treatments were not all the same; some of the women who had been given implants, and were more likely to develop uterine hyperplasia than the others, did not take the progestogens prescribed for seven days each month, and more than half of them developed hyperplasia, compared to 15 per cent of the others. When the progestogen regime was lengthened from seven days to ten days that percentage dropped to 3; when it was lengthened again to thirteen days it disappeared altogether (Studd *et al.*, 1980, 1981).

This is the kind of evidence upon which the prescription of progestogens to oppose the action of oestrogens on the womb lining is based. It does not do to ask about the more than nine out of ten women in Studd's sample who did not develop uterine hyperplasia when given unopposed oestrogens; everyone must take the progestogens because of the minority who will exhibit uterine hyperplasia if they do not. Evidently nobody knows how to identify the one out of ten. Nobody knows just how little progesterone you can get away with, whether you need to slough the womb lining every twenty-eight days, or every six months or once a year. This would not be a problem of course if taking progestogens was fun, but progestogens make many women feel sicker than ever menopause did. It is unlikely that a British woman will be allowed to make her own assessment of the cost-benefits of taking progestogens, however, as her doctor is likely to have come to his own conclusion in the matter and will not sanction the use of oestrogen unopposed by progestogens, even though progestogens are thought to undo a good deal of the beneficial effect of oestrogen.

Progesterone is the hormone that acts upon the lining of the womb in the second half of the menstrual cycle, the secretory phase. It blocks the accumulation of oestrogen in the endometrium, and it promotes the formation of an enzyme that changes oestrogen so that it prevents the over-stimulation of the endometrium that is thought to lead to an increase in endometrial cancer in women taking replacement oestrogens. Progesterone itself is inactive if taken by mouth, because it is broken down by the digestive juices; for oral administration the synthetic progestogens norethisterone and norgestrel were developed. If oestrogens can make women feel good, progesterone can make them feel terrible because

it increases the use of energy by the body and affects the amount of salt which the kidneys excrete. It may make the skin greasy and may induce acne. It may also be responsible for breast-tenderness, depression, backache and abdominal cramps as well as 'bloating'. These side effects may be reduced by lowering the dose and varying the type of preparation. (Evans, 45)

Oestrogen is thought to confer some protection against diseases of the heart and blood vessels; the likelihood is that progestogens reverse this. A conference on 'Prevention and management of cardio-vascular disease in women' held in July 1987 found that while oestrogens exert a protective effect by increasing triglycerides, decreasing low density lipids (the risk factors) and increasing high density lipids, progestins reverse the protective effect. The association of the contraceptive pill with an increase in the incidence of deep vein thrombosis and pulmonary embolism is undeniable; it used to be thought that the oestrogens were the culprit, but it seems far more likely that the progestogens are the risk factor that makes a woman on the pill five times more likely to suffer from either than a woman who has never taken it. The Royal College of General Practitioners' Oral Contraceptive Study of 1977 found that the incidence of arterial disease in women who had used oral contraceptives was not related to the variations in the doses of oestrogen to which they had been exposed but to the amounts of progestogens in the pills they had taken. Women wanting to take responsibility for their own health ought to balance the increased risk of heart disease and deep vein thrombosis against the increased risk of endometrial cancer in women taking unopposed oestrogens, but they will find the statistical evidence inscrutable. The American experience contrasts sharply with the British experience; attitudes to cyclical progestogen vary from sceptical to downright suspicious and unopposed oestrogen is always considered as a viable option. The copious instructions to prescribers and patients that must be included with every pack of Premarin by order of the US Food and Drug Administration note tersely that

Although the evidence must be considered preliminary, one study suggests that cyclic administration may carry less risk than continuous administration . . . If concomitant progestin therapy is used, potential risks include adverse effects on carbohydrate and lipid metabolism . . .

John Studd, the very man who gave progestogens over thirteen days to prevent uterine hyperplasia, is still saying in the Foreword to the revised edition of Dr Evans's book that was published in 1988:

We must also determine if there is a cancer risk and, if so, what balance of hormones must be used to avoid overstimulation of the lining of the womb.

While they are determining, many women are obliged to give up HRT because they cannot tolerate the progestogens that they may not need.

Who is likely to develop endometrial cancer from oestrogen replacement? No one. The chances of getting the disease at all are one in a thousand or less, so likely is not the right word. If you already have a tumour that produces oestrogen, in another site, for example the ovary, your chances of also having an endometrial cancer are as high as one or even two in five. Women who develop endometrial cancer are more likely than others to develop a breast tumour and also to suffer from high blood pressure. Women who have a late menopause and women who are obese are both more likely to have endometrial cancer than thin women who have a relatively early menopause, but women who have had children are less likely to have an endometrial cancer than women who have had none.

Though everyone is terrified of the least risk of cancer, and doctors devoutly believe that no risk of developing a potentially fatal condition should ever be run, no one seems unduly concerned about the much greater likelihood of post-menopausal women developing heart disease or circulatory disorders, which together cause four times as many deaths as all cancers of the womb, cervix and breast. In the statistical analysis the rise in the number of diagnoses of endometrial cancer was nowhere balanced against the decline in the number of deaths from heart attacks. A group of researchers from South California School of Medicine examined the case histories of all the women in a large retirement community who died of coronary artery disease and found that women who had been treated with oestrogen were less than half as likely to die of heart disease. Heart attacks in American women declined more than 30 per cent between 1976 and 1981 since oestrogen replacement became common practice.

Age-adjusted deaths from I[schaemic] H[eart] D[isease] in white females in the US are over four times the combined death rates of breast cancer and endometrial cancer. If the protective effect of oestrogen replacement therapy on the risk of fatal IHD is real, this benefit would far outweigh the carcinogenic effects of oestrogens. (Ross *et al.*, 860)

The bids are by no means all in. Though we know that women without ovaries and after ovarian failure are much more likely to die from diseases of the heart and arteries than women who are secreting oestrogen, we do not know why. We all know by now that cardiovascular disease is commoner in people with high levels of cholesterol, triglycerides and lipoproteins in their blood. Menstruating women have much lower levels of all three than men or post-menopausal women, and their levels of cholesterol are lowest when oestrogen levels are highest. However, oestrogen does not lower the levels of all blood lipids; it is well known to raise the level of triglycerides which increase the risks of blood-clotting; of the lipoproteins, it raises the level of high density lipoprotein, which can be reabsorbed through the artery walls carrying cholesterol with it, and lowers the levels of the dangerous low density lipoproteins. By and large, then, replacement oestrogen would seem to confer a measure of protection against cardiovascular disease.

In an article in *Geriatrics* (May 1990), Lila E. Nachtigall, Professor of Obstetrics and Gynaecology of the New York University School of Medicine, and Dr Lisa B. Nachtigall review the evidence presented by Burch *et al.* (1974), Gordon *et al.* (1978), Hammond *et al.* (1979), Pettiti *et al.* (1986), Bush *et al.* (1983, 1987), Barrett-Connor *et al.* (1989) and Knopp (1988) and come to a conclusion which is heard more and more often, that protection against cardiovascular disease should be the prime reason for prescribing oestrogen replacement, with relief from vasomotor disturbance and mitigation of oesteoporosis as mere fringe benefits. In the words of Cummings *et al.*,

even a small beneficial effect of estrogen therapy on the risk of coronary heart disease would far outweigh any increased risk of deaths from either endometrial cancer or breast cancer. (2448)

The effect on the protective mechanism by which oestrogen lowers cholesterol and raises the HDL count of adding progestogens to the oestrogen is not at all clear. The pharmacology of progestogens is complex, but it seems clear that we need newer and better progestogens if we are to reduce side-effects and maintain the quality of the life we are interested in prolonging. Henderson *et al.* argue that C21 progestogens provoke fewer side-effects, but the same article argues too that

during the progestogen phase of HRT beneficial effects on lipoprotein levels are partially negated if not reversed . . . [this] varies with different progestogens and is dose-related.

This partly explains why British researchers can find no evidence of a beneficial effect of oestrogen on 'the risk of stroke and myocardial infarction'. Thompson *et al.* (1989) can only say:

There is no evidence that the use of HRT as recently prescribed in the UK constitutes a major cardiovascular risk or benefit.

What the Americans would say is that by insisting on opposing oestrogens the British were undoing its most important effect.

Endometrial cancer is detectable and more easily dealt with than degenerative disease of the heart and arteries, but the potency of the dread word 'cancer' is such that no risk, no matter how small, of any cancer, no matter how treatable, is considered worth running. The treatment for endometrial cancer, namely hysterectomy, is one of the commonest operations carried out in our hospitals, yet no woman is allowed to decide for herself that the risk of having to undergo a hysterectomy is one that she is prepared to run. Endometrial cancer can be detected in the early stages by aspirating the uterus; even in women who are taking sequential treatments and putting up with the progestogens a periodical review of the womb lining is considered advisable.

Examination of the womb lining used to require dilatation and curettage under general anaesthetic. Nowadays the endometrium can be sampled without anaesthetic. Dr Evans is unusually revealing on this point:

These curettes can usually be easily passed through the cervix. About 4 per cent of women find this uncomfortable. As a patient myself, I have found the newer Isaacs aspirator can be inserted without discomfort. These techniques constitute a major breakthrough in the treatment of menopausal women. Women on treatment, especially without a progestogen, are advised to have these examinations periodically to monitor any changes in the endometrium, as required by their medical adviser. (105)

Not, you will notice, as required by them. It is useless of course to demand of a GP that he start messing about in his surgery with a curette or a cannula, if it is more than you can do to get him to give you a thorough examination, or indeed to touch you at all. Even your gynaecologist, if he has not been trained in the use of the small curette or the aspirator, will refuse to use it, usually on some ground other than his own ignorance.

The supporters of HRT see distress at change of life as the result of a deficiency, as diabetes is a result of a deficiency in insulin. If, as Dr Barbara Evans says, 'It is unwise to take oestrogen without clear evidence of deficiency, because the risks may not be justified', it must always be unwise to take oestrogen, for the evidence of deficiency is anything but clear. For the evidence to be clear, we would have to have found out something about the levels of oestrogen in women who are not finding the menopausal transition unmanageable. The studies described by Barry M. Sherman and his colleagues showed that

the menopausal transition, by irregular menses, is not a time of marked oestrogen deficiency . . . very low oestradiol concentrations characteristic of menopausal women may not occur until six months or so after the onset of amenorrhea. Because episodes of abortive follicular maturation and vaginal bleeding are often widely-spaced, perimenopausal women may be exposed to persistent oestrogen stimulation in the absence of regular cyclic progesterone secretion, a situation that may be related to the dysfunctional uterine bleeding common during this time.

In other words, menopausal women may be suffering from too much oestrogen rather than too little. We are not surprised to find that the first question Dr Sherman could not answer in discussion was:

Is there any correlation between oestradiol levels and menopausal symptoms? Some of our patients with menopausal symptoms have quite adequate amounts of oestradiol and other oestrogens. (Parkes *et al.*, 48)

Dr Sherman was obliged to answer:

There are not many systematic studies on the correlation between hormone levels and symptoms. Our studies show that individual women may have high menopausal levels of gonadotrophins and irregular cycles preceding any symptoms by many months. During continuous blood sampling over 24-hr periods we detected no relationship between changes in oestrogens or gonadotrophins and the individual episodes of hot flushes. The mediation of these symptoms is unknown.

So much for 'clear evidence of deficiency'. It seems at least as likely that climacteric distress is caused by too much oestrogen as too little.

Though Sherman's work is ten years old and a good deal has been done since, the mechanism by which administration of oestrogen relieves climacteric distress is still unknown. Older women do not suffer from hot flushes and night sweats, because, it is assumed, their bodies have become used to functioning on the low level of oestrogen derived from the androstenedione secreted by the adrenals supplemented by a much smaller amount secreted by the ovaries, which together amount to no more than a fifth of the pre-menopausal level (Vermeulen, 1983). Women who accept HRT, on the other hand, may have more than five times the amount of oestrogen in the bloodstream that they had before menopause, so it is small wonder that when they come off it their symptoms can recur with a vengeance. What is puzzling is that this does not happen for all of them. If the climacteric syndrome is actually a deficiency disease it ought to last as long as the deficiency. The truth is that it is nothing of the kind.

Giving suffering women more oestrogen may represent inadvertent homoeopathic prescribing by committed allopaths. The principle of homoeopathic prescribing is to supply more of the element that is causing the imbalance, so that the body stops secreting it and equilibrium can return when the added substance is gradually withdrawn. It could be that by dosing women with much more oestrogen than they ever produced themselves their bodies are persuaded that there is no need to pump out oestrogen to fend off ovarian failure.

What if those female bodies that fight menopause by flooding themselves with FSH and keeping up oestrogen secretion are robbing other vital functions in the process, so that the organism has to go short of endorphins and corticosteroids? Some such dysfunction would explain some of the strangest manifestations of menopause, for example, joint pains and crawling skin, and even the famous hot flushes. In which case the deficiency would be seen not in oestrogens but in other body chemicals. Nevertheless prescription of oestrogen would relieve them, because it would take the pressure off the hypothalamus to produce more and more FSH and oestrogen, and let it revert to its usual patterns.

Until we know if women without symptoms have something that women with symptoms do not, we have no logical ground for describing menopausal distress as a deficiency disease. It would make more sense, in view of the fact that older women adjust to very much lower levels of oestrogen, to ask what the biochemical trigger is that facilitates the switchover, and try to prime that pump. As we are not within thousands of research hours of doing that, we prefer to treat the problem symptomatically. What we are really doing is denying the process that is trying to occur, and pushing the woman off the rung of the life ladder that she has arrived at, to a lower one, where she will wait indefinitely to complete the fifth climacteric.

Unfortunately, despite her apparent rigour, Dr Evans herself falls for the deficiency disorder theory:

... if [the patient's] main symptoms are hot flushes or sweats with vaginal dryness and urinary frequency the evidence is plain for all to see that she is short of oestrogen. (101)

When in doubt, give oestrogen and see if the patient feels better; this is what Dr Evans's caveat actually amounts to. What cannot be denied is that patients usually do feel better on oestrogen, a great deal better, so much better that they realize for the first time just how unwell they had felt before oestrogen. Endless studies can demonstrate how the therapy works not only on the vagina, the bladder, and the urethra, but also on the brain, on depression, mood control, nervous instability, stress, anxiety, sleeplessness, libido, orgasm, bones, skin, hair, the heart and blood vessels, longevity, marital felicity, intellectual performance and so forth, until one is obliged to question the morality of withholding oestrogen, rather than the wisdom of prescribing it. Nevertheless, having found this panacea, most doctors will prescribe it only for certain patients and for limited periods. As Dr Evans remarks:

Each doctor employs his own criteria, dose, type of hormone, alone or in combination, as well as the route by which treatment is to be given. Women are not all alike and differ in response to and need for treatment. (102–3)

Getting the right fit between doctor and patient would seem to be a matter of luck.

Though HRT, like 'the Pill', is talked of as if it were a single thing, the array of options (as with the Pill) is bewildering to say the least. Treatment may be long-term, or short-term, or even for the term of one's [un-]natural life. The hormones may be taken by mouth, by injection, as a sub-dermal implant, as a topical application, or absorbed through the skin from a cream, gel or patchet. Which of these you get from your GP has more to do with the effectiveness of the latest medical salesman to visit him than with any objective evaluation of the suitability of any particular system for your particular case. Even if your doctor knows that 'women are not all alike', there is no way he can assess how they differ. He can only write a scrip and ask you to tell him how you get on. If you accept a sub-dermal implant, of course, it doesn't matter how well or how badly you get on, because it can't easily be taken out again.

Not all oestrogens are suitable for treating menopausal symptoms. The cheapest ones, the synthetic oestrogens derived from coal-tar used in contraceptive pills, do not raise the circulating levels of oestrogens in the blood. Natural oestrogens, which are derived from living tissues and are therefore more costly to produce, do, and so does a combination of natural and synthetic oestrogens. The preparations prescribed for menopausal distress are all either natural hormones bound with a carrier, as in Premarin, Harmogen and Progynova, or semi-synthetic oestrogens like ethinyloestradiol and mestranol.

If you prefer to take medications by mouth, you have the choice of the oestrogen preparations Premarin, Harmogen, Progynova and the generic ethinyloestradiol. These are by no means all versions of the same thing. The oestrogen in Premarin is derived from the urine of pregnant mares. There are three strengths, signified by three colours; the yellow pill is twice the dose of the maroon, and the purple is twice the yellow. Harmogen, which is piperazine oestrol sulphate, comes in only one strength. Progynova is oestradiol valerate, suitable for short-term treatment; it is marketed in two strengths. The generic ethinyloestradiol is also sold in two strengths. The array of choice here is not offered to the consumer, of course, but to her doctor. He too will decide whether she should take the pills continuously, whether she should take them for three weeks and then rest, whether she should take them for three weeks and then take a progesterone preparation, to oppose the effect of the oestrogen on the lining of her womb, or whether she should take them for three weeks, take progestogens as well in the third week, and rest in the fourth week.

There are eleven different kinds of progestogen preparations available, using seven different hormones, all of which have different modes of operation and different side-effects. The permutations of oestrogen plus progesterone plus posology amount to hundreds of options, all slightly different. The chances of any doctor, even in a specialist menopause clinic, knowing his way round even half of them, are nil. Progestins are sometimes prescribed for women who cannot tolerate oestrogens as a preventative of osteoporosis and hot flushes, although why they should be able to do this if the climacteric syndrome is caused by a deficiency in oestrogen is unclear. One of the most urgent requirements for successful HRT would seem to be the development of better progestogens, and better ways of administering them.

There are at present in Britain three kinds of sequential HRT packages: Cycloprogynova, which offers eleven tablets of oestradiol valerate (white) followed by ten tablets of the progestogen norgestrel (orange) followed by seven days of no tablets at all. This is recommended by the manufacturers for long-term use. Prempak-c, on the other hand, offers uninterrupted twenty-eight-day cycles of Premarin, supplemented over the last twelve days by additional tablets of norgestrel. Trisequens comes in a circular calendar pack; the patient works her way round it through twelve blue tablets which contain oestradiol and oestrol, ten white tablets that contain oestradiol, oestrol and the progestogen norethisterone, and six red tablets that contain lower doses of the same. During the red phase the patient is supposed to see break-through bleeding.

Why should the regimes be so different and which one should you go for? We have not exhausted the options by considering hormones to be taken by mouth. Interestingly, if we consider the hypothesis that it is caused by an oestrogen deficiency, the climacteric syndrome can be treated by injections of depot testosterone. Schering have withdrawn their combined testosterone-oestradiol valerate preparation, Primodian Depot, on grounds that have never been explained. The combination was intended to avoid some of the undesirable effects of unopposed oestrogens, listed as haemorrhages, fibroids, and breast problems, and androgens alone, namely virilization. The side-effects listed by the manufacturers included increase in libido, feeling of fullness, nausea and vomiting, anorexia, dizziness, irritability, breast tension, gain or loss in weight, and allergic skin reactions and, in some susceptible female patients, deepening of the voice. The hormones were in esterized form, held in an oily solution; they dispersed over a period of weeks, when the injection was repeated.

In England implants that last six to nine months have ousted injections in popularity. These are pellets of oestradiol, or oestradiol and testosterone, or testosterone alone, inserted under the skin; for some reason this technique of administration works best in restoring lost libido. Certainly the administration of testosterone will bring about an instant increase in genital sensitivity, but the patient is very aware that this touchiness is unrelated to sexual response as she knows it. If a peri-menopausal woman is not part of a heterosexual couple, she will not be offered this treatment, for the diffuse genital tension she will feel can only lead into dangerous and compromising situations or humiliating bouts of masturbation. Lack of libido in a single woman is not a ground for treatment.

When we dose middle-aged married women with testosterone to increase libido we are not treating a woman but a couple; the ethics of such an approach are dodgy to say the least. In view of the fact that no studies have ever associated decreased libido in middle-aged women with deficiency of either oestrogen or testosterone, we are entitled to ask whether decreased libido is a disease entity at all. When we give a male hormone to a married woman who has lost interest in sex, we are consciously tailoring her sexuality to fit her husband's; the whole business smacks of women's willingness to try anything for a quiet life. Still, even Dr Evans says,

The method is useful for women who have severe psychosexual or marital problems. (109)

The medicalization of everyday life is here taken to its absurd extreme. The husband has become the wife's health problem, and testosterone in her body the treatment for him. If the wife's problem was desire for a husband who was impotent or not interested in her, testosterone would hardly be the drug of choice; if her psychosexual problem was that she lusted for young boys or girls, testosterone would be stringently withheld. The hormone is being given to her for the sake of another; she is to desire someone whether he is desirable or not, because she is his wife.

Women who have an implant are advised to take progestogens by mouth for seven to ten days a month, in order to induce a small bleed; indeed, they are not simply offered the progestogen but must promise to take it as a condition of getting the implant, which is known to exert a stronger effect upon the womb than oestrogens taken in other forms. We know from the behaviour of the women in Studd's programme at Dulwich that they found the effects of the progestogens disturbing and that they tended to stop taking them. Oestrogen absorbed from an implant does not affect blood lipids; progestogens absorbed by mouth do. Some of the symptoms that caused the women at Dulwich to stop taking the progestogens may have signalled quite serious side-effects of progestogens unopposed in the bloodstream. The evidence seems to show that women who have suffered from thromboses in pregnancy should certainly not be given oral progestogen to oppose non-oral oestrogen, and probably should not be given progestogens at all.

In some cases, menopausal symptoms like the itching and painful intercourse caused by the atrophy of the vagina are treated by the local application of hormone creams. Curiously, though these are the symptoms most obviously associated with oestrogen deficiency, they do not always respond to oestrogens taken by mouth, and sometimes the creams are prescribed in addition to oestrogens by mouth. The worry here is that oestrogens are readily and rapidly absorbed through the vaginal wall to act directly upon the uterus; some experimental programmes running at the moment are trying vaginal delivery for contraceptives, with good results. Oestrogen vaginal creams and pessaries can cause uterine hyperplasia, therefore, and oral progestogens may be prescribed along with them. Other creams and gels have been devised for absorption through the skin, and are meant to be rubbed on the abdomen. One of the most curious aspects of HRT in England is that the method most used in France is to all intents and purposes unavailable. Oestrogell®, manufactured by Besins, is an oestradiol gel which is rubbed on to the thighs, which French women find more acceptable than a sticky patchet. The rationale behind transcutaneous methods of administration is to lower the dose of oestrogen and still achieve an adequate level of oestrogen in the bloodstream, by-passing the liver where the effects of stored oestrogen are anything but good. They are so successful that the continued preference for oestrogen by mouth must be seen as irrational.

The fastest riser through the HRT popularity charts is the patchet, devised by Ciba-Geigy. These are small round transparent purses containing tiny amounts of the hormone in a transparent gel; the patchet is simply stuck on to the belly or upper thigh and the gel is absorbed gradually through the permeable layer next to the skin. There are three dosage strengths, all very much less than would be conveyed in an oral oestrogen pill. The delivery method is patented by Ciba-Geigy; patchets are expensive and doctors are not anxious to include them in their prescription budget.

Oestrogen replacement, then, would seem to be turning the clock back for the menopausal woman by mimicking her earlier hormonal state, rather than helping her to accomplish the transition upon which her later health depends. What cannot easily be assessed is whether the use of exogenous steroids in the peri-menopause interferes with the establishment of the default system, in which oestrogen secretion is taken over by the adrenal glands. Very few trials have so far attempted to establish the levels of the oestrogen precursor, androstenedione, in the bloodstream throughout the climacteric, either with or without HRT (e.g. Vermeulen, 1983; Brody *et al.*, 1987), and the picture is far from clear. Women secrete other hormones besides oestrogens and progesterone, including testosterone; testosterone levels fall at menopause but only to about two-thirds of the pre-menopausal level.

Dr Barbara Evans's little book *Life Change* is the only book for the layperson that does not simplify the genuine intricacy of the question of whether or not to accept HRT. She does not conceal the fact that all the few double-blind trials of HRT have displayed a disconcertingly high placebo effect.

This was well demonstrated in some studies which were made at the Chelsea Hospital for Women, in which women who agreed to take part in two double-blind trials were either postmenopausal, or were at the stage where their periods were infrequent with at least three-monthly intervals between each period. In one short study which lasted four months the women, who all had severe symptoms, were given a placebo for two months and this was replaced by oestrogen for the next two months. Women with milder symptoms cooperated in another trial which lasted for a year, during which they took a placebo for six months and then took oestrogen for six months. They filled in a questionnaire at the beginning and at two-monthly intervals during the trials. (47)

During the short trial some of the women on the placebo reported improvements in the conditions specifically related to ovarian failure, namely hot flushes and vaginal dryness, as well as insomnia, irritability, headaches, anxiety, frequency of passing water, memory, spirits, optimism, skin and appearance. It is impossible to tell, of course, whether the improvements they claimed would have happened without even the placebo, let alone whether the psychoprophylactic effect of being given an important treatment, and more attention than is usually given to out-patients in our public hospitals, released the consoling endorphins from the hypothalamus and actually made the women feel better, or whether their subjective impression of symptoms was wrong in the first place.

The results of the longer trial were if anything more puzzling. The placebo did not work for hot flushing and vaginal dryness, whether the women took it in the six months before they had replacement oestrogen or the six months after. The return of hot flushing was so marked in the women who took the placebo after they had oestrogen that they were all aware that they were in fact being given a placebo, and the trial was no longer double-blind. What no one paused to inquire was whether the withdrawal of HRT might not actually exaggerate vasomotor disturbance. Despite such evidence it is now considered unethical to administer placebos when women report menopausal distress, because ostrogen is known to relieve their symptoms; the consensus statement signed by Wulf Utian in *Maturitas*, 1990, probably signals the end of double-blind cross-over trials of HRT.

A sharp return of flushes was also experienced by women who were taken off HRT and given a placebo in a trial set up by Dr Jean Coope in Macclesfield in 1981; one group of patients was given HRT for six months, a placebo for two, and a second placebo that was identical in appearance to the oestrogen tablet for another six, while another group was given the HRT last. Both groups improved equally in the first two months, then only the HRT patients continued to improve, but the others did not deteriorate.

The evidence of a beneficial effect of HRT on psychiatric disorders of menopause is hardly more impressive:

Dr F. P. Rhoades, who studied 1,200 post-menopausal American women suffering from poor memory, depression and fatigue, which he regarded as psychiatric in origin, found that 95% improved during two years' treatment with oestrogen. (Evans, 50–51)

Well he would, wouldn't he? If the finding of Dr Barbara Ballinger that the psychiatric disorders of menopause appeared 'before the periods had finally stopped, and commonly lasted only about a year' (Evans, 52) is correct, Dr Rhoades's HRT cases might have performed better if he had left them alone (cf. Lozman *et al.*).

Wendy Cooper, author of *No Change*, another easily available discussion of HRT, is a journalist who wrote her first story on HRT for the London *Evening News* in 1973.

Just once in the life of a working journalist, there somes a story so exciting, important and demanding that it refuses to be written out or written off. You may present it in a dozen different ways for a dozen different papers and magazines. In the process *you* may become exhausted, but the subject does not. Instead of public interest and response declining, they increase. The law of diminishing returns fails to operate. In the end you have to recognize that instead of *you* running the story, the story is running you. (9)

These admissions should function as a warning. No journalist should ever allow herself to be so taken over by a crusade, let alone a crusade that advertises a panacea, let alone a crusade advertising a panacea pushed by one of the most powerful commercial lobbies on earth, namely the multinational pharmaceuticals manufacturing industry.

After Wendy Cooper's life was taken over by HRT and her house filled with literature on the subject, including 5,000 letters from suffering women, a process that took no more than two years, she decided to write a book that would encourage women to use steroids to eliminate the menopause. She called it *No Change*. Her argument is based upon a number of premisses that women might wish to question: she believes

that women have the right to age in a way that parallels the ageing process of a man, with no abrupt decline, no accelerated ageing, and no atrophy of the sex organs to make intercourse painful, sexual response impossible, and middle-aged marriage a misery. (13)

Women's happiness consists, it seems, in becoming a more exact fit to a man. Just as the definitions of sexual intercourse current in the later twentieth century sought to confer upon women an orgasm as much like a man's as possible, now a woman's ageing pattern is meant to keep step. Hormone replacement therapy is most effective, and most obviously effective, in halting and reversing the gradual atrophy of the vagina. Wendy Cooper notes that it continues where contraception left off:

The battle for modern contraception has been won . . . women in their fertile years have achieved for the first time the ability to control their own biology, to plan their families and their lives, and compete at last on something like equal terms with men . . . So, with Biological Lib within the grasp of the younger woman who wants it, the same knowledge of the complex chemistry and workings of the sex hormones, which led to the development of the contraceptive pill, has now been used to bring about a second biological revolution, just as radical and profound, for the older woman. (16)

When in the early 1950s Carlo Djerassi and Geoffrey Pincus realized the potential application of steroids derived from Mexican yams in suppressing ovulation, their 'knowledge of the complex chemistry and workings of the sex hormones' was very imperfect. The first pills were known to suppress ovulation, but the effects of steroid ingestion on the whole body chemistry were completely unknown. The dosage levels were eventually drastically lowered, but not until after some distressing episodes. Even now we do not know the biological pathways traversed by the steroidal agents that women put in their mouths. After nearly forty years the contraceptive pill must still be taken on a daily basis, is still ingested by mouth, still affects the entire endocrine system instead of a single target function, and still makes women feel anything from slightly less to intolerably less than well. Where the contraceptive use of sex steroids is concerned Wendy Cooper is a Pangloss, imagining that what we have is the best that could be had. Her approach to HRT is hardly more judicious.

If the numerous studies claiming to have proved the protective action of HRT on practically every organ of the female body are to be believed, there can be no justification for denying the treatment to any woman, or for ceasing the treatment once she is on it. However, other studies of the actual take-up of the therapy and its duration indicate that the rate of usage is low. A campaigner would say that this is because doctors are either unsympathetic, or conservative, or don't care about the sufferings of women middle-aged or older. Pressure-groups have already been formed to raise the profile of HRT and the level of patient demand. These groups utilize the rhetoric of women's rights, claiming that all women have a right to HRT which anti-feminist doctors are withholding. Certainly doctors' behaviour is neither consistent nor logical; most British doctors prescribe HRT only for the shortest time and for the severest symptoms, as if it were a kind of painkiller-cum-tranquillizer. Some, mostly American, doctors prescribe HRT before menopause symptoms appear and try to keep the patients on it for the rest of their lives. The German Master in Menopause, C. Lauritzen, believes that HRT must be continued for a long period:

Substitution should in any case be continued over a long period. With regard to osteoporosis 10–15 years' treatment seems necessary to prevent the disease for life. Lasting positive effects on cardiovascular diseases are noticed after five years' medication. However substitution for life is seldom and most patients drop out for various reasons. (1990)

In fact no preventive effect of HRT on the development of osteoporosis has actually been demonstrated, because the longitudinal cohort studies have simply not been done. It is a hard sentence indeed to be obliged to take a daily medication for a disease that one may never suffer from.

Patricia Kaufert and Penny Gilbert pointed out that doctors in Manitoba, like doctors in Montreal in an earlier study by Margaret Lock, were found to follow a diverse collection of clinical models, some giving oestrogen to virtually all their patients, others being more selective in their prescribing habits. The one common factor was that each physician believed absolutely in the correctness of his own approach. (1986)

Kaufert and Gilbert were concerned that, as the health costs of caring for ageing women rise, the pressure upon menopausal women to accept hormone replacement therapy could intensify to the point of becoming irresistible. In a recent Danish study of ten years of HRT, a questionnaire was sent to all women born in 1936 living in four Copenhagen suburbs. Of 597, 526 replied. Of these 37 per cent had had HRT at some time; 22 per cent were still using it. Forty-two per cent of the ever-users had begun using HRT during the pre-menopause (including forty women who had been hysterectomized). Of the 40 per cent of women who had deliberately interrupted the treatment, 28 per cent claimed they had got no relief of their symptoms while 44 per cent reported adverse reactions such as weight gain, nausea, irregular bleeding and engorged breasts, 7 per cent had become ill from unrelated causes and 12 per cent had negative attitudes, i.e. disliked the bleeding, or were afraid, or found the drug too expensive. The average duration of use by the ones who stayed until the end of their course was twenty-three months; two-thirds of the women used only one preparation, although one woman tried six. This pattern of use, with a high drop-out rate, and a short duration even among the people who claim to be benefited by the treatment, is fairly typical of the countries with the highest rate of take-up. A recent Canadian study, surprisingly, showed a much lower take-up (McKinley, 1987; cf. Barlow et al., 1991; also Rees and Barlow, 1991). Women's use of HRT is still a long way from justifying the promoters' optimism.

Doctors tend to warn women off talking to other women about their experiences with medication. Given the fact that the vast majority of studies of HRT are directly funded or supported in some other way by the manufacturers, women must collect their own case histories of HRT use and make their own analysis of the cost benefits and the risk benefits that will accrue to them if they accept it. Women should also come to their own conclusions about the mode of administration that might suit them and not allow themselves to slip into the easy error of supposing that HRT is one, single and miraculous cure for what ails them. Only if women continue to refuse to be pressured into making do with what is at present available will the pharmaceutical multinationals be forced to continue trying to devise a series of hormone cocktails that will provide the desirable effects without the undesirable ones.

9

The Treatments – Traditional

When Philippa, the tall and handsome daughter of William the Good, Count of Holland and Hainault, landed at Dover two days before Christmas, 1327, on her way to meet her childhood sweetheart and proxy husband, Edward III of England, she brought with her her mother's herbal. All women, even the greatest, were then expected to doctor their households. Most of them were illiterate and used recipes that they had seen their mothers use, varying them according to time and place. Philippa, far from her homeland and her mother, would have to rely on her beautifully lettered book, which included descriptions of the properties of herbs in Latin and in English, little diagrams of the affected parts, and drawings of English wild plants. Philippa bore her husband seven sons and five daughters.

We should not be surprised, then, to find Queen Philippa's herbal to be full of medications 'for to bring out the secundyne' (afterbirth) and 'provoke menstrues', to 'deliver the dead child' and 'cleanse the mother' (i.e. the womb) as well as for the 'flux of the menstrue' and for 'women that have their terms too much or too often'. There are one or two that might be thought to relate to older women, the use of myrrh, for example, 'for to comfort the mother in a woman and waste the humours that are in her' or 'calametum' 'to draw the superfluity is in a woman', but they are more likely to apply to infection in breeding women than to the discomforts of menopause.

Queen Philippa is unusual among self-medicating women

because she has a written text to go by which makes at least nominal use of a male authority, for it includes a version of 'Circa instans' by Mattheus Platearius. The secular scholars of the Italian school were not shy of prescribing for women's troubles; the monks who made copies and translations of their works for use in the infirmaries and dispensaries of their monasteries left out much that referred to women and their organs of generation, for reasons which are fairly obvious. The nuns who cared for women were poorer and less literate and made do without great parchment tomes. Once the eminent gentlemen, monkish or other, had established their authority, they had to defend it, not against women or practitioners but against their male rivals.

The early documentary history of medicine is largely a hierarchy of texts, with very little empiric evidence of how remedies worked in practice. Most of the people on earth at the same time as the most famous of the ancient practitioners were dosed for what ailed them, not by the likes of Hippocrates, Galen or Paracelsus, but by their mothers and their mothers' mothers, who did the best they could with what they had. The 'old women' set bones, washed wounds, let blood, delivered infants, drove out infestations, anointed buboes and chafed sore joints, with an array of embrocations, vulneraries, electuaries, tinctures, syrups and tisanes that altered from place to place, from climate to climate, from season to season. Despite the activities of male scholars, this vast body of knowledge was never systematized. The written herbals that survive represent only a minute fraction of medication as it was always and everywhere practised.

Sometimes the women cured; mostly they did not interfere with healing. Much of their activity soothed and comforted the patient rather than fighting his disorder. There was a marked element of psychoprophylaxis in the magical and semi-magical rituals that attended much of the dosing. The herb-women of old could hardly have had ways of deceiving themselves into health, even if they had time, and it seems that in fact they did not. What nostrums there are for menopausal distress are hidden in general prescriptions not for bringing down or staying of women's courses, but for sleeplessness, lethargy, melancholy or fits of the mother.

Few or none of the hundreds of specifics to bring on menstruation listed in all the ancient pharmacopoeiae should be understood as treatments intended to delay the cessation of the menses. The 'obstruction' or 'suppression' of the menses in younger women was regarded as a serious symptom, principally because menstruation was considered a necessary evacuation of superabounding blood together with evil humours; the treatments vary with the suspected cause and the somatic type of the individual. A few of the treatments for excessive blood loss could be profitably used by older women, but the metrorrhagia of the menopause, though inconvenient, can be easily observed to be a self-limiting phenomenon that did not threaten life. Haemorrhaging in younger women was all too often a cause of death; the high visibility in the old herbals of treatments to stay or allay women's courses principally relates to this greater need.

One of the ancient herbal treatments for treating the climacteric syndrome is 'agnus castus', which is still in use. The name refers to a plant of the verbena family, properly named *Vitex agnus-castus*. Among the earliest vernacular medical texts that have survived is a series of Middle English manuscripts that begin with the words (in various idioms) 'Agnus Castus is a herb that men clepe Toutsaine or Parkleaves': after a minute account of the habit and habitat of that member of the Verbenaceae we are told that the 'vertue of this herb is that he will gladly keep men and women chaste' (Brodin, 119). The translators suppressed the detailed reference to the use of the herb in treating women to be found in their Latin original (BL MS Sloane 2948):

et virtus eiusdem est: conservare in hominibus castitatem, unde et mulieres ratione illius herbe frutices secum conferre consueruerunt in mortuorum exequiis, quando propet honestatem pudicam oportuit continentiam necessarie obseruare . . . Item fomentum decoctionis agni casti matricis exsiccat superfluitates et ipsum orificium coangustat, menstrua autem provocat . . . (21)

According to Dioscorides (I, 103) and Pliny (*Naturalis Historia*, XXIV, 59), Athenian women anxious to avoid lascivious dreams in the absence of their husbands put the leaves in their beds; for its known anaphrodisiac property it is also known as chaste tree. Because monks ground it and sprinkled it on their food in an attempt to suppress sinful desire it was called monks' pepper. The Cistercian monk Andrew Boorde, writing *The Breuiary of Helthe*, of which the first of many editions appeared in 1547, includes agnus castus in 'a receipte to kepe a man or a woman lowe of corage', i. e. free of concupiscent desires: the whole recipe is worth citing, for it bears a family relationship to nostrums for climacteric syndrome:

To kepe one lowe, is the vsage of eatynge or of drenkynge of veneger or smellyng to it, and so dayly vsed, Rewe and Camphire for this matter is good to smel to it. And Tutsane otherwise named Agnus castus and Singrene otherwise named Houseleke, and stronge purgacions, watche and study . . . (Boorde, fol. xxxvii^v)

According to Malcolm Stuart's *Encyclopedia of Herbs and Herbalism*, the seeds of agnus castus 'contain hormone-like substances which reduce libido in the male and are of benefit to women with certain hormonal problems. Chaste Tree is now included in several gynaecological formulations.' Dr Stuart is quite clear that agnus castus is only anaphrodisiac in males, thinking perhaps that the plant steroids it contains are similar to oestrogens. In fact it seems clear that agnus castus helps with menopausal distress not because it turns the clock backward by imitating oestrogen secretion or acting as a precursor of oestrogen but because it is an androgen antagonist and suppresses testosterone secretion in both sexes.

Other proven uterine sedatives in the ancient herbal pharmacopoeia are derived from the dried root bark of *Viburnum prunifolia*, the black haw, and the dried stem bark of her sister, *Viburnum opulus*, the guelder rose or cranberry tree, both of which have proved of benefit in controlling the metrorrhagia of menopause. The black haw is common in America where it is to be found in several native pharmacopoeiae, while the guelder rose, which is common in English gardens, is still retained in central European pharmacopoeiae. The extract of the flowering plant of the greater periwinkle, *Vinca major*, which is an invasive nuisance in most gardens, also has a marked effect upon smooth muscle. As it also reduces blood pressure and dilates both coronary and peripheral blood vessels, it is useful for women in whom menopausal distress is complicated by hypertensiveness. The 1826 edition of Culpeper's *Herbal* says that 'The French use it to stay women's courses. It is a good female medicine, and may be used with advantage in hysteric and other fits.' Culpeper advises either an infusion of the green plant or the expressed juice of it, 'to the quantity of two ounces for a dose', which seems excessive.

Another of the few herbs named in connection with the menopause specifically is *Alchemilla mollis* or lady's mantle. Prolonged use of the dried leaves, taken as an infusion, relieves both metrorrhagia and menopausal distress. The little sister of *Alchemilla mollis*, *Alchemilla alpina*, is considered more effective but is correspondingly more difficult to come by. Culpeper suggests sitting in a warm bath in which lady's mantle leaves have been steeped as a preventive of miscarriage; the same utero-sedative effect could be useful for menopausal symptoms.

Perhaps the most important plant in treating menopausal symptoms is *Hyoscyamus niger* or henbane. Its persistent association with witchcraft is probably a reflection of the fact that older women have used it as medication since ancient times. It is known to be sedative, analgesic and anti-spasmodic; the alkaloids hyoscyamine, atropine and hyoscine, all of which still have useful therapeutic function, are to be found in the leaves.

Henbane causeth drowsinesse, and mitigateth all kinde of paine: it is

217

good against hot & sharp distillations of the eyes and other parts . . . To wash the feet in the decoction of Henbane causeth sleepe; and also the often smelling to the floures. (Gerard, 87–8)

It is a saturnine plant. The leaves are good for cooling hot inflammations in the eyes, or other parts of the body; and being boiled in wine and used as a foment, it will assuage all manner of swellings . . . also the gout, sciatica and pains of the joints, if proceeding from a hot cause. Being applied with vinegar to the forehead and temple, it helpeth the head-ach, and causeth those to sleep who are prevented by hot violent fevers. (Culpeper, 72)

It has been used successfully in modern times to treat hysteria. In Boorde's *Breuiary of Helthe* (1547), insomniacs are advised 'to make' a dormitary of henbane, and lay it to the temples' (Pt. II, fol. xxi^v).

Almost none of the medical texts refers directly to the psychological stresses of the climacteric. Though works on hysteria and melancholy abound, and each is a portmanteau term that describes a wide variety of conditions, none concerns itself specifically with the mental sufferings of the menopausal woman. The classical notion of hysteria derives from Hippocrates, who considered that the womb was no mere organ like other organs, but an imperious, mysterious, rebellious, in-dwelling creature that could torture the woman who did not satisfy its demands by rising upwards in her body and suffocating her. The withering away of the womb represented, if anyone considered it at all, a liberation from its tyranny and its furious hunger, which forced women to risk their lives again and again in the lottery of pregnancy and childbirth. The view that the stresses of menopause represented the death-throes of the wild womb lingered on in some quarters until the mid eighteenth century. We find Moreau de la Sarthe, for example, in *L'Histoire naturelle de la femme* (1803), arguing that if a woman survived to the climacteric, the womb rebelled against the forced relinquishment of its power over the organism. The menopausal uterus bouleverse tout le système vivant, et occasionne surtout des affections nerveuses et une altération profonde dans les fonctions digestives [overthrows the whole system and brings about nervous afflictions and a profound alteration in the digestive functions].

For adherents of this theory menopausal anxiety, sleeplessness, palpitations, and even hot flushes, which were observed in younger hysterics as well, were variants of hysteria, and to be treated in the same ways.

A systematic discussion of women's diseases in the vernacular medical texts is, alas, too much to hope for. Though accidents and plagues befalling men's organs of generation may be discussed at length, the 'privities' of women are considered improper subjects. Even in Queen Philippa's herbal the generic patient is referred to as 'a man'; the early printed texts follow the same convention. When a woman is writing, as Mary Trye wrote in 1675 in defence of her father, Thomas O'Dowd, against the aspersions of his rival Dr Stubbe, reluctance to discuss female ailments is, if anything, more marked. At the end of *Medicatrix, Or the Woman-Physician*, Mary, whose generic patient is also 'a man', after an advertisement for her own practice and the medications she had learned from her father, remarks of the 'Diseases attending Women',

As Histerical Fits, or Fits of the Mother, Green-Sickness, Wastings, Barrenness, Obstruction, Fluxes of Several Kinds &c. The Diseases incident to this Sex are many, and not proper here largely to be discoursed on; therefore I purposely omit them . . . (Sig. K4ᵛ)

Similarly the theoreticians of melancholy saw little to distinguish menopausal depression from female melancholy in general. The classic theory of melancholy explained the condition as the result of a superfluity of one of the four humours that make up the human constitution, namely black bile. The word 'humour' began its career in English as meaning a bodily fluid, gradually took on

the association with a state of mind, until the anatomical constitu-
ent of the idea eventually perished, leaving only the secondary
meaning. Texts like Robert Burton's *Anatomy of Melancholy* move
freely back and forth along a psychosomatic continuum, so that
biochemistry is seen as causing mental and spiritual distress, which
in turn aggravates the biochemical imbalance. It would seem then
that we might expect a better understanding of the complex
nature of climacteric syndrome from the students of melancholy
than from the medical theorists, if only they would concern
themselves with older women; in fact they were only mildly
interested in female melancholy of any kind. Timothy Bright's
Treatise of Melancholie (1586) suggests a treatment for depression
leading to amenorrhoea that is one of the few that could be taken
to apply to older women:

> If this melancholy falleth unto maidens, women, and their ordinary
> course faile them, the vaines of the hammes or ancles are to be cut, and
> drinkes of opening rootes, fenell, persley, butchers broome, madder and
> such like, with germander, goolds, herbe grace, mugwort and nep are to
> bee much used, with sittinges and bathinges in mallows, cammomile and
> nep, peniroyall, bay leaves, fetherfew ... decocted in water, wherein so
> much honie has been dissolved, as will give it a taste of sweetnes.
> (264)

Though the opening medicines Bright names in the first part are
not the ones usually recommended for older women, the baths he
recommends, but for the inclusion of pennyroyal, are sedative and
anti-spasmodic. He adds, moreover, that the venesection should be
performed at the new moon for the younger women but at the
full 'for the elder sorte'. Similar spasmolytics appear in the recipes
for the soothing baths for melancholy that feature in several
surviving receipt-books, such as Mary Fairfax's of 1632:

> To make a bath for Melancholy. Take mallowes pellitory of the wall,
> of each three handfulls; Camomell flowers, Mellelot flowers, of each one
> handfull; holly-hocks two handfulls; Isop one great handfull, fenecrick

seed ... one ounce, and boil them in nine gallons of Water, till they come to three, then put in a quart of new milke, and go into it bloud warme or somthing warmer. (Fairfax family, 16)

A handful is a precise measurement: it is as many twelve-inch sprigs of the herb as may be held in the hand at once. One can hardly imagine an older woman going to all this trouble for herself; if a younger woman, a granddaughter perhaps, made up such a delicious bath to relieve someone else's suffering, the evidence of tender care or 'cherishing', as it was known, must have constituted a large part of the effectiveness of the therapy.

Hypochondria is another heading in the old texts under which we might expect to find the symptoms of climacteric syndrome. The disorder was thought to arise from windiness in the gut, which in turn caused anxieties and tremulousness.

Though it might be fun, it is hardly realistic to try to re-invent the practices of the old herb women in our time. Most women have no option but to seek the aid of the medical establishment in dealing with difficulties encountered at the climacteric. A study of the treatments offered before the panacea of HRT became available provides little more, however, than food for thought. Though the name 'menopause' was not invented till de Gardanne coined the term in 1821, the phenomena associated with the cessation of the menses were observed long before. At first the disturbances of the menopause were thought to result from the fact that menstruation no longer discharged excrementitious humours from the womb, and a good deal of the apprehension felt by women entering the climacteric was due to this notion. In *The Anatomy of Melancholy* (1628, 1632) Burton summarizes the theory 'out of *Hippocrates, Cleopatra, Moschion* and those old *Gynaeciorum Scriptores*' in describing the melancholy of 'more ancient Maides, Widowes and barren Women' whose

heart and braine [are] offended with those vitious vapours that come from menstruous blood ... offended by that fuliginous exhalation of corrupt seed, troubling the Braine, heart and minde; ... the whole maladie proceeds from that inflammation, putredity, black smoakie vapours, &c and from thence comes care, sorrow & anxiety, obfuscation of spirits, agony, desperation & the like ... to Nunnes and more ancient Maides ... 'tis more familiar. (I, 414)

Burton accurately describes hot flushes and palpitations:

The midriffe and heart strings doe burne and beate very fearefully, & when the vapour or fume is stirred, flyeth upward, the heart it selfe beats & is sore grieved and faints ... they are dry, thirsty, suddenly hot, much troubled with wind, cannot sleep &c ... so farre gone sometimes, so stupefied and distracted, they think themselves bewitched. (I, 415)

An ancient, barren woman could hardly have put it better herself. Though Burton was a bachelor and led 'a Monasticke life in a College', he was quite convinced that the cause of these manifestations was 'enforced temperance'. His observations bear out the impression that historically the climacteric was associated with women who had not perished in the lottery of childbirth, who were mostly virgins, widows and the sterile. Burton, who would have been more familiar with labouring women who were prevented from marrying by their servile status, had also noticed that they did not manifest the same kind of distress.

... seldome shall you see an hired servant, a poore handmaid, though ancient, that is hard kept to her worke, and bodily labour ... troubled in this kinde ... (I, 416)

Burton's ideas, which have as much to do with the history of Pre-menstrual Syndrome as that of Climacteric Syndrome, are no more than the sum of medical orthodoxy of his time. In 1683, in a letter written in Latin to his colleague, William Cole, Thomas Sydenham, MD, declared that menstrual blood was none other than the sustenance supplied for the foetus in the womb, which had to be shed if impregnation did not ensue in due season. In the letter, which was published in his *Opera Universa* in 1685 and in a translation by John Pechey, a Licentiate of the College of Physicians, in 1701, Sydenham had little to say about older women except to offer a treatment for excessive blood loss during the climacteric:

But as to the Flux . . . [that] . . . comes most commonly a little before the Time the Courses are about to leave them, *viz.* about the Age of Forty-five if they flow early, but about Fifty if they come somewhat later; from these as it is said, a little before they quite go away (like a Candle burnt to the Socket which gives the greatest light, just as it is about to go out) they flow impetuously, and subject the poor Women almost continually to Hysterick Fits, by reason of the quantity of Blood which is continually evacuated . . . (337)

Sydenham began his therapy by letting blood:

Let eight Ounces of Blood taken from the Arm, the next Mor[n]ing give the common purging Potion, which must be repeated every third day for twice and every Night at Bedtime through the whole Course; let her take an *Anodyne* made with one Ounce of *Diacodium*.

Sydenham does not give his reason for letting blood or for the purging which was also universally prescribed for climacteric syndrome. Both were intended to reduce the tendency to 'plethora', which is what was thought to cause the symptoms in the first place. Plethora, as the name implies, was 'a morbid condition generated by excess of blood'; some considered that the blood itself was of poor quality, being 'full of excrementitious matter' by reason of defective excretion of wastes whether by inadequate sweating, salivation, defecation, urination or menstruation. Purging and bleeding were to be practised if plethora was suspected, in order to avoid haemorrhage, and as a measure to reduce the violence of what was considered to be not the menstrual discharge of blood without fibrin, but a haemorrhagic flow of whole blood. The hysterics Sydenham describes was probably a reaction of sheer terror, for heavy bleeding in younger women was too often a precursor of death.

John Pechey had already, in 1698, published Sydenham's therapy as his own in *A Plain and Short Treatise of an Apoplexy, Convulsions, Colick, Twisting of the Guts, . . . and several other Violent and Dangerous Diseases*: his intention in doing so was that

This little Book may be an assistant to Charitable ladies and Gentle-women in the Country . . . here they may find plain directions, and the most celebrated medecines. (Preface, [i])

He spells out the recipe for the 'common purging potion' which is identical with that to be found at the beginning of another translation of Sydenham's prescriptions, published in 1694 as *The Compleat Method of Curing Almost All Diseases*:

Take of Tamarinds, half an Ounce, of Sena two Drams, of Rhubarb one Dram and a half; infuse them in a sufficient quantity of Fountain-water, and in three ounces of the strained liquid, dissolve of Manna and Syrup of Roses solution, each one ounce. (23)

By 1701 Pechey was advertising his own purging pills at the end of his translation of Sydenham's *Opera Universa* for sale at the relatively high price of one shilling and sixpence. His were the antecedents of a long line of 'female pills' for self-medication which continued to be sold at high prices until the middle of the nineteenth century (BMJ, 1907, ii, 1653–68; Brown, 1977).

Though Sydenham's anatomical understanding was empirical and scientific, his prescribing seems to have been affected by the Paracelsian doctrine of sympathies; the most effective aspect of the ball of medicinal nougat that he instructs the apothecaries to confect for middle-aged ladies suffering heavy and continuous blood loss is that it is the colour of blood.

Take of Conserve of dried Roses two Ounces, of Troches of Lemnian *Earth one Dram and a Half, of Pomegranate-peel and Red-coral prepar'd, each two Scruples, of Blood-stone, Dragon's-blood and* Bole Armenick, *each one Scruple; make an Electuary with a sufficient quantity of simple Syrup of Coral; let her take the quantity of a large Nutmeg in the Morning, and at five in the Afternoon . . .* (338)

Earth from the island of Lemnos was not only considered to be astringent but was quite evidently red; nothing has more red colour than pomegranate; coral has no medical property beyond the associations of its fresh redness and the fact that in water it is a plant but exposed to air becomes a stone; syrup of coral is probably a herbal preparation, perhaps of coralwort, *Dentaria bulbifera*, which was taken as a powder in wine to stay fluxes; bloodstone, Pliny's heliotrope, was a kind of jasper streaked with red that was thought to have the property of staunching blood; dragon's-blood, which was the red resin of a Mediterranean species of palm, is to be found in Queen Philippa's herbal as 'Sanguis draconis for women that have their terms too much'; 'Bole Armenick' was a pale red earth from Armenia used internally against fluxes of all kinds. Interestingly, when the recipe for this electuary appears in later pharmacopoeiae derived from Sydenham's, it is not recommended specifically for the metror-rhagia of menopause.

With her red electuary the patient was required to drink 'six Spoonfuls of the following Julep' made up of workaday local materials in use for hundreds of years.

Take of the Waters of Oak-buds and Plantain, each three Ounces, of Cinnamon water bordeated and of Syrup of dried Roses, each one Ounce, of Spirit of Vitriol a sufficient quantity to make it pleasantly acid. (338)

The product of distilling the buds of the oak-tree just before it comes into leaf had long been used by herbalists to 'stop all manner of fluxes in man or woman' and 'The juice of plantain clarified ... stays all manner of fluxes, even women's courses, when they flow too abundantly' (Culpeper, 1826). Sydenham's syrup of roses, cinnamon water and vitriol was intended merely to disguise his julep's humble origins. Time, effort and money were not to be spared in treating the sick lady whose still-room must have been crowded with people preparing her therapy. Sydenham ordered a second purge to be prepared adding to plantain (*Plantago major*) stinging nettles, an invaluable astringent and anti-haemo-rrhagic:

> Take of the Leaves of Plantain and Nettles, each a sufficient Quantity; beat them together in a Marble Mortar and press out the Juice, then clarifie it: Let her take six spoonfuls cold three or four times a day, after the first purge applie the following Plaister to the Region of the Loins.
>
> Take of Diapalma, and of the Plaister ad Herniam, each equal parts, mingle them and spread them on Leather.

Diapalma was a desiccating mixture of palm oil, protoxide of lead and sulphate of zinc, which Sydenham suggests mixing with another compound used externally to shrink hernias, perhaps in some understanding that the shrinking of the uterus which begins in the peri-menopause will soon put a natural end to the metror-rhagia of menopause and should be aided rather than opposed. Thus dosed with her red electuary, her astringent julep, her red purge and her green, resting under her plaster, 'the Sick' was allowed a treat, which seems to have been an intrinsic part of popular treatments for menopausal distress.

> A cooling and thickening Diet must be order'd, only it will be convenient to allow the Sick a small draught of Claret-wine, once or twice a day, which tho 'tis somewhat improper, by reason 'tis apt to raise the Ebullition, yet it may be allow'd to repair the strength; . . . this is very beneficial to Women thus affected . . .

The cooling diet was part of the herb women's treatment for menopause. When Madame de Sévigné was taking the waters in 1675, Bourdelot physicked her with 'melons and ice' (I, 150) to the horror of her friends, who were sure the treatment would kill her. The Marquise was forty-nine; it seems likely that the treatment was intended for the metrorrhagia of menopause. A few months later she was complaining of joint pains:

> . . . the same stiff neck was in truth a very pretty fit of rheumatism; it is a disorder attended with violent pain and want of rest or sleep; but it gives no apprehension respecting the consequences. This is the eighth

day; a gentle dose of medicine and a sudorific will restore me again. I have been bled once in the foot and now abstinence and patience will put the finishing stroke to the disorder. (I, 185)

The Marquise's discomfort was actually far from over, for the 'cure' caused her to swell alarmingly and for many weeks she complained of 'flying pains' which may be a mistranslation of 'ardor volaticus', the Latin name for hot flushes. Her son Charles put his mother's sufferings down to 'repletion of humours' and earnestly entreated her to take 'Delorme's powders'. His sister's protest against this prescription gives further ground for believing that the Marquise's indisposition was originally climacteric distress considerably worsened by her medical treatment (I, 190).

Are you mad, brother, to think of giving our mother antimony? She wants nothing but a little dieting and a cooling medicine occasionally.

In May the Marquise betook herself to Vichy, where she drank the water, was pumped upon and sweated and bathed.

The sweats, which weaken everyone else, give me fresh strength, which is sufficient proof that my disorders proceeded from a redundancy of humours. (I, 224)

Given the labours of Sydenham and Pechey, it is curious that the official historian of menopause, Joel Wilbush, D. Phil., Fellow of the Royal College of Obstetricians and Gynaecologists of Canada, affirms without any sign of doubt that

The first reference in English to discomforts associated with the female climacteric occurs in a guide for women published early in the 18th century (A physician 1727).

He is referring to *A Rational Account of the Natural Weaknesses of Women and of Secret Distempers peculiarly Incident to Them*, of which no copy of the first edition survives. Wilbush cites it by the title of the third and seven subsequent editions, *The Ladies' Physical*

Directory or a Treatise of all the Weaknesses, Indispositions and Diseases Peculiar to the Female Sex from Eleven Years of Age to Fifty or Upwards. He quotes from a later edition of 1739:

... between forty and fifty years of Age, their *Courses* begin first to dodge and at last to leave them; for then they are frequently troubled with a Severe pain in the head and Back, and about the Loins; oftimes also with Cholick Pains, Gripes, and Looseness, at other Times with Vapours to a Violent Degree; likewise with feverish Heats, wandering Rheumatic Pains and general Uneasiness. (1)

Though he gives his own recipes, the anonymous physician refuses to identify some of the ingredients, such as his 'mineral powder', because his main intention is to sell his own specifics. His account of the brewing of his 'uterine drops' makes quite clear that it is beyond the scope of even the best-equipped still-room and quite justifies the high price of three shillings and sixpence that he is asking. The sufferer from metrorrhagia is to be let eight ounces of blood from the arm and purged, as recommended by Sydenham, then given 'the Cooling Anodyne Powder', the 'Restraining Electuary' and the 'Consolidating Apozem', in all costing fifteen shillings and sixpence. The anonymous man-midwife gives no rationale for his treatment; his prescriptions are derived from no pharmacopoeia, classic or otherwise, but he sternly admonishes his clientele to accept no imitations.

Wilbush sees in this quack-salver's advertising pamphlet the emergence of menopause into medical literature, which he relates to increased rates of survival of women who, once they had reached the age of twenty, were likely to live nearly ten years longer in 1730 than they were in 1680. In truth the anonymous author is less interested in advancing the state of medical knowledge than in exploiting the newly emergent semi-literate female middle class. He makes use of no authorities and, except to vilify a rival who plagiarized his own book and increased its saleability by making references to female masturbation, no reference to his medical colleagues, if indeed he was a qualified physician at all. He contemptuously dismisses the remedies used by 'Midwives, Nurses and other Good Women who chiefly undertake the Cure of the Secret Indispositions of the Female Sex' (1742, Sig. A2).

Isinglass boiled in milk, Turpentine Pills, Clary fried with Eggs, Arcangell Flowers, Armenian Bole, *vulgarly called* Bole Armonick, Sperma Ceti, Confection of Alkermes, Penny-royal Water, *Dr* Stephens Water, and compound Bryony water, *commonly called* Hysterick Water *are in a manner their whole Magazine of Remedies.*

For diagnosticians the difficulty was to decide whether the cessation of the monthly flow represented the natural cessation of ovarian function or the suppression of the menses. Concern that the failure of the menstrual flow led to the development of dangerous symptoms persisted well into the nineteenth century. Bucknill and Tuke in 1858 recorded that

Amenorrhoea is a frequent cause or consequence of, or concurrent phenomenon with mental disease; and its removal leads to recovery of sanity. (436)

The observation was essentially correct; Bucknill and Tuke are unusual in that they confess that they do not understand the connection between amenorrhoea and mental disturbance, but clearly they thought that if you could correct the amenorrhoea your patient would recover her sanity. (Nowadays we would reverse the emphasis and take the return of the menses as a symptom of recovery.) Earlier doctors were not always so conservative nor so rigorous. Though both Sydenham and the anonymous author of *A Rational Account* did not believe that the disorders of menopause were the direct result of the failure of the menstrual discharge to cleanse the blood of 'excrementitious humours', most other male practitioners did. They treated distress in the early part of the climacteric by setting up or encouraging 'vicarious menstruation'. Any bloody discharge in a menopausal patient was to be encouraged and on no account to be stopped. If no such discharge, from a bleeding ulcer, from haemorrhoids or from the nose, for example, was to be observed, then a vein was to be opened and the woman cupped, or leeches were to be applied to the anus or the groin. Better still, a continuous issue could be provoked, by opening a wound and keeping it open with setons, threads drawn through the flesh and left in place. Though this approach is clearly derived from classic medical literature, which was never relevant to female healing practice, Wilbush attributes these invasive practices to women practitioners:

Female healers first tried to ensure a continuation of natural 'excretion' by emmenagogues, leeches applied to the genitalia or, with the help of barber surgeons, directional phlebotomies. When these measures failed they opened other routes of excretion, purgation, issues, cauteries, setons or others. (2–3)

He quotes the example of the lady in *Gil Blas* who retained her youthful beauty by means of an issue in each buttock, and forgets to add that the issues in question were regularly opened by a male surgeon, which is the point of the episode.

All of these measures were used in fact by male practitioners, even distinguished male practitioners. Some went so far as to push the seton needle through the neck of the womb itself. Wilbush writes:

Though treatment was far from pleasant, women were only too eager to follow it. Haunted by the threat of losing their sexual attraction, and with it much of their status, they were ready for any measures which promised results. (3)

He cites no authority for this observation. What the scant evidence seems to show is rather that these grim procedures remained popular with doctors for more than a hundred years, despite the protests of their patients. C. Locock, writing of the disorders of 'the dodging time' in *The Cyclopedia of Practical Medicine*, published in 1833, makes clear his own position:

The production of artificial discharges by means of issues, setons or perpetual blisters, so much in vogue formerly, is now no longer fashionable, from the dislike patients have to such remedies; but viewing what is often effected naturally, we cannot doubt but that their more frequent employment would be highly advantageous.

Perhaps because he was under the impression that the torturers of menopausal women were other women, Wilbush is very ready to identify a significant iatrogenic element in their sufferings:

It is significant that, with the partial exception of several items like feverish heats [? hot flushes], rheumatic pains [? osteoporotic pains] and vapours [? emotional disturbances], the complaints detailed by the anonymous physician [in *A Rational Account*] are largely iatrogenic. They are, in all probability, due to the medications ... Backache and pains 'about the loins' were probably due to emmenagogues, for these often affected the urinary tract causing strangury. 'Cholick pains, Gripes and Looseness' were due to purgatives, Headaches and 'Uneasiness', being general complaints, could be either functional or iatrogenic. The same applies to the vapours and, to some extent, to 'Rheumatik Pains' and 'Feverish Heats'. The iatrogenic character of the symptoms listed therefore constitutes strong evidence of a tradition of treatment for climacteric stress. (3)

Female patients generate their own symptoms, unless the doctors are female, in which case they generate the symptoms. Wilbush is untroubled by any circularity in a position which identifies climacteric syndrome by its symptoms and then accuses the (female) people trying to deal with them of having caused them. In fact the symptoms were both endogenic and iatrogenic; the worst suffering was caused not by the women so contemptuously dismissed by the men-midwives but by the grand doctors who regularly tortured monarchs and their children like Indians at the stake, to use Macaulay's phrase. Among literate women there was a strong tradition of distrust of doctors. The painful surgical procedures inflicted on menopausal women were justified principally by a masculine conviction that menopause was *'l'enfer des dames'*, hell on women. The purpose of such propaganda was, as it is now, to create a vast and lucrative medical speciality.

The American doctor William P. Dewees noted that for some months prior to the cessation of the menses there is more frequent blood loss, sometimes very heavy blood loss, interspersed by long periods with no losses. Unlike other doctors he did not treat the amenorrhea of menopause. Most of his treatments were for the flooding of menopause, which was considered by him and the more enlightened of his contemporaries as the only dangerous aspect of the process. The consequences of metrorrhagia are vividly described by Dewees.

The woman also finds that some alteration has taken place in her general health: she becomes pale, debilitated and nervous; arising how-ever from the too frequent returns of this discharge, or its too great abundance . . . (146)

Dewees's treatments are conservative and sensible.

At this period of life, nothing will so effectively secure the woman against injuries which may arise from the irregularities of the menstrual discharge as a well-regulated regimen . . . a milk and vegetable diet, together with pure water as a drink; regular exercise not carried to fatigue; keeping the bowels open by well selected food, as the fruits of the season in proper quantities; the bran bread if necessary, but not by medicine, unless absolutely required. (149)

During heavy bleeding the patient was to lie down, and all motion, even turning in bed, was forbidden. The room was to be kept cool, all food and drink was to be cold and ice-packs were to be laid against the woman's body. Her legs and feet, however, should not be permitted to get cold.

We should also give by mouth two or three grams of the acetate of lead, every hour or two, guarded with a sufficient quantity of opium or laudanum. (150)

To prevent 'excessive return', blood-letting and other poisons, extract of cicuta or hemlock, were necessary and 'all kinds of liquor, and spices should be absolutely forbidden'. Dewees was very well aware that he had little success in controlling excessive bleeding in menopausal women and he gives a curious and very rare glimpse of an alternative practitioner who was more successful than he. He tells us that one of his patients 'was told by some old woman that hiera picra was a certain cure for her complaint'. Hiera picra is a name given to many preparations in the ancient Greek pharmacopoeiae. The name means 'holy bitters' and describes a purgative compound of aloes and cinnamon bark which was in constant use for hundreds of years. Hiera picra figures in Timothy Bright's clyster for melancholy, along with marshmallows, hollyhocks, pellitory of the wall, camomile, hops, melitot and other plants decocted in ale or beer with honey 'wherein Rosemarie-flowers have been steeped' (262).

Dewees did not scruple to express his contempt for such hickery-pickery (for the name was synonymous with quackery), but to his chagrin the 'old woman' cited two cases that she had treated successfully. Dewees was honest enough to interview the ladies who 'warmly recommended' the treatment, which was half an ounce of hiera picra dissolved in a pint of gin, a wine-glass to be taken at bedtime. His patient took it and was drunk all night and sick all the next day; that evening she tried again, thinking her reaction the second time might not be so bad, and suffered equally (152). Dewees had pills made up in which a much smaller dose of hiera picra was mixed with oil of cloves and syrup rhaei, which procured the desired result.

The first whole book on the menopause was C. F. Menville's *Conseils aux Femmes de l'Epoque de l'Age de Retour*, which appeared in 1839, and in a second edition as *De l'Age critique chez les Femmes* in 1840. Menville believed that the last death throes of the womb caused the inconvenient symptoms that women experienced. The physician's job was to correct the derangement of the nerves and the digestion, which in any case was temporary.

... lorsque les forces vitales cessent de conspirer vers l'utérus, elles augmentent celles de l'esprit et du reste du corps. Passé l'âge critique les femmes ont l'espérance d'une plus longue vie que les hommes, leur esprit acquérit plus de netteté, d'étendue et de vivacité. [When the vital forces cease to work together in the interest of the uterus, they go to join those of the mind and the rest of the body. The critical age passed, women have the hope of a longer life than men, their thought acquires more precision, more scope and vitality.] (47)

Samuel Ashwell, writing a few years later, noted that women of the plethoric type 'who have been healthy prior to the change often become corpulent after its completion and are more than usually liable to attacks of apoplexy, paralysis, pulmonary obstruction and cough'. Nevertheless he did not approve of the measures taken to reduce plethora.

I have now under my care a lady who has ceased to menstruate for three or four years, and who, by the adoption of a spare and vegetable diet and the almost daily use of purgatives throughout the whole time, has become gradually so exhausted, irritable and neuralgic that her life is a burden. (200)

Ashwell's therapy for women whose menstruation had not yet ceased included purgatives, small bleedings, exercise and abstinence from 'wine, spirits and malt liquor'. So frequently do the ladies' doctors repeat the prohibition of alcohol, it seems reasonable to suspect that there was a popular tradition that encouraged women suffering menopausal distress to drink more than was usually thought proper.

I have lately attended several cases of decided insanity consequent on the improper use of wine and spirits during the period of catamenial decline ... In one ... these stimulants had been employed in the hope that they would relieve the languor and *depression*. The affection assumed all the characters of violent mania; eventually however subsiding into what we feared would be incurable madness. Nevertheless the patient entirely recovered in two years: the efficient remedies being *frequent leechings* of the cervix uteri, moderate purgatives, nutritious diet with malt liquor and light wines, and extreme tranquillity in the country. (202)

Gin, which is sometimes called 'mother's ruin', is assumed on that ground to have been a specific in procuring abortion. It is more likely, on linguistic and medical grounds, that the name refers to the fact that women of menopausal age were encouraged to use gin to combat 'low spirits', whereas alcohol is generally prohibited to women of breeding age. For a visible number of middle-aged women, alcohol dependency was the fairly rapid outcome. The stereotypical gin-bibber of the nineteenth century is not the drunken young mother of Hogarth's Gin Lane but Dickens's Sairy Gamp.

Ashwell also implies that the theory of 'vicarious menstruation' was not yet dead and the provocation of blood loss was still being practised:

On setons and issues great stress was formerly laid, but they are not often necessary . . .

Ashwell prefers less wrong-headed procedures:

Other measures of a derivative kind will naturally suggest themselves, as mustard hip baths and pediluvia, frictions with stimulating embroca-tions, and the flesh brush, the continuance of sexual intercourse, and the encouragement by any gentle means of the catamenial flow. (201)

The use of counter-irritants in the menopause was a bone of contention over which the ladies' doctors delighted to quarrel. For no sooner had the menopause attracted the attention of professional gentlemen than they began competing with each other, belittling each other's theories and methods, writing books to justify (and to publicize) their own practice, and perfecting a bedside manner that would bring society ladies of a certain age flocking to their rooms. Edward John Tilt is a perfect example of the ladies' doctor. After studying at St George's Hospital in London he went on to qualify in Paris, where through the efforts of de Gardanne, Menville, Moreau de la Sarthe, Brierre de Boismont and Dusourd, awareness of climacteric syndrome was much higher than in England. After travelling as the family physician with the family of Count Shuvaloff, he settled in London in 1850 and practised there as a fashionable ladies' doctor.

Tilt strongly disagreed with those of his medical contemporaries who declared that nothing significant happened in the 'seventh septenniad' of women's lives, quoting Brierre de Boismont's sample of 107 women of whom eighty suffered considerably, and his own experience of 539 women of whom he had 'only met 39 who have not suffered'. On the other hand he refused too to espouse the view that the menopause was in itself dangerous. His descriptions of the climacteric in *The Change of Life in Health and Disease* are based upon the rare practice of listening to women themselves and are thoroughly sensible. Tilt saw the climacteric as a period of exceptional somatic stress, out of which 'arise a beautiful series of critical movements, the object of which is to endow woman with a greater degree of strength than she previously enjoyed' (4). He noted that older women were far less prone to infection than younger ones and had greater endurance than women who were still subject to the demands of menstruation, pregnancy and childbirth. He saw a new role for older women as the guardians of the mothers and the arbiters of taste and manners.

One observation applies to the treatment of all the diseases of this epoch – the necessity for time. Nature cannot work at a railway pace. A habit of 32 years cannot be interrupted without periods of hesitation, trial and infirmity previous to health being regained. (116)

It would never have occurred to Tilt to try to postpone or counteract the natural processes of the climacteric. A womb that is shrinking should not be stimulated; ladies who might be contemplating matrimony at this time were considered by him to be risking their physical and mental health. He quotes examples of middle-aged women treated for occluded menses, when actually they had ceased to ovulate, who were driven into melancholy and mania after a series of heavy break-through bleeds. Whenever Tilt encountered, in the absence of an external stimulus, increased sexual interest in a middle-aged woman he immediately suspected the cause to be pathological, and he had found diseases of the womb in enough cases to be confirmed in his suspicions. In the case where the external stimulus was to be found, the uterine excitation of courtship put the woman's life in danger. At no time does Tilt refer to the sexual demands of a husband. His sole concern is for the woman herself. In each case he built up a picture of the patient's entire reproductive career starting with her experiences at puberty, and he treated each one in a manner suited to her type, which he classified under one of three heads, 'plethoric', 'chlorotic' or 'nervous'.

'Visiting different medicated springs' was, according to Tilt, 'at once the most agreeable and effectual mode of restoring health at the change of life'. This was no more than orthodoxy, and popular orthodoxy at that; ladies of a certain age were a conspicuous proportion of the floating population of Bath and Tunbridge Wells long before the springs were roofed over and became places of fashionable resort. Dr Tilt liked to send his patients further afield, to Aix-en-Savoie, now better known as Aix-les-Bains, 'combining varied medicated waters with good society and a country abounding in beautiful scenery'. His patients were also encouraged to avoid sexual excitement, to take a tepid bath three times weekly and to spend several hours each day 'on the sofa'. They should eat less, take only 'one dinner' a day and avoid red meat.

Dietary restrictions upon older people have a long and mostly unwritten history. Though the medical establishment may have had little understanding of or interest in the physiology of ageing, it seems likely that the carers, the women upon whom the care of older people devolved, did understand the changing dietary needs of older people. In 1775 an unknown lady replied to a 'Gentleman' who complained 'that he could not eat meat, owing to the

Looseness of his Teeth' with a poem that was printed in *The Gentleman's Magazine*.

> You told me, Sir, your Teeth were loose,
> And soon would be unfit for use;
> And, if I rightly recollect,
> My answer was to this effect:
>   That Nature meant they should be so,
> As I imagined you must know:
> For what our stomachs cannot bear
> Ought never to be placèd there . . .
>
>   (Lonsdale, 1989, 336)

The poet's ground for advising against the eating of red meat is simply that it will be unchewed; however, there is a case to be made for older people giving up red meat, for the action of the phosphorus in red meat speeds up bone resorption.

> 'What! not eat meat!' you made reply,
> 'Why, Madam, I should starve and die;
>   . . . what can men eat
> So wholesome, or so good as meat?'

The list the poet supplies begins badly with boiled milk and flour-and-water puddings, but it gets better:

> When tired, as you may be, of these,
> I give you leave to eat some peas,
> With greens and every wholesome root
> The gardener's art can furnish out.
> Plain soups, or boiled or stewed, I hold
> Not much amiss for young or old;
> But such as aldermen would choose
> 'Twere death for aged men to use.
>
>   (337)

It should also be noticed here that aldermen's feasts were often the death of aldermen, as well as aged men. Our poet's low-

cholesterol/high-fibre regimen continues with a grudging conces-
sion and good advice about eggs and fish:

> Eggs for a meal may sometimes please,
> But sparingly regale on these:
> And would you follow my advice,
> Of nothing eat so much as rice . . .
>   Now then I say that I could wish
> That twice a week you'd eat of fish . . .
>   Yet one thing more – and then you will
> Of eatables have had your fill –
> And that is, fruit of every sort
> That with your pocket will comport,
> From apples-John to apples-pine,
> And the rich product of the vine . . .
>
> (337)

The anonymous poet's advice could well be followed today by
older women, for the sake both of their health and of their
pockets. If we were to substitute wholewheat flour pancakes or
chapatis for the flour-and-water puddings that head her list, we
would have a perfect diet for older people. The poet assumes that
her gentleman friend has access to a kitchen garden, and her
recommendation of all kinds of vegetables presupposes their freshness.

Tilt's recommendation that the menopausal woman cut down
on her food intake is probably based on his clinical experience
rather than on the commonsensical fund of female knowledge that
our poet was calling on seventy years before, but the conclusion is
equally just. He too is adamant about the inappropriateness of
alcohol as a treatment for the climacteric syndrome.

> By no means . . . seek a comfort for languor, weakness or nervousness,
> in wine, cordials and spirits, by which a temporary support only can be
> obtained at the expense of an increase in the faintness, flushing and
> nervous symptoms. (123)

This observation is certainly true. It seems that alcohol burns off the small supply of oestrone which, if she is lucky, keeps the menopausal woman on an even keel; there is a curious association here, for *Oenothera*, used by some women as a precursor for oestrogen, is an alcohol antagonist, hence its Greek name. Tilt's approach aims to help the organism to do what it was already trying to do and speed the accomplishing of the change. Like his predecessors, in the case of heavy bleeding in the peri-menopause he recommends bleeding by venesection or by leeching, but only for patients of the 'plethoric' type. By our standards Tilt was rather too keen on administering purgatives. The preferred sedatives for those of his patients who were 'driven to the verge of insanity by ovario-uterine excitement' were camphor, lupulin, hyoscyamus and opium.

Hyoscyamus is an invaluable remedy in the treatment of diseases of women, whether given as an extract in pills, or a topic in plaster. (97)

Hyoscyamus is our old friend henbane. Tilt insists on using the fresh extract, pressed out of the macerated plant, but unfortunately he gives no hint of the degree of dilution, and henbane is highly poisonous. Camphor is obtained by distilling the aged wood of the camphor tree, *Cinnamomum camphora*, which is indigenous to China and Japan. Its medical properties had been known since Avicenna (980–1037); in the twelfth century the Abbess Hildegarde of Bingen used it. In the eighteenth century 'camphire' was considered an ideal antimanic. Inhaled it relieved fainting fits and convulsions; rubbed on the skin it caused inflammation and was used as a counter-irritant; taken internally it caused vomiting, diarrhoea and sweating, and 'exhilarated' or, in larger doses, 'refrigerated' the nervous system; in larger doses still it functioned as convulsive therapy. The constituents of the crystals and in white oil of camphor are safriole, acetaldehyde, terpineol, eugenol, cineole, *d*-pinene and phellandrene. Camphor is listed in the pharmacopoeiae as weakly antiseptic, carminative, mildly expectorant, mildly analgesic, rubefacient and parasiticide. It is not immediately obvious why Tilt should say that camphor 'was made for women with whom it always agrees, while it always disagrees with men' (105), but it has been used internally as a sedative in cases of hysteria, as well as abating convulsions and epileptic fits. In Cuba it used to be used as an anaphrodisiac, which together with its use in cases of 'hysteria' seems to indicate that it was thought to act directly on the uterus. Certainly there is no reason why a woman seeking relief for climacteric distress should not inhale spirits of camphor, which seems a better idea than taking it by mouth.

Tilt prescribes 'lupulin' or extract of hops (*Humulus lupulus*) because of its function as a soporific and, as he thought, anaphrodisiac. He favoured pessaries and instillation through the anus as a way of administering sedatives. Not all his chosen specifics were as respectable as the ones discussed above; he was not shy of using opium or belladonna, or Epsom salts, or sulphur 'for all the diseases of ageing'. He had also succumbed to the Swiss enthusiasm for cherry laurel water, which is prepared from the leaves of *Prunus laurocerasus* by distillation. Its function as a sedative, which would be due to the presence of cyanide derivatives, has never been demonstrated and the preparation is now considered too dangerous for use.

Generally Tilt's attitude was in complete contrast to the modern approach which treats menopausal distress as a deficiency disease. He would have thought it unethical and mischievous to dose women with hormones so that they would continue to experience or respond to sexual desire. He prescribed ambergris 'to withstand the over-exciting effects of the present civilization on the nervous system by deadening the reproductive stimulus which only lingers on to disturb health'. As he understood it, the processes of the menopause were as natural as the processes of childbirth and his job in both cases was the same, to make them easier and the attendant suffering less. If the body sweated excessively during menopause, the treatment was not to attempt to dry up or inhibit the secretion but to encourage it, principally by bathing, for the warm bath functioned as 'a giant poultice' for the whole body. He was not keen on the application of leeches to the uterus, or on the use of counter-stimulants and blistering, as favoured by Fothergill and Ashwell, and he returned again and again to the most popular and successful treatment of all:

Travelling is a great strengthener of the nervous system, for it places the patient in entirely new circumstances, every one of which makes a fresh call on her attention, solicits her interests, captivates her faculties, and completely leads her from trains of thought, to which, perhaps, she had been long enchained. (127)

Another Fothergill, not Tilt's antagonist this time but Dr J. Milner Fothergill, published in 1885, three years before he died from diabetes at the age of forty-seven, *The Diseases of Sedentary and Advanced Life: A Work for Medical and Lay Readers*, in which he spelt out his own attitudes towards 'the change of life'.

. . . females at the change of life, or the menopause, are often in feeble health. They are not infrequently stout, with flabby muscles; the heart, being a muscle, is weak; and there is an incapacity for exertion, with palpitation on effort. The nervous system is often debilitated, and self-control is impaired, and the sufferer becomes pettish or fretful, or irritable or nervous. (113)

Dr Fothergill would have been incensed if anyone had taken an equally uncharitable view of his own poor health. He was in fact mountainously obese and notoriously bad-tempered.

The bowels are apt to become irregular, while the diet becomes capricious. As to the uterine functions, the changes in them take various directions. Sometimes a barren wife becomes a mother, like Sarah of old, when all hope of offspring is dying out. Or a widow or spinster, who hitherto has led a decorous life, suddenly develops strong erotic tendencies. . . (113–14)

Perhaps because he was tormented by gout, Fothergill tended to see it everywhere. Painful menstruation in the peri-menopause was probably cause by 'latent or suppressed gout'. Morever,

Flatulence is not rarely also present; and then this adds to the disturbance of the heart, and aggravates the condition of nervousness present. Attacks of breathlessness, or palpitation, come on at other times than upon effort. Sometimes they are set up by flatulence; possibly at other times they are set up by latent gout affecting the vaso-motor nerves. Or the patient wakens up, with one or both, out of her sleep, and is gravely alarmed . . . (114)

The only preventative of such derangement is 'a regulated regimen' and light food.

A generous wine may be indicated; and some stimulant be at hand when attacks of palpitation, etc., come on. It is well to lie down when not feeling well, so as to limit the demand upon the body powers. Some tonic should be given, as digitalis and strychnia, or lily of the valley or belladonna, and be combined with a carminative, or cascarilla, or other aromatic. (115)

Though the bowels must be kept open, the menopausal lady is not to be distressed by griping and she is to drink nothing cold.

If these matters be not attended to, the lady will be very liable to change her medical adviser, until she finds some one who understands her condition, and her requirements. (115)

Fothergill is afraid that the dissatisfied customer might strike back. With or without the benefit of an adviser the climacteric eventually passes:

After the perturbations of the menopause are past and over, woman passes into a period of calm; relieved from those tumults which mark the period of her reproductive life, and continues an almost sexless existence; except in very rare cases, of which the illustrious George Eliot was an unfortunate instance. (115)

It is slightly shocking to discover that Dr Fothergill is prepared to refer to George Eliot as a fatality caused by unseasonable passion in a work published for the general reading public only four years after her marriage and death. On 9 April 1880 the distinguished surgeon Sir James Paget called on Eliot and, after a long consultation, advised her to accept Johnny Cross's third proposal, despite the fact that she was sixty, twenty years older than Cross (Haight, 1969, 536).

During the honeymoon, in Venice, Johnny Cross, who never before or since in his long life showed any signs of mental derangement, jumped from the balcony of their hotel room into the Grand Canal. He was pulled out by gondoliers, given chloral to calm him, and his wife telegraphed for his brother Willie to come and help nurse him. He recovered, and they continued with their trip through Austria and Germany. Cross lived on until 1924 but 'the illustrious George Eliot' died a few months later. The Venice incident was given out as an intestinal complaint. (For further discussion of George Eliot's marriage to Johnny Cross, see p. 340). Though Eliot's biographer, Haight, did not discover the truth until 1968, Fothergill seems quite secure in his opinion that George Eliot did feel a sexual passion for her husband and did not scruple to refer to her among his colleagues as an acknowledged case of fatal uterine excitement in tacit criticism of his distinguished colleagues, Her Majesty's Sergeant-Surgeon Extraordinary, who had advised her to put her life in jeopardy.

By the turn of the century women were already being dosed with the extracts of animal glands, most of which were inert. Doctors had become intensely aware of fibroids, which they were attempting to extirpate by highly experimental and often quite dangerous methods, including surgical hysterectomy, castration by X-ray, and ablation of the endometrium by electro-cautery. Though the learned gentlemen would have rebuffed the charge that they hated and feared the womb as much as any old scholarly medieval celibate, they inflicted outrages upon it in so exemplary and inventive a fashion as to defy explanation. No matter how grisly the procedure, there was never any shortage of middle-aged ladies delighted to discover that their womb was the cause of all their woes and prepared not only to undergo torture by uterine sound, by curette and by electrified rod but to pay through the nose for the privilege.

The Treatments – Alternative

As professional men increased their penetration into the care of the sick, inflicting upon them all kinds of invasive procedures, some of the patients, notably those who were not too sick to take defensive measures, recoiled. If the traditional medical procedures of healing the body by blasting it with purges and vomits, inducing copious sweats, letting blood, sometimes in enormous quantities, to the point of inducing convulsions and syncope, worked at all, it seems they must have worked as aversion therapy or shock treatment. Perhaps a patient felt relief when the treatment had run its violent course simply because the assault upon her body was over. When alternative systems of health care were advertised, women of a certain age were among the first to offer themselves as suitable cases for treatment, whether the prophet of the new system was a charismatic male or not.

Common to many of the alternative treatments is the idea that the body is not a hostile entity, with an innate tendency to go painfully wrong, but a homoeostatic mechanism which will cure itself of most disorders, if given a chance. Coupled with this notion there is often a corollary, that modern civilization is hostile to the demands of the body, exposing it to toxic levels of stress, as well as a multitude of environmental poisons. The typical alternative view that 'We become ill when we violate nature's laws' is not actually tenable. The sufferer from malaria or sleeping sickness is obeying a natural law which decrees that the malarial parasite or trypanosome can survive only within his body. The diseases of ageing also follow a natural law: all that is born must die. Nevertheless most of us would accept the paired dicta of Hippocrates that the body should be aided in its self-adjustment and that the cure should not be more destructive than the disease.

Though life in the non-industrialized countries is shorter and more painful than life in the industrialized world, most of us would agree that industrialization and urbanization have consequences deleterious to health. The middle-aged woman who understands that she needs plenty of exercise if she is to minimize the risk of developing osteoporosis can do very little about it if she lives in a city and cannot take long walks in safety or without stifling in traffic fumes. The city-dwelling woman who has no job is doomed to become a couch potato; if she has an office job, she must suffer all the inconveniences of sedentary office life and commuter travel, neither of which is what the alternative doctor would order. The middle-aged saleswoman has the worst option, for she is obliged to stand all day, and is probably too tired to run all the way home, even supposing it would not be foolhardy. Given the fact that most women cannot observe the basic conditions of alternative health care, most are best advised to try to take advantage of the only treatment the establishment can offer for climacteric syndrome and the inconveniences of ageing, namely HRT, a drastic therapy for a brutalized life-style.

With the onset of menopause one thing becomes clear, that is, that we must work at being healthy. We can no longer abuse the organism and get away with it. A positive commitment to health might involve the decision to move away from the city, but people who have grown up in an urban environment could find life intolerably dull or arduous if they were suddenly transplanted to the country. Still, there are strategies for self-purification that can profitably be undertaken without moving away from overcrowding and pollution.

Among the rites of passage that the middle-aged woman can choose for herself there should be the ceremony of renouncing her addictions. Sugar and tobacco, as well as coffee, tea and alcohol, exacerbate vasomotor disturbance, so the time of hot flushing is the ideal time to give them all up. Alcohol burns off the small post-menopausal oestrogen supply and interferes with calcium metabolism; evening primrose oil, usually suggested to women as an oestrogen precursor, might be more important to menopausal women for the function signified by its botanical name, *Oenothera*, as a counteractive to alcohol. Coffee and salt can cause calcium to be excreted and should be banned from the middle-aged woman's regimen. Taking calcium supplements by mouth is no way to compensate for failure to eschew coffee, salt and alcohol, being more likely to cause kidney stones than to prevent bone resorption.

It is the most difficult thing in the world to tail off an addiction; a dramatic renunciation often works much better. The most dramatic renunciation of bad food habits is giving up food altogether, i.e. fasting. Fasting is no more difficult than acquiring, preparing, serving, and eating food, not to mention clearing up after it. Fasting might sound duller than eating, but the processes of excretion that are activated by fasting are quite dramatic, spectacular enough to take your mind off what you are not eating. Many alternative health regimes involve longer or shorter periods of fasting, intended as jolts that will cause the system to jump the rails of a noxious habit and enter upon proper self-regulation. Alternative practitioners will tell you not to fast without supervision; indeed, some will want you to fast from everything but distilled water for weeks at a time in a hospital. In a Natural Hygiene hospital like Herbert Shelton's Health School, patients are confined to their rooms and obliged to rest while fasting:

Control of patient behaviour is made easier because most are suffering from chronic ailments for which they are desperate to obtain help. Many have vainly spent years seeking cure or relief from orthodox medical sources. They are usually women in their 50's or 60's who see this perhaps as a final opportunity to turn the tide of deteriorating health ... (Roth, 21)

Such a regimen is every bit as punitive as the tortures devised for complaining women by conventional allopathic medicine. We are not surprised to find that with such an other-directed system there is a good deal of backsliding. Patients behave like naughty children and persuade or bribe the staff to bring them food, or sweets or alcohol. The average middle-aged woman has quite enough common sense to decide how she will fast and for how long; if the decision is hers she is much more likely to carry it out. Many religions require the faithful not involved in childbearing or heavy labour to fast one day a week. One day a week on nothing but water will do no harm and may do good. Naturopaths recommend aiding the body in the excretion of toxins during fasting by the use of a long-handled 'skin brush' to stimulate the circulation under the skin. Another way of doing the same thing is to take a sauna bath and gently switch the skin with young birch twigs.

Many alternative therapies take time and determination to follow, and can absorb the mental energy that otherwise might be spent hankering after old addictions. Instead of longing for a sweet or chocolate or a cigarette, the woman who is looking for a change can follow one of the simplest and oldest ways of purifying the body, by drinking lots of water. Because drinking lots of our tap water could be a way not only of flushing out the kidneys and bladder but of ingesting large quantities of chlorine and nitrates, the self-purifying ritual should involve efficient filtration of tap-water or finding alternative sources of H_2O. Developing a discriminating taste in water and finding the perfect water can be every bit as demanding as choosing wine; it is, moreover, a good deal cheaper. People who have grown up on chlorinated recycled water imagine that water is tasteless, but people who have never had piped water know the different characters of the different springs in their area, and are well able to distinguish what water comes from where. Once you can distinguish the different tastes of water, you are in a fair way to have detoxified yourself.

Since the beginning of human history springs have been endowed with sacred, magic and medicinal properties. The therapeutic effects of drinking spring water with a high mineral content have been understood since the earliest times; where the water that gushed so inexplicably from the earth was unsuitable for drinking, the human animal found other ways of using it to relieve his aches and pains, or to clean infections and parasites off his skin. Copper age implements have been found in sulphur baths on the island of Malta. Sea-bathing was used for similar purposes; before entering the salt water, patients buried themselves in the hot pebbles or sand or mud of the beach. Older women have always constitituted a significant proportion of the clientele at mineral baths and sea-water bathing establishments. Twenty years ago, groups of grandmothers were the only people to be seen on the beaches of Sicily that are now covered with younger bodies in search of a tan. Middle-aged women may be shy of exhibiting themselves in such company but swimming is one kind of exercise that the city-bound woman should take if possible.

Hydrotherapy, the system of self-medication based upon a belief in the healing properties of plain water, is one of the earliest of the alternative systems of medical care.

This can include applications of hot and cold water, either externally or internally in the form of baths, packs, compresses, sprays and douches or sitz-baths (hip) in which the lower half of the body is immersed in hot or cold water, while the feet are put in water of a contrasting temperature. (Westkott, 140)

Hydrotherapy developed in reaction to the conditions prevailing at the fashionable spas, including the spread of contagion from diseased persons, exposure to the elements, the shortage of attendants, lack of privacy and offences against modesty brought about by the lack of dressing facilities and the mingling of the sexes (Donegan, 1986). Private use of cold water baths as a treatment was first advocated by John Floyer in *Psychrolusia, or History of Cold-Bathing*, first published in London in 1702 and five times subsequently by 1722.

Floyer's were ideas whose time had come; he was followed by the American, John Smith, who published *The Curiosities of*

Common Water in 1723. Tobias Smollett was a follower, if we may believe his *Essay on the External Use of Water* (1752) and John Wesley in *Primitive Physic* (1747). The great prophet of the water-cure as a panacea, however, is Vincent Preissnitz, who developed a whole system of wetting and sweating. In 1826 he opened a water-cure centre at Grafenburg in Silesia; there he applied a whole regimen which involved not only the water-cures but also plenty of fresh air and exercise and a diet of coarse, heavy food, invariably served cold. By 1840 he had accumulated a clientele of the rich and great, who were astonished at the improvement in their condition brought about by what was in fact a gradual process of detoxification. In America hydropathy became an enduring craze that claimed a million followers.

The next of the more venerable European alternative therapies is homoeopathy, a system of treatment devised by Samuel Hahnemann in the early nineteenth century. The homoeopathic approach to discomforts of ageing and the climacteric is first of all to relate the symptoms to a complete profile of the sufferer. It is assumed that symptoms are generated by the body's own response to factors operating upon it. By imitating the distorted function, the homoeopathic treatment of opposing like with like makes it possible for the organism to cease its deranged operation. An inflammatory condition will be treated, for example, by an inflammatory substance. Which inflammatory substance will be decided upon the basis of the patient profile. All the remedies consist of minute traces of the active agent to be taken in granule form on an empty stomach. Before any homoeopathic treatment the patient must renounce all toxins, including coffee, tea, alcohol and nicotine. A homoeopathic practitioner who does not insist upon this as a condition of prescribing is wasting his patient's time and money. At first the remedy may cause the symptoms to worsen, in which case it is the right remedy. As the symptoms disappear, the remedy should be taken in smaller and smaller quantities until it is discontinued altogether. The effectiveness of homoeopathic prescribing may be no more than a combination of detoxification and the placebo effect; however, I have found homoeopathic remedies effective for treating chronic disorders in animals, when neither needed to be taken into account.

In one Finnish study doctors found that ginseng 'helped dry vagina, hot flushes, sweats, tension, anxiety and palpitations', according to Patsy Westcott, whose *Alternative Health Care for Women* devotes two and a half pages out of more than 170 to the menopause. Ginseng is the most widely used of all medicinal herbs. Its botanical name, *Panax*, comes from the same Greek root as the word 'panacea', meaning universal remedy. The Chinese name transliterated as ginseng comes from words meaning 'shaped like a man', referring to the root, which has a thick trunk with limb-like lesser roots attached. There are in fact various varieties of ginseng: *Panax pseudoginseng*, which is native to damp, cool woodland in Manchuria and Korea, *Panax quinquefolium* or American ginseng, *Panax fruticosum*, used as a food and a medicine in some parts of Polynesia, and Siberian ginseng, *Eleutherococcus senticosus*. The most important of these is *Panax pseudoginseng*, which comes in various commercial grades, the most valuable being Red Korean ginseng. Centuries of collecting mean that ginseng is rarely found in the wild in China and Korea, where commercial cultivation of the root, which takes nine years to mature, is undertaken on an increasing scale and carefully controlled by the government. The virtues so long extolled by Oriental pharmacists have now been recognized by western pharmacognosy, which has coined a new word, 'adaptogen', to explain the combination of tranquillizing and energizing functions of ginseng. Ginseng root contains

Volatile oils, comprising sapogenin and panacen (stimulating the central nervous system); a saponin, panaxin; panax acid; ginsenin (with hypoglycaemic activity); a glycoside, panaquilon (acting as a vasoconstrictive stimulant); ginsennosides; phytosterols; hormones; vitamins B1 and B2; mucilage; several other substances; all combining to produce a complex total effect. (Stuart)

As their names indicate, most of these constituents are found in no other plants. As an adaptogen ginseng is particularly indicated as a therapy in times of exceptional somatic stress, and therefore in the peri-menopause. The difficulty for the woman treating herself with ginseng is to understand how much she needs to take and in what form. The drug is available in a bewildering variety of expensive commercial preparations, all of which make different and conflicting claims for the effectiveness and suitability of their own mode of administration. For women who are feeling agitated rather than listless, ginseng is not the drug of choice.

The first person to use hypnosis in treating the sick was Franz Anton Mesmer. He was trained as a philosopher, and graduated MD from Vienna in 1766 with a treatise on the influence of heavenly bodies upon human health. He followed the English physician Richard Mead in describing the influence that the sun and moon appeared to exert as 'animal gravitation'. His first experiments consisted of placing magnets on the affected parts; when he found he could obtain the same astonishing results with his hands he coined the term 'animal magnetism' to explain the mechanism. When his colleagues in Vienna rejected him, he took his discoveries and his practice to Paris, where he elaborated his theories and his treatments. Patients sat in a darkened room, and to the strains of soft music were connected up to an enormous tub of magnetic fluid by iron branches passing through its perforated lid; the aim was to induce a trance-like state that would in turn lead to healing convulsions. When he set up a Society of Harmony to train other practitioners, the French medical establishment demanded an investigation of his claims, which dismissed the very idea of magnetic fluids in the body. None could deny the effectiveness of his treatments; eventually it was understood, but not by Mesmer, that hypnosis worked through the mind and not through bodily fluids.

Hypnosis is still used, not only for mental disorders but in the treatment of complex physical symptoms, including climacteric syndrome. It might be possible to stimulate the production of oestrone from adrenostenedione by hypnosis. The marked placebo effect in HRT trials would seem to indicate that removal of the fear of being without oestrogen, of 'not being a woman any more', by hypnosis, would have a marked effect upon the patient's subjective impression of well-being and this in turn would stimulate her internal secretions. Dr Caroline M. Shreeve, author of *Overcoming the Menopause Naturally*, would recommend that the woman with sexual difficulties at menopause

. . . seek out a hypnotherapist. Stress reactions and anxiety, coupled with an inability to relax, lie at the heart of very many psychological disturbances, phobias and anxieties that arise in women in their forties and fifties . . . Hypnotherapists are qualified to deal with depression and anxiety, phobic fears, unwanted habits such as drinking problems, smoking and nail-biting, compulsive activities such as having to repeat an action several times to release worry, and psychosomatic illnesses . . . (91)

Though Dr Shreeve is herself a hypnotherapist, she gives rather more importance to the process of auto-hypnosis, as described by a fifty-three-year-old widow (66). The sufferer hypnotizes herself by, after bathing, relaxing in a dimly lit room and concentrating on a candle-flame, counting backwards to ten, telling herself that she is going further and further into trance. When she is in a trance and can see herself in her mind's eye, she tells herself: 'I am cool and calm. My memory is getting better and better. I feel happy, serene and relaxed' and she believes herself. The key it seems is relaxation, which may be achieved not only by hypnosis or autohypnosis but by 'autogenic training', in which the subject is taught first how to stretch all her muscles, and then let them go limp, until she is completely floppy and concentrating on the physical process of breathing, when she is to visualize individual parts of her body and tell herself how they feel, so that she experiences them that way. Because the technique reduces tension, Dr Shreeve's reporter, a fifty-two-year-old unmarried school-teacher, had hot flushes much less often and dealt with them by auto-suggestion.

The London Centre for Autogenic Training mentions a number of stress-related disorders for which autogenics has been found helpful. They include: 'Tiredness, insomnia, anxiety, examination nerves, circulatory problems including stress-related heart disorders, high blood pressure, migraine ... being overweight, nervous sweating, alcohol and tobacco problems, feelings of depression, inferiority, tension and hostility. Gynaecological problems, including pre-menstrual tension and menopausal symptoms, and dependence upon anti-depressants, tranquillizers, sleeping tablets, blood pressure drugs and other types of medication.' (60)

Other ways of exerting mind over matter include yoga, meditation transcendental and otherwise, and bio-feedback. One thing is common to all of them; if they are to work the woman herself must make a positive commitment to them. The methods simply systematize the woman's own attempt to take control of the situation and herself: all are different ways of doing the same thing, examples not of right and wrong therapies, effective and ineffective, but of the different strokes natural to different folks. Women who are unable to 'discipline themselves' in the matter of alcohol, nicotine, caffeine or food abuse find it easy once they have made an investment of time and mental energy in a system of self-regulation. Instead of saying no to a host of compulsive behaviours, they are saying yes to a new idea of self. They are born again without religion. Traditionally, of course, women past their childbearing were born again within religion; they fasted and meditated and prayed to something outside themselves, but when they did it wholeheartedly the result in terms of tranquillity and detachment was the same.

Therapies which require the woman to submit to another person's control, allow herself to be put into trance, or needles to pierce her flesh, or pressure to be placed upon her feet, her ear lobes, her acupuncture points, or her joints to be manipulated or her body to be anointed with aromatic oils, will not perform the function of persuading her that the locus of control is within herself which, psychologists tell us, is essential to well-being. The climacteric is the time of taking control; part of the shock of the climacteric is the cold water effect of discovering that one has no choice but to do so. Having professional alternative therapists work upon one's body can be very pleasant; the uncaressed woman may well feel invigorated after her skin has been stroked and gently pummelled. If the treatment has cost a good deal of money the woman has an interest in making it work. If the woman has no money she will not be able to afford hours of massage or acupuncture or psychotherapy, no matter how much she would like it.

The best way to approach the climacteric is to be in shape. At this time of life food needs are declining sharply. The menopausal woman should cut down her total food intake, and avoid protein and cholesterol. Discomfort at night can be eased to some extent by common-sense measures like eating less at the evening meal. A spoonful of honey at bedtime can help to raise night blood-sugar levels and avoid waking in fright. The menopausal woman should also avoid her favourite drugs, be they coffee, tea, chocolate or gin, all of which add to the chemical uproar in her body.

Alcohol is often attractive, because of the momentary enlivening-cum-sedative effect, but its eventual effect is exhausting. My own belief is that alcohol burns up the little oestrogen the fifty-year-old woman has at her disposal and adds to her general malaise. Certainly the woman who routinely drinks at suppertime is much more likely to wake with a pounding heart and drenched with sweat when the alcoholic effect has burned off. Allopathic doctors are utterly incurious about the bad health practices of their patients, especially where alcohol is involved. They do not ask what a patient's daily intake is, nor do they insist as a condition of giving treatment that alcohol use be discontinued. This may be taken as evidence of the extraordinary power and influence of the liquor lobby, which has penetrated so far into our culture that hotels are allowed to use the money you have paid for your bed to buy small bottles of brandy to leave on your pillow. The woman who drinks the 'free' brandy is unwise, to say the least. Very little of the research into menopause evaluates the cumulative effect of bad habits like smoking, alcohol consumption or continual coffee- or tea-drinking on the successful negotiation of the menopause rapids.

Since the beginning of medicine men and women have been in search of the fountain of eternal youth. Though the classic comedies of Greece and Rome provide us with examples of the decayed beauty duped into believing that she has held age at bay by the flatteries and manipulations of an adroit quack, most modern rejuvenation therapy was devised by men for men. One of the advantages of eternal youth, after all, is that it enables the successful senior male to enjoy all the young females who fall to his lot. Historically, many of the seekers after eternal youth were convinced that they could steal youth from another living creature by destroying it and absorbing some part of its living body. Stories abound of despots who had young virgins killed in order that they might stay young by drinking or bathing in their blood. Others merely inhaled the breath of young girls or sucked milk from their breasts. Murder and cannibalism are not within the range of privileges allotted to civilized man; the later purveyors of eternal youth plundered non-human species. Hindu rajahs afflicted with torpor and general debility ate the testicles of tigers. From 1889 when Professor Charles Brown-Séquard, who was seventy-two years old, injected himself with an extract of animal testes and proclaimed himself rejuvenated, the emphasis has been upon virility. Brown-Séquard was followed by Arnold Lorant, author of *Old Age Deferred*. Serge Voronoff transplanted hundreds of glands from the testicles of chimpanzees, popularly known as 'monkey glands', into the scrota of human males. Alexis Carrel, who kept a chicken heart alive and growing for nearly thirty years, believed that 'man' wore out prematurely because of insecurity, overwork and an inappropriate nutrition. Ilya Metchnikoff believed that ageing was caused by the ravages of intestinal bacteria and recommended daily ingestion of yoghurt to neutralize them, encouraged perhaps by the extraordinary longevity of Georgian peasants who

eat yoghurt every day. Alexander Bogolometz, who is believed to
have injected Stalin with his elixir, antireticulocytotoxic serum, in
attempt to prolong his effective life, held that

A man of sixty or seventy is still young. He has then lived only half of
his natural life. Old age can be treated just as any other illness because
what we are accustomed to regard as old age is actually an abnormal,
premature phenomenon. (Hannon, 50)

The most successful elixir of youth was the saline solution of
fresh cells from the organs of lamb foetuses which was injected
into degenerating tissues in what was known as Niehans's cellular
therapy. The average age of Niehans's patients was forty-five. In
his view men began to age at sixty when glandular secretions
began to fail; women's biological age was determined by
menopause ten years or more earlier. Evidently Niehans did not
consider that cellular therapy could keep the ovaries from senes-
cing. Niehans treated thousands of powerful men and a few women,
among them Gloria Swanson, Queen Victoria Eugenia of Spain,
Marlene Dietrich, the Gish Sisters, Hedda Hopper and Ann Miller.
  Women are ill-represented among the clientele of the youth
doctors; generally the youth doctor assumed that while the ageing
man wished to retain sexual potency, the ageing female wished to
retain her attractiveness. According to a *Daily Express* article by
Jean Soward, Dr Peter M. Stephan

suggested that, ideally, a woman should begin injections at about age 30,
then with further injections every five years, keep at her peak throughout
life . . . 'I don't promise she will not age,' Stephan was quoted, 'but she
will age well and comparatively slowly . . . She will most likely look
anything from ten to fifteen years younger than she is all her life.'
(Hannon, 106)

According to Soward, with Stephan's version of the Niehans
therapy, which he called 'Therapeutic Immunology', memory
improves, tiredness vanishes, skin, hair and nails improve, muscles
refirm, lines fade and face sags less and less. In 1980, David

Abbott, the Wendy Cooper of Therapeutic Immunology, wrote his own version of *No Change*, calling it *New Life for Old*. He included case histories, some of which sound as if they might have come out of Ms Cooper's post-bag. Patient B 'female' first approached Stephan when she was forty-five; he diagnosed 'total exhaustion' and treated her with extracts of various animal tissues after which she announced:

> The whole success and development of my life has been made possible by the cell treatment and a great skill and knowledge which [*sic*] [Peter Stephan and his father] applied it. I live an 18 hour day to the full and have my health, vitality and looks that reflect both. (Abbott, 126–7)

Abbott was convinced that Therapeutic Immunology was about to be adopted on a national scale. Stephan stood at the crossroads; he awaited only the indoctrination of all the GPs and the education of secondary school students in the necessary ancillary techniques to sweep aside all other systems of medication and confer upon mankind 'the secret of eternal youth'.

Royal jelly, another of the elixirs of youth, has likewise survived discreditment. Though it was proved by the AMA to contain no more than vitamins of the B group, and US shipments of royal jelly were impounded in 1962, it is still to be found, and at a high price, on the shelves of health food shops. Individuals can be found who 'swear by it'. When Dr Ana Aslan, who combated ageing with H3 or 'Gerovital', which was simply procaine hydrochloride, visited England in 1959 this therapy too was discredited, though Dr Aslan too had patients who swore that they felt much younger and healthier than before they took her elixir. When the first hormone replacers began their careers they were anxious to dissociate themselves from the pedlars of rejuvenation, but the planeloads of women who arrived from all over the world at the Atlanta clinic of Robert Greenblatt in the early seventies came with the same suggestibility that worked so well for Stephan, Aslan and the royal jelly industry.

The term 'aromatherapy' was invented by René Maurice Gattefosse in 1928; the techniques were further developed by Dr Jean Valnet, who used essential oils from plants first to treat severe burns and battle injuries and then in psychiatric practice, and founded the Société Française de Phytothérapie et d'Aromathérapie. Like virtually all alternative medical systems, aromatherapy claims to treat the whole person, rather than an afflicted part; illness is seen as an imbalance of the energies in the body which can be rebalanced by the absorption of selected volatile oils distilled from plants, either through direct application to the skin, by massage or hot and cold compresses, in creams, lotions or aromatic waters, or as baths. Nevertheless, *Aromatherapy: An A – Z* by Patricia Davis, Principal of the London School of Aromatherapy and one of the founders of the International Federation of Aromatherapists, does not at all illustrate the idea that the absorption of the volatile elements in the oil of plants acts upon the whole organism. The patient is divided up into parts and encouraged to medicate herself using methods familiar from Queen Philippa's herbal; indeed, Davis claims that aromatherapy has been in use for 4,000 years. Human beings have deliberately inhaled pleasant and unpleasant scents for longer than that and have been sensible of effects varying from nausea to drowsiness. Under 'Menopause' Davis describes a treatment which is not so much aromatherapeutic as eclectic:

Every woman's experience is different, and the aromatherapist needs to take this into account when considering treatment. Many of the essential oils which help with menstrual irregularities earlier in life can be used to minimize the physical problems. In particular, Geranium which is a hormonal balancer and Rose, which tones and cleanses the uterus and helps to regulate the menstrual cycle. Camomile is another oil which is often found helpful, being gently calming, soothing and anti-depressant. All the anti-depressant oils, such as Bergamot, Clary Sage, Jasmine, Lavender, Neroli, Sandalwood and Ylang Ylang can be helpful.

Many women at this time feel that their femininity is fading, and Rose, again, can help them to feel feminine, nurtured and desirable. (222–3)

Queen Philippa would have been surprised to learn that attar of roses 'has a powerful effect upon the uterus', 'cleansing, purifying, regulating and tonic', invaluable for women 'who have menstrual irregularities or are tense, depressed and sad' (290). The best is Bulgarian or French, being obtained by the enfleurage method in which rose petals are laid on fat spread on sheets of glass which are stacked in wooden frames so that the oil is gently squeezed out into the fat. Each day the petals are renewed until the fat can absorb no more. Then the fat is shaken in alcohol to separate out the essential oil. It is tempting to consider whether the efficacy of attar of roses is not directly related to its costliness, which acts as an objective indicator of the user's worth to herself and others, not least the aromatherapist who is charging her for all this tender loving care. An easier way to extract oil from one's own roses is to spread the petals on muslin impregnated with refined olive oil laid on glass and stacked, changing the petals each day. After three weeks you should be able to press out or distil a usable body oil. Any roses of the Gallica, Damascena or Centifolia group can be used.

By geranium, Davis means *Pelargonium odoratissimum* which is sometimes used in men's perfumes and has no medical application outside aromatherapy. Davis claims that Culpeper describes this plant as under the dominion of Venus, which she takes to mean that it has some special affinity to the female organs of generation. In fact, Culpeper does not describe *Pelargonium odoratissimum* at all. He describes two of the geranium family, herb Robert and cranesbill, neither of which has or had any application in female problems.

Of the anti-depressant oils, most have no medical application outside aromatherapy. Bergamot has no connection with the plant English gardeners call by that name, being instead the cold-pressed oil of the rind of *Citrus bergamia* from Sicily. Clary sage is *Salvia sclarea*, which has been used to scent wine for hundreds of years. Elsewhere Davis claims that oil of jasmine is 'a valuable uterotonic', an effect not noticed anywhere but in the literature of aromatherapy; if it is, its usefulness when the uterus is in the involutional phase must be questioned. Neroli is the oil of Seville oranges, and has presumably a similarly uplifting effect to bergamot. Ylang ylang is the oil of *Cananga odorata*, an Asian tree.

However, aromatherapy does not consist entirely of overwhelming the patient with smells. Davis's entry on menopause goes further:

Supplements of Evening Primrose oil and the whole spectrum of vitamins, with emphasis on the B group, as well as minerals and trace elements, become even more important at this stage in life. Calcium supplementation is advisable, because as the production of oestrogen decreases, the bones may become more brittle . . . Fennel is a plant which contains plant oestrogens, so fennel tea is a valuable drink. (223)

Under the heading 'Fennel', Davis makes extraordinary claims for this common herb:

Fennel is one of the plants that has been known for thousands of years for its effects on the female reproductive system. It now seems probable that this is due to a plant hormone – a form of oestrogen – in the structure. It can help to regularize the menstrual cycle . . . It is useful at the menopause in reducing the unpleasant symptoms caused by wildly fluctuating hormone levels, and it stimulates the production of oestrogen by the adrenal glands after the ovaries have stopped functioning. Oestrogen is needed by everyone, both men and women, to maintain muscle tone, elasticity of the skin and connective tissue, a healthy circulation and strong bones; so maintaining the supply can postpone some of the degenerative effects of aging. (131–2)

If Davis means *Foeniculum vulgare*, its known constituents do not appear to include a 'plant oestrogen'; the constituents of the seed are *d*-pinene, camphene, *d-alpha*-phellandrene, dipentine, 50–65 per cent anethole; fenchone, methyl chavicol, adehydes, anisic acid and sometimes 1, 3-dimethyl butadiene. In cultivation the character of fennel can alter very much; the swollen base that we eat blanched or otherwise as *finocchio* is very different from the dried flower used as a flavouring and different again from the dried twigs used to flavour grilled fish. What parts of the plant dried or fresh are to be used for the 'tea' Davis describes and how the 'plant . . . oestrogen' survives this treatment are nowhere described.

Valuable steroids have been found in plants; the sex steroids used in contraception are extracted from Mexican yams of the dioscurea family. Agave, sarsaparilla, some of the *solanum* family, and soy-bean all contain plant steroids or phytosterols. Davis may have confused fennel with fenugreek, *Trigonella foenum-graecum*, which is sometimes called *Foeniculum graecum* (Ross and Brain, 1977, 150–58). Fenugreek, which is grown as a forage crop, and the seeds and leaves of which are used in cooking, is an important source of steroids; it is also the 'fenecrick' of Mary Fairfax's bath for melancholy.

Aromatherapy, like other forms of alternative medicine, claims effectiveness only on the condition that the patient reform her diet, exclude toxins, such as tea, coffee, tobacco and alcohol, and take adequate exercise. If these conditions are fulfilled, no further therapy may be necessary; if in addition the patient takes vitamins and herbal diuretics and carminatives, the contribution of aromatherapy to the improvement in her condition is impossible to assess.

Despite such caveats, it is obvious that aromas do exert powerful immediate effects on living organisms, whether to attract or repel them. Nasal receptors communicate rapidly and forcefully with the brain. In the 1960s, when Ivan Popov, the medical adventurer who first introduced placenta and embryo extracts into cosmetics, was working for the French scent manufacturer Anton Chiris, he drew out a chart of 400 aromatics, assigning to them eight basic characters: fresh, stimulant, exaltant, erogenous, heavy, narcotic, tranquillizing, anti-erogenous. When Patrick McGrady interviewed him for his book *The Youth Doctors*, Popov was sure that

if anything is going to revolutionize the field of rejuvenation in the next few years . . . it's going to be aromatics (especially stimulant and tranquillizing aromatics). Alone, they have incredible properties. Used in conjunction with other treatments, they often possess a powerful synergism, greatly accelerating and augmenting the regular beneficial effects. Moreover, their application is utterly simple. (McGrady, 179)

Popov was also interested in reflexotherapy.

[Reflexotherapy] was much talked about during the inter-war period. But it was dropped since so much nonsense was written about it. Reflexotherapy has to do with simply smelling the aromatics. Through action of certain extremities of the central nervous system they can have a direct effect on the brain. It is now being studied in the Paris Medical School. They are burning certain parts of the nasal mucosis and getting effect elsewhere in the body. But this is too brutal and not natural. They cured many illnesses, including certain cases of paralysis. They affected hormonal disturbances. (179)

Rather than reflexotherapy, Patricia Davis chooses twenty years later to discuss reflexology, in which pressure is applied manually or with a special vibrating device to selected points on the feet in order to produce reactions in the rest of the body (P. Davis, 1988, 284). A spot under the instep is associated with the adrenal glands; and the uterus is reflected in two, one just behind the heel and another six inches or so higher on the leg. According to Westcott (154), foot massage is particularly useful in problems of menopause.

The idea that volatile substances acting on the extremely sensitive nose might affect the brain, and enter the bloodstream by inhalation and through the skin, is not in itself improbable. The idea that the foot is connected by mysterious sympathies to every organ in the body is more difficult to credit, especially when we are also told by the acupuncturists that the organs are connected by meridians conducting energy through the length of the body, or the ear or the hand. The justifications of treating one part of the body by inflicting pain on another sound no more convincing than the notion of counter-irritation that justified some of the most painful therapies of the eighteenth century. When we find electric currents being passed through acupuncture needles in order to stimulate the flow of endorphins, we might call to mind all the other attempts to affect disease processes in the body by sending electric currents through it.

The woman seeking a remedy for what ails her will find in the old herbals many treatments for insomnia, flushing, nervousness, rumbling guts, lethargy, depression, bloating, and the like. There is no reason why she should not try her own combinations and her own modes of administration, bearing in mind that herbal substances are anything but harmless. Agnus castus, for example, is also called wild pepper, and can scorch the throat if taken in infusion. Nightshade (*Solanum dulcamara*), used for treating night sweats, and henbane are too poisonous for internal use in any form. Oil of henbane or a poultice of fresh leaves is valuable in treating joint pain; women wanting to try henbane for menopausal distress might like to experiment with external plasters, or Andrew Boorde's 'dormitary' which I take to be an impregnated compress of fresh extract. Otherwise minute quantities of henbane tincture are still used in homoeopathic prescribing.

An easy and pleasant way for a woman to avail herself of the relaxing effects of the volatile oil contained in the female strobilus of hops is to collect the hops from the hedgerows in autumn, dry the seedheads (not in sunlight) and stuff a small pillow with them, so that during spells of insomnia she can rest her cheek upon it and inhale the soothing scent without having to leave her bed or disturb others. Such a sleep cushion should consist of an inner butter-muslin bag of herbs and a pillow-case of fine lawn, which can be easily laundered. The ladies of Queen Elizabeth's bedchamber strewed it with meadowsweet (*Melilotus officinalis*) by her order; an alternative to green stains on the carpet could be a few sprigs of this fresh herb or any other of the fragrant soporifics in a variant of the sleep cushion. Another way to use herbal sedatives is to add a few drops of the essential oil to a bedtime bath and inhale the active constituents that way.

Most dried herbs sold in commerce are not only old and valueless, but can be contaminated by the presence of other material and may not correspond at all to the label. The usual quality controls do not apply to herbal preparations, which are often costly. Preparations of fresh material are not only more reliable, but are usually very much more effective and should be used in much smaller quantities. Juice expressed from the fresh plant ferments very quickly and may become dangerous, while refrigeration may destroy its effectiveness. All the traditional remedies are slow-working and need time to exercise their effect. When collecting fresh material it is important to consider whether it is affected by herbicides or other poisons, such as lead from vehicle exhausts. In some circumstances, for example if they are grown in greenhouses, overfed and overwatered, herbs may have grown lax and weak and lack the properties they develop in the right cultural conditions.

The naturopathy of old wives cannot be approached like the modern standardized commercial pharmacopoeia. It is pointless to set off to the health food shop to buy remedies that have in the past been associated with various kinds of distress, imagining that they can be taken like aspirin. Ideally the sufferer should collect her own plant material, carefully following any indication she can find of the part of the plant that should be used, the time it should be collected, and the way it should be treated. Fresh plant material can be prepared in infusion or decoction, macerated and steeped in oil or white wine, or carefully dried away from sunlight. Some valuable plants, like rocket and watercress, which both contain calcium, should be eaten raw. There are two good ways to get to know how plants behave and what they are likely to be good for; one is to study them in their natural habitat, the other is to grow them. Walking or working among living plants is very much the best way of absorbing their active constituents, which rub off on skin and arise from bruised leaves. If you are scrambling across a mountainside with a swag of fresh herb on your back, you are absorbing its volatile elements into a well-oxygenated bloodstream in ways that cannot be duplicated on the therapist's couch or in your bathroom.

The efficiency of absorption of therapeutic substances into the bloodstream by the nasal route has probably not received sufficient attention. Plant oestrogens are known to exert a powerful influence upon animal behaviour; the oestrus of many species is triggered by the presence of plant oestrogens in pasture in springtime, probably not by ingestion but by inhalation. Human beings seem to be like other species in this respect – 'in the spring a young man's fancy lightly turns to thoughts of love', etc. Most people feel exhilarated in springtime whether the sun is shining or not. Some women have noticed that even if they are having a majority of anovulatory cycles they will ovulate in spring. Our receptors for phytosterols, if they do act upon the human organism, are most likely in the nose or the upper respiratory tract. We are unlikely to be able to devise a mode of administration of any derivative of phytosterols which does not offer the same problems of overdosing and inappropriate biological pathways that we find in our use of equine steroids.

Millions of women between the ages of forty-five and fifty-five discover gardening. Other people imagine that this is because they have nothing else to do. In fact there is always something else to do, as every woman who gardens knows. The time spent in the garden is time stolen from some other less rewarding task. Gardening cannot be recommended as good exercise, because too much time is spent virtually motionless and in awkward positions, while muscles chill and bones seize up, and feet get colder and colder, even if they are not wet. Though low back pain and gardening go together, gardeners feel very much better for gardening, back pain and all. The effect is so like the 'mental tonic' effect of HRT that we may be justified in suspecting that there are volatile oestrogens in living plants that do not survive in treated plant material.

When she was fifty-seven, sophisticated, intensely gregarious Lady Mary Wortley Montagu astonished her friends and family by turning gardener. She wrote to her daughter in 1748:

I have been this six weeks, and still am, at my Dairy house, which joins to my Garden . . . which is my greatest amusement . . . It is on a Bank forming a kind of Peninsula rais'd from the River Oglio 50 foot, to which you may descend by easy stairs cut in the Turf . . . My garden was a plain Vineyard when it came into my hands not two year ago, and it is with a small expence turn'd into a Garden that (apart from the advantage of the climate) I like better than that of Kensington. The Italian Vineyards are . . . planted . . . in clumps fasten'd to Trees planted in equal Ranks (commonly fruit Trees) and continu'd in festoons from one to another, which I have turn'd into cover'd Gallerys of shade, that I can walk in the heat without being incommoded by it. I have made a dineing room of Verdure, capable of holding a Table of 20 Covers . . . it is far from large but so prettily dispos'd (thô I say it) that I never saw a more agreable rustic Garden, abounding with all sorts of Fruit . . . I beleive my Description gives you but an imperfect Idea of my Garden. (II, 402–4)

Two weeks later she wrote again:

I am realy as fond of my Garden as a young Author of his first play when it has been well receiv'd by the Town, and can no more forbear teizing my Acquaintance for their aprobation . . . I must tell you I have made 2 little Terrasses, rais'd 12 steps each, at the end of my great walk . . . I have mix'd in my espaliers as many Rose and jessamin Trees as I can cram in, and in the square design'd for the use of the Kitchin have avoided puting anything disagreable either to sight or smell having another Garden below for Cabbage, Onions, Garlick. All the walks are garnish'd with beds of Flowers, beside the parterres which are for a more distinguish'd sort . . . Gardening is certainly the next amusement to Reading . . . (II, 407–8)

With the letter she sent her daughter a little plan showing her plot divided by covered walks and her dining arbour with a cupola above it. She may not have known it, but her wobbly drawing is on exactly the same plan as the medieval *hortus conclusus* which figured the Garden of Eden. A garden is a kinetic work of art, not an object but a process, open-ended, biodegradable, nurturant, like all women's artistry. A garden is the best alternative therapy.

Misery

The misery of the climacteric comes from two sources, from without and from within. It is less sharply painful than grief and differs from grief in that no mourning will appease it or express it. Misery is the dull pain or dreariness that cannot find relief in tears. Misery is degrading; there is no loftiness or nobility in it. The ageing woman feels misery because she has become in the eyes of the world a 'poor old' someone; the external cause of misery is to be found in the attitudes of others. The internal source is the awareness of the stigma, which persists despite the classic response, the denial that one is a menopausal woman or, worse, an old woman. The only strategy for dealing with stigma is to assert and reassert that one does belong to the stigmatized class, confident that one is so different from the stereotype that the stigma can be clearly seen to be nothing but bigotry.

To call someone, anyone, an 'old woman' is to insult him. It will take a great deal longer to teach the world that 'old is beautiful' than it took to teach people not to use the word 'black' as pejorative. 'Old' is familiar, shabby, belittling. The 'old woman' is the part of ourselves that we must drive out. When Joseph Addison mounted an attack upon what he called 'old Women's Fables' in 1711 in the twelfth number of his new magazine *The Spectator*, he took as his text a quotation from the Roman satirist, Persius: *Veteres avias tibi de pulmone revello*. We must, he argued, 'pull the old woman out of our Hearts (as Persius expresses it . . .)'.

In 1785 William Hayley dedicated *A Philosophical, Historical and*

Moral Essay on Old Maids . . . in Three Volumes to the 'Poet . . . Philosopher and . . . Old Maid', Elizabeth Carter, without her permission. He assumed that everybody, including Miss Carter, would agree that old maids were universally afflicted with 'curiosity, credulity, affectation, envy and ill-nature', only partly counteracted by their potential for 'ingenuity, patience and charity'. Miss Carter illustrated his case by failing to accept the dedication with the 'polite good humour' that he stipulated. She was offended; there was no way the expression 'old maid' could be anything but derogatory. 'Old' plus a female noun, 'old woman', 'old girl', 'old cow', 'old bitch', is always insulting. The insult lies in the combination of the age with the sex; to be called 'old man', 'old boy' or even 'old dog' is not in the least insulting.

We are not here concerned with male anophobia so much as with the anophobia of women themselves, which so complicates their own inescapable ageing. It is understandable, but not therefore forgivable, that young women, whose oppression is often dealt out to them by older women, should react against them with bitterness and ridicule. Schoolteachers, overseers, manageresses, mothers-in-law, social workers, health visitors, all are likely to be older women whom the younger woman perceives as interfering in her life, criticizing her, disapproving of her. It is a permanent aspect of all kinds of oppression among human groups that the oppressed are forced to act out institutionalized oppression and exert pressure on those immediately beneath them in the power structure. The sales manageress who herself was never allowed to sit down never allows a younger saleswoman to sit down, although (because) her own legs and feet are screaming from the pain of such abuse over the years. The younger saleswoman damns her in her heart and aloud. A cruel system is then seen to be personified in the old bitch who notices how long a saleswoman stays off the floor when she goes to the toilet but not how pale and tired she is from trying to keep up with the demands of husband and family. The odd thing of course is that a man could behave in exactly the same way and it would not be so bitterly resented.

Female writers, regardless of their own grey hairs, were quick to root the old woman out of their hearts, and to write as intolerantly of older women as any man. If we scan the works of George Eliot for fifty-year-old female characters, for example, we find very few. There is Adam Bede's mother, Lisbeth, 'an anxious, spare yet vigorous old woman' (54), athough probably not yet fifty, who does nothing but whine and wail. Eliot gives vent to her own rejection of her own ageing in the construction of this character; her identification with a perpetual daughter is repellently clear in the writing: 'The long-lost mother, whose face we begin to see in the glass as our own wrinkles come, once fretted our young souls with her anxious humours and irrational persistence' (56). An older woman's concerns are not concerns but 'humours', and her pressing of her case is not persistence but 'irrational persistence'. All old women are hags; all old hags are batty old hags. Needless to say, Eliot is not interested in Lisbeth, and does not dwell upon the change in her life and character that ensues when her alcoholic husband tumbles into a stream and drowns. One day, perhaps, a woman novelist will write *The Deliverance of Lisbeth Bede*.

Hostility expressed by younger towards older can be found at all levels of female development; *old* is part of practically every insult spoken or thought by a younger woman towards an elder; in the mind of a twelve-year-old a silly bitch is a silly *old* bitch even when she is not yet thirty. Youth in women is prized by men, and therefore, by women themselves; a younger woman is prompted by a thousand cultural goads into thinking of herself as a newer and therefore better model. There is in our throwaway culture no suspicion that an individual might improve with age and accumulate desirable characteristics.

The tradition of ridiculing older women seems neither to surprise nor to infuriate them. They watch without complaining as television commercials show them to be too stupid to understand the instructions on a detergent packet or too bigoted to see that new chemicals might make it possible to wash soiled clothes in cool water. Fifty-year-old women laugh along with everyone else when male comedians guy whiskery-chinned shrieking old bags in ridiculous hats, their bums stuck out in a nanny's stoop and their feet bulging with bunions. They do not see how much of the hatred of Mrs Thatcher derives from the fact that she is old and female, or how much the high-principled rhetoric of the opposition parties makes use of the animus against the aged female.

The creation and imposition of these stereotypes of older women involve the cooperation of women themselves. While there are few women writing television commercials or working as art and campaign directors in the agencies, there is no lack of actresses prepared to caricature themselves and their mothers. In order to popularize new services and new tariffs, British Telecom makes use of a forty-five-year-old Jewish actress to caricature a fifty-five-year-old Jewish mother adept at creating confusion on the telephone. The campaign is funny but, like lots of British humour, it is also sexist, racist and ageist. It goes less than no way towards helping a middle-aged woman feel less inadequate or less marginalized. Such a campaign relies for its acceptability on the fact that no one cares about older women, not even the women themselves.

If the British Telecom campaign relies upon casual contempt for older women, some lager commercials have relied on hatred. The figure of the older woman in the lager-drinking environment is treated with loud derision. She is usually shown in a coven with other witches, gabbling and cackling incomprehensibly. As the male hero of the commercial sips his synthetic lager the eldritch noises retreat in his consciousness and he is set free of malign elderly female influence.

The importance of advertising in our culture can hardly be exaggerated. Market research investigates attitudes and responses in order to establish the imagery that will be effective in presenting products as desirable or indispensable for their target audience. That imagery is based in prejudice and relies on prejudice for its subtext. Advertising cannot but reinforce the prejudices existing in the community. Only the subtlest and most intelligent, and hence the least effective, advertising can buck the system. With the ageing of the population a new rich market exists for new services and new products, retirement homes, pension plans, fiscal services of all kinds, health products, treatments, tourism and so forth; the problem is how to sell them. Old faces, old bodies sell nothing, if only for the reason that most people perceive themselves as essentially younger than they are. A car advertised as specially suitable for a senior citizen would not be bought by senior citizens, none of whom want to be stereotyped in that way. No old person wants to go on a tour that has only old people on it. One rather cunning campaign for an airline showed an old lady having a fantastic knees-up in five exotic locations while her married son and his family worried about whether she was not too frail to make the trip at all. They did not show the old lady hobbling around Hong Kong and Singapore in a drove of dazed blue-rinse widows. The old lady was the embodiment of a fantasy frequently indulged in by older women, for she was the only old lady on the screen, the centre of attention in a younger world, more disarming, cuter and more rewarding than any of the younger women around her.

The woman who aligns herself with old women and objects, on behalf of old women, to the casual abuse of old women, will be told that she is not old. Present company is excluded so that old women in general can be vilified and mocked.

A long tradition associates the climacteric with mental disorder. Dr Ashwell was of the opinion that of the disorders of the menopause, the commonest was 'functional derangement of the brain and nervous system'. The mental aberrations included 'timidity, a dread of serious disease, irritability of temper, a disposition to seclusion, impaired appetite or broken sleep, with physical weakness and inquietude . . . Hysteria, of marked intensity, not infrequently exists, and with two patients formerly under my care, a stranger, seeing the extent of mental aberration, might, without careful investigation, have concluded that they really were insane.' Happily, Ashwell thought they were not, otherwise they might have joined the throngs of women walled up in madhouses, their temporary aberration forever complicated by institutional psychosis. The tendency nowadays is to find that the stress of the climacteric does not cause temporary pschiatric disorder, but rather prompts latent psychiatric disorder to become manifest.

The first psychiatrists included among the psychoses what they called involutional melancholia, which afflicted women of climacteric age and men ten years older.

An involutional psychotic depression is a depressive episode of major proportion occurring for the first time in the involutional ages without a prior history of manic depressive illness . . . The onset is gradual, with a slow build up of hypochondriasis, pessimism and irritability, finally flowering into a full-blown depressive syndrome. The most prominent features are motor agitation and restlessness, a pervading affect of anxiety and apprehension, an exaggerated hypochondriasis (sometimes with bizarre delusions), and occasional paranoid ideation which infrequently dominates. These distinguishing symptoms may be thought of as superimposed on a basic depressive substrate with insomnia, anorexia and weight loss and feelings of guilt and worthlessness. The depressed affect is described by some as shallow as compared with that seen in other depressive patients. Retardation is sometimes described as absent or masked by the agitation. (Rosenthal, 23)

The syndrome was first identified in the fifth edition of Kraepelin's *Psychiatrie*; he recommended bed rest, diet and prevention of suicide.

In the 1920's enthusiastic investigators reported excellent treatment results with whole ovary and corpus luteum extracts, which in later years were shown to be inert. (Rosenthal, 24)

In the 1930s oestrogen was found to work wonders with involutional melancholia, but these results were difficult to repeat and the treatment was as often derided. In 1944 electro-convulsive therapy – shock treatment – was used successfully on women whose melancholy failed to respond to oestrogen. The groups of women studied were all small, there was no double-blind and many of the guinea-pigs had been institutionalized for years.

In 1951, John C. Donovan of the University of Rochester set about identifying a climacteric syndrome by regularly interviewing 110 patients referred to him. He found that more than half of them had many current symptoms that could not be explained by their menopausal status, or had symptoms that varied from visit to visit, or had a past history of similar complaints, or were highly suggestible. After the other cases had been further worked up, they too tended to resolve into the same three categories; if they demanded treatment, Donovan often gave them saline injections, pretending that they were hormone, and the patients all claimed to feel better as a result. Dr Donovan was irresistibly led

to speculation that if a woman has been able to withstand the stress of living without prominently resorting to symptom formation and if the menopause has no catastrophic emotional meaning for her, she will experience the menopause without undue difficulty. (1287)

In 1979 involutional melancholia was deleted from the Diagnostic and Statistical Manual of Mental Disorders, for it had been proved that women of all ages suffered depression with no significant peak in the climacteric (Weissman).

It is no consolation to find that depression at menopause is pretty much like any other depression. In some ways it is helpful to think that a physical process can be blamed for mental phenomena, especially when that process is understood to have a beginning, a middle and an end. If a woman is allowed to think that she is tearful, irrational or aggressive because she is having a bad menopause, she can escape part of the burden of guilt that attaches to such misbehaviour. She 'has not been quite herself' as the expression goes, and she can therefore return to a self unsullied by her temporary aberration. Once the idea gains ground that the sleepless, exhausted, touchy middle-aged woman is so because she is a 'bad coper', she can be pardoned for regarding a future of failing to cope with ever-increasing problems without the least enthusiasm.

Though involutional melancholia proved to be a phantom of theorization founded on anecdote, the basic assumption that psychological upheaval was characteristic of the climacteric was slow to die. Indeed, it cannot be said to be quite dead yet. In 1924, when forty-year-old Helene Deutsch addressed a meeting of psychoanalysts at Würzburg on the subject of the climacteric, the notion of the 'dangerous age' was still current. The paper she gave is the basis of the last chapter in *Psychoanalysis of the Sexual Functions of Women*, published in German by Freud's publishing house in Vienna in 1925.

Woman's last traumatic experience as a sexual being, the menopause, is under the aegis of an incurable narcissist wound. In complete parallel to the physical process, this represents a retrogressive phase in the history of the libido, a regression to abandoned infantile libidinal positions.

The real frustrations of this period in life, which do not run parallel with the disappearance of libidinal needs, create a psychical situation coping with which is a task which makes big psychological demands . . .

At the menopause everything that was granted the female being at puberty is taken back. Simultaneously with the processes of genital retrogression, the beautifying activity of internal glandular secretions ceases, and the secondary sexual characteristics come under the aegis of the loss of femininity.

The libido, now without the possibility of cathexis and with a diminished capacity for sublimation, has to go into reverse and seek out earlier positions, i.e. set out on the path that is familiar to us from the formation of neurotic symptoms. (Deutsch, 1984, 56)

None of this argument is susceptible to proof, nor is any of it logically necessary. It represents a masculine view, of course, being very little more than the systematic application of Freudian theory to an event about which Freud never theorized. The 'complete withdrawal of the libido from the genitals' cannot be shown to be the inevitable consequence of the involution of the uterus or the cessation of ovarian function; the assertion demonstrates a degree of biological determinism that would seem to imply that all adult females who had never had congress with the penis had to be insane. Deutsch places the beginning of the climacterium at age thirty, when

> Though still capable of conception, the woman already feels the threatened devaluation of the genitals as an organ of reproduction, and on top of this there are the external frustrations to which that function is exposed (social difficulties, etc.) . . . the genitals fight to regain their position. It has often been suggested that a purely hormonal process lies behind the pre-climacteric increase in libido . . . (57)

Clitoral masturbation is mobilized again, as the ageing female regresses towards her pre-genital condition, and she becomes sexually rapacious.

> The impulse is provided by the progressive devaluation of the vagina in its significance as the organ of reproduction as well as failure in the outside world resulting from the greater difficulty of object finding, after which an increased libidinal hunger persists in the narcissistic need to be desired and loved. The tragi-comic result is that the older and less attractive she becomes, the greater is her desire to be loved. Under the pressure of failure the vagina gives up the struggle . . .
> The analogy between the beginning of this regression and puberty makes clear to us the psychology of women in the early climacteric, the so-called 'dangerous age'. (57–8)

Given the element of disguised autobiography in this article, it is not irrelevant to ask oneself how much the stereotype of the 'dangerous age' had to do with explaining and containing Deutsch's sexual aberrations in her thirties. It might make more sense to relate a marked increase in sexual interest in women in their late thirties, supposing any such change had ever been observed in any but Deutsch herself, to completed family size and/ or the removal or otherwise of fears of pregnancy. According to Deutsch, in the pre-menopause women who have hitherto coped with frigidity now break down; masculinized women 'fall ill over the femininity complex at menopause'; clitorally centred women suffer castration anxieties. The incest prohibition breaks down and the pre-menopausal woman begins to fantasize about repeating the

Oedipal situation with her son; Deutsch cites three cases in illustration, for as we all know, the reason behind attraction of older adults to younger ones and vice versa is the ubiquitous Oedipus complex.

The reversion of the libido to objects that are subject to the incest prohibition that now sets in as well as the inversion of the psychical life by unconscious fantasies lead to a characteristic personality change as well as numerous organic symptoms that generally have the quality of conversion formations. (59)

It would be interesting to know if Deutsch recognized the 'characteristic personality change' when it started happening to her for, as we have seen, women who have actually experienced menopause do not agree that anything drastic or permanent has happened. Far be it from me to suggest that to proceed from an assumed physical process, described by Deutsch as if it were the disappearance of the genitals, to psychic manifestations and then back to physical manifestations, which are then denied any connection with bodily events, is arbitrary or preposterous. Climacteric distress, according to Deutsch, is caused by unavoidable frustration: the adolescent's 'too early' is neatly balanced by the pre-menopausal woman's 'too late'.

The typical irritability of the unsatisfied, their liability to depression, numerous equivalents of anxiety (giddiness, palpitations, high pulse rates etc.) closely resemble the numerous complaints that appear at puberty . . . Of the numerous organic symptoms such as headaches, neuralgia, vasomotor disturbances, heart sensations, digestive troubles etc., a large number must be regarded as conversion symptoms . . .
The psycho-neurotic events that take place in the phases of the early climacteric . . . come under the heading of hysteria. Later pathological developments come under the pre-genital, that is to say the post-genital heading, i.e. they are obsessional, melancholic, paranoid. (59–60)

Deutsch's conviction that the management of menopause should be the symmetric equivalent of the handling of puberty is supported by a quotation from Professor Wiesel, a Viennese specialist in internal medicine:

It has struck me that the disturbances of the gastro-intestinal tract, for instance, which come to our notice during puberty, also introduce the menopause with extraordinary frequency, with quite similar symptoms in both cases. It can further be observed that in cases in which hyperthyroidism occurs at the age of development and later disappears without appearing again in the course of life, the menopause also begins under the aegis of thyroidism . . . (60)

Nowadays gastro-intestinal disturbances are not included among menopausal symptoms; their survival in this context may reflect the survival of old ideas about hypochondria, which was thought to be caused by windiness in the epigastric region. People with a tendency to irritable bowel will characteristically display stress through bowel disturbance; the stress may be menopausal, while the symptom is chronic or idiopathic. The tenuousness of this relationship has meant that sceptical investigators, like Donovan in 1951, who have deliberately given suffering menopausal women placebos and smugly reported that they appeared to work, have interpreted this as an indication that no 'real' symptoms are experienced at menopause. Professor Wiesel also appears to be identifying 'thyroid storm' as a menopausal symptom, another identification which nowadays no doctor would make.

It is worth returning to the entry on the menopause by E. Borner in the American *Cyclopaedia of Obstetrics, and Gynaecology* (1887) in order to hear the voice of common sense:

The climacteric, or so-called change of life in women, presents, without question, one of the most interesting subjects offered to the physician, and especially to the gynaecologist, in the practice of his profession. The phenomena of this period are so various and changeable, that he must certainly have had a wide experience who has observed and learned to estimate them all. So ill-defined are the boundaries between the physiological and the pathological in this field of study, that it is highly desirable in the interests of our patients of the other sex, that the greatest possible light should be thrown upon this question.

It must be understood that Deutsch was not writing about the significance of menopause in the general population, but of the mechanisms behind symptom formation in the climacteric; however, women will only cope successfully with the menopause if they can maintain 'male-oriented relations to life' or continue 'psychical motherhood in relation to the outside world', i.e. they must either have careers or continue nurturing. Though Deutsch would not have held with the notion of an involutional melancholia as such, she recommended 'an analysis begun just before the menopause' as a precaution against eventual symptom formation. Neither the putative analysts nor the putative patients responded with enthusiasm.

Simone de Beauvoir certainly knew Deutsch's work; it seems not unlikely that Freudian determinism affected her extremely bleak view of her own ageing. De Beauvoir wrote *Force of Circumstance* between June 1960, when she was fifty-two and March 1963. At thirty-nine she had had a rather unsatisfactory affair; at forty-four, when she was already obsessed by the spectre of advancing age, Claude Lanzmann asked her to go out with him. De Beauvoir was so pathetically grateful for this attention that she burst into tears. They began an affair.

Lanzmann's presence beside me freed me from my age. First, it did away with my anxiety attacks. Two or three times he caught me going through one, and he was so alarmed to see me thus shaken that a command was established in every bone and nerve of my body never to yield to them; I found the idea of dragging him already into the horrors of declining age revolting. (De Beauvoir, 1965, 297)

The cause of the anxiety attacks, it would seem, was a phobia, an irrational fear of old age. In *The Second Sex* de Beauvoir prefigured her own condition:

Long before the eventual mutilation, woman is haunted by the horror of growing old ... she has gambled much more heavily than the man on the sexual values she possesses; to hold her husband and assure herself of his protection, it is necessary for her to be attractive, to please ...

What is to become of her when she no longer has any hold on him? This is what she anxiously asks herself, as she helplessly looks on at the degeneration of this fleshly object that she identifies with herself. (1984, 587–8)

When de Beauvoir wrote *The Second Sex* she was forty-one. It seems unlikely that all her love affairs would have ended because her body was ageing, rather than because of growing incompatibility or boredom or dislike. What seems more likely is that de Beauvoir interpreted male loss of interest as evidence of ageing, and internalized the value judgement that she had foisted on to her lover/lovers. It is not intrinsically improbable that her lovers felt unable to reassure her, given the intensity of her anxiety, and unequal to the demands her anxiety made upon their failing sexual prowess. Helene Deutsch would have explained de Beauvoir's phobia as what happens when a successfully masculinized identity is undone by the femininity complex of the pre-menopause, and predicted that an Oedipal affair with a much younger man was on the cards.

De Beauvoir does not show any signs of realization that her view of old age was wildly distorted. She certainly seems not to consider the possibility that living in propinquity with a much younger man is not likely to assist adjustment to one's own ageing. Ten years later the affair had fizzled out and she had settled into a shallow but interminable depression:

I no longer have much desire to go travelling over this earth emptied of its marvels; there is nothing to expect if one does not expect everything . . . To grow old is to set limits on oneself, to shrink. I have fought always not to let them label me; but I have not been able to prevent the years from enmeshing me . . . I have written certain books, not others. At this point, suddenly, I feel strangely disconcerted. I have lived stretched out towards the future, and now I am recapitulating, looking back over the past. It's as though the present somehow got left out . . . once my worktable is left behind, time past closes its ranks behind me . . . suddenly I collide again with my age. (1975, 654)

There is not much point in preserving people to live to be full of years if they are to spend the reclaimed time in futile repining. Simone de Beauvoir is, she tells us repeatedly, an intellectual; notwithstanding, she faces the future as unprovided as any empty-headed beauty queen.

Old age. From a distance you take it to be an institution; but they are all young, these people who suddenly find that they are old. One day I said to myself: 'I'm forty!' By the time I recovered from the shock of that discovery I had reached fifty. The stupor that seized me then has not left me yet . . .

Often in my sleep I dream that in a dream I'm fifty-four, I wake and find I'm only thirty. 'What a terrible night-mare I had!' says the young woman who thinks she's awake . . . (656)

De Beauvoir regards this obsession – she says herself the nightmare recurs 'often' – as no more than reasonable. She is excessively revolted by her own appearance: before the mirror

I often stop, flabbergasted at the sight of this incredible thing that serves me as a face. I understand la Castiglione who had every mirror smashed . . . When I was able to look at my face without displeasure I gave it no thought, it could look after itself . . . I loathe my appearance now: the eyebrows slipping down towards the eyes, the bags underneath, the excessive fullness of the cheeks, and that air of sadness round the mouth that wrinkles always bring . . . when I look, I see my face as it was, attacked by the pox of time for which there is no cure. (656)

This despondency seems to be specifically related to menopause. The conviction that her death has already begun, because it 'haunts' her sleep, is quite irrational. De Beauvoir could have died at any time, and did not in fact die for another twenty years. Though we might imagine that our death comes on stealthily, we have no way of knowing if it is thundering towards us or is still forty years away. Characterizing ageing as dying is the kind of category mistake that a woman as well instructed as de Beauvoir should blush to make. It is ironic that she is unashamed to present herself as a nightmare-ridden narcissistic phobic, but ashamed to offer an explanation in terms of the menopausal syndrome. On the one hand she had everything that any middle-aged woman could ask, health, work, independence, fame and friends; on the other, she had never been a beauty. Perhaps her desolation is the outcome of the impoverishment of existential philosophy itself: she can find no joy in the idea that she is drifting away from an earth whose injustice and misery disgusts her. It is as if she has no interior landscape.

One after another, thread by thread, they have been worn through, the bonds that hold me to this earth, and they are giving way now, or soon will.

Yes, the moment has come to say: Never again! It is not I who am saying goodbye to all those things I once enjoyed, it is they who are leaving me; the mountain paths disdain my feet. Never again shall I collapse, drunk with fatigue, into the smell of hay. (657)

Why ever not? we must ask. There is no lack of fatigue, no lack of hay. There may be no truth in the idea of involutional melancholia, but there does seem to be something radically wrong with fifty-four-year-old Simone de Beauvoir, who has already suffered for ten years or more from anxiety attacks, which she gratuitously identifies as one of the 'horrors of declining age'. If one were to coin a word to describe her state it would be 'anophobia', irrational fear of the old woman. It would seem to be deeply rooted in fear of the mother and rejection of the mothering role, and in the kind of insecurity that requires male conquest as a condition of self-approbation. Her condition is not so different from that of the old concubine in Aphra Behn's *Oronooko*:

This *Onahal*, as I said, was one of the Cast-Mistresses of the old King; and 'twas these (now past their Beauty) that were made Guardians or Governantees to the new and the young ones, and whose Business it was to teach them all those wanton Arts of Love, with which they prevail'd and charm'd heretofore in their turn ... certainly, nothing is more afflicting to a decay'd Beauty, than to behold in itself declining Charms, that were once ador'd; and to find those Caresses paid to new Beauties, to which once she laid Claim; to hear them whisper, as she passes by, that once was a delicate Woman. (Summers, V, 147)

De Beauvoir's self-defeating mental processes, her vivid aware-ness of death, her nightmares and obsessions, are the misery of the climacteric. Like the sweats and the pins and needles, they will recede, but if this brief agony has reminded us of our weaknesses and inadequacies, it should have left us sadder, wiser and more merciful than before. We can no longer permit ourselves to say as de Beauvoir does that

my species is two-thirds composed of worms, too weak ever to rebel, who drag their way from birth to death through a perpetual dusk of despair. (1965, 654)

The healthy, wealthy, literate woman who lives to menopause only to find herself brought low, struggling to get from one day to the next, knows that life is all but too hard for all of us, and hardest for the poor and hungry, who nevertheless create as much joy and beauty as or more than we do. The woman who can write that two-thirds of her species are nothing but worms seems to have lost her bearings; her disillusionment seems to have reached toxic levels.

... that unique sum of things, the experience that I lived with all its order and randomness ... If it had at least enriched the earth; if it had given birth to ... What? A hill? A rocket? But no. Nothing will have taken place, I can still see the edge of hazel trees flurried by the wind and the promises with which I fed my beating heart while I stood gazing at the gold-mine at my feet: a whole life to live. The promises have all been kept. And yet, turning an incredulous gaze towards that young and credulous girl, I realize with stupor how much I was gypped. (658)

So wrote Simone de Beauvoir in 1963 when she was just fifty-five, untroubled by any suspicion that thinking she had come on earth to change it might be considered megalomania, or that mining companies and the military industrial complex utter hills and rockets every other day. No one diddled her; she deluded and diddled herself. Her disappointment with her life is endogenous; it arises in her.

We have to assume that Simone de Beauvoir's attitude to the actual cessation of the menses was more negative than negative, if only because she refuses to mention it. Thirty years later we are told that researchers have charted a gradual change in attitude towards menopause from negative to more positive, which is considered a good and helpful phenomenon. In so far as women's anxiety about menopause may be lessened by the inculcation of less negative notions perhaps it is, but if the net effect is to lessen the already scant sympathy that others feel for the woman struggling with menopause the change in attitudes can only be a bad thing. Studies of attitude to menopause are misleading, however. In 1963, Neugarten and Kraines devised an ATM (attitudes towards menopause) test, which they administered to four groups of women: women in their twenties, women between thirty and forty-four, those from forty-five to fifty-five and those from fifty-six to sixty-five. Attitudes were divided into seven categories: negative affect, post-menopausal recovery, extent of continuity, control of symptoms, psychological change, unpredictability, sexuality. More than half the women in their twenties and the women actually traversing the climacterium thought that menopause was an unpleasant experience, and slightly less than half the others. Two-thirds of the women over forty-five thought that women felt better when the menopause was over, in sharp contrast to younger women, of whom only 19 per cent in their twenties and 27 per cent of the others agreed. Likewise, under the heading of continuity, three-quarters or more of the older women tended to think that menopause did not change a woman in any way, but only half the women in their twenties. If a woman is the sum of her changes it is puzzling to know what they can have made of the question about continuity; older people are not the same as younger people. Life would be very dreary and rather pointless if they were; the question seems to test ego strength rather than 'continuity'. Under control of symptoms was registered the attitude that women who had problems at menopause were those who expected them, and, surprisingly, three-quarters of the older women agreed. When under 'psychological change' we find the example 'women often get self-centred at the menopause', we must wonder how far these notions were prompted; in any event, only half or fewer of the women under fifty-five agreed, and only a third of the older women.

A constant feature of attitudes to menopause is the resentment of the young. Virtually all the studies of attitudes to menopause show that they are more negative among the young (Eisner and Kelly, 1980; Dege and Gretzinger, 1982) than among the middle-aged themselves. The loaded description of menopausal women as 'more self-centred' in the Neugarten and Kraines sample might have been substituted by 'less self-sacrificing', 'more preoccupied', 'less accessible' or 'less predictable' or 'less biddable'. Mothers and wives are, in my experience, seldom self-centred to begin with, especially by comparison with both their husbands and their children. The perception of a less obliging female as more self-centred seems to carry part of the resentment felt by family members if the mothering function ceases to be the focus of a woman's life.

When it comes to having a 'positive image' of the menopause, the mind begins to boggle. It is hard to feel positive about vasomotor disturbance, painful intercourse and ageing; if saying that you reckon you can handle it is regarded as the expression of a positive attitude, the notion of positivity that is being invoked would seem to be paler than pallid. The truth seems to be that the question itself instructs the 'coping' response; women who appear to be coping best may in fact not be facing the situation at all. They may be sparing their partners and family members from facing it too. Though such gallant behaviour will be perceived as positive, it is actually anything but.

Researchers might ask about a woman's attitude to the loss of her reproductive function and be told that it makes no odds at all. If family size was completed years before, even fifteen or twenty years before, and contraception has been a problem ever since, it would be strange if a woman should regret the cessation of ovarian function. If the same woman were to be asked how confident she felt in her power to attract male attention whether in bed with her partner or in the forecourt of the petrol station, the answer might be very different. While she sees men of her age having no difficulty at all attracting the attention of women, and holding it, and flirting as much as they ever did, she knows that she has become invisible, and she is expected to be inaudible. She has a choice, to become the kind of stentorian bully who can be heard apostrophizing saleswomen from the other side of the store, or to fade out of sight and hearing. The combination of ageism and sexism in our society is what makes menopause utterly negative; asking the woman herself whether she shares the negativity is to challenge her own self-esteem, and to call forth the classic response to stigma.

The menopausal woman herself is not likely to be heartened at the conclusion of a survey by the International Health Foundation (AKZO) that Subjective Adaptation (satisfaction with daily life, health, physical appearance and daily tasks and view of the future), Role Identity (dependency on others, identification with traditional female, maternal and sexual roles), Immediate Family Relations and Wider Social Relations *all* deteriorate with age, some with a dip at menopause, some not.

Despite their findings, the authors of the Swiss survey in the discussion section of their report frequently use the term 'menopausal crisis' and it is difficult to concur wholly with their final conclusion, namely that 'it is clear that for many women the menopause is a period of disorientation, physical problems and psychological imbalance' (49). The impact of the menopause per se on most of the psychological and social characteristics of middle aged women in this survey appears to be relatively benign, certainly in comparison with that of chronological age. (Greene, 79)

What this means, of course, is that most of the misery of menopause will not go away, but will steadily, quietly and inexorably worsen. Likewise it seems that loss of interest in sex is not menopause related but age related.

In 1975 C. B. Ballinger undertook a survey of all the women between the ages of forty and fifty-five listed in six general practices in Dundee in order to find out how many of them were suffering any kind of latent or manifest psychiatric illness. As well as a questionnaire about their menstrual cycle and family situation the women were all sent the General Hospital Questionnaire, which lists sixty symptoms and asks respondents to mark which ones they have; a score of eleven identifies a suitable case for treatment. No fewer than 30 per cent of the 539 women who responded were identified as probable psychiatric cases; among women between forty-five and forty-nine the figure was as high as 40 per cent. The case seemed to be proven. In fact it was not, for hot flushes are included on the symptom list, and six items relate to disturbed sleep, which in menopausal women can be caused by vasomotor disturbance. Neither should have been included as a psychological symptom. Ballinger's publications (1975, 1976, 1977) are all based on this study, which, though its flaws have been stringently analysed by J. G. Greene (1984, 55–6, 80–81, etc.), is itself the authority for dozens of articles on the psychotropic effects of HRT.

It is only to be expected that allopathic medicine would place all the emphasis on the biochemical basis for depression in fifty-year-old women. Though we find, as Aylward (1973) found, that menopausal women are low in indoleamines, and in particular tryptophan, we ought perhaps to consider the possibility that these substances are not secreted in sufficient quantity because patients are depressed. Low levels of tryptophan are as likely to be a symptom as a cause. The organism may react to grim and painful conditions by failing to secrete the chemical of joy and serenity. Administration of oestrogens may free bound tryptophan, but given the pronounced placebo effect noticed in all double-blind trials of oestrogens, it is impossible to conclude from that that oestrogen will 'cure' the misery of middle-aged women. It seems equally possible that the display of genuine interest in the middle-aged woman and the expression of concern for her state of mind and health will raise her spirits, and the objective sign of raised spirits will be higher levels of tryptophan. It would seem from the marked placebo effect noticed in studies of menopause that a very little help and support goes a long way with menopausal women.

According to Dr Barbara Evans:

The menopause does not appear to give rise to a specific pattern of psychological symptoms. In relation to the general increase with age of psychiatric illness in women, the effect of the menopause is relatively small, in spite of some conflicting reports. Admissions to mental hospitals increase with age in both sexes, but more steeply in women, with a peak in the climacteric age group, but there is no evidence that the menopause induces psychiatric illness or psychological changes apart from adding to the stress upon a woman already predisposed to anxiety and depression. (55)

Those of us who see that women's lives predispose them to anxiety and depression can see pretty clearly that not only menopause but also ageing can cause both to intensify in mid-life. Sofia Andreyevna Tolstoy was married at eighteen; her husband, the great novelist, was thirty-four. Sofia Andreyevna loved him with the kind of mature, genitally centred passion that Deutsch would have regarded as appropriate; he responded to her intensity and then hated himself for it, not least because he made her pregnant thirteen times. Sofia Andreyevna learned the full extent of his contempt for her when she read his diaries, in which he claimed that he had to get away from her, that a wife like her would drive anyone mad. One of the torments of her life was that her husband showed the diaries to other people. Though he called her his ordeal, he continued to use her body when he felt the need, until the last year of his long life. After these episodes of compulsive sex, he would treat her with even colder contempt than before.

She never gave up her struggle for his love, but he never granted what she yearned for, tenderness, intimacy and respect. The verdict of history is that she was a paranoid, hysterical nightmare who tormented the great man beyond endurance. As he lay dying, she was prevented from being by his side in case she should upset him.

A woman whose ego is under such pitiless onslaught can hardly be expected to deal calmly and quietly with her change of life. By the time of her fiftieth winter on earth in 1895, Countess Tolstoy was in a sorry state. Her last-born child, Ivan, was her joy and consolation, but he was frail and often ill. Tolstoy never took her place by Ivan's bedside for a moment. To her worry and exhaustion was added the stress of the climacteric:

> Something is broken inside me – I ache inside and cannot control myself. (12 January)
> My body has stopped – my body and soul have come to a halt. (14 January)
> I am exhausted by Vanechka's illness and my own situation. I feel weak, and breathless from the slightest exertion. (16–17 January)
> I have never learned to do anything properly! . . . It's fine, 6 below freezing, a moonlit night. But I am still depressed and my soul is asleep. (19 January)
> I am in poor health, constantly bothered by asthma and palpitations. If I walk fast my pulse shoots up in five minutes from 64 to 120. (1 February)
> I am passing through yet another painful period . . . it is so terrible, so difficult, and so clear to me now that my life is going into a decline. I have no desire to live and thoughts of suicide pursue me ever more relentlessly. Save me lord, from such a sin. Today I again tried to leave home; I think I must be ill. I cannot control myself. (21 February)

Demented by 'the old grief of having loved him so much' when he never loved her, she had run off in the snow in her nightclothes and slippers.

> He has killed my very soul. I am already dead . . . Having tortured my soul, he then called in the doctors to examine me . . . so the neurologist

prescribed bromide and the specialist in internal diseases prescribed Vichy water and drops. Then the gynaecologist Snegirev was called in, referred cynically to my 'critical time of life' and prescribed *his* particular medicine. I haven't taken any of it.

On 23 February little Ivan died. Sofia Andreyevna wrote in her diary, 'My God, and I am still alive!' For two years her diary lay untouched. By the time she took up her pen again her condition had changed. She had ceased to menstruate and accepted that she was in the 'critical time of female life'.

. . . today I left the room in which I have slept for 35 years and moved into Masha's old room. I have started to want more privacy, besides it was stiflingly hot in the bedroom and I am drenched in sweat all day as it is. (3 July 1897)

However much my children criticize me, I can never be again as I was. I am worn out, my passionate maternal feelings are exhausted . . . I feel happier with outsiders, I need new, more peaceful and straightforward relationships with people now . . . (23 July)

Needless to say, Tolstoy was bitterly jealous of his subject wife's attempts to find in other relationships the esteem that he withheld. Simone de Beauvoir sees the storminess of their relationship as merely the psychopathology of age; according to her Sofia Andreyevna had 'always hated' sleeping with Tolstoy, for whose contradictory attitudes towards his own sexuality de Beauvoir seems to have considerable sympathy. She notes quite neutrally that Tolstoy 'slept with' his wife on his seventieth birthday (1977, 398), with no sign of awareness of how the old man's cold and selfish lust devastated Sofia Andreyevna. (A better account of the sexual economy of the Tolstoy household can be found in Andrea Dworkin's book, *Intercourse*.)

Dr Evans is principally concerned to make a distinction between the endocrinological and the psychological causes of climacteric depression. As she has seen HRT relieve the symptoms she goes for the endocrinological version, even though the doses used in one of the few trials of oestrogen in cases of depression were up to ten times higher than the doses used for vaginal atrophy and vasomotor disturbance. Interestingly Klaiber, who ran this American experiment, decided that severely depressed women had actually become resistant to oestrogen. We could reverse the order of bio-feedback in the case of mood-regulating hormones as well and argue that angry women will not tolerate their own tryptophan, rather than assuming that they are angry because they do not have enough of it.

It does not do to argue in a world where a woman's only friend and counsellor is her doctor that there may be causes for women's misery that are not endogenous. The doctor must treat the patient as a closed loop system, because the socio-cultural wheels that grind her cannot be moved by medical prescription. The doctor, who cannot operate upon the body politic, can only attempt to adjust the patient to it.

A good deal of the misery of older women is actually associated with menopause, and fades when the stress of the climacteric is past. When Anna Inchbald was forty-five she was well and busy rehearsing her play *Lovers' Vows* in London. She declared herself 'Happy but for a suspicion amounting almost to a certainty of a rapid appearance of age in my face.' A year later she described herself as 'extremely happy but for the still nearer approach of age'. Two years later, in 1801, when she was mourning the death of her 'best friend in the world Mrs Robinson', she made one of the very few references in literature to the menopause as 'the suspicion of never more being as a young woman again', adding that she was 'very happy but for my years'. The next year she declares herself 'very happy but for ill health, ill looks, etc.'. But by 1803, despite leaving her London home for ever and fearing an invasion of the French, she simply described herself as 'very happy'.

Nevertheless, there is an ineluctable social dimension to the dreariness that enwraps some post-menopausal women. Margaret Powell, in *The Treasure Upstairs*, tells us that when she was a door-to-door canvasser she met many women who were pathetically grateful for someone to talk to.

One middle-aged and quite well-to-do widow assured me that she always filled in every form sent to her by the council or the government, 'because,' she said, 'for a brief while it gives me the feeling that I'm alive and my existence is noted somewhere. Otherwise every day is so much like another that I could be in a dream and not in the real world at all.' (104)

When the only person a woman has a right to talk to is her doctor, and only the doctor is obliged to listen, we cannot be surprised that so many women seek consultations, thus putting themselves in mortal danger, for the doctor must prescribe, and nothing a doctor can prescribe will make an empty life worth living. Over-prescription of tranquillizers threatens the health of women of all ages, including women in the climacteric. Over-prescription of tranquillizers is the price we pay for pretending that misery is disease and not an appropriate response to oppressive circumstances. Though there is no psychopathology that arises from the cessation of ovulation and the involution of the uterus, there is a psychopathology that threatens the older woman's mental health. It is a complex of sexism and ageism complicated by greed, intolerance, impatience and callousness. Giving women medicines to help them to deal with it is another case of medicating one person for another's illness.

Grief

'Old woman, why are you crying, it is not allowed here. No one must make any noise. . .' (Aidoo, 30)

One of the most subtle changes during the fifth climacteric is the encroachment on the consciousness of the idea of death and, even less acceptable to most people, the idea of one's own death. Quite suddenly and without warning or deliberation, after fifty years of feeling immortal, we begin to see an end to our journey on earth. Rachel Brooks Gleason, a woman doctor who with her husband ran a hydropathic establishment, used to tell her patients that

The menopause tells us that we are looking toward the sunset. But is there not a brighter morning in that land where there is no night, where no one is sick, none is sad and all are satisfied? (217)

History does not record whether her patients found this observation cheering, or whether they fled howling. Dr Gleason was not terribly sympathetic to women's anxieties; she admitted to wishing that her more anxious patients suffered in reality from the infirmities that they imagined that they suffered from, so that she could send them home to die. Nowadays a therapist who allowed, let alone encouraged, menopausal women to spend any time trying to understand death would be accused of dereliction of duty. The middle-aged woman's new consciousness of the finiteness of the individual life, which involves an awareness of the limitations on what can be accomplished in a single life, is another of her guilty secrets. In consumer society everything may be talked about, the most intimate anatomical and personal matters may be discussed in any company, but not death.

In 1969 Iris Murdoch wrote a strange and interesting novel called *Bruno's Dream*. At its centre is Bruno, an old man who is bedridden, waiting for death. He is a curious figure, with a huge head and withered limbs, who might be thought to resemble one of the spiders that have fascinated him all his life. A spider is not only capable of living for months without nourishment, with only the thinnest flicker of vital force that will nevertheless suffice to launch it into killing mode if prey should come within its reach, in dreams the spider prefigures the womb, and Bruno's is a dream. Though in treating this odd old man whose head is 'a mass of crumpled flesh' as a figure of the womb in process of involution there is a considerable risk of appearing solemnly absurd, and Iris Murdoch would be the first person gently to ridicule any such reading, the novel makes a good deal of sense if we pursue the analogy. Bruno continues to die throughout. His fortune resides in a collection of stamps which is eventually lost. It would be too much perhaps to insinuate that the stamps are like the undeveloped ova, blueprints for something of immense value that can never be built. They are lost, of course, in a flood.

Around Bruno's deathbed revolves a cast of characters who dovetail like a Chinese puzzle: Danby Odell, the womanizer, who married Bruno's daughter, Gwen, who died when she dived into a river, the same river that will flood in the novel, to rescue a child; Miles Greensleave, Bruno's son, who married Parvati (goddess of plenty), who died (pregnant) in a plane crash, and then Diana (goddess of chastity), and Diana's sister, Lisa, the unfulfilled spinster, ex-Poor Clare, actually in love with her sister's husband, together with the low-life trio of Adelaide the Maid, Nigel the Hippy, and his twin brother Will, the unreflecting male animal. Bruno himself had betrayed his intense wife Janie with a prostitute called Maureen, whom he had to give up when his wife discovered the affair by coming across them both in a fitting-room in Harrods. Bruno wants to reconcile himself with his son, Miles, but

GRIEF

the meeting causes only greater bitterness. It also brings Danby into contact with Miles's wife, Diana.

Diana, the calm, the beautiful, the orchestratress of existence, is menopausal, 'nearly fifty' as she says.

She had spent so many years waiting for children and only lately had consciously told herself that the wait was over. She had occupied so many years – how had she occupied them? . . . She still counted herself fortunate. Though lately, perhaps prophetically, collected quietly in the kitchen at night, she had found herself looking a little with new eyes, had felt a vague need for change, had sensed even the possibility of boredom. (90–91)

This is the view from inside of the menopausal woman's bad behaviour, and it is not so very bad after all. Diana begins a *flirt* with Danby, meaning to hold off physical intimacy, but needing the excitement and the confidence that the flirtation gives her. She wants the romance and courtship signified by old-time dance music.

I am middle-aged, thought Diana, looking around the ballroom at the dreamy couples who were so far from young. I belong with these people . . . Had Diana now reached an age where there had to be, at last, one novelty after another? (93)

Two crushing blows knock her once for all out of the game. Her new suitor has barely declared himself before he falls intensely in love with her younger sister, Lisa, and then Diana's husband finds that he is in love with Lisa too. Diana is stripped of everything she has lived for. It is as if she has realized that her lovers are all in love with herself when young, and she is moving inexorably away from them to a realm where they cannot follow.

Because 'April is the cruellest month' the novel is obsessed with barrenness amid the fresh lushness of early spring, the season of narcissi and anemones. Danby courts Lisa, who to other eyes than his is simply 'a gaunt untidy middle-aged schoolmistress', in Brompton Cemetery. Actually she is the angel of death, and the cemetery is a mass of tiny graves like the follicles of the dying ovary.

295

Behind her were the graves of children, tiny pathetic stones half lost in the meadowy vegetation. The silent sleepers made a dome of quietness. (146)

Bruno is a dome, inside a dome, the cage of his bed, a sarcophagus that contains a barely living body. Though it is risky to assume that a writer is not in control of her material, the return of these elements within *Bruno's Dream* suggests something not quite worked out, indeed, something not quite confronted. The contrasting women of the novel are like aspects of the same woman before, after and during her changes, one mourning her never-born children and one her lover and one her youth.

Adelaide the Maid is Danby's housekeeper, and his mistress.

Adelaide, though putting on weight and no longer very young, was really quite beautiful . . . She was heavy about the hips and stomach but her shoulders and breasts were classical. She had a round face and a naturally rosy complexion and a great deal of long hair of a rich brown colour. (Her hair was dyed, only Danby had never realized this.) (20)

Adelaide's reaction to losing Danby to Diana seems accurately pre-menopausal, although she is too young to be described that way.

She had that heavy graceless fat feeling which she identified as the feeling of growing old, the feeling of no return. She had made some sort of life-mistake which meant that everything would grow worse and never better. Was there no action which she could perform which, like the magic ritual in the fairy tale, would reverse it all and suddenly reveal her hidden identity? But she had no hidden identity. (133)

Adelaide is a kind of living proof of those researches that show that uneducated blue-collar women suffer more at menopause than women who have options not connected with sexual and reproductive function. Adelaide cannot cope with Danby's loss of interest. She deliberately does dreadful things, smashes fragile china, steals a valuable stamp, destroys a camera, and then painfully regrets them. She is rescued by Will's constancy; they marry despite everything, though the bride is fearfully flushed and hot and tearful. Adelaide alone proves fruitful. Her husband becomes a knighted actor, and her tall twin sons, Benedick and Mercutio, a Russian expert and a mathematician, respectively. Adelaide's happy ending is Murdoch at her most perverse. It is told out of synch, before we reach the real ending which must be Bruno's death. In Adelaide's case Eros wins and Thanatos is held at bay, but it is Thanatos we are really concerned with. The consignment of Adelaide to life is perfunctory.

Diana knows about her husband's love for Lisa as soon as he does. She tells him, 'things will never be the same again, never, never, never' (174); the whole book cries out that 'the most precious thing is gone, lost forever'. What is lost was not truly valued until it was lost. The bitter pangs of regret that rack the pages are typical of menopausal mourning, but Murdoch does not allow herself to dwell upon the mental state of any single character. We move in and out of the mental states of all the characters in what seems to be an omniscient fashion but, though we see the tears shining on Diana's cheek as she lies rigid in bed alongside her husband, we do not feel them. The experience is held at bay. The book speaks to itself in riddles. Lisa gives Miles up, sentencing him to 'real death' and declares her intention of going to India.

If only they had gone away, thought Diana, I could have survived. Of course it would have been terrible. She tried to imagine the house suddenly empty, deprived of that dear familiar animal presence. They had lived together for so long like animals in a hutch. But all she could feel was the hollow misery of her irrevocably transformed marriage. 'Things will never be the same again, never.' But if they had gone, she thought, then all the energy, all the pride, all the sense of self would have been on the side of survival . . . Every way I lose. She has taken him from me, she has destroyed our married love, and I have no new life, only the dead form of the old life . . . My pain and my bitterness are sealed up inside me forever. I have no source of energy, no growth of being, to enable me to live this hateful role . . . I am humbled by this to the point of annihilation . . . (233)

At this point Diana does not know that Danby too loves her sister. She is told it by Nigel, the *deus ex machina* who when she asks 'what about me?' instructs her:

'That is what they all cry. Relax. Let them walk on you. Send anger and hate away. Love them and let them walk on you. Love Miles, love Danby, love Lisa, love Bruno, love Nigel.' (239)

The doctrine is a hard one, but it is the only one that can help a suffering woman to cope with the death of her womb. Diana must extract her ego from the business of loving; she must rise above the narcissism that is luring her to the quintessentially narcissistic act of self-murder. Nigel takes the sleeping pills out of her handbag and returns them to the place she pinched them from. The black tide of the river rises; Adelaide and Bruno both fall into the water and the stamps are lost. Somehow everyone survives and the story resumes the next spring, in Brompton Cemetery again, where Diana and Miles are walking 'like an old couple'. Suddenly Lisa reappears and offers herself to Danby because she wants all the things she has always denied herself, 'warmth and love, affection, laughter, happiness'. The angel of death is humanized and takes what is on offer, although it is only second best. Diana meanwhile has to contemplate the slow demise of Bruno and grows to love him.

And now, she thought, I have done the most foolish thing of all, in becoming so attached to someone who is dying. Is not this the most pointless of loves? Like loving death itself . . . He could give her nothing in return except pain. And it seemed to her as the days went by and Bruno became weaker and less rational, that she had come to participate in his death, that she was experiencing it too. Diana felt herself growing older and one day when she looked in the glass she saw that she resembled somebody. She resembled Lisa as Lisa used to be. Then she began to notice that everything was looking different. The smarting bitterness was gone. Instead there was a more august and terrible pain than she had ever known before. As she sat day after day holding Bruno's gaunt blotched hand in her own she puzzled over the pain and what it was and where it was, whether in her or in Bruno. (309)

The mourning is not easy, nor is it soon over.

The pain increased until Diana did not even know whether it was pain any more, and she wondered if she would be utterly changed by it or whether she would return to her ordinary being and forget what it had been like in those last days with Bruno. She felt that if she could only remember it she would be changed. But in what way? And what was there to remember? What was there that seemed so important, something she could understand now and which she so much feared to lose? She could not wish to suffer like this throughout the rest of her life. (310)

But eventually her grieving has accomplished its work, and run its course.

Let love like a huge vault open out overhead. The helplessness of human stuff in the grip of death was something which Diana felt in her own body. She lived the reality of death and felt herself made nothing by it and denuded of desire. Yet love still existed and it was the only thing that existed.

The old spotted hand that was holding on to hers relaxed gently at last. (310–11)

A novel is perhaps not the best way to confront the anguish of the middle-aged woman, but it is one way to tease out the elements of the conundrum without appearing to beg for diagnosis, treatment and cure.

For many of our female poets grief was a medium in which they worked all their lives, but even in such cases the grief of the climacteric is distinct, tougher, more grinding, for it is grief that cannot ask or expect to be assuaged. Elizabeth Barrett chose invalidism and reclusiveness until her virgin fastness was invaded by Robert Browning. Their love-story is commonly perceived to be without blemish; in fact a degree of ennui and irritation seems to have crept in before Elizabeth's death at the age of fifty-five. In the volume of poems published the year after her death, there is one that strikes the note of climacteric grief. It is to Robert Browning's credit that he did not attempt to expunge it from the Barrett Browning canon, for it specifically denies the myth that Robert and Elizabeth lived happily ever after.

> You see we're tired, my heart and I.
>   We dealt with books, we trusted men,
>   And in our own blood drenched the pen,
> As if such colours could not fly.
>   We walked too straight for fortune's end,
>   We loved too true to keep a friend;
> At last we're tired, my heart and I.
>
> How tired we feel, my heart and I!
>   We seem of no use in the world;
>   Our fancies hang, grey and uncurled
> About men's eyes indifferently.
>   Our voice which thrilled you so, will let
>   You sleep; our tears are only wet:
> What do we here, my heart and I? . . .
>   (566)

Understandably, such poems do not make a poet's reputation. The celebration of middle-aged dreariness does not have the glamour of blighted love or premature disillusion, but to the middle-aged woman herself it is a comfort, if a cool one, to know that other women have stood on the same bleak promontory and wondered if there was any point in surviving the crossing. Elizabeth seems in fact to have given up, for her health declined rapidly in this period; within a few months of penning these lines she was dead.

Christina Rossetti, who deliberately chose the life of a celibate semi-recluse in preference to the kind of middle-class marriage that was offered to her, who loved in secret and writhed in life-long frustration, expressed the bereavement of the climacteric in typically encoded form:

> Never on this side of the grave again,
>   On this side of the river,

On this side of the garner of the grain,
  Never.

Ever while time flows on and on and on,
  That narrow noiseless river,
Ever while corn bows heavy-headed, wan,
  Ever.

Never despairing, often fainting, rueing,
  But looking back, ah never!
Faint yet pursuing, faint yet still pursuing
  Ever.

(405)

Her brother William was uncomfortable with this kind of writing, which he found harsh and unfeminine. He would have been even more uncomfortable if he had paused to consider the imagery of the ungathered ears of corn and the silent channel beside. Rossetti often thought of herself as a spiritual athlete; the imagery of life as an uphill climb reaches its apogee in another poem of the same period:

From depth to height, from height to loftier height,
  The climber sets his foot and sets his face,
  Tracks lingering sunbeams to their halting-place,
And counts the last pulsations of the light.
Strenuous thro' day and unsurprised by night
  He runs a race with Time and wins the race,
  Emptied and stripped of all save only Grace,
Will, Love, a threefold panoply of might.
Darkness descends for light he toiled to seek:
  He stumbles on the darkened mountain-head,
  Left breathless in the unbreathable thin air,
Made freeman of the living and the dead:–
He wots not he has topped the topmost peak,
  But the returning sun will find him there.

(412)

Now that more and more women are publishing poetry, and more and more of that poetry deals with women's reality rather than parodying the preoccupations of men, we can perhaps expect better insights into the emotional world of the ageing woman than were available to us before. In 1978 the distinguished American poet Linda Pastan published a book of poems called by the name of the last poem in the collection, *The Five Stages of Grief*. On the jacket May Sarton is quoted as saying:

Nothing is here for effect. There is no self-pity, but in this new book she has reached down to a deep layer and is letting the darkness in.

What distinguishes the older woman's grief is precisely this absence of self-pity. Her lament is not about herself, nor is it complaint. It is sterner than either and more austere, repellently so perhaps to the young, who repeatedly fail to understand its 'still, sad music'. The epigraph to the book (from Shakespeare's *Richard II*) could be lettered on the T-shirt of every woman who is looking her destiny in the eye:

> You may my glories and my state depose,
> But not my griefs. Still am I king of those.

The five stages of grief are Denial, Anger, Bargaining, Depression and Acceptance. Perhaps menopause comes as such a shock to so many women because they have been denying their advancing age for so long. The complaint, that it has come too soon, is heard by many doctors.

> Consulting summer's clock,
> But half the hours remain.
> I ascertain it with a shock —
> I shall not look again.
> The second half of joy
> Is shorter than the first.
> The truth I do not dare to know
> I muffle with a jest.
> (Emily Dickinson, 697)

Denial is over, of course, as soon as a woman registers the truth that she has been denying. Linda Pastan may only have realized that the first group of poems fitted into a denial group when she had passed that stage herself.

> In this season of salt
> leaves drop away
> revealing the structure
> of the trees.
>
> Good bones,
> as my father would say
> drawing the hair from my face.
> I'd pull impatiently away.
>
> Today we visit my father's grave.
> My mother housekeeps, with trowel
> among the stones,
> already at home here.
>
> Impatient, even at forty
> I hurry her home.
> We carry our childhoods
> In our arms.   (Pastan, 3)

This small poem is full of ironies; the home that the daughter hurries her mother to is also the grave, impatient even (still? already?) at forty, denying the place where her mother actually lives, refusing to see where she herself is heading, and yet the poem knows. The exploration moves quietly on through the sequence, while unfamiliar darkness gathers around familiar imagery:

> At the edge of the grass
> Our deaths wait like domestic animals.
> They have been there all along,
> patient and loving.
> We must hurry
> or we may miss them
> in the swelling dark.
>
>   (4)

The imagery of bereavement is complicated by themes of adultery, of the departure of a lover/husband, and by the poet's fear of the end of her creativity; the painfulness of the underlying theme of the death of the womb is almost too deep for utterance, though there is no other way of reading a poem like 'Egg'.

> In this kingdom
> the sun never sets;
> under the pale oval
> of the sky
> there seems no way in
> or out,
> and though there is a sea here
> there is no tide.
>
> For the egg itself
> is a moon
> glowing faintly
> in the galaxy of the barn,
> safe but for the spoon's
> ominous thunder,
> the first delicate crack
> of lightning.
>
> (5)

In the angry phase of her grief, the poet cries out against those who reject her, by dying, by their unthinking superiority, by adultery ('all men are babies, my mother said'), by leaving her. In the last poem in this section, 'Exeunt Omnes', she takes the only way out (having shrunk from suicide) by detaching herself from the life that does not satisfy her, in which she has failed, being no more than an 'average' mother/wife, to satisfy the ones she loved.

> Let everything happen
> off-stage
> Leave me
> with the scenery:
> with the stream which this morning

is all surfaces;
the hills which alter
no more than their colours;
with the old passion
of the seasons
changing.
Let the only dialogue
be between hawk and crow
in their innocent
murderous play.
Go away
all of you.

(22)

Detachment is not so easily accomplished. In the next stage in realizing grief the poet's struggle to cling to the life that is rejecting her continues, but the young more and more are appearing as an alien race. The pain of bereavement breaks open at the old site; the companion insists on leaving, having no need to feel as she does, indeed dreading the sharing of her feeling.

Don't leave now.
We have almost
survived
our lives.

(28)

The failed negotiation leads to 'Depression'.

You tell me nature is no mirror
yet in the broken surface
of the lake I find
jagged pieces of my face.
Ask nature what love is.
Silence is answer enough.

(37)

All the poems in this section are bleak; the familiar imagery of the beloved country is replaced by hotel rooms and 'the city'; her

mother's voice on the telephone crackles 'like a brush-fire soon to
be put out'. Life is a test that she has failed.

> I studied
> so long
> for my life
> that this morning when I waken
> to it as if for the first time
> someone is already walking
> down the aisle
> collecting the papers.
>
> (42)

This is the authentic regret of the climacterium, with its special
feeling that if only one had been allowed a reprieve one would
have done better. The notion that life is out of one's control, the
decisions affecting one's whole existence have been made and
acted on behind one's back, dominates the most unbearable phase
of the sea-change. When we have identified the delusion, we are
already on the way to refuting it.

> I studied
> so long
> for my life,
> and all the time
> morning had been parked
> outside my window,
> one wheel of the sun
> resting against the curb.
>
> Can so much light
> be simply
> to read by?
> I open the curtain
> to see,
> just as the test
> is over.
>
> (43)

The test is over; the results are unimportant. Study has ended and the living is about to begin. The programmed life of response to the expectations and demands of others has ended. But for the moment the woman is blinded by the harshness of the light and can hear only the cawing of the crows. She can find no joy yet in her own observations in '25th High School Reunion':

> We come to hear the endings
> of all the stories
> in our anthology
> of false starts:
> how the girl who seemed
> as hard as nails
> was hammered
> into shape;
> how the athletes ran
> out of races;
> how under the skin
> our skulls rise
> to the surface
> like rocks in the bed
> of a drying stream.
> Look! We have all
> turned into
> ourselves.
>
> (45)

We have arrived at the point of 'Acceptance' but this time the poet does not find herself walking towards the sun and away from night, as Kate does in her dreams in *The Summer Before the Dark*. Her agony is not yet over; her grief is a circular staircase and she is back where she started, ready to deny, rage, and bargain all over again.

The middle-aged woman will not find it easy to get her mourning done. Our culture demands a smiling face; it is bad enough to know oneself for an old trout, without having to add the epithet 'miserable'. We have no tolerance for female images that are solemn, thoughtful or severe. The menopausal woman finds that she is obliged to buck up, to pull herself together. If she wants to sit and think and cry a little or a lot, she is made to feel that these are bad wishes, and may not be indulged. Such behaviour makes other people feel bad. Yet such feelings are not only just and proper, but necessary. Though Freud might be surprised to find his theory of mourning applied to the death of the womb, because he did not understand the forms in which the womb received cathexis, it applies nonetheless.

Mourning occurs under the influence of reality-testing; for the latter function demands categorically from the bereaved person that [s]he should separate h[er]self from the object since it no longer exists. Mourning is entrusted with the task of carrying out this retreat from the object in all those situations in which it was the recipient of a high degree of cathexis. That this separation should be painful fits in with what we have just said, in view of the high and unsatisfiable cathexis of longing which is concentrated on the object by the bereaved person during the reproduction of the situations in which [s]he must undo the ties that bind h[er] to it. (333)

The death of the womb straddles Freud's two categories of physical pain and mourning, and bears all the narcissistic weight that physical pain does, with the same propensity for 'emptying the ego'. The mourner can ignore her condition only at her peril; somehow or another the loss must be acted out. The form that the acting out takes will depend not only on the personality of the mourner but upon her circumstances. Many of the older descriptions of climacteric syndrome noticed that it involved a desire for solitude, a desire that solicitous persons felt obliged to deny. Even when mourning was considered proper and carried out in public, people who assumed that women's emotions exist in order to provoke responses in other people could see no value in a woman's unwitnessed tears.

One exception is the author of *What Every Woman of Forty-five Ought to Know*, published in the United States in 1902.

Emma F. Drake was a woman doctor who likened the climacteric to 'early fall housecleaning', which is perfectly manageable unless demanding guests arrive. Though she fell for the lurid descriptions of mental and physical derangements associated with menopause, and advised her readers to 'be quiet and patient and all will be well' (67), she was prepared to suggest radical strategies that would permit the menopausal woman to get her grieving done. To women panicking that their youth is gone, she recommends taking time out to face just how far away it is.

Run away from yourself and your surroundings for awhile and forget for a little the every-day cares. Hunt up some old friend, the more closely associated with faraway times the better, and get away to her where you can talk over unmolested all the girlhood days. (92–3)

She encourages women to examine the life that has hitherto been unexamined, assuming, probably correctly, that all the woman's time has been monopolized by others. Long before anyone had identified a 'me generation' she was advising women to take time for themselves. She counselled a sea voyage, 'with a friend who will not tire, or be putting you in mind constantly of things you have left behind'.

If you are in the city and cannot get away from home, buy a tent and set it up in the yard and sleep with nothing but canvas between you and the sky ... Get away from home as often as you can. It will do the family good to miss you ... Never mind what social functions are demanding your time, get away from them all ... (94)

The purpose of getting away is to reflect, to mourn and to let go. Dr Drake teaches her patients, besides the necessity of taking stock, techniques of relaxation, of letting go.

Learn to be a child again, and go back to your childhood days, to remember the recesses and the restfulness. Swing your hammock under the trees. (110)

Nowadays one reason given for menopausal mourning is 'the empty nest', the house that the children have grown up and left.

In the large American families of 1902 this was one explanation that did not apply, for the middle-aged mother's nest was still full of shrieking young. Dr Drake understood that mothers undergo many separations from their children, and miss their babies long before the young persons they have grown into have flown the coop.

Your darlings are not yours quite the same as they were before, and you mourn without meaning to do so ... Do not go to friends, where you will need to talk much of the very changes that trouble you so, but go among strangers and rest. (117)

Strangers will not be irritated or panicked by the ageing mother's melancholy, nor will strangers interpret it as a strategy.

Once involved in the inner drama of the climacteric the ageing woman should retreat into her own spiritual world and come to terms with herself. She should not be jollied out of it, or bullied or ridiculed. To be patient she must be allowed to be quiet. Dr Drake quotes the scripture in reference to the grief of single women at menopause, likening them to 'Rachel weeping for her children' and refusing to 'be comforted, because they are not'. All mothers weep for their children's childhood, for the disappearance of those magical small people, who understood so well how to give love and how to take it. It is at least as sad for a woman to know that the love affair with her babies will never come again as never to have known it, especially now that a grandmother's physical hunger for her grandchildren is a thing of no importance.

Our culture has very little tolerance of grief. We are forbidden to mourn even the death of those nearest and dearest. A woman whose child dies is not allowed to sit with other women crying and keening, much less required to do nothing else for a certain prescribed time. A woman whose parent dies is not allowed to veil her head and withdraw from human intercourse in order to understand what has happened to her. What should be a time of recapitulation, of constructing an overview of a long and protean relationship, is expected to pass at the same ragtime pace as the rest of our lives, which are seen as a continuum. The most heartening thing that writers can find to say about the menopause is that there need be 'no change', as if human life was anything but change. The refusal to recognize change is what causes maladjustment. Sorrow is not itself evidence of maladjustment but of the adjustment process itself.

In 1984, Inner City Books, a publishing company set up to promote the application and practical understanding of the work of Carl Gustav Jung, produced a very unusual and important book by the Jungian analyst Ann Mankowitz. *Change of Life: A Psychological Study of Dreams and the Menopause* dealt with the case of 'Rachel', who was fifty-one and had 'just had her final menstruation'. Her marriage had endured, her children were grown up; her husband's parents and her father had died several years before, her mother a year before. Rachel was not complaining of particular difficulties; she simply wanted to understand how to approach the second half of her life, but together she and Mankowitz discovered that there was unfinished business that had to be got out of the way before she could be reborn as herself. Out of Rachel's dreams came evidence of profound desolation and loss.

The first dream was the image of the house in the country where she had lived when her children were small as a burnt-out ruin, which struck in the dream with the kind of physical shock that endures long after waking. The second was a scene inside the burnt-out house where an unburnt woman lay upon an unburnt bed, but she was dead. The next was the barn of the burnt-out house, full of dust and ashes, where four wisps hung from four ropes and the dreamer recognized them as babies burnt in the fire and turned away, unable to bring herself to look more closely. At this dream Rachel baulked, unable to face the reality of her own recognition of the death of her womb. She became preoccupied by the deterioration of her sight, and by the deterioration of what she saw in the mirror.

It was some weeks before she could return to the dream of the dead babies.

When she first described them as looking mummified her eyes filled with tears and the connection with Mummy, which the children always called her, and which she called her own mother, became clear. The number four at first puzzled her, until she remembered her miscarriage; then she realized that these wisps represented not just her live children but all the fruit of her womb . . . (55–6)

Once she had confronted the meaning of her dream symbols, Rachel went through several emotional stages, of shock, of revulsion, and then of the anguish of maternal deprivation. She became angry with the analysis, seeing it as the cause of her feelings of grief and hopelessness, rather than submerged grief and hopelessness as the causes of the recourse to analysis.

For a few sessions she mourned her 'dead children', her dead hopes. She talked about the little creatures in the barn and wept over them; she remembered in detail her births and pregnancies and her miscarriage; she reminisced over her children as infants and toddlers and had nightly dreams of babies. She savored the deep nostalgia that surrounded the whole generative process from beginning to end . . . Then she said farewell to it all. It was gone forever. When this mourning was over she reported that she felt purged of what seemed now to be irrational grief, and she felt ready for what might come next. (58)

Margaret Christie Brown, contributing to an International Symposium in 1975, ended by saying

I should like finally to make a point that the menopause is a time of loss and women should not fall into the trap of feeling guilty about their sadness or of putting doctors into the position that they must produce a panacea so that no distress is felt at all . . . a process of gradual letting go . . . is one of the purposes of mourning.

Brown does not tell us what it is that the menopausal woman is mourning. Some would say that it is the passing of her beauty; others that it is the children that she did not have; others that it is the children she had who died; others that it is the children she had who grew up. Elizabeth Barrett Browning, in a late poem called

'Little Mattie', gently chided the bereaved mother for her desperate grief, teasing her because her child in heaven could no longer be a baby.

> There's the sting of 't. That, I think,
>   Hurts the most a thousandfold!
> To feel sudden, at a wink,
>   Some dear child we used to scold,
> Praise, love both ways, kiss and tease,
>   Teach and tumble as our own,
> All its curls about our knees,
>   Rise up suddenly full-grown.
> Who could wonder such a sight
> Made a mother mad outright!
>
> (557)

On the other hand the grief could be a kind of penitence for having survived the role of lover-mother, for having failed quite to annihilate oneself in altruism. At menopause an old denied self reappears like a ghost, and may indeed reproach us for having delivered our lives over to the control of others who may now appear uncaring and unappreciative. The furious reproach, that one has given 'the best years of one's life' to this or that or these or those is mostly self-reproach. The people we upbraid will tell us that they did not require or demand the sacrifice; at menopause we are charged by ourselves with having thrown the best years of our lives away. Images of waste, of squandering, and even of charade crowd our dreams waking and sleeping. We have done our best to fulfil the conflicting demands of the female condition and after thirty-five years we have been dishonourably discharged.

The personal has survived the impersonal role of lover-mother and it is not too late, but the grief of the climacteric causes temporary blindness. The end of the old life feels like death. It is a kind of death, from which we will be reborn, but first we must mourn the passing of the other self. Her exequies should include a celebration of her contribution, but in an anti-matrist society a eulogy of the mother is unlikely to be forthcoming.

The middle-aged woman's new thoughtfulness about death may lead her back to the church of her childhood or to her lawyer's office to make a will. If it does, she is unlikely to discuss the matter with anyone other than her lawyer and her priest. Though we might not agree with Prospero, the Duke of Milan, who decided after his daughter was married to make every third thought a thought about his death, we ought to accept the fact that death is a part of life, and one that can be handled well or badly. The way we handle it will be as much an expression of our personality as anything else we have ever done, unless of course it is taken out of our hands, unless we die not knowing that the great moment is at hand. The older woman knows the truth of the advice that the Duke gives Claudio in *Measure for Measure*, but she should not say so:

> Be absolute for death; either death or life
> Shall thereby be the sweeter.

In the late twentieth century the woman who admits that she sees the climacteric as the entry into the antechamber of death is in grave danger of psychiatric interference. Such weird insights are better kept to oneself. If she admits that death is on her mind, it will be understood that something is wrong with her. She is not allowed to be sad, or sorrowful or melancholy; these conditions are translated into others that signify disturbance or illness. She will be described as despondent or depressed. Thinking about death is considered to be itself a morbid symptom; if its presence is suspected, some brain-deadening treatment will be ordered. If thinking about death is associated with insomnia, severe psychological disturbance will be suspected and more drastic intervention justified. Given this intolerance for grief, it is not surprising that women themselves convert their censored feelings into symptoms. To be sad is wrong; to be sick is not your fault.

Sooner or later death must be thought about. We must get used to the idea at some stage. The climacteric is a time of mourning, whether deaths in the immediate circle of family and friends occur at that time or not. The menopausal woman should be allowed her quiet time and her melancholy. There is work to be done, setting the psychic house in order, organizing the basis of a new life, with a new focus and new concerns. It often falls to the lot of menopausal women, who do not themselves feel well and capable, to attend to the needs of a querulous parent or, worse, to see them through a protracted end. How often have you seen the fifty-year-old woman guiding the seventy-five-year-old around the hospital, the supermarket, the theatre foyer? You will not often see a grandchild performing this labour of love; the middle-aged women are the only ones free to do it, and the whole responsibility tends to fall on them.

It is a bitter irony that most of the caring for aged parents has to be undertaken by their menopausal daughters, who may be least able to cope with the anxiety and depression and the bone-deep tiredness that such care involves. Perhaps in that great storm of emotions the passing of menstruation is a mere bagatelle. Then again, perhaps day to day dealing with the ending of life makes the climacteric worse, by underlining the theme of loss, endless irreplaceable loss. To the weight of depression is added the weight of exhaustion and grief. The world suddenly seems all loss and death; the irreversible law of entropy becomes so obvious to the middle-aged daughter who day after day watches her mother struggling with confusion and pain that it seems a law of futility.

There can be no cure for this pain, only the compassion of people with enough imagination to see how vast the sorrow of the middle-aged woman can be. The younger generation soon makes clear that it does not want to be troubled by the details of grandmamma's plight; indeed, the middle-aged woman knows that screening the grim truth is part of her duty towards them. She carries the whole weight in her heart and moves dry-eyed from day to day doing what has to be done.

There was a time when mourning was not forbidden but compulsory, and in many 'primitive' or 'backward' countries it is so still. When my Tuscan friend, Angiolina, lost her mother, she was in the throes of a climacteric so painful that she had bouts of what appeared to be mental derangement; for the first time in our twenty-year association she stole from me. Sometimes she was disoriented and confused. Her mother's decline was slow and difficult, and Angiolina fretted that she was far away in the house of her daughter-in-law, who did not know how she liked to have her hair braided or how much she longed to see the wild blue hyacinths on our hills where she was born. When Angiolina's mother died, her body was brought home to our small cemetery. Every day for as long as they lasted Angiolina gathered the hyacinths and took them there. Every day she would sit for hours by the grave, talking to her mother. Nobody interfered with her; nobody tried to cheer her up. Instead, neighbours did her household tasks while she gave herself up completely to her grief. She put her bright-coloured headscarfs away and wore a black one. She saved up all her spare money and paid for masses to be said for the repose of her mother's soul.

In those weeks when Angiolina came up to work, we would sit together and sew, and she would talk to me. Her mind was running on her childhood, on her mother's struggle to protect her children from their father's severity, on the way her mother hoarded her egg money so that the children could have small treats, on her mother's suffering when the Nazis shot her eldest son before her eyes. Normally Angiolina was unreflective; she could not read or write and she had no way of keeping a record. Under the stimulus of her grief for her mother, her memory accomplished extraordinary feats of recall. She would tell me every detail of those far-off days, the way the wind blew, whether the trees were in leaf or in bud, how good the harvest had been, what road she had taken with her goats. She told me how her father threw her out when she refused to give up the poor boy who had courted her for sixteen years. On their wedding night they had no covering to their bed, but Angiolina's mother risked a beating from her husband to creep up the hill by night bringing them the brand new blanket that was their only wedding present, a luxury in those grim years of the *miseria*.

Angiolina's love for her mother was a passion that had never found its full expression during her life; now that she was dead, Angiolina needed to talk to her. I would hear her in the vegetable garden, earnestly talking away as if her mother were there beside her, explaining, protesting, wheedling. Sometimes she would sit and rock for a few moments with her apron held to her eyes. Then, when her grieving was done, she laid by her black kerchief. She still goes to her mother's grave every Sunday before Mass. And she still says when the dark blue hyacinths begin to open on their purple stems, '*alla povera mamma piacevano tanto*' and we both love them the more on that account. In mourning her mother so wholeheartedly Angiolina brought her life under a measure of imaginative control. When her mourning was over her menopausal distress had vanished with it.

The time is long gone when Anglo-Saxons gave vent to their grief. Friends do not hasten to your house when you have suffered a bereavement, in order to sit by the body with you, and weep with you. Grief became first a private thing, veiled and silent, then a secret thing, and then a shameful thing. Sadness, though it is possibly the most rational and explicable state of mind, has become odd and inappropriate. If we were allowed to wear mourning we would discover as I discovered in Sicily that people are quick to offer sympathy, and under the gentle pressure of compassion to recall their own bereavements. The Sicilians would ask me for whom I mourned, when he died, what he was like. Each time I told them my heart felt eased of some of its burden of regret for the things unsaid and the things undone, the roads not taken.

Not only does grief demand expression, the expression of grief brings relief. Some of the finest poetry in our language has been written in the throes of mourning. It might do the grieving woman's heart more good to read it and find release in tears than to dose herself with tranquillizers in an attempt to ignore her justified pain. Failure to mourn makes light of loss, and undervalues the one lost. An unmourned death is made meaningless. Meaninglessness causes despair and despair kills the soul. The ageing woman cannot afford to compromise the life of her soul; her continuing ability to feel is an index of her vitality. As Karen Blixen said, quoting William Faulkner, 'between grief and nothing I choose grief'.

13

Sex and the Single Crone

Most discussions of the sexuality of the fifty-year-old woman have concerned themselves exclusively with the category 'married woman, husband present'. Writers seem to share the view of Frances Brooke, who was married and in her early forties when as 'Mary Singleton' she published *The Old Maid*, who says of herself:

I am afraid I am on the verge of fifty . . . an old maid is, in my opinion, except an old bachelor, the most useless and insignificant of all God's creatures . . . (2)

Miss Singleton is anxious to tell us that she 'had offers' and once a year on her birthday she re-reads her old love letters 'by the help of spectacles'. Our interest in her is concentrated on her one abortive attempt at a monogamous heterosexual union, as if nothing else of interest had ever happened to her.

This discussion of the sexuality of fifty-year-old women will reverse Mrs Brooke's emphasis, so that the last shall be placed first. There are in Britain nearly three-quarters of a million women over the age of fifty who never married, about half as many divorcees and more than four times as many widows. About half the female population over fifty is without a male. Fifty-year-old maids, widows and divorcees all have sexuality and all would be interested to know what changes they might look forward to in their sexual feelings in the course of the climacteric. The truth is that the options seem as varied as ever they were.

'Until recently there has been a paucity of factual data on the effects of the climateric on women's sexuality.' So writes Tore Hallström, of the Department of Psychiatry of the University of Göteborg in Sweden, and we may believe him (Parkes *et al.*, 1979, 160). There is a paucity of data, and an even more marked paucity of factual data on women's sexuality generally. Dr Hallström goes on to define his particular inquiry: 'The basic questions here are: do changes occur in sexual behaviour, sexual interest or responsiveness during the climacteric years? If so, what are the variations and how are they caused?'

The value of the Göteborg study, which was reported at the Eighth IPPF Biomedical Workshop in 1978, is rather compromised by the first question asked Dr Hallström by Dr Helen Ware:

> How many of the women interviewed did not know what an orgasm was or whether they had experienced one? ... I know from an exploratory study ... that working-class women in Australia know what a male orgasm is, but they do not necessarily know that there is a female orgasm or what it is. (Parkes *et al.*, 172)

Dr Hallström's reply could be thought to reveal some inadequacies in his approach.

> I should have mentioned that. A few women, about 2%, would [not?] talk about sexual matters – that is another group to be added to the 11% [drop-out] I described. There were some women who hesitated or did not want to answer specific questions. About orgasm, I cannot give a figure.

You would have thought that as a necessary preliminary to finding out how many women experienced a decline in sexual interest or responsiveness during a particular period, you ought to establish how much sexual pleasure they expected to get. A woman who has never had any pleasure cannot very well experience a decline in it during the menopause. Curiously, though he said he did not know what women understood by 'orgasm', Dr Hallström included in his tables figures for 'Increase in capacity for orgasm'.

The notion that menopause often brings a surge in women's sexual urges dies hard. Its origins are lost in the annals of prejudice. In *The Spectator* No. 89, Joseph Addison, counselling women against 'the folly of Demurrage', warned them darkly about the craziness that lay in wait:

First of all I would have them seriously think on the Shortness of their Time . . .

In the second Place, I would desire my female Readers to consider, that as the Term of Life is short, that of beauty is much shorter. The finest Skin wrinkles in a few years, and loses the Strength of its Colouring so soon, that we have scarce Time to admire it . . .

There is a third Consideration which I would likewise recommend to a Demurrer, and that is the great Danger of her falling in Love when she is about Three-score, if she cannot satisfy her Doubts and Scruples before that Time. There is a kind of *latter Spring* which gets into the Blood of an Old Woman, and turns her into a very odd sort of an Animal. I would therefore have the Demurrer consider what a strange Figure she will make, if she chances to get over all Difficulties and comes to a final resolution in that unseasonable Part of her Life.

Byron expresses sympathy for Catherine the Great, whose 'climacteric teased her like her teens' though 'her dignity brooked no complaining'. His suggestion that the climacteric is a period of adjustment similar to adolescence was shared by the most enlightened opinion of his time.

The belief that menopause can turn virtuous women into sex maniacs still persists. Professore d'Alba, writing in answer to readers' letters in the Italian magazine *Cronaca Vera* in April 1990, told a reader whose wife had been seduced by his African lodger that he was to blame for leaving her alone in the house with the young man. According to the 'professor', women approaching 'the tunnel of the menopause', as he called it, are often troubled with uncontrollable sexual desire, and are therefore particularly susceptible.

Ann Mankowitz feels that, though she can cite no examples, she can say with impunity:

In fact, the pain and anger brought on by a woman's awareness of the decline of her feminine power in middle age can even increase her apparent sexual desire, sometimes to the point of frenzied promiscuity. (5)

The authors of the Göteborg study dismiss this as myth.

Even in up-to-date texts the old concept of a specific increase of the sexual drive in the climacteric is mentioned (e.g. Helen Kaplan, 1974 – *The New Sex Therapy*). The present investigation, however, gives no support to the opinion that sexual interest tends to flare up at the climacteric. Those women who report increasing sexual interest or capacity for orgasm are few in number at these ages and become steadily fewer with rising age . . . (Parkes *et al.*, 166)

They then cite their own table, which gives 16 per cent of respondents reporting increased interest at age thirty-eight, 12 per cent at forty-six, 4 per cent at fifty and 2 per cent at fifty-four. The numbers reporting increased capacity for orgasm were higher; 21 per cent at thirty-eight, 18 per cent at forty-six, 13 per cent at fifty and 6 per cent at fifty-four. These are significant numbers even in so small a sample, and do provide evidence that the sexually aggressive menopausal female is to be found with sufficient frequency for most men to have encountered one. The problem of course is to decide what the increased interest is being compared with, and whether any of the respondents at fifty had already experienced increased interest at thirty-eight and forty-six, and were being asked to calculate an increase over an increase. Nevertheless Dr Hallström reports confidently:

The idea of an increased sexual drive in these years is based on mere anecdotal evidence and must now be regarded as a myth. (166)

As far as Hallström is concerned, if everybody does not have it, nobody has it. The truth is that many women, especially those with high circulating levels of testosterone, will feel increased clitoral sensitivity during the climacteric, and a disturbing level of genital tension, occurring regardless of the presence or absence of a partner and often irreconcilable with the presence of a partner used to a different pattern of response. Women using testosterone to alleviate the discomforts of menopause may find the ensuing genital irritation and diffuse sensations of arousal so unmanageable and disconcerting as to necessitate the cessation of the treatment. Middle-aged women, having perforce cast off the narcissism of younger women, are quite likely to be more direct in their sexual advances and to make quite clear what it is they are after, especially if, for the first time in their lives, what they are seeking is not love but a fuck. If this is the case, it will be the first time in their lives that they have understood the male pattern of arousal and the male search for release.

The Göteborg study, which began in 1968 and ran for ten years, had as its object 'to demonstrate any possible effects of the climacteric on mental health and sexual behaviour'. What the connection might have been between the two was possibly obvious to Dr Hallström; certainly he did not feel any need to define it. Of the total random sample of 899 Göteborg women, only 800 were interviewed. The study concerned itself only with 'married women and unmarried women cohabiting with a man'; no questions were asked about female sexuality, except as it was expressed in heterosexual intercourse. There was no mention of masturbation whatsoever, though the best way to assess 'capacity for orgasm' is by asking about masturbation rather than the pattern of response to a (very possibly perfunctory) male partner.

In Sweden divortiality is standing at more than forty-five divorces per 100 marriages. Divorced women living with their children must have made up a significant proportion of the population of Göteborg. There would have been some widows, and there were the 6 per cent or so of women never married, who, we are told, do not make up a deviant or residual group of people left behind, but are part of the community, and usually a distinguished part of it, for the never-married female is typically a high achiever in the highest social class. None of the numerous members of these classes of women has sexuality worth studying, it would appear. In selecting their random sample of cohabiting women, the designers of the study must have ignored a sample almost as large as the one it 'randomly' selected.

Revulsion at the demanding of conjugal rights by old men is a staple of European comedy. Usually the wife of the old man is a young woman repelled by the deathly touch of old age and afire for contact with flesh as taut and warm as her own, but similar revulsion could be felt by any woman, regardless of her age. It is quite impossible to 'interiorize' the objective fact of one's age, and hardly more possible to gear one's sexual response to individuals of the right age group. Simone de Beauvoir sees that women are less aware of physical appearance in sexual partners than men are, but does not understand that this is only so in the dialectic of unliberated sex. Women who must be parasitic on men if they and their children are to survive will respond to the evidence of power and wealth, rather than beauty. Women who are financially independent may choose something more delectable; women who are rich can have their pick of very handsome, very much younger men, of the kind who will be only too happy to live off them.

The men who see women only as dependants and treat them as perpetual children do not feel the need to add physical attraction to the services they are prepared to perform. They tend to take little care of their looks and fitness. Most shave when they get out of bed rather than before they get into it. One of the surprising things that can happen to the older woman who achieves her own independence and a degree of authority is that she decides to seek sensual pleasure before it is too late. Her own sensuality leads her in the same direction as men are led, towards youth and beauty. She cannot, however, take her pick of beautiful youth with the same impudence as a man and the relationship is fraught with hazard for both parties. The tragedy of the marriage of May and December has been a theme of European literature since it began but December in this case is always a man. The marriage of female December and male May has always seemed comic.

It is generally assumed that youth is sexually attractive and age is not. From one point of view this is simply objective fact. Young people give off the pheromones that attract sexual interest. Older people simply do not. While it is understood that men respond to the appeal of young bodies, it is assumed that women are unmoved by it. Paedophily, the sexual love of children, is understood to be a male attribute. Most women will reject a boy in favour of a man. This was not always the case; Eros is depicted as a youth, and boys have been seen as proper objects for the love of both sexes. This is the older woman, Venus, wooing the boy, Adonis, in Shakespeare's poem:

> 'Thrice fairer than myself,' thus she began,
> 'The fields chief flower, sweet above compare;
> Stain to all nymphs, more lovely than a man,
> More white and red than doves or roses are . . .'

Venus is unlike the heroines of romanticism in that she feels sexual desire and is sexually aggressive. Shakespeare guys her aggressiveness in the poem, but he is equally mocking of the youth's cold rejection of the queen of love. In the libertine culture a very young man was expected to be taught the arts of love by an older woman; one of the routes to preferment for a young nobleman lay through the bed of a powerful woman. He was expected to use his juvenile charms in his own interest much as we now would expect young women to do. This is Aphra Behn's description of the male love object, in this case in the form of a young friar in 'The Fair Jilt':

. . . he wanted no one grace that could form him for love, he appear'd all that is adorable to the fair sex, nor could the mishapen habit hide from her the lovely shape it endeavour'd to cover, nor those delicate hands . . . (Summers, V, 78)

Such young men were desirable precisely on account of their effeminacy, their slenderness, their silky curls, the pink and white of their hairless cheeks. Both men and women were presumed to desire this kind of beauty which, though it lies in a realm beyond gender, did not exclude sex. The exaggerated potency of young men was a part of their attractiveness and a fitting counterpart to the feared potency of females. As one of the 'women who deserve to be praised' says in *The Perfumed Garden of Sheik Nefzawi*:

> I prefer a young man for coition and him only
> He is full of courage, he is my sole ambition
> His member is . . . richly proportioned in all its dimensions;
> It has a head like to a brazier.
> Enormous, and none like it in creation;
> Strong it is and hard, with the head rounded off.
> It is always ready for action and does not die down;
> It never sleeps owing to the violence of its love.
>
> (Luria and Tiger, 129)

Many epochs have understood that a woman of taste and appetite is best served by a delicious boy who can ejaculate many times to the older man's once. What this meant in practice in pre-revolutionary Europe was that a married woman in her twenties could take as her *cavaliere servente* a youth in his teens. Clearly in Elizabethan England, and throughout the reigns of the Stuarts, male display played an important role in heterosexual affairs. At other times men who exploited their beauty have been more likely to be homosexual and to find male protectors.

Lady Mary Wortley Montagu wrote excitedly in a letter from Vienna in 1716 when she was twenty-seven.

I can assure you that wrinkles, or a small stoop in the shoulders, nay, grey hair itself, is no objection to the making of new conquests. I know you cannot easily figure to yourself a young fellow of five-and-twenty ogling my Lady [Suffolk] with passion, or pressing to lead the Countess of [Oxford] from an opera. But such are the sights I see every day, and I don't perceive any body surprised at them but myself. A woman, till five-and-thirty, is only looked upon as a raw girl, and can possibly make no noise in the world till about forty . . . 'tis a considerable comfort to me, to know there is on earth such a paradise for old women . . .
(I, 269–70)

In 1755, when she was sixty-six, she decided that 'no Man ever was in love with a Woman of 40 since the Deluge. A Boy may be so, but that blaze of straw only lasts till he is old enough to distinguish between Youth and Age, which generally happens about 17; till that Time the whole Sex appears angelic to a warm Constitution,' (II, 98). In April 1736 she had met a handsome, cultivated, clever, twenty-four-year-old Italian, Francesco Algarotti, and lost her forty-seven-year-old heart. Algarotti was also admired by Lady Mary's homosexual friend, Lord Hervey, and played them off against each other. In September, after he had left England, she wrote time and again to him in France, humbling herself in repeated confessions of love; in October Algarotti replied in time, she said, to save the remains of her understanding. She went on writing to him in Venice, with a most improper suggestion:

If your affairs do not permit your return to England, mine shall be arranged in such a manner that I may come to Italy. This sounds extraordinary, and yet is not so when you consider the impression you have made on a heart that is capable of receiving no other. My thoughts of you are such as exceed the strongest panegyric that the vainest man on earth ever wished to hear made of himself . . . (II, 110–11)

Algarotti, who was used to the effect his sumptuous good looks and passive charm exercised over the great and good, thought, correctly, that he could probably do better than commit himself to either of his English lovers, both of whom continued to write to him despite his slowness to reply. In March 1739 he wrote to tell Lady Mary that he could not return to her in England if she did not send him money. She did and he returned to live in splendour at Lord Burlington's house, where she saw him often. In July 1739 she left England to meet him in Italy, while he set off with Lord Baltimore on a visit to Russia. On the way back he met the young Prince Frederick of Prussia, who, when he came to the throne in June of the next year, summoned him to court and gave him a Prussian peerage. When he and Lady Mary met again in Turin in the spring of 1741 she realized how misled she had been:

At the time (of foolish memory) when I had an unbridled preference for you, the desire of pleasing you (though I understood the utter impossibility of it) and the fear of irritating you stifled my voice when I spoke to you . . . I have studied you, and so well that Chevalier Newton has not dissected the rays of the sun with more exactitude than I have deciphered the feelings of your soul . . . In you will always be found taste, delicacy and vivacity. Why is it then that I encounter only coarseness and indifference? It is that I am so dull as to excite nothing better, and I see so clearly the nature of your soul that I have as much despair of touching it as Mr Newton would have of adding to his discovery with telescopes, which by their own properties dissipate and change the rays of light. (II, 237, author's translation from the French)

It was of no consequence that Algarotti was homosexual. Lady Mary was looking for the ideal companion with whom to share her life; she believed that Algarotti loved her taste, delicacy and vivacity, as she loved his, and that the evidence of age in her face and body was irrelevant. For many middle-aged women the most suitable choice of companion seems to be an effeminate young man, a 'walker' as he is nowadays called, who will assist her in her social life, advise her and console her, amuse and stimulate her. All kinds and degrees of affection can subsist in such a relationship. Her letters show that Lady Mary was passionately in love with Algarotti. Her other homosexual friend, Lord Hervey, on the one hand reminded Algarotti of her lack of physical attraction —

> To make her lover pleased as well as kind,
> She should be never mute, you always blind.
> (Halsband, 157)

— and on the other reassured Lady Mary that at fifty-two she was not too old for love and should simply choose a new love-object. Lady Mary knew better. After five years of unrequited love, the frenzy had left her for ever. She was left with what she herself called 'the passion of her life', namely her love for her daughter Mary, Lady Bute, to whom she wrote punctually every fortnight for more than twenty years.

Byron, himself a beautiful youth, who had no financial or social need to capitulate to the older women who wooed him, created Regency versions of the type in *Childe Harold* and *Don Juan*. The gravitation of young men towards older women principally came about because unmarried women could not risk entering the marriage market as used goods. Fornication was out and adultery was in. Our present culture of fornication and serial monogamy, though costly in terms of both money and of human suffering physical and mental, seems doomed to be with us for some time longer. It is, of course, the system that is most injurious to the interests of the older woman, who fares better even under polygamy. However much one might desire a revival of the sex culture that expected young men to be initiated by older women, in order generally to improve the quality of sexual interaction, it is unlikely to eventuate in a society where sex is not merely available but practically inescapable for the young of both sexes.

The last great work to depict the vestiges of the matching of experienced women and very young men is Colette's masterpiece, *Chéri*. At the beginning of the novel the heroine, Léa, is fifty; for the last six years she has been having an affair with a man twenty-four years younger than she. It has been suggested that the novel was inspired by Karin Michaëlis's *The Dangerous Age* (see p. 27), but it was actually based on an affair of one of her female friends, Suzanne Derval.

At forty-nine years of age, Léonie Vallon, known as Léa de Lonval, was coming to the end of a happy career of *courtisane bien rentrée* and *de bonne fille* whom life has spared flattering catastrophes and noble regrets. She concealed the date of her birth; but she confessed readily, letting a glance of voluptuous condescension fall on Chéri, that she had reached the age of allowing herself a few little *douceurs*. She liked neatness, fine linen, mature wines and careful cooking. (Colette, 1920, 11, author's translation)

Among the *douceurs* she has permitted herself is Chéri, barely twenty at the beginning of the liaison, now twenty-six. The affair was initiated by the boy. Léa is not slim; she does not pretend to be younger than she is, by contrast with Chéri's eventual mother-in-law, Marie Laure. Her *nourrisson méchant* loves her partly because she is motherly; he sleeps always with his head pillowed on her left breast, unaware that she is often awake. Léa deliberately insists upon her seniority; Chéri is not to call her *ma chère*, as if she were his chambermaid, or a girlfriend of his own age; she is *madame* (68). Her household is perfectly run; the champagne she chooses for him as old as she is. Her love for him is the love of a connoisseur . . .

Colette keeps reminding us that Léa is overripe; her eyelashes are still dark, but . . . her eyes still a striking blue, but . . . In two years she will have Louis XVI's chin. 'She had a good body, guaranteed to last, a big white body flushed with rose, long legs, a flat back, *la fesse à fossette*, and a high slung bosom, all guaranteed to see her out until Chéri was married' (14).

As the novel turns out, Léa is wrong. Chéri is not just a love that she has conducted with great pleasure and impeccable taste; he is the love of her life. When he leaves her to be married, for the first time in her life Léa feels grief, grief that grows more painful and bitter with every passing day. She goes away, leaves no forwarding address, travels around France, ostensibly amusing herself, in reality bored and desperate, but at no time does she contemplate trying to make contact with Chéri. At this point she is absent from the novel, for Colette is concerned with its hero, the young man. If Léa's situation is difficult, Chéri's is tragic.

Chéri, unable to play the role of husband, longing for his cradle in Léa's bosom, returns to Léa. She admits that by selfishly keeping him by her side she has prevented him from growing up. They are both defeated in the end by the twenty-four years that separate them; for a moment Léa allows herself to believe that they have some time left, but Chéri knows better. He has come back to a different Léa. The morning after their reunion in her enormous bed of polished steel and brass, he does not jump up as he used to, demanding his coffee and brioches, but pretends to be still asleep. He watches her 'not powdered yet, a thin twist of hair dangling on her neck, her double chin and her devastated neck' (229). She is quick to understand the alteration in him: 'You have come back to an old woman' (245). She begs his pardon for having loved him 'as if they were both to die an hour after' and not thinking of his eventual destiny. In a moment of cutting psychological realism, after she has watched Chéri pause on the doorstep, and allowed herself vainly to hope that he might be about to turn back, she catches sight of herself gesticulating in the mirror. 'A panting old woman in the mirror repeated her gesture, and Léa asked herself what she could have had in common with that madwoman' (251).

Still Colette sees that the real casualty is not Léa, who will survive, but Chéri who does not. In *La Fin de Chéri*, Chéri, still unable to adjust to the role of returned serviceman and husband, commits the folly of calling on Léa in a new apartment, smaller, different from their love-nest in every way. He discovers a huge white-haired old woman, as jolly and unaffected as an old man, who expresses concern for his worn face and attributes his misery to his kidneys, suggesting a good restaurant where he might be able to eat the kind of food that would make him well in soul and body. Only her laugh seems to belong to his Léa; he waits in a sort of mad hope that the real Léa will jump out of this vast fleshy stranger who slaps her thigh as if it were the crupper of a horse. In the end Chéri cannot handle time's revenges; he shoots himself.

Colette does not give us the answers to Chéri's anguished questions. When did Léa stop dyeing her hair? When did she leave off her corset? When *Chéri* was published, Colette was forty-nine. She had been working on the idea since 1911; it was not until 1921 that she fell in love with her husband's son by his first marriage, Bertrand de Jouvenel, who was to be the model for Phil in *Le Blé en Herbe*. The relationship lasted until late 1924.

Chéri made it possible for women of Colette's generation to take young lovers; if *La Fin de Chéri* proved that taking young lovers was a blood sport, the possibility did not deter the rash young men who entered freely into relationships with the likes of Colette and her friend, Marguerite Moreno. In 1924, while she was finishing *La Fin de Chéri*, Colette met Maurice Goudeket; she was fifty-two, he thirty-six. He had a jealous mistress, and the situation was strained at first, but Colette assumed command. She wrote to Marguerite Moreno: 'I got that crazy confidence that people get, when they fall from a belfry, and stroll for a moment in the air *dans un confortable féerique*, and feel no pain anywhere.'

Evidently Colette was thinking, as most women in her situation would do, that the love affair with Goudeket would soon come to a bruising end. The play of *Chéri* was on tour when Colette and Maurice used to meet in the property he had rented in the south of France, and she was amused by the correspondence between the fiction and her reality, but it was limited after all. She and Maurice lived together for thirty years. In April 1935, Colette and Maurice were married so that they could travel together on the inaugural voyage of the *Normandie* and stay together in prudish American hotels. They remained together, except for a terrible period during the war when Maurice, who was Jewish, was twice arrested, once deported and always obliged to hide, until her death in 1954. In her last years she never let him see her without her powder and kohl, never exposed her devastated body to him. From 1942 she was bedridden by arthritis and her maid, Pauline, helped her to bathe and change her clothes. Her arthritis was undoubtedly complicated by osteoporosis and her overweight. Maurice Goudeket has left an account of his life with Colette, which explains in some measure how she kept her charm for him; Pauline, to whom she had to show the reality behind her powdered mask, has, of course, left none.

Simone de Beauvoir devotes a significant part of *Old Age* to a discussion of the sexuality of the aged. Everybody knows, she writes, that the frequency of coitus lessens with age. The most salient factor is the marital status of the individual; the married continue to have relations, because difficulty in achieving and maintaining erection, and of satisfying a partner, are less catastrophic in a settled relationship than in a chance encounter. De Beauvoir's point of view in this discussion is, as usual in *Old Age*, repellently male-oriented. She does not appear to realize, let alone care, that she has failed to consider whether the fumblings of an aged spouse are gratifying to his wife, nor does she suggest that the frequency of coitus ought to have anything to do with a wife's desires. Worse still, though she treats masturbation as if it were equivalent as a sign of active sexuality, in this discussion there is no mention of female masturbation at all. There is never any suggestion that the changes in the female genitalia that are consequent upon menopause might make genital sexual activity not only pleasureless but painful, and that the demands for reassurance on the part of aged males who see in their penis their alter ego might be experienced by their wives as an oppression.

We have de Beauvoir's own discussion to remind us that interiorly women do not see themselves as old. Every woman being mounted by an old man with a half erection, who will paddle for hours trying to bring himself off, is, in this sense, a young woman. Colette's Léa considers making love to the middle-aged men who still court her, and rejects the idea of accommodating a paunch and a wrinkled faceful of false teeth with disgust. A woman of taste would of course prefer to hold in her arms the boy of whom Lady Mary spoke, whose semen flows like tap-water, the same boy as is depicted on a Greek vase in the Fitzwilliam with the legend in Greek, 'The boy, yes, the boy is beautiful.' A blaze of straw is better than no fire at all, and there is more to love-making than insertion of the sacred phallus. There is also closeness, sleeping together, waking together, sight, smell and touch. The sex that de Beauvoir discusses is sex without sensuality.

De Beauvoir carries her male-centred discussion even further from a female viewpoint, however. In speaking of masturbation she interpolates an observation of her own.

When he is old he grows tired of a companion he knows too well, even more so since she has aged and he no longer finds her desirable . . . And no doubt many elderly men prefer their fantasies to their wife's age-worn body. (1977, 359)

She can find no good reason for a wife's refusing to have bad sex with her husband, for she goes on, 'And then it happens either as a result of old complexes, or because consciousness of her age makes love repellent to her, the spouse refuses' (359–60). A man may be repelled by his wife's ageing body, but a woman may not be likewise disgusted. De Beauvoir herself might have argued that this observation was not sexist but simply realistic. There do exist gerontophiles of both sexes who are poignantly attracted to and desire sexual congress with old men, but no man, says de Beauvoir, feels sexually attracted to a woman old enough to be his grand-mother. She finds that there is nothing to prevent a woman remaining sexually active until the end of her days, because she does not have to fear impotence, and because she is less sensitive than a man to the appearance of her partner. She might have seen in this failure to demand an effective stimulus evidence of women's continuing oppression. In any event we might be justified in seeing in her failure to allow women any valid reason for rejecting sex with an aged man a failure to recognize their right to sexual autonomy. In *Force of Circumstance* de Beauvoir had argued that the greatest success of her life was her relationship with Jean-Paul Sartre. She was to see in the years that followed that Sartre needed her less and less, and needed a succession of clever and attractive young female disciples more and more. If she suffered the jealousy that she describes in *Old Age*, her last years must have been tormented indeed. De Beauvoir needed no one but Sartre, but she could not interest him sexually and so, eventually, she lost him – if indeed she ever had him, for Sartre was never heard to say that the greatest achievement of his life was his relationship with de Beauvoir.

Simone de Beauvoir was writing on the eve of the 'sexual revolution'; the stress she places upon coitus is part of a deliberate strategy of liberation of sexuality, a liberation which has now become promotion and even prescription. It might be argued that though there is no cultural pressure that would drive young men into the arms of older women, older women are now as free as men to look for and exploit sexual opportunities. Such an argument presupposes that women have enough money to frequent places of popular resort (can run a car for example) and present themselves in an attractive manner. Even in cases where these things are equal (and they seldom are), the older woman cannot cruise the sex scene the way that a man of the same age can. She is simply not perceived as a sexual entity, unless she makes an unsubtle display of herself, which amounts to a statement of availability, which is a turn-off to all but the least desirable partners. She then exposes herself in a buyers' market, and the results to her physical and mental health, to her very life, can be ruinous.

There is one such woman whom I see almost every day. She always wears tightly belted dresses with short skirts, very sheer stockings and very high-heeled shoes. Her dyed hair is teased into strange lumps and coils and piled on top of her head, with some curls bobbing over her eyes. Her face is so matt with powder that it looks like a furry mask; her lips are a greasy red bow and her eyes smudged with black, for make-up is harder to put on as you grow more long-sighted. She contrives forever to be walking with tiny steps and switching tail through the most public parts of the building where she works. For all I know she is beautiful and clever; she is certainly my age or older but all anyone can see of her is an advertisement crying 'Notice me! Desire me! Love me!' She is as depressing a sight as any other beggar I have ever seen.

The fifty-year-old woman, if she wishes to remain in the sex race, has got to make herself visible by some such means. Men do not have this difficulty. Though youth is always more attractive than age, there are objective differences in the ageing process between men and women which can mean that men become more attractive with the arrival of grey hairs, and there are good

335

sociobiological reasons why they should. Sperm production and testosterone secretion continue in men indefinitely; though the level of secretion drops it does not cease until death. Once women cease ovulating, they look and feel quite different. Older men never lose reproductive function and can continue to attract sexual interest, and even start a new family, in a way that women of the same age cannot. As if these objective differences were not enough in themselves, they are paralleled by differences in perception. Women are far more likely than men to be attracted to individuals older than themselves. They are less susceptible to the sensual attraction of youth and much more likely to respond to the external signs of authority, power and wealth exhibited by an older man. Women are so obliging that they tend to find men not only attractive but actually sexy if they are in positions of power, regardless of what they actually look like. The women of the United States of America once voted Spiro T. Agnew the sexiest man in the country, although he was over sixty. After his disgrace, and loss of influence, his sex appeal diminished markedly and he was never mentioned in a list of sexiest men again.

Men therefore may find their sexual attractiveness actually increasing with age; very few women will find this to be the case once they have passed the less attractive phases of puberty. The commonest image of a middle-aged woman is someone who is lumpy, dumpy and frumpy, Tina Turner and Lena Horne notwithstanding. The exceptions simply prove the rule. Many a non-lumpy middle-aged woman has had the experience of being whistled at by men in the street walking up behind her, only to have them turn to look at her face and burst out into sneering remarks because the neatness of her behind and her un-frumpy clothes misled them as to her evident age. It is not enough for a middle-aged women to be attractive or to take care of her figure. In the competition with younger women for available men she needs to be young.

Some of the widows and divorcees will marry after the age of fifty, and a few of the confirmed bachelor women. Single men of

336

the same age who are not gay, and some who are, are considered supremely eligible and much sought after as house guests and dinner party guests. Their female counterparts are nowhere near as popular. If they have spent their adult years bringing up children and now find an empty bed as well as an empty nest, they will not find it easy to make new contacts. They are unlikely to have enough money to dress well and have the best beauty care, but even if they could make the best of themselves, they are still the same, old, selves.

The fifty-year-old woman who cannot contemplate manlessness for the rest of her life has a problem. Some women, the lucky ones, I shall argue, lose interest in sex after menopause. For others, in Byron's phrase, the climacteric teases like their teens. My friend Flora told me that after three weeks or so without a man she would walk in the street staring at men, longing to 'lick their bare arms'. She projects a deliberately unsubtle image of availability; her hair is dyed a crude shade of yellow; she wears either tight short skirts with slits in the back or trousers, invariably with high heels, usually of the strappiest kind, a gold chain around her ankle. Some part of her peek-a-boo brassière is usually visible. Standing with her in a bar I can see men on all sides staring at her, in full receipt of her message. The men with female companions sneak looks at her by bending down to pick something up and turning in her direction, or looking behind a newspaper held up, or standing behind their womenfolk and looking past them, in a manner that I find positively frightening. Everywhere we go she picks somebody up, and each time it is a shabbier, drunker, less interesting somebody. When I suggested once that she could end up beaten to death on a vacant lot, she looked at me in despair and said, 'Don't you see? I don't care.'

Flora was married at twenty, and for more than half her married life carried on a series of extramarital affairs, sometimes more than one at a time. 'Love' is what has made her life worth living. If she is not involved in a passionate affair with a man, she said to me over and over, she feels only 'half-alive'. To make matters worse her elder brother is about to marry for the second time; his new wife is an heiress in her late twenties, and they mean to start a family. 'It's not fair,' says Flora over and over again. 'It's not fair. They [men] get to start over and over. He's beginning and I'm finished.' Her ex-husband, meanwhile, though he took a long time to get over the divorce, is also beginning to enjoy himself. His girlfriends are career women, independent, interesting and undemanding, and ten years younger than his ex-wife. 'It's not fair,' says Flora again. Her terror of manlessness means that she will take no steps to provide for a single old age. Some kind of a man will just have to turn up.

The last kind of a man who turned up represented a distinct deterioration from Flora's husband and from her former lovers. Usually her lovers were young, good-looking, and fairly interesting, although not as interesting as Flora thought them. They were mostly penniless young artists of one sort or another, who valued Flora not only for her beauty but for her intelligence, her culture and her connections. Her last boyfriend was something else. Not only was he slightly paunchy, unshaven, balding, with bloodshot eyes and broken veins in his cheeks, he smelt bad, of rancid sweat and unwashed underclothes. Like many another of her boyfriends he was a film-maker, but as he had only one film to his credit and he was approaching forty, he could hardly have been called promising. Nevertheless Flora entered into all of his concerns, studied his single film until she could recite the shot list by heart, and completely absorbed its political ideology.

According to Flora, the sex she had with this unprepossessing character was the best she had ever had. I asked her to consider the possibility that this was not because of something virtuosic in the man's performance but because of the emotional intensity that she was bringing to a fairly banal affair. They had met at a luncheon party; she was going on to a party in the evening and he offered to accompany her. They stopped at her apartment so that she could change her clothes and 'fell into bed'. They never went on to the party; indeed they never appeared together in public anywhere. He saw her irregularly, mostly late at night at her apartment.

She was soon completely hooked. She thought about him continually. She was tormented by desire for him. Night after night she sat in her apartment waiting helplessly for him to call. She neglected other friends because of her utter need to be available for him. She was obsessed and there was nothing she could do but wait until he found time for her. She believed that he was travelling, working on arranging showings for his film. She tried to help by bringing the film to the notice of some of her connections. Just talking about it and him helped to relieve her insistent need for him, a need which she believed he also felt for her. It was unbearable to think that she was not the only woman in his life, and so she did not think it, although it ought to have been fairly obvious. The affair, cold-blooded on his side, tumultuous on hers, corroded her self-esteem. She knew that she had become abject. In despair she confronted him. Yes, there was another woman and yes, it would be better if they did not see each other again.

The loss of what little she had of him affected her so severely that she found herself weeping helplessly on trains and buses, wandering aimlessly in the street. She let her pretty apartment become dirty. Her daughters, who both love her dearly, came to her rescue, making sure she was not too much alone, but they knew that there was little that they could do to relieve her utter desolation and her crying physical need. Eventually she realized that there was not just another woman, there had always been other women. His decision to end the affair with her was simply that he was tired of her as he was not tired of the others. Her humiliation was complete. All she could do was wait for another man who would probably treat her even worse. Her husband, who remains her good friend, thought she might suffer less once she had actually gone through menopause. She thought that she would find life without sexual desire joyless and utterly without savour. She began to think that she might kill herself.

Some women will not understand how a highly educated and brilliant woman could be so enslaved to sex. Yet even Simone de Beauvoir found the idea of life without sexual intrigue dreary and repellent. She never found the activity of thought, of which she was supremely capable, sufficient to fill her days with excitement. Her reactions on finding the first signs of advancing age are to be expected in a woman who has never had anything but her looks and physical presence to boast of; in an intellectual such vanity and poverty of spirit as de Beauvoir exhibits in *Force of Circumstance*, with devastating honesty it must be said, undermine the importance of her thinking, which could not bring her serenity or self-command. It seems that she actually despised the detachment of age, seeing it merely as a withering away of the capacity to feel. Like Flora, she felt that without a man she was only half alive.

Some older women do find love, and sometimes from younger men, even much younger men. Perhaps Flora, who is intelligent, cultured, and really beautiful despite her calculatedly sluttish exterior, will find a younger man sensitive enough and virile enough to discern what is special about her. The odds are long, but other women have done it. When forty-nine-year-old Marian Evans aka George Eliot aka 'Mrs' Lewes first met John Cross in Rome in 1869, he was twenty-nine. She adopted the play role of his aunt and when George Lewes died in November 1878 Johnny was her chief consolation. By August 1879 they were in love. They read the *Divina Commedia* together. She wrote to him in October, on black-edged paper:

Best Loved and loving one:
the sun it shines so cold, so cold, when there are no eyes to look love on me . . .

The letter is signed 'thy tender Beatrice'.

Johnny several times asked George Eliot to marry him; twice she refused. In 1877 when Thackeray's daughter Anne married Richmond Ritchie, who was nearly twenty years younger than she, Eliot wrote to Barbara Bodichon that she had known several instances of 'young men with even brilliant advantages' choosing 'as their life's companion a woman whose attractions are wholly of the spiritual order'. Lady Jebb, who was a house-guest with the newly-weds with the Bullock-Halls at Six-Mile-Bottom, wrote:

George Eliot, old as she is, and ugly, really looked very sweet and winning in spite of both . . . In the evening she made me feel sad for her. There was not a person in the drawing-room, Mr Cross included, whose mother she might not have been, and I thought she herself felt depressed at the knowledge that nothing could make her young again. She adores her husband, and it seemed to me to hurt her a little to have him talk so much to me . . . (163–4)

I should rather have thought it was Johnny Cross who was more acutely aware of his wife's age; she would have found his relative youth familiar, for she had once been thirty-eight herself, and it is easy to feel rejuvenated by a young spouse. Besides Johnny Cross had been treated by her as an aunt, which is after all a version of a mother. They fell in love when she was mourning the death of her husband and he the death of his mother. George Eliot died before the first year of their marriage was out. Johnny Cross did not marry again.

By her will, George Eliot left her husband nothing. Apart from a few personal bequests, everything was left to Charles Lee Lewes, who was sole executor. Cross began work on a peculiarly hagiographic biography which was ridiculed when it was published two years later. It seems fairly likely that Johnny Cross married George Eliot because of attractions 'wholly of the spiritual order', only to discover that she expected him to carry out his conjugal duty. The manner of his discovery may have been the catapult that sent him flying out of the window of the Gritti Palace.

Margaret Powell, the charlady turned authoress, describes another case of a sixty-year-old woman in love with a man in his thirties, in terms which Marian/George and her Johnny would find wounding and coarse. Her voice is, however, the voice of common sense. In *The Treasure Upstairs* she tells how her employer,

Thora Ellis, made the acquaintance of some young Canadians when she took her out to a pub in Hove:

> ... Miss Ellis – or Thora – was entranced by her Pete. I didn't at that time realize how much she'd been taken in by him. When we left together at closing time she talked about him all the way back to her home: what an interesting life he'd had, what good manners he'd got . . .
>
> What I didn't know was that she'd given this Pete her address and invited him round to the flat. So I was very annoyed when, on the following morning, he called at eleven o'clock, and I had to make coffee for three instead of two. This was the start of regular visits. He felt that he'd got her where he wanted her . . . he captivated her so quickly that no warnings from me would have had any effect. I knew she was giving him money. One day he came in wearing a new watch, and on another he'd a gold cigarette case. It annoyed me how a woman of her age could be so deluded. Surely she should have known that a young man of thirty-five couldn't have fallen in love with even an attractive woman of over sixty, let alone a plain one with a hairy old mole. Eventually I did try telling her that he was just after her money, but she wouldn't listen to me. 'He's like a son to me,' she kept repeating. 'A right bastard son you'll find him to be,' I flung at her in my exasperation . . .
>
> Then things got worse. This Pete moved into the flat, sleeping in the spare room, and he used the place as if it belonged to him. He now quite openly asked Miss Ellis for money, even in front of me, and I could tell it wouldn't be long before he had me out of the place . . . (131–2)

What happened in this case is that Margaret Powell wrote to Miss Ellis's lawyer brother, who threw the opportunist lodger out of the flat and took his sister home with him to Manchester . . .

> It was this that made me feel so awful about having written to him. I had, as it were, turned the calendar back forty years. She was again keeping house, just exchanging a martinet of a father for a martinet of a brother . . . When I said goodbye to her, she didn't reproach me. I think she felt that the moment of happiness she had had made everything worthwhile. She'd had her taste of what, to her at any rate, was romantic love . . . (133)

Neither Margaret Powell nor lawyer Ellis considered for one moment the possibility that 'this Pete' was turned on by women twice his age, especially with hairy moles on their chins. I have known gay men who were sincerely gerontophile and did not fancy a man unless he was much older, but I have yet to encounter a man who sincerely lusted after women twice his age and considered himself uninterested by and impotent with younger women, though doubtless some exist. Most women would still agree with Lucy Bentham in George Moore's novel, *Lewis Seymour and Some Women*, speaking of her affair with Seymour, twelve years younger than she:

A year and a half, nearly two years, had passed since she saw Lewis for the first time in Mr Carver's shop. She was then thirty-four, now she was thirty-six. A year of the short time allowed a woman for love had been wasted, and in ten years she would be no longer fit for love. She might keep him for ten years, but after ten years she would have to hand him over to another woman ... would she suffer at this surrender of her happiness, and retire gracefully into middle age? (128)

This is not of course a woman speaking, but a womanizer speaking in the person of a woman; nevertheless most women would accept this version of their fitness or otherwise for love. A hundred years before, Mary Wollstonecraft recalled a sprightly writer who asked 'what business women of forty have to do in the world'. Moore allows Mrs Bentham rather more time:

She might retain him for some ten or a dozen years, till she was forty-five; at fifty a woman's life is really over, and she began to wonder how the sensual coil would break, if weariness or some accident would break it; or the arrival of another woman, a misfortune that might befall her at any moment, for she could see that all attracted him, he being a very young man. (128–9)

In the event Lucy Bentham was lucky; she got to forty-five before the blow fell.

'A woman dies twice,' she said, 'and in a very few years it is borne in upon us that our mouths are no longer fit for kisses. His mouth, too, will one day cease to be attractive.' (202–3)

At least Moore allows that men too eventually become unfit for love, but Mrs Bentham is unusual among female characters in novels in that she is a sensualist, and she loves Seymour for his beauty. If we accept Moore's premiss that really only the young are fit for love, then we are obliged to conclude that women have mostly been forced to endure the embraces of people unfit for love. Perhaps many women are aware of being kissed rather than kissing, and feel that as long as one mouth is succulent, that is sufficient. Certainly most women could not contemplate the kind of sex in which the male is indifferent and simply allows himself to be caressed. They cannot simply wish to press greedy old mouths against firm young flesh for the sake of feeling, smelling and tasting it. It is as if women's sensuality has always been obliterated by narcissism. Even in a male brothel a woman would expect her partner to enjoy her, and would be more concerned or at least as concerned about that as about her own orgasm. We are often told that male prostitution is on the verge of becoming big business, and that female buyers exist for soft pornography displaying male bodies and that the new kind of female executive will know where and how to find satisfaction and will have the money to pay for it, but the phenomenon never eventuates.

Old women are commonly assumed to be sexually repulsive; the mythology of temptation is full of beautiful maidens who turn into hell hags with no more gruesome attributes than the normal attributes of age. Conversely, as in *The Magic Flute*, a lecherous old hag miraculously turns into Papagena. Cronishness used to come early; it can now be indefinitely postponed. The most significant advance in the unmaking of the crone is the perfection of the art of orthodontistry. Women who are not left with toothless gums do not suffer the downward curve of the nose that meets the upward curve of the chin to create the familiar witch profile. Women do not allow bristles to sprout freely or warts and wens to proliferate. Nevertheless the fifty-year-old woman knows that her body is not what it used to be. No matter how fit she is, or how flat her belly, her skin is thinner and less elastic, her muscle tone less firm. Oestrogen replacement may slow down such changes, but it cannot stop them or undo them. It becomes more and more difficult for a middle-aged woman to undress before a stranger, especially if he does not know her age and she does not know what he expects. She may resort to subterfuge, to soft lighting and luxurious underwear, or drugs or alcohol, to blur the first impressions that she feels so crucial. And still the man, nourished on a diet of inauthentic imagery of womanhood, may take to the windowsill and chuck himself into the canal if he discovers that he has a crone to his portion.

The elderly lover may discover after she has exercised all the arts of love-making that she has ever learned, so that matters have been brought to a relatively satisfactory conclusion, that the man is tremendously pleased with himself for having performed so well against such tremendous odds. The younger he is the more likely are his remarks to be of a crassness so wounding that the entire experience becomes painful to recall.

Nothing is more protean than taste; doubtless we could all be re-educated to believe older bodies to be as attractive as young ones and to perceive them as such. There is a concerted effort to show older people as more attractive now that populations in the developed world are becoming older. (This is a shorthand way of saying that as people are having fewer children and living longer, the mean age of the population is rising.) Marketing now has specific targets among large groups of relatively aged people, but even so, they would seldom use models of the same age as the target population. Advertising used to bracket people into children, teenagers, young married, yuppie and cuddly antique. Now the gap between yuppie and cuddly antique has to be filled by acceptable consumer types. The distinguished executive has been around for some time; he is now being joined by the fit retiree.

However, women over forty are still usually shown as pains in the neck, mothers-in-law in silly hats. The sexy middle-aged woman is not even a gleam in the ad man's eye, even though she may have significant buying-power. The ad man knows that to sell to her he may as well use a younger woman with whom she too would rather identify.

The received opinion now is that the older woman should be having sex. The logic is that everybody has a right to sex; women have the same rights as everyone else, therefore they have a right to sex. This is probably experienced by women as a series of rather mocking demands on them, namely, that there should be someone in their lives who wants to have sex with them, and they should also be wanting sex with that person. What this means in practice is that you should be a married woman, you should have hung on to your husband and not allowed him to die or go off with someone else, and you should still fancy him. These are all tall orders, if only because they are all out of the individual woman's control. Husbands continue to die in the most inconvenient and inconsiderate fashion. Some, as they rise in affluence and influence, begin to desire more effective sexual stimuli than a familiar old wife can offer, and a female of a newer model with increased horsepower, who will be a better indicator of status than a wife who learnt her cooking during the lean years. Many a middle-aged woman has to accept an unwanted divorce. Others seek the divorce themselves.

The right of the middle-aged woman to sexual self-expression is not one that she can exercise in the absence of an interested partner. If she has never had sex, there is not much chance that she will start getting it when she is over forty, and less chance than ever when she is over fifty, unless of course she is in one of those caring institutions where the old men and women are urged to get it on together. If she has lost her husband by death or divorce she cannot demand a replacement. It is all the more important then that she not allow herself to be convinced that without the psychic release of sex she will become a 'frustrated', bitter, cruel, dried-up,

SEX AND THE SINGLE CRONE

envious old stick. The symptoms of the climacteric should not be misinterpreted as signs of mental imbalance or emotional disturbance caused by sexual deprivation. The general rule holds; doing without sex if you have been used to having it is not easy, but you can do it. If you have survived so far without it, you will find life getting easier with every month that passes. Whatever the case, one possibility remains as long as life remains: the recollected soul can always flame into love. At fifty Emily Dickinson wrote:

> The Thrill came slowly like a Boon
> Centuries delayed
> Its fitness growing like the Flood
> In sumptuous solitude –
> The desolation only missed
> While Rapture changed its Dress
> And stood amazed before the Change
> In ravished Holiness –
>
> (629)

14

The Aged Wife

In all the editions of his *Diseases of Women: A Clinical Guide to their Diagnosis and Treatment*, George Ernest Herman, MB Lond., FRCP, could still aver that

> After menstruation has finally ceased, the genital organs atrophy. The uterus becomes small, the vagina becomes smooth, and its orifice, if it has not been enlarged by child-bearing, shrinks. These changes are not important to women who have been married at the most suitable age; but to women who have been married late, to husbands younger than themselves, they may be. (1898, 582–3; 1903, 582–3; 1907, 592–3; 1913, 574)

The good doctor, and he seems to have been a sensible compassionate man, assumes that a woman who has married at the right age and to a person of the right age, i.e. somewhat older than she, by the time she arrives at menopause has no further use for her vagina. The only woman who may be embarrassed by the unserviceability of her orifice is the one whose husband is younger than she and still makes demands on her.

Nowadays we know better than to treat the vagina as if it were part of the furniture set aside for a husband's use; we have come to believe in female libido. Current sexual orthodoxy teaches that women have sexual desires and, not simply the *right* to express them, but a *duty* to express them in the interests of better health. Whereas Dr Herman may well have felt that there were few good reasons for continuing intercourse after menopause, nowadays there can only be bad reasons for discontinuing it.

Theodore Faithfull, Consultant Psychologist and Sexologist and Member of the Royal College of Veterinary Surgeons, is quite certain that decline of sexual interest in the ageing female is evidence of the wrong kind of sexual interest in the first place:

If the sex life of a married couple has been fornication, that is glandular relief for the male and instinctive satisfaction by occasional pregnancies for the female, there can be in both males and females in the middle years of life a lack of desire for physical intimacy as the glandular function decreases. (104)

Faithfull has his female patients in a cleft stick. If admitting loss of interest is to admit that one's marriage has been fornication, then no woman of spirit is going to admit it. Faithfull is fairly typical in that he does not concern himself in the least with the ageing female who is not in a heterosexual union. For Faithfull the females who never achieved their destiny as wives and mothers are doomed to ill-health whatever they do. The females who have allowed their husbands to leave them by death or any other means are equally absent from his consideration in *The Future of Women*. Though Faithfull's account of female orgasm is nonsensical and *The Future of Women* is a strange and cranky book, he is by no means untypical in his treatment of female sexuality as half of that perfect whole, the couple. Most doctors nowadays would treat this case of Faithfull's in exactly the same way:

A few years ago the wife of a man holding a responsible post in the teaching profession came to see me. She considered that her life was as good as over. The climacteric was finishing, her son would soon be leaving home and she felt her husband would be far happier with a younger woman. I told her she was talking nonsense. (104)

Clearly what she is talking is not nonsense, although she may well have been wrong. But Faithfull went on:

That if she put herself right she would be a help to every young married woman in her social circle and she and her husband would

349

enjoy marital intimacy for many more years. A few months later I one day noticed a smile on her face and asked her what it meant. 'Oh!' she said. 'I suppose I must tell you. When my husband finished last night he said my dear, you are now giving me more happiness than in all the 25 years of married life.' (104–5)

When her husband finished what, we may ask. Whatever Faithfull may consider he has done for this mythical female he has not succeeded in getting her to stop living for others. He does not explain how she 'put herself right'. He might have felt less smug if his patient had told him that she was standing over her husband with a whip, or kicking him with high-heeled red shoes, or allowing him to tie her up, beat her or defecate on her. In this kind of discourse the husband's unexamined requirements are assumed to be legitimate; the wife's need is to satisfy them.

The distortion in thinking about the sexuality of married people partakes of a general distortion to be found in all thinking about heterosexual intercourse. Though homosexuals male and female are assumed effectively to achieve orgasm by all kinds of sex play which does not by definition involve the penetration of the vagina by the penis, heterosexuals are considered abnormal if they prefer sex in any other form than the kind guaranteed in fertile persons to result in impregnation. This is the reason the condition of the ageing woman's vaginal mucosa is crucial to her relationship with her husband. Though it has been proved time and time again that women's orgasms do not originate in the vagina and that other forms of love play are more effective in pleasuring women and that constant exposure of the cervix uteri to the glans penis represents a health risk to women, the emphasis on intromission as the only form of heterosexual intercourse is unweakened. Not even the terrors of the AIDS epidemic have succeeded in weakening it. When we consider the question of sex between ageing spouses we assume that they will do it 'like grown-ups' in Márquez's phrase (see below). At no time in her life is a woman to be permitted to declare the vagina off-limits and take her pleasure by more certain means. If she is one of the many women who have been fucked when they wanted to be cuddled, given sex when what they really wanted was tenderness and affection, the prospect of more of the same until death do her part from it is hardly something to cheer about.

There is a darker side still to the emphasis laid upon continuing sexual activity as the one sign of vitality in a marriage. Purveyors of pornography often justify their activities on the grounds of the services they provide for bored couples who are enabled to copulate by having their fantasy stimulated by looking at images of others doing sexy things. It is hardly necessary to scrutinize commercial pornography to register the fact that all the images are directed towards the flaccid penis rather than the dry and unresponsive vagina. Indeed it is unlikely that the dry and unresponsive vagina would become excited by visual stimuli in any case, for women are not yet as genitally fixated and fetishistic as men. It cannot be too often or too clearly said that all our commercial pornography is sado-masochistic and degrades the individuals depicted in it, the overwhelming majority of whom are women. The sex inspired by it is not just not worth having, it is fundamentally destructive.

In 1957 Maxine Davis, writer on medical subjects for *Good Housekeeping* magazine, encapsulated the current thinking about the role of women in married sex in her best-selling book, *The Sexual Responsibility of Women*. 'Ardent young couples,' she writes, assume that 'the book of sexual life suddenly closes with the finality of the first clod of earth on a coffin' (190). How wrong they are, she enthuses. An old couple 'have sound reason to expect to enjoy their sex lives together after an evening spent baby-sitting for their third great-grandchild'.

Their sexual activity naturally will not be nearly so frequent, so prolonged or intense as it used to be but it will still be possible, in a mild way, for it to be complete enough to give happiness and meaning to their lives. (190–91)

This blessed couple has evidently managed to gather four generations of family around them and keep them there but, in order for happiness and meaning to enter their lives, they still need to manoeuvre the penis into the vagina. Not for Davis the suggestion that it might be rather more useful to retain the power to make each other laugh. Heaven forbid, they might laugh when they were working on the penis. A sense of the absurd in such a situation could be most inconvenient.

Life is not like Davis's paradigm. It is fearfully difficult to orchestrate human whims and susceptibilities so that they coincide. A perfect fit between lovers, whether sanctified or not, is so rare that no one should ever feel guilty at not having managed it. We are all like the imprisoned men in Genet's film *Chant d'Amour*, straining to express tenderness through lavatory pipes and cracks in concrete walls. The ageing couple that does not celebrate its closeness by a weekly symphony on the bedsprings has nothing to apologize for. The literature of menopause implies that loss of interest in genital congress after twenty-five years of marriage is a relatively rare and severe symptom:

> More serious psychological problems may call for the help of a psychotherapist and for psychotherapy. Both husband and wife may benefit from psychosexual counselling and re-education. Failure to stimulate the partner, persistent premature ejaculation on the man's part and inability to relax on the woman's part are the main factors which cause sexual activity to fail. (Evans, 98)

The current orthodoxy is that psychosexual difficulties themselves may cause the formation of symptoms at menopause. Younger doctors are as interested as Theodore Faithfull in getting women to 'put themselves right' and they tend to attempt it by the same means, by talking to them. If not enjoying sex with your husband is evidence of a serious psychosexual problem, the pressure is on you to submit to any kind of brainwashing to get well. Nobody wants to be permanently stigmatized as 'mentally ill'. If the menopausal woman already feels that she is losing her mind, the suggestion that her not wanting sex with her husband is a symptom of a psychosexual problem needing treatment is particularly mischievous.

'Failure to stimulate a partner' is clearly a heinous crime. Psychosexual counsellors would all claim that both partners in heterosexual intercourse should be given all necessary stimulation. They seem not to realize that the partner whose stimulation is essential to sexual intercourse is the male; once he is stimulated, especially if he is fundamentally bored, it is important to proceed to the business before his synthetic enthusiasm wanes. Stimulation moreover obeys its own law of diminishing returns, which is why some men are carried into the casualty departments of our hospitals every year with their penises flayed because they have put them into the suction nozzle of a vacuum cleaner. Just how much time, energy and money needs to be devoted to the providing of adequate stimulation is nowhere quantified. The umpteenth best-selling book on how to seduce your husband is once more on the market; it contains instructions for hundreds of masquerades, all involving expenditure not only of money for costumes, flowers, alcohol, telegrams, etc. but of enormous amounts of time. The view of its author is that the humblest suburban bedroom can be the scene of exotic sex play that would bring a blush to the cheeks of the courtesans of ancient Alexandria. The woman who refuses to dress up as a French maid one day, a nun the next, and a schoolgirl the next, and come on like an expensive whore, is clearly holding out on her husband, failing 'to stimulate a partner', therefore the couple is failing to have right sex, therefore *she* has severe psychosexual problems, therefore she needs counselling.

If sex has never been particularly rewarding, if time and energy have been put into it and regular twice-a-week bliss-for-two has not resulted, turning fifty might be a good time to give up the struggle. If giving up sex meant giving up marriage, divorce statistics would be much higher even than they are. The re-enactment by spouses of sacramental intercourse is not necessary, although it might be pleasant. To assume that resumption of sexual activity is an infallible sign of a revivified relationship is to fall into an egregious blunder; to assert that it is a condition of revivifying marriage is tyranny. To dose women with steroids for the sole purpose of keeping them receptive to their husbands' advances is outrageous.

There are surely many middle-aged women who have husbands alive and living with them, and who desire sex with those husbands and are desired by them. If such women experience the condition of their vaginas as an obstacle to the fulfilling of their own desires, then clearly they are entitled to replacement oestrogen, either as a cream to apply directly to the vagina or as tablets to be taken by mouth. However, if the woman only wants to be able to have intercourse with her husband so that she can have a quiet life, it is quite improper to dose her with sex steroids so that she can endure an activity that she has never much enjoyed. If a man has never been a considerate or imaginative lover, he may just conceivably become so as his own sexual potency wanes and the matter becomes less urgent. If he does not, if his expression of desire becomes more mechanical rather than less, more masturbatory rather than less, if he finishes earlier and falls asleep even sooner than in the first years of marriage, the middle-aged woman may quite conceivably prefer to opt out of the whole business. She might prefer to opt out too if he takes a good deal longer about it, if he wakes her up at odd times in the night, if he only feels like it after a couple of drinks or after reading some of the magazines he buys from the top shelf at the newsagent's.

In the popular literature on menopause, a husband is assumed to have conjugal rights of access to his wife's body, when in fact he has no such rights. A husband's desire is also assumed to be more or less constant over thirty-five years. The sexologists tell us on the other hand that in men

From adolescence onwards, there is a continuous decline in sexual interest, arousal and activity, without a sudden discontinuity in any group . . . sexual arousal is slower and requires more intense stimuli, ejaculations are less forceful, detumescence after orgasm is quicker and the vasocongestive increase in testicular size during sexual excitement is decreased, as is the psychosexual pleasure. (Vermeulen, 1979, 5)

What this would seem to add up to is that the ageing male must work harder for less pleasure and his partner of many years is going to have to provide more intense stimuli, somehow, if they are to get it on at all.

Although many factors play a role in determining the frequency of sexual activity, among which impotence, boredom with the sexual partner, stress, fear of failure, or a period of forced abstinence are the most important, an age-dependent physiological decline is also undeniable. This age-dependent decrease is also observed in domestic animals, for example, bulls, many of which are discarded early in life because of gradual sexual apathy. (6)

In the discussion of this phenomenon at the Eighth IPPF Biomedical Workshop, the learned gentleman kicked around the idea that encroaching male apathy could be staved off by dosing with testosterone, but this suggestion was thrown out because of the danger of suppressing endogenous testosterone secretion, and of increasing the risk of myocardial infarction and prostatic hyperplasia. The contrast between this conservatism with regard to their own ageing bodies, and their radicalism when confronted with the problem of female loss of interest was marked.

Our culture encourages men to demand effective sexual stimuli; as their own sperm production declines, they need even more effective stimuli. The ruling class, which is and always has been and must be male, has always had its pick of young flesh of both sexes. After twenty-odd years of marriage the wife of Bob Slocum, the anti-hero of Joseph Heller's *Something Happened*, is a more cooperative partner than she ever was, but, though her husband succeeds in responding, her willingness avails her little.

Nowadays my wife is much better. Nowadays my wife is completely different about this whole matter of sex; but so am I. She is almost always amorous nowadays, it seems, and ready to take chances that horrify even me. I can usually tell that she's been thinking about it the instant I walk in, by a self-satisfied, slightly twisted smile. I know I am right if she has left her girdle off . . . (124–5)

His wife is doing everything she can to keep him interested in her; she dresses well, looks good, is a superior 'hostess' and flirts aggressively with other men. She drinks before he gets home to loosen herself up. She has stopped asking him if he loves her. She is actually acutely miserable; her increased libido is evidence of anything but spiritual well-being.

My wife is unhappy. She is one of those married women who are very, very bored and lonely, and I don't know what I can make myself do about it (except get a divorce and make her unhappier still. I was with a married woman not long ago who told me she felt so lonely at times she turned ice cold and was literally afraid she was freezing to death from inside, and I believe I know what she meant.). (71)

Nameless Mrs Slocum displays some of the negativity of the menopause, though, as far as we can tell, she is a few years off it.

She thinks she has gotten older, heavier, and less attractive than she used to be – and of course she is right. She thinks it matters to me, and there she is wrong. I don't think I mind. (If she knew I didn't mind she'd probably be even more unhappy.) My wife is not bad-looking; she's tall, dresses well, and has a good figure, and I'm often proud to have her with me. (She thinks I *never* want her with me.) She thinks I do not love her any more, and she may be right about that too. (71)

Though Slocum has had many other sexual relationships and is sexually obsessed by at least one other woman, he cannot bear the thought that his wife might take one of his business colleagues as a lover.

I think I might really feel like killing my wife, though, if she did it with someone I know in the company. My wife has red lines round her waist and chest when she takes her clothes off and baggy pouches round the sides and bottom of her behind, and I would not want anyone in the company to find that out. (509)

Slocum is not intended as a hero, nor is he some kind of archetype, nevertheless the theme of *Something Happened* is the dreadfulness of ordinariness. One is at least as likely to encounter the Slocum family in middle America as the mythical forty-year monogamous love-affair that doctors imagine they are able to perpetuate through HRT. Though with a reticence rare among male novelists Heller never pretends to be able to read Mrs Slocum's mind, we may suspect that she gets half-drunk and tears at her husband's fly-buttons because she is terrified that he will divorce her. Faithfull might say that she had never enjoyed sex, because when she was younger she used to fight her husband off, and therefore she was only able to use sex as manipulation, and then when it was too late.

Men who bathe and shave when they leave their wives' beds, rather than before they get into them (i.e. the majority), probably do not consider whether their wives find sex with them uncomfortable, unexciting or even revolting. It is possible that even the wives themselves have not considered the matter. Dr Barbara Ballinger could get only 114 of her 539 respondents aged between forty and fifty-five to discuss sex with her. Of them, thirty-four said their sexual responsiveness had deteriorated and five said it had increased; twenty-four had never enjoyed sex at all; twenty-seven found sex satisfactory; five had refused to have intercourse at all for periods ranging from five to seventeen years. Only ninety of the women had husbands; of them twenty-one said the relationship was poor, twenty-five fair, and forty-four good. Only 40 per cent of the women with poor libido had good relations with their husbands, compared to 66 per cent of those with unimpaired libido (Ballinger, 1975). These figures are thought to constititute a case for hormone replacement. Get your libido fixed and your chances of a good relationship with your husband improve from

40 per cent to 66 per cent. Actually the chances are not even as good as that, for only thirty-two women had unimpaired libido, and only twenty or so of them had good relations with their husbands; the impaired numbered almost twice as many. None of these discussions ever asks whether a husband is attractive, or a good lover. Loss of interest in sex is never a rational response, always a symptom. Robert A. Wilson, MD, used to put a three-pointed star on the files of the women who seemed to him to be in love with their husbands, who were only 20 per cent of his patients.

Yet the majority of women, when asked, 'Do you love your husband?' cannot give a straight answer.
    'I respect him very much.'
    'He is a very good man.'
    'He is very kind to me.'
That's one set of responses. They don't qualify for the three-pronged star, but the prognosis is still good. Then the answers may run like this.
    'He's very busy – I don't see him very much.'
    'He's very tired – even falls asleep watching television.'
    'He is not well – wish he would take off some weight and take better care of himself.'
Usually these remarks are uttered without any emotion. I know then something besides estrogen is needed to restore this woman to a fully feminine role. (118)

The prognosis in such cases is bad, presumably. The husbands described in these terms are uninterested and uninteresting, tired, obese, distracted and worse, but it is still a sign of inadequacy in the wives that they do not find them attractive. Though as a gynaecologist Dr Wilson cannot offer to treat these husbands, he does allow that they may need treatment:

Clearly there is something wrong here. But it is not likely to be lack of hormones in a man. More probably, it is lack of interest. The man is simply bored. The fault may be a dull mind, a dull job, or a dull wife. Whatever it is, it is unendurable and deadly. (128)

The wife has already been told how to dress, how to suggest

new adventurousness in sex, how oestrogen will make her breasts taut and so forth. Nobody has even suggested that *her* problem might be lack of interest. Hers too might be a dull mind, a dull job or a dull husband. Yet people whose minds are not stimulated are likely to have dull minds; housework is a dull job and the kinds of jobs generally done by women outside the home are dull jobs, and husbands can be very dull, especially if their best efforts have already been expended on people they consider more important, in their workplace or their playplace. The situation is as unendurable and deadly for a woman as it is for a man and she should not be encouraged to dose herself with steroids rather than put an end to it.

An older man is by no means as likely to be unattractive to his spouse as an older woman. Women are conditioned generally to prefer men older than themselves; they tend to look for the lineaments of a father in a husband and may very well tolerate a greater degree of physical ageing than men, who have been conditioned to desire and to demand a sexual partner younger than themselves. In September 1990 the cruise liner *Crown Princess* was launched into Brooklyn Harbour by fifty-six-year-old Sophia Loren, resplendent in an enormous tawny wig. Her famous cleavage was well displayed in the glittering gold lamé dress she wore to the dinner on board, to be photographed hand in hand with her husband, Carlo Ponti, now eighty-one, small, sweet and frail. Though Sophia has always towered above him, and seems to come from a different breed of gorgeous humanity altogether, her name has never been linked with any other man. She expects all observers to accept the fact that she finds this little old man attractive, and it seems that they have no difficulty in doing so. Moreover Sophia escapes the rueful reflections of Joanne Woodward (born 1930), married to male pin-up Paul Newman, reported in *Stern* magazine in November 1990.

While Paul is supposedly becoming more and more attractive, I'm becoming an old wreck. Anna Magnani once said that she had earned every wrinkle on her face, and when I was young I agreed with her. What a lovely old face! But when I had that old face, it stopped seeming beautiful to me . . . Fortunately, I inherited good skin. But I'm getting old, I'm getting wrinkles and at a certain age one stops being a pin-up. There's no female Robert Redford or Paul Newman.

There are very few male Robert Redfords and Paul Newmans if it comes to that. Most men do little if anything to render themselves presentable; if they take pains with their appearance, they are required to conceal the fact. Despite the fact that the cosmetics lobby tells us year after year that men are on the brink of wearing make-up there is still something suspect in a man's attempts at self-beautification. Though women are advised at every turn to stay attractive, men are never advised to be attractive or to behave attractively. Such was not always the case; in past epochs even British men practised the arts of flamboyant display and sexual blandishment. In the late seventeenth century and eighteenth century men painted their faces and corseted themselves in order to deny the encroachments of age, because it was understood that old men were no more attractive than old women.

The character of the *senex amans*, the old man in love, is a stock figure of European comedy from classical times. When syphilis was brought back to Europe from the Americas by the explorers at the beginning of the sixteenth century, poets sought to explain the phenomenon in a series of verse allegories in which Love and Death quarrelled, dropped their quivers and got their arrows mixed up. Some of Death's lead-tipped arrows remained in Cupid's quiver, so that young lovers were killed when he aimed at them, and Death occasionally let fly one of Cupid's gold-tipped arrows, so that an old person who should have died fell in love instead. In the popular *commedia dell'arte* the old man in love becomes the pantaloon, who exists to be mocked by the young lovers who will enjoy their right to sexual pleasure in spite of him.

In 1790, Despina, the maid in *Così fan tutte*, could get a laugh by answering Don Alfonso, when he says he has need of her, that she has no need of him. 'I want to do something for you,' he insists, and she answers again, 'For a young girl like me an old man like you can't do anything.' Yet Don Alfonso is not decrepit; he is described in the libretto as 'a man of the world'. He is witty and charming and in tune, but, as he says himself, his hair is grey. That is enough to indicate to Despina that he is incapable of pleasuring her. There are two assumptions at work here and in the audience for whom Lorenzo Da Ponte wrote the libretto, one that Don Alfonso's sexual energy is not adequate to a young woman's needs, and another that he is not attractive enough to excite her.

The middle-aged theatre-goers of the seventeenth and eighteenth centuries, who watched ridiculous figures of their own age persecuting beautiful young people with inappropriate demands and expectations, were being warned off. They were being shown how repulsive they seemed to the young people to whom they might be attracted. In so far as the ridiculous old men had financial and political power they could force their attentions upon young women, and thereby greatly increase the quantum of human misery. The comediographers were defending the rights of the young against the dead hand of paternal power and selfishness, which tried to arrogate all pleasure, including sexual pleasure, to itself. The truth is, of course, that only in the theatre could Chronos be castrated by his sons. In real life old men with money and power could take their pick of young marriageable women and did so. Poets since the time of Chaucer have dealt with the misery caused by the marriage of May and December. The outcome was usually the betrayal of the old husband by the young wife, who succumbed to a natural attraction for a younger man. This outcome could be seen as merely funny or desperately tragic, if the betrayed older man decided to avenge himself on wife and/ or lover. Everything depended upon whether the audience could believe the older man capable of sexual passion. If he wasn't the story was funny; if he was the story was tragic. Sometimes, as in *I Pagliacci*, it was both.

By the time *I Pagliacci* was written theatre-goers had stopped laughing at sex. Once sexuality had been defined as a locus of disease rather than sin, sex became deadly serious. Right sex, good sex was credited with mystical powers, so that no one with any intellectual pretensions dared laugh at Lady Constance with forget-me-nots woven in her pubic hair worshipping the phallus of Mellors the garden god. Ordinary people, of course, continued to find sex funny, and told as many 'dirty jokes' as ever, but their common sense was banished from literature into the 'illegitimate' theatre.

For women writers the emphasis was, as might be expected, rather different. A young woman, compelled to tolerate the sexual attentions of an older man with whom she is not in love, might very well be considered to be in a more desperate situation than the young woman married to an impotent old man. Aphra Behn argues against the denial of female sexuality entailed in marrying young women to old men, rather than the oppression of submitting to the repulsive embraces of palsied eld. The most sophisticated treatment of the theme is the case of Dorothea in *Middlemarch*. Dorothea does not betray her old husband; by her misplaced idealism, she betrays herself. George Eliot rescues her by putting her husband to death in the nick of time, so that Dorothea can marry a man who is more likely to satisfy her sexual and emotional needs.

These commonplaces are all now outdated. What is considered obscene nowadays is the idea of age itself. We are not now allowed to call ourselves old, still less is anyone else allowed to call us old. We are now supposed to stay young, and both sexually attractive and sexually active until the utterly unmentionable end, death. We no longer refer to 'dirty old men' in the same way that we did forty or even thirty years ago. 'Dirty old men' were the ones who had a prurient and creepy interest in the sexuality of the young, although in those days we presumed that there was little that they could do about it. The 'dirty old men' were the ones who offered children sweets and talked suggestively to them, who put their hands up their granddaughters' skirts when they were sitting on their knees, who sniffed bicycle seats. They were disgusting rather than dangerous.

Now that we are not permitted to call anybody old, we must not assume that anyone is impotent either. Impotence is not a natural condition but an affliction to be treated with all the ingenuity that modern technology can assemble. There are even such things as vacuum condoms that will exert negative pressure to produce tumescence in the floppiest old penis. With it comes more cultural pressure than ever to create anxiety about loss of interest and the floppiness of the penis. Even so, there is a residue of common sense which provokes men into announcing their incapacity. Denis Thatcher, asked what he was doing in the election campaign of 1987, said, 'Helping, I suppose.' When pressed he replied rather tartly, 'Do? There's not much I can do at my age.' As a rejection of the prurience and silliness of the English gutter press his retort was quite justified, but many people must have shaken their heads over his 'negativity'. Time was when the fading of sexual desire was seen as a liberation. Consumer culture being predicated on self-pleasuring, such an attitude is untenable. Someone who is not seeking sexual pleasure is simply not playing the game.

The argument of this chapter is simply that continuing sexual interest and perfect sexual adjustment between partners who have been together for thirty years is so difficult and rare that no one should feel guilty or inadequate for not having managed it. When it has been managed it has been extraordinary and wonderful, so extraordinary that there are few accounts of it. The ones we can find are the more fascinating for that.

Forty-seven-year-old Jane Digby gave up on love in 1854, when, after three marriages, she had been rejected by her Arab lover for a younger woman and decided that she and her friend Eugenia would grow old together surrounded by their cats and dogs. She could hardly have imagined that the love of her life was about to sweep her away with him to the desert. Sheik Abdul Medjuel El Mezrab, who ruled the desert around Palmyra, saw her, loved her and continued to love her for thirty years. When they were married in 1855, she said, 'If I had neither a mirror, nor a memory, I would think myself fifteen years old' (Blanch, 176).

We do not know how Jane Digby El Mezrab kept the love of her dark desert king for thirty years, during which she did not live as the usual suppressed and invisible Arab wife, but rode alongside her husband like an Amazon. The Sheik for his part refused to use her money and took no other wife. Isabel Burton met her in 1868 and wrote:

> She was a most beautiful woman, though at the time I write she was sixty-one, tall, commanding and queen like ... [she wore] one blue garment, beautiful hair in two plaits to the ground. (183)

Though she adopted Arab dress, Jane Digby El Mezrab kept her silver and damask and her fine bed linen; after fifteen years she succeeded in persuading her husband to use a knife and fork. She chose a Christian burial, at which her grief-stricken husband, mounted on her favourite black mare, rode up unannounced, took one last look and wheeled off into the desert.

The love of Sheik El Mezrab for the middle-aged English lady might inspire middle-aged people to think themselves into falling in love instead of talking themselves into resignation. There are some signs that a new mythology of geriatic love is springing up as the population ages; as more and more leisured elderly people re-invent the social events that were the framework of courtship, tea-dances and picnics, and sporting events of an unstrenuous nature, flirtation must ensue and old men and women must dream dreams. It would be invidious to suggest that Gabriel García Márquez had this readership in mind when he made his own highly significant contribution to the myth of geriatric love in *Love in the Time of Cholera*. The plot follows the tradition of old romances; Aucassin, in this case Florentino Ariza, must wait all his life and traverse untold hazards, mostly affairs with other women, before he can enjoy his true love, Fermina Daza. Because this is the twentieth century the fulfilment of the ancient lovers must be described in concrete terms, but Márquez, who was nearly sixty when he wrote *Love in the Time of Cholera*, has some difficulties. The first physical contact is disappointing.

Both were lucid enough to realize, at the same fleeting instant, that the hands made of old bones were not the hands they had imagined before touching.

'Not now,' she said to him, 'I smell like an old woman.' (329)

Admittedly these lovers are very old; Márquez is quite deliberately pitching his preposterous story as far into old age as his imagination will take him. He may be deliberately invoking images of the charnel house in insisting on the smell of the very old, who are not rotting, or as he would have it, fermenting. Old people smell less, not more, than young people, because they secrete less (see Chapter 6). A clean old person is quite likely to have the same powdery smell as a baby. Nevertheless, Márquez insists that his ancient lovers smell not just bad but awful.

Florentino Ariza shuddered: as she herself had said, she had the sour smell of old age. Still, as he walked to his cabin, he consoled himself with the thought that he must give off the same odor, except his was four years older, and she must have detected it on him, with the same emotion. It was the smell of human fermentation, which he had perceived in his oldest lovers and they had detected in him. The widow Nazaret, who kept nothing to herself, had told him in a cruder way, 'Now we stink like a henhouse.' They tolerated each other because they were an even match: my odor against yours. (335)

So depressed are the lovers by the evidence of their own unbiological 'fermentation' that they can proceed no further in their genital affairs until Fermina drinks anisette. Then, a blow having been struck for the liquor lobby, they are off and running:

. . . he dared to explore her withered neck with his fingertips, her bosom armored in metal stays, her lips with their decaying bones, her thighs with their aging veins. She accepted with pleasure, her eyes closed, but she did not tremble, and she smoked and drank at regular intervals. At length, when his caresses slid over her belly, she had enough anisette in her heart.

'If we're going to do it, let's do it,' she said, 'but let's do it like grown-ups.'

She took him to the bedroom and, with the lights on, began to undress without false modesty . . .

She said: 'Don't look . . . Because you won't like it' . . .

He looked at her and saw her naked to the waist, just as he had imagined her. Her shoulders were wrinkled, her breasts sagged, her ribs were covered by a flabby skin as pale and cold as a frog. (338)

There is a certain perversity operating here too; if Fermina does not want Florentino to see she ought not to undress, let alone with the light on, which is evidently what she means by doing it 'like grown-ups'. There is no law of taste or morality which demands that people fuck naked or by the light of the overhead bulb. Fermina seems to be doing her utmost to revolt Florentino, so Márquez can revolt us. How Florentino knows that the 'flabby skin' is cold without touching it is mysterious; Márquez's intention in invoking frogs is not. Old bodies are not as revolting as young people think; Márquez's invention of heroic fucking against tremendous odds, as if the two old people were galvanized corpses, is actually profoundly ageist. Underlying it are two unpleasant and invalid assumptions: that old people will only transcend their oldness by imitating younger people, and that old people are revolting.

. . . she stretched out her hand in the darkness, caressed his belly, his flanks, his almost hairless pubis. She said: 'You have skin like a baby's.' Then she took the final step: she searched for him where he was not, she searched again without hope, and she found him, unarmed.

'It's dead,' he said . . .

He took her hand and laid it on his chest: Fermina Daza felt the old, untiring heart almost bursting through his skin, beating with the strength, the rapidity, the irregularity of an adolescent's. (340)

While it is probably a truism that the end of one's sexual career is as incompetent as the beginning, it seems unduly cruel that the old lovers have to approach each other as baldly and dispassionately as any pair of pick-ups after a town-hall dance, and that Fermina should think less of wrapping her new lover in her arms than of 'searching for him', by which I suppose Márquez means groping for his penis, and finding it 'unarmed', i.e. limp. Eventually, on the second encounter, penetration is effected Márquez calls it 'making love'.

It was the first time she had made love in over twenty years, and she was held back by her curiosity concerning how it would feel at her age after so long a respite. But he had not given her time to find out if her body loved him too. It had been hurried and sad, and she thought: Now we've screwed up everything. But she was wrong . . . (341)

In the world of magic realism vaginas do not atrophy. Fermina Daza might well have suffered excruciating pain, and torn or bled; her lover's frail erection, for the glans penis does not often become completely turgid in eighty-year-old men, would have found penetration very difficult, if not impossible. Why the two ancient lovers have to imitate the act of generation, why they cannot pleasure each other in any of the myriad ways human beings can but must achieve 'normal' or 'grown-up' sex, seems to argue a certain lack of imagination on the part of the lovers, and their creator. Márquez invents for them a normal married life in which Fermina waits as devotedly on Florentino as ever Colette's Pauline waited on her.

. . . she helped him to take his enemas, she got up before he did to brush the false teeth he kept in a glass while he slept, and he solved the problem of her misplaced spectacles, for she could use his for reading and mending . . .

Locked in the boat doomed to sail for ever in the pestilential river as the corpses float by, Florentino and Fermina enact true happiness. The ending of the novel has the hollow ring of mere pious feeling. Eric Segal could hardly have written it worse.

They made the tranquil, wholesome love of experienced grandparents . . . they no longer felt like newlyweds, and even less like belated lovers. It was as if they had leapt over the arduous calvary of conjugal life and gone straight to the heart of love. They were together in silence like an old married couple wary of life, beyond the pitfalls of passion, beyond the brutal mockery of hope and the phantoms of disillusion: beyond love. For they had lived together long enough to know that love was always love, anytime and anyplace, but it was more solid the closer it came to death. (345)

After such flummery, 'love is never having to say you're sorry' sounds like hard-headedness.

Behind the prescription of unending sexual intercourse between spouses from the altar to the grave lies the domestication of passion. It is nowadays generally held that sex is good for you. Despite the fact that women and children are commonly subject to sexual abuse and sex is suspected as a motive in the murder of every woman and every child, the certainty that sex is at least as good for you as bran has been successfully established. The sexual revolutionaries' belief that sex was only destructive when distorted by repression has been shown to be wrong, for the incidence of all kinds of sex-related crime has risen steadily over the last twenty years. Nevertheless the belief in a domestic brand of sex, which is regular, benign, wholesome and affectionate, has completely driven out any idea of love as essentially related to death. Sex has been purged of all obsessiveness, all hostility, all jealousy, all guilt. It has been reconciled with familiarity and predictability. It is exclusive without being possessive. It is inexhaustible. To suspect, let alone believe, that this is a delusion, is to be a modern heretic. To admit holding any such belief is to reveal oneself as a reactionary crone.

The version of sex as the cement of the family is a new one upon the earth and may indeed constitute a delusion, particularly as it has gained the ascendant at the same time and at the same rate that divorce has reached the level of one in two marriages in the United States, with the western European nations close behind. Older societies have acted on the principle that sex is basically unpredictable, dangerous and uncontrollable. Traditionally the sex relation between spouses has been carefully contained within a family structure, and monitored by other family members, aware of the constant potentiality for abuse and physical violence within it. Recent reporting of the frequency of spouse rape in Britain would seem to show that we cannot afford to continue pretending that sexuality has been domesticated. Most human societies have understood that young men are particularly dangerous and should be kept away from children and other men's wives, disciplined by apprenticeship or national service or the authority of an older patriarch, so that their aggressiveness did not disturb the nurturing home where women and children were meant to feel safe from outrage. The extent of our failure to ensure that mothers and children are secure can be assessed from the horrifying figures for child abuse and for wife battery and rape that every year strike us as incredible, but in which we are constrained to believe. The tiny nuclear family built about the copulating couple is unsafe for women and children. It is arguable that it is unsafe because of the primacy given to the sex relation between the couple, the maintenance of which may be thought to justify all kinds of distorted behaviour and certainly conflicts with the demands of small children.

The pressure then upon the ageing wife to continue playing the sex game with her husband, who may be still interested, or may require more effective stimuli than she can offer, or may be completely uninterested, is part of the same process that has apparently already succeeded in brutalizing family life. If this is the case, which is admittedly suggested rather than demonstrated, the ageing wife would be better advised to opt out, to insist upon a different relationship with her husband in which different values were paramount. What is so clear as to be obvious is that she should have the right to opt out of the sex relationship without appearing to invite desertion.

Peasant populations generally have very clear notions about the stage in life when sexual activity should cease. For women this is usually when the first daughter reaches the age of marriage; though this may be long before menopause, it is felt inappropriate for two generations to be in the childbearing phase at the same time. And so we find very commonly in peasant populations a long period of what is called 'terminal abstinence', which is very important in limiting fertility, as it limits a potential childbearing season of thirty years to sixteen or so (Caldwell and Caldwell; Ruzicka and Bhatia; Gayanake).

Terminal abstinence would be considered by most developed societies an unbearable limitation on human sexual expression. In most societies that practise it, it is considered merely normal. Older people no longer feel '*la furia*'; they have other indulgences – food, alcohol, tobacco, power, money, business, politics. It is understood, moreover, that old bodies are not attractive; those who can may buy young bodies for their gratification. In some societies the powerful old men commandeer all the young women for their own use, while young men and older women alike go without. Bride-price in some societies functions as a way of supplying young women exclusively to those who can raise the payment, so that young men are obliged to watch the women of their own generation mated with the generation of their fathers. This may or may not be seen as a tyranny, largely depending upon whether there is a semi-sanctioned culture of adultery that goes along with it.

There are many different ways of organizing human sexual response and human sexual relationships. Human beings are not monogamous; they are not programmed like the species that once mated can never part, none of whom rely upon continual intercourse to keep them together, but only mate when they are reproducing. Human love does not depend upon the need to mate or the need for orgasm; the greatest love can survive distance and even death. When in 1750 at the age of sixty Susannah Highmore realized that she was dying, she hid notes for her husband all about their house, so that he would find them after she was gone. The notes were to tell him how deeply she loved him (*Gentleman's Magazine*, January, 1816).

15

The Hardy Perennials

Though it is clearly not true that life begins at forty, and even more obviously absurd to claim that life begins at fifty, many women may expect to live as many years after menopause as they have already lived as adults. For some women, especially women who have felt themselves most alive when functioning as the lover and beloved of a man or men, this is by no means good news. Simone de Beauvoir inveighed bitterly against the decline not only of her sexual attractions but of her interest in sex: she wrote in 1963, when she was fifty-five:

Never again a man. Now, not my body alone but my imagination too has accepted that in spite of everything, it's strange not to be a body any more. There are moments when the oddness of it, because it's so definitive, chills my blood. But what hurts more than all these deprivations is never feeling any new desires: they wither before they can be born in the rarefied climate I inhabit now. (1965, 657)

However, there have been women who saw their influence over a man or, even more difficult, over more than one man, continue to grow long after menopause had come and gone. The essentials for such a career seem to be first of all good health, and its concomitant, good spirits, then intelligence, and then style or its equivalent. Great mistresses of the arts of civilization continue to enchant regardless of whether they are allowing physical intimacy to one or other or all of their followers. Even courtesans, provided they were endowed with taste, wit and energy, have been able to continue living in the grand style though neither they nor the habitués of their salons were interested in sex. Such a one was the great French courtesan Ninon de Lenclos.

In the spring of 1671, when she was fifty-one, Ninon de Lenclos fell in love for the umpteenth time. The object of her passion was Charles de Sévigné, a smooth-faced angelic-looking young man of twenty-three. His mother, the Marquise de Sévigné, wrote to her daughter, 'Your brother wears the chains of Ninon; I wish they may do him no harm. There are minds that shudder at such ties. Ninon corrupted the morals of his father' (Letter XXV, I, 47). Many years before, when the Marquis de Sévigné was a handsome rakehell who had left his virtuous wife at home to be assiduously courted by her cousin, he had caught Ninon's roving eye. As was usually the case with her, she tired of him in a few weeks and amused herself by making a conquest first of one of his wife's admirers, the Sieur de Rambouillet, and then another, the Marquis de Vassé. Madame de Sévigné could avenge herself for this series of humiliations only in her letters. Now in middle age Ninon seduced her son, whose latest amorous exploit had been to take the actress Champmeslé away from Racine.

Mademoiselle de Lenclos promenaded with Charles in the Cours, and let herself be seen slapping him hard for looking at other women and then kissing him to make up. Furiously jealous of the young actress, she demanded that he yield up to her Champmeslé's letters, which he did. Nothing Ninon did could awaken the spirit of gallantry in him, however. He let her exhibit him at delicious suppers in Saint-Germain but he made no attempt to hide his lack of real interest in fashionable manners and elegant conversation, at which Ninon was universally acknowledged to excel. Meanwhile his mother and her friend Madame de Lafayette were struggling to awaken in Charles some sense of the indelicacy of his position. They persuaded him to get Champmeslé's letters back, but before they could prevail upon him to give up his relationship with Ninon, she threw him out. 'He is past belief,' said Ninon, 'with the mind of a milksop and a heart like an iced pumpkin.' The affair had lasted a month.

Ninon used to say that three months was her limit with anyone; she had had hundreds of lovers and history would go on to credit her with more. She was supposed to have taken pity on Charles Paris d'Orléans, son of the Duc de la Rochefoucauld and Madame de Longueville, who begged her to save him from his mistress, 'that fat Marquise de Castelnau'. She is thought in her sixties to have had an affair with a Swede called Jean Banier and in her nineties to have extended her favours to two licentious *abbés*, Gedoyn and Châteauneuf, and at the same age to have tried to seduce Bourdaloue. Such stories, some of which are derived from conflicting statements made about her by Voltaire, whose father was her lawyer, are somewhat blighted by the fact that Ninon died in 1705 at the age of eighty-five.

More reputable biographers have argued that she gave up physical passion after Charles de Sévigné. She replied to a flattering letter from her dear friend Saint-Evremond:

I learn with pleasure that my soul is dearer to you than my body, and that your good sense leads you as always to the better part. To tell truth, the body is no longer worthy of attention, and the soul still does have some glow that supports it and renders it responsive to the memory of a friend, whose absence has not dimmed his image. (Colombey, 119–20; author's translation)

Madame, the King's sister, the Duchesse d'Orléans, wrote to a friend:

Now that Madame de Lenclos is old, she leads a very strict life. She maintains, so they say, that she would never have reformed if she herself had not realized how ridiculous the whole affair was.

Though she had given up physical passion, Mademoiselle de Lenclos did not give up passion. She devoted herself to the cultivation and maintenance of friendship.

Durability in friendship is at least as rare as durability in love. Time was when I cared only for the latter, now I long for the former. (Magne, 214–15)

She befriended Madame de la Sablière, the unhappy wife of her old lover, the Sieur de Rambouillet, and was a frequent visitor at her house in Saint-Roch, where she shared Madame de la Sablière's hospitality with the likes of Molière, La Fontaine, Mignard, Tallemant and Boileau. The same luminaries visited her exquisite house in the Rue de Tournelles, where newcomers were as astonished by the liveliness of their hostess's wit as by the freshness of her complexion. Her explanation of her youthful appearance was simply that in a lifetime of offering her guests the best wines she herself drank nothing but pure water.

She avoided late nights and all excess of eating and drinking, the sources, she was wont to say, of premature senility. (229)

Saint-Simon wrote in his *Mémoires*:

Everything at Mademoiselle de Lenclos' is done with a respect and decorum which is rarely enjoyed even by the best-loved princesses in the conduct of their affairs. She had, therefore, the noblest and most attractive people at Court for friends . . . it became the fashion to be received at her house, and people used to like to go there on account of the people they met. There was no gaming, ribaldry, nor brawling, and no one discussed politics or religion. Humour and elaborate wit, talk of things ancient and modern, news of everyone's love affairs, were the order of the day; but everything was discussed delicately and tolerantly, with no hint of malice, and the hostess knew how to keep conversation going by her intelligence and her great wealth of information about this and every age. (Magne, 231)

The Sun King himself dreaded the scalpel touch of Ninon's irony. For thirty post-menopausal years she was the arbiter of taste for *tout-Paris*; princes, statesmen, philosophers and artists all knew that her verdict on their performances carried more weight than the screeds of bought praise that appeared in print. And some of them persisted in writing love poems to her. As for Charles de Sévigné, he became a monk.

Though Ninon was a rarity so fabulous that noble travellers in Paris insisted on being taken to meet her, she was by no means unique. The mistresses of the kings of France set a formidable precedent in durability. The Abbé Brantôme claimed to have seen the legendary Diane de Poitiers at the age of seventy 'as beautiful of face, as fresh and kindly as at thirty years'. Unfortunately for this evidence, Diane de Poitiers died at the age of sixty-six. Six months before her death, again according to Brantôme, she was lovely enough 'to move a heart of rock'; her horse had fallen with her in the streets of Orléans and her leg had been broken, but she gave no sign of pain. 'Far from it; for her beauty, her grace, her majesty, her handsome appearance were all the same as they had always been.' Above all, her skin was dazzling though she used no rouge or powder. Dreux du Radier thought her dazzling complexion the result of washing her face every morning with *eau de puits*, well water. She rose at six, rode, and then went back to bed and read till noon, and this combination of strenuous exercise and rest is thought by some to be the secret of her undiminished vitality in later life.

When Diane's lover became Henri II of France in 1547 he was thirty-one; Diane was in her forty-eighth year. She had been a widow for fifteen years and had never changed her *petit deuil*. To the end of her life she wore only black and white. The court was quickly staffed with her associates. The King made her Duchesse du Valentinois and gave her not only an enormous sum of money with which to rebuild her own Château d'Anet, but the huge domaine of Chenonceau as well. Diane ruled him in everything; it was she who told him when to sleep with the Queen, Cathérine de Médicis; when Cathérine's children were born Diane was placed in charge of them. In 1552 the Venetian ambassador Contarini wrote:

. . . he greatly loved, he greatly loves her, and old as she is she is his mistress. It is true that although she has never used rouge and perhaps by virtue of the minute care which she takes, she is far from looking her age . . . His Majesty . . . does . . . in this and in everything else what she wants. She is informed of everything, and every day as a rule the King, after his dinner, goes to her and remains an hour and a half to consult with her and to tell her all that happens. (H. W. Henderson, 182–3)

In 1554, at the height of her power, Diane was obliged to beg the King to leave her for a time. She was unwell, and evidently did not wish him to see her at anything but her best. Her biographers do not tell us, and probably could not tell us, if her malady was connected with menopause. The King went to Saint-Germain-en-Laye. When he returned his neglected wife had arranged a ballet, to exhibit the charms of a governess of the Scots princess who, she thought, might succeed in drawing her husband away from his middle-aged lover. The King fell for his wife's stratagem and fathered a son upon the little Scotswoman, but the second part of the ruse failed. When Diane was fully recovered the King was once more by her side. When the Queen became pregnant for the eleventh time, he gave up going to her bed for good.

The love of Henri II for a woman nearly twenty years older lasted until he was mortally wounded in a tournament in 1559. As he lay dying the Queen, with whom he had had no relations for the last six years, was called to his side and sworn in as regent. When Diane came to take her leave of the man she had loved for thirty years, the doors were shut against her. She was evicted from her apartments in the palace and Chenonceau was taken from her. She said that she would die with her lover; she lived on until 1566, leaving us a single realistic portrait of her in middle age to compare with the dozens of idealized depictions of her tall, graceful, long-legged, high-breasted person as the goddess Diana, in words by Marot or du Bellay, in sculpture by Jean Goujon or Benvenuto Cellini, and painted by François Clouet or Léonard Limosin.

Madame de Maintenon is an even more remarkable example of a woman's power to fascinate long after what was commonly perceived as her beauty had decayed. She was born Françoise d'Aubigny in 1635; at eighteen she married the crippled playwright

Paul Scarron, who died in 1660, leaving her destitute. In 1669 Madame de Montespan appointed her governess of the children she had borne to Louis XIV of France, then living near Vaugirard; in 1674 the King decided that his children should be at court, and Madame Scarron came with them. By September 1675 she had already undermined the position of Madame de Montespan so effectively that her erstwhile patroness was sent away from the court. Meanwhile the King's architect had been sent to supervise the restoration and embellishment of the house at Maintenon that Madame Scarron had bought with the money she earned from Madame de Montespan. Her champions excuse her of all calculation in the matter.

Her gentle nature and retiring disposition soon gained for her Louis's esteem; he chose her to read to him and gradually admitted her more and more to his confidence. In 1678 he advanced her small estate of Maintenon ... into a marquisate. From the first moment of her influence over the King she used it for the good of France and himself. Once she had finally succeeded in ousting Madame de Montespan from favour, she cleansed the Court of much of its looseness, made friends with the poor neglected Queen, who trusted her and liked her, and after that lady's death was secretly married to Louis ...

It is always romantic when a pretty young commoner marries a powerful king. In this version of the Cinderella story the commoner was a fifty-year-old widow who was rumoured to have been before her marriage to the playwright no better than a prostitute. She was an old friend of Ninon de Lenclos, and had had a long affair with one of Ninon's ex-lovers. Evidently Madame de Montespan did not expect her to use an appearance of virtue to discredit her. There were many at court who saw the Marquise de Maintenon as a designing hypocrite, among them the King's sister-in-law, Elisabeth-Charlotte of Bavaria, Princess Palatine, Duchess of Orléans, Madame de France, who could never bring herself to speak of Madame de Maintenon without including the epithet 'old':

The old Maintenon woman amuses herself by making the King hate all the members of the Royal family and bend them to her will . . . the Dauphiness is . . . daily ill-treated at the old hag's instigation . . . The old hag has already tried a dozen times to embroil me with the Dauphiness. (Stevenson, I, 74)

Despite the high-bred fury of the royal families of Europe at the unconscionable power wielded by this woman of low birth, the King married Madame de Maintenon secretly in 1685. His sister-in-law wrote in 1688 in answer to queries about his marriage from her aunt, the Duchess of Hanover:

One thing, however, is certain, the King never loved any of his mistresses as devotedly as he loves her. It is very amusing to see them together. If she is anywhere about he cannot let a quarter of an hour pass without whispering in her ear, or withdrawing to talk to her in private, and this although he has spent the whole day with her. (I, 80)

Four years later she writes again:

On journeys like these the Great Man lives in the same house as his old slut, but does not sleep in the same room, and a mystery is made of the whole affair. You will understand therefore that he has not yet acknowledged her as his wife. That, however, does not prevent him from shutting himself up with her every day when they are together and keeping the whole court waiting at the door . . . (I, 107)

And again in 1696 she tells of the King's severity with two of his illegitimate daughters, who had been making rude songs about their stepmother:

. . . it appears that he did not mince his language, and he seems to have been more annoyed on Madame de Maintenon's account than because of what they said about himself. The love he bears that woman is quite extraordinary. (I, 45)

So unchallenged was Madame de Maintenon's power at the court of the most powerful monarch in Europe that Madame referred to her, when she was not calling her 'the old bawd', as 'the Pantocrat'.

In September 1698, Madame had the satisfaction of reporting:

The Pantocrat is very powerful, but from all accounts she is not very happy and often weeps bitterly. And she often talks about Death, but I expect that is only to see how people will reply to her ... (I, 169)

In July 1699, Madame was displeased to discover that when she visited 'the all-powerful Dame' she was offered only a footstool to sit on, because the King visited so often and no one could have a seat in his presence, except Madame de Maintenon, who was 'allowed one because of her bad health' (I, 185) which dissipated before 1710 when she was still 'the all-powerful Maintenon':

When the King is going neither to shoot, nor to Marly, he spends the whole afternoon with Madame de Maintenon, and he works in her room with his ministers every evening. (II, 55)

In 1712 she told her aunt:

Although the old woman is my bitterest enemy, I nevertheless wish her a long life, for the King's sake, because everything would be ten times worse if the King were to die at this juncture, and he is so devoted to the woman that he would assuredly not survive her, therefore I hope that she may live for many years to come. (II, 58)

When she was seventy, Madame de Maintenon 'complained to her confessor that she still very often had to lie with the old king' (De Beauvoir, 1965, 187n). After his death, she withdrew to the girls' school she had founded at Saint-Cyr, where she died four years later at the age of eighty-four.

In order to understand the high visibility of older women in the French court, we have to understand that the culture of pre-revolutionary France placed a high premium on refinement of taste and manners. Such depth of polish took many years to acquire; it began with discipline and after years of practice became second nature. Though everyone was aware of the bloom of young women and quick to caress them, no one visited the great *salonnières* to marvel at beauties that were more easily observed and enjoyed in milkmaids. This state of affairs still prevailed in the 1780s when, according to Madame de La Tour du Pin, the older women were 'all-powerful' (86). After the revolution,

gatherings of all the generations [became] things of the past and . . . to M. Talleyrand's great regret, old ladies are no longer to be met in society. (95)

Men and women alike willingly submitted to the rule of the doyennes in order to learn from them the complicated and subtle movements of the social dance. Though there were salons in England, and they were run by older women, the greater segregation in British society is manifest in that they were never central. When Molière made fun of *Les Femmes Savantes*, he was singling out women whose pedantry offended against the standards of behaviour set and observed by ladies of refinement. When women who dared to discuss matters of aesthetics and philosophy were guyed by English satirists, there was an added element of sheer intolerance for having to listen to a woman at all.

The English version of the venerable *salonnière* is Mary Delany, who at eighty-eight 'blushed like a girl'. When she was seventeen she was married off to a disagreeable sixty-year-old man who died five years later without making his will, leaving her without the fortune her family had hoped for. She was courted by various gentlemen, including Lord Baltimore, but she did not remarry until she was forty-three, when Swift's friend Patrick Delany came over to England to ask her to be his second wife. He was much her inferior in rank and connections, and not a wealthy man, but she accepted him and they lived happily until his death in 1768. In her second widowhood she became a favourite of the royal family, who visited her every day. She was remarkable for her taste, her good breeding, her charm and her vivacity, which she retained until her death in 1788. George III commissioned her portrait by Opie and it hangs still in Hampton Court.

Louisa Maximiliana, daughter of Gustavus Adolphus, Prince of Stohlberg-Gedern, after eight unhappy years as the wife of the elderly, debauched and drunken Young Pretender, then living in exile as the Count of Albany, ran off with the great Italian playwright Vittorio Alfieri and lived with him as his mistress until his death in 1803, when she was fifty. Though her grief was intense, within a few months Alfieri's place at her side was filled by their mutual friend, the young French painter Fabré, who lived with her until her death in 1824 and was her sole heir.

We may speculate that these women all had attractions of other than a physical kind. In the case of Ninon and Madame de Maintenon we may judge that theirs were charms of personality. Other middle-aged women who were successful in love were so because of their rank and fortune; the most obvious example of a woman who used rank to entice into her bed men much younger than herself is Catherine the Great, who behaved as Empress in much the same way that male monarchs behaved, taking her pick of the most vigorous and attractive sex objects appearing at court. The greatest middle-aged stars sparkling in our firmament are those of the screen; not a week passes without one or other of them appearing on the arm of a new lover. Elizabeth Taylor (born 1932) is never seen these days without thirty-eight-year-old ex-construction-worker Larry Fortensky by her side. Some commentators suggest that he may be her bodyguard. What her rich and distinguished ex-husbands think of the situation is not on record. 'Miss Taylor' told *People Weekly* that she does not intend to marry Mr Fortensky:

I think I've outgrown that. In today's society you don't need to be married. You don't need to tidy up. Not at my age anyway.

On 22 September 1990, a popular British weekly featured on its cover a portrait of a sixty-year-old lady, or rather of her porcelain teeth, her lipstick, her eye make-up, her brass earrings and her wig. There was some obvious air-brushing about the chops and the barest touch of chicken-skin across the bosom, but otherwise, you had to say it, she looked terrific. (Besides, everyone in the beauty business has her photograph touched up these days; as far as the glossies are concerned, none of us actually looks good enough.) 'Exclusive' ran the banner in caps to the left of her. 'Joan Collins introduces her secret love to us and talks frankly about marriage and fulfilment'. And on the right, 'I think I'm happier now than at any time during my life.' The same photograph appeared in larger format inside, this time showing her only slightly crêpey arms and ringless hands and an exposed knee. Not an age spot to be seen. Opposite, the heading ran: 'Joan Collins: A fulfilled woman who's found love and achieved a lifelong ambition.' The same white dress appeared in another photograph, revealing that it had a floor-length skirt split up to mid-thigh, showing just enough leg and a good deal of very high-heeled white shoe.

'Joan's used to being told how great she looks: "I'm quite proud of being the age I am, with the knowledge and experience and productivity that I have – and still looking pretty good",' a caption read. She went on: 'And if I have a few lines, that's only to be expected.' You had to look hard to find the lines, or the name of the man who had photographed her in eight outfits, an assortment of wigs and postiches, and twelve or more locations. If you looked at the close-ups you could see the lights reflected in the middle of Miss Collins's pupils; one of her skills is that she knows how not to screw up her eyes when she is being dazzled by the vast wattage that will light out any lines and make her eyes shine. No mention at all was made of the person who looked after make-up and hair or the person with the airbrush who finished the prints. The mythology must make it seem that Joan looked as good as she did by virtue of inner radiance. For most of the outdoor shots she wore dark glasses; only one showed that her eyes were clogged by make-up and she had to keep a small half-smile if the jowls were not to droop. The photostory is a triumph, for whatever else Joan Collins might be, she is thoroughly professional.

She is not easily drawn on the subject of her close friend art-dealer Robin Hurlstone. But after three-and-a-half pretty secret years, 57-year-old Joan Collins has just openly acknowledged their special companionship and disclosed Robin's best qualities. It's 'to Robin' she dedicates her second book, 'for his patience and support. With all my love'.

Patience and support are not what younger women might thank a lover for; the cynical reader might be pardoned for suspecting that Joan and Robin, a never-married old Etonian in his early thirties, are indeed just good friends, or even that Robin is what is known in the business as a walker, supplying the 'harmony, compatibility and friendship' that the star says are the most important aspects of a loving relationship.

Under all the make-up and false hair Joan Collins was actually coming on not like the witty theatrical professional that she is but like a dear old grannie, who wanted us all to know that what she had learned after sixty years was that 'there are only two important things in life – health and being happy'. The magazine was anxious to parlay the relationship with Robin into a searingly passionate love-affair, but had to be content with such unromantic items as the fact that Robin found the site for Joan's new house in Provence. Unfortunately the tabloid gossip columns a few days later ran a story about Miss Collins's attempt to buy a portrait of Mr Hurlstone from his close friend the Marquess of Bristol, for whom it had been executed. According to Nigel Dempster, when she named her price, she was told by the nobleman that it would suffice only to buy pictures of rather a different kind, depicting both Mr Hurlstone and the Marquess in attitudes that she would not find particularly attractive.

The *Hello* interviewer reverently prompted her:

You've said yourself that in some small way you've been a pioneer in the cause of women's sexual equality, and also in overcoming the age barrier that sets a cruel double standard for so many women.

'Miss Collins' took up the challenge.

That's right, and the issue which was rammed down my throat from such an early age, I found utterly shocking. One's usefulness as an actress, it was disgracefully assumed, was over at the age of 23. 23! I was determined that was not going to happen to me, though other girls were quite resigned to it.

. . . I happen to come from a rather youthful-looking family.

The extraordinary structure of these unsayable sentences is the only indication of the contradiction of being a four-times married mother of three adult children inside a carefully reconstructed nubile 'Miss Collins'. The interviewer was probably too young to care whether Miss Collins's notion of 'health' included HRT and certainly too reverent to ask whether any plastic surgery had been had, possibly because she had read Miss Collins's emphatic denials elsewhere. In the same magazine we could see that another Miss Collins, Jackie this time, staring-eyed in a welter of hair lacquer and lip-gloss, was celebrating the publication of a new book. We could also see Teddy Kennedy's estranged wife, in off-the-shoulder lilac, making her daughter seem dumpy and old at her own wedding. It was not easy to reconcile these images with others in the same magazine. The sixty-one-year-old woman who trains the Queen Mother's horses seemed a creature from a different planet; Jane Goodall, sitting with her chimps, seemed like the mother of nations carved in stone; the vivid face of sixty-year-old Elettra Marconi looked intelligent and loving, rather than appetizing; C. Z. Guest looked like a picturesque ruin of a high-bred woman. To say that you liked these images better than the seventeen dazzling studies of 'Miss Collins' is to stand a confessed gerontophile; nevertheless they were images of something spiritual, like the asymmetrical faces of the great Roman portraits of the first century. Here is no question of packaging or of product. Reconstructed middle-aged women all look more or less the same, despite variations of colouring and shape; in the unconstructed female face we see the flame working through the clay.

It has been said that if you are to fight age you have to decide between the face and the body. A cruder version says, 'It's either your bum or your face.' Jane Fonda (born 1937) has concentrated on her bum, with rather dire results for her face. At the time of writing 'Miss Fonda' is engaged to be married to the President of CNN; she has shared with her public the fact that to go with her opal and diamond ring she has had augmentation mammoplasty. No matter how hard you work out, it seems, there is nothing you can do for the bosom but pump it up. Whether she is also having hormone replacement therapy is not known, but how actual breast tissue stimulated by oestrogen would react to the synthetic prosthesis is one thing that one must hope she has considered in the midst of love's young dream.

At fifty-eight, British-born film star Anne Heywood has married the former Assistant Attorney General of New York State, George Danzig Druke. Her hair, though thin, is still a flaming titian; her bosom is every bit as full and taut, her tummy as flat as Robert A. Wilson could desire. Via *Hello* magazine (No. 137, 26 January 1991, 18) she had encouraging words to say to every woman approaching sixty:

People have to understand that older women are just as marketable, as they get older, as men are. We women have to remember that we are sexually attractive just the way men think they are until well into their old age. And not only have we got to educate men to think that, but women themselves have to believe in it deeply.

There is an intriguing sub-text here. It seems that old men only think that they are attractive; Joanne Woodward too referred to men *supposedly* becoming more attractive as they age. Both these women are married to old men, but Anne Heywood's husband is no Paul Newman. In the wedding pictures his vague smile and unfocused watery gaze made him look twice his wife's age, despite the thin curls carefully combed over his bald skull. Anne Heywood's use of the word 'marketable' needs no commentary; she might be surprised to learn that at her age many women have rejoiced in being able once for all to cease thinking of themselves as commodities. It is 'Miss Heywood's' dearest ambition to star in a film about abortion rights with Glenda Jackson. This is no more likely to happen than that Barbara Bush should agree to play 'the fate of the untreated menopause' in a movie opposite Nancy Reagan.

Zsa Zsa Gabor is a different matter. Nothing on earth would induce her to call herself marketable because she is in fact priceless. She had almost despaired of her eighth husband, Prince Frederick von Anhalt, because, though handsome and rich, he was a humourless Prussian. The crumbling of the Berlin wall made possible a fairy-tale outcome. Zsa Zsa is now a proper princess, who may wear, besides her brand new diamond and emerald tiara, the sash of a royal order across her shapely bosom. The prince has retrieved three castles belonging to the family, Ballenstedt, Roehrkopf and Moosykau, together with 200 old masters and countless other works of art. It is not often that the showgirl becomes a princess at the age of (undisclosed), having shed seven husbands along the way.

After more than thirty years of marriage to the same man, Helen Gurley Brown is the prototype of the eternal bride. As one of her friends told James Kaplan for an article in *Vanity Fair* (June 1990), 'It must be *exhausting* to be a girl at sixty-eight.' The eternal bride has no children if she can help it, and gets rid of the ones she has as smartly as possible so that she can fix what Kaplan calls her 'heat-lock eyes' on her husband and give his least action her full, dazzled attention. Whenever they are likely to be observed she must gaze at him with parted lips as if they are on the brink of some kind of sex marathon. As she must appear girlish, the eternal bride does not get her bosom pumped up. Usually she has no body to speak of; her face on the other hand is large, stretched shiny-tight by surgery and split by a gash of lipstick and porcelain. The other great prototype of the eternal bride is Nancy Reagan, but if she works out for an hour and half each day to keep in shape as Gurley Brown does, we have not been told.

In January 1991 fifty-eight-year-old jazz singer Bertice Reading celebrated the first anniversary of her marriage to twenty-seven-year-old astrological psychotherapist Philip George-Tutton, telling *Hello* magazine:

It's the best marriage I ever had. Philip is very kind and sweet and he takes care of me.

There are astonishingly attractive older women who do not find it necessary to flaunt male conquests. Neither Tina Turner nor Gina Lollobrigida nor Shirley MacLaine nor Raquel Welch finds it necessary to indicate their continuing marketability by flaunting new conquests, though they may indeed make them. Tippi Hedren, at fifty-five still as slim, fragile and dazzlingly blonde as ever, lives on a ranch with seventy animals, including tigers and leopards, but does not find it necessary to produce a walker or a fiancé.

None of the great perennials, Diane de Poitiers, Ninon de Lenclos or Madame de Maintenon, could have had recourse to cosmetic surgery. None had her jowls pared, her tummy flattened by liposuction, her eyes tidied up, her breasts plumped out. Neither did they have hormone replacement therapy. It did not take them three or four hours to ready themselves for their public, for they were not principally valued for the effect their appearance had on strangers standing at a distance or on cameras. The dazzling old sex objects *de nos jours* are a curiously garish bunch, better to see from a distance than to come close to. They seldom state their age, though everybody knows it; they do not make a point of having triumphed over menopause. Nor are they willing to admit being on HRT. Strange to relate, though the effects of HRT are spectacular, the Masters in Menopause tell us, no one can tell from looking at her whether a woman is on HRT or not.

The chairman of the Amarant Trust is Conservative MP Teresa Gorman, whose heavily made-up face appeared in an airbrushed photograph on the front page of the Trust's first newsletter, which urges women to demand HRT as a right. Mrs Gorman is vociferous about her own hormone replacement and appears sure that her own appearance is encouraging. *She* magazine cooperated in what seems an unusual promotional campaign, featuring Mrs Gorman in a full-page colour photograph with all the lustre that make-up, hair-lacquer, pale pink jacket, diffused lighting and airbrush can bestow. The result may be less encouraging than Mrs Gorman imagines. Though she may think she looks terrific others might easily disagree, especially when they see her in the televised sessions of the House of Commons when she has not had the attentions of make-up artists, hairdressers and lighting cameramen. On the one hand, Mrs Gorman's contribution in the Commons in my view has been neither so judicious nor so venturesome as to inspire emulation and, on the other, if Mrs Gorman should develop a malignancy or a thrombosis or gallstones and be as public about it as she is about her HRT, the consequences for Ciba-Geigy, Organon, Schering and all could be disastrous. If after all the fuss Mrs Gorman has to come off HRT, the result for the industry will be hardly more satisfactory.

Generally, women in high places are ashamed to admit that they are taking replacement hormones and far less willing to function as advertisements for it than Mrs Gorman. Mrs Thatcher would rather we knew about the practitioner who gives her electric tingles in her bath than about her patchet – if she has one. Mrs Gorman successfully sued for libel when she was incorrectly quoted as saying that Mrs Thatcher was a user of replacement hormones. Mrs Thatcher has so far not sued any of the sources that have said that she is, but she herself refuses to divulge whether she is or not. It would have been worth rather more than a king's ransom to the pharmaceutical multinationals if Mrs Thatcher could have been persuaded to announce that she was on HRT. Once she has retired from politics there will be nothing to stop her doing a deal, but by then she could prove to be more of a liability than an asset. Funnily enough, the Amarant Trust newsletter features an editorial by Teresa Gorman, MP, BSc which asks:

Can we grow old with grace and dignity like the Queen Mother or must we face the indignity of declining health with the prospect of ending life in a home incapable of living an independent life?

Is this to say that the Queen Mother is on HRT or simply that HRT confers all the benefits that accrue from the Queen Mother's income? Presumably Mrs Gorman did not refer to the Queen in this context because she stopped smiling at menopause while the Queen Mother's smile, in the manner of the Cheshire Cat's, bids fair to outlast the century. The implication that hormone replacement can guarantee good health in extreme old age is absurd. In Mrs Gorman's confused editorial there is little evidence of the mental tonic effect claimed for HRT by the Masters in Menopause. The main reasons only 2 per cent or so of British women have taken up HRT at the time of writing may be, not their own timorousness and the reluctance of doctors to take their problems seriously, but their own inbuilt scepticism and common sense.

16

The Old Witch

To disbelieve in witches is the greatest of heresies.

Malleus Maleficarum

Witches are to be found in every human society, throughout history, all over the world. Though young women and men have been accused of sorcery and paid the price, the archetypal witch is both old and female. Women who outlive their husbands, or worse, their children, are anomalies in societies where high maternal mortality has been the norm. Their very survival has something in it of the not-natural; it is inevitable that illiterate villagers will assume that childless, widowed women who live long have thrived at the expense of others and that the younger people who sickened inexplicably and died have been eaten up by them. The old women may even believe it themselves. For peoples who have no other explanation of infertility, sickness, and death, belief in witches is a necessity. The ideal candidate must be somebody who will function as a scapegoat. She must therefore be without allies and expendable. 'Of all other women, lean, hollow-eyed, old beetle-browed women are the most infectious,' said Reginald Scot. Bodin agreed, 'For every male witch there are fifty female witches . . .' (fol. 245–245^v)

In 1563 Johann Wier, in *De Praestigiis Demonum*, had argued that witches were 'poor, mindless old women', 'childish old hags', 'old women of melancholic nature and small brains' to be pitied rather than feared. By the beginning of the eighteenth century enlightened men like Addison were arguing that there had never been such things as witches, only superstition, timorousness and prejudice, to which mischievous old women added by their own irrational and meddlesome practices. Yet when Addison wrote deploring the cruelty and superstition that led to their persecution, witches were still being sentenced to death by fire.

There should be no more shame in being a witch than in being old, for witches have a long and distinguished history which reaches far back beyond the invention of writing, to the time when women protected the birthplace and the dangerous transitions between life and death. Much of the story is the story of the criminalization of female power and the discrediting of female knowledge in order to corrode and eliminate the rights and privileges of mothers. In a society where there is still a degree of matrifocality we are not surprised to find positive images of the powerful old woman. A remarkable example is the folk-tale of Mwipenza the Killer told by the Hehe people of Southern Tanzania. Mwipenza is overcome by a very old woman, who was old twenty years before when Makao, the female protagonist of the tale, had gone with her mother to get a medicine for her sister who was dying. The old woman's dark powder had saved the girl's life. Now Makao needs a medicine for her mother but she is attacked by Mwipenza, who lies in wait for her outside the old woman's hut. Her husband finds her dying, but before he can pull out the stick that is pinning her to the ground, the old woman comes out of her hut and calls to him for help.

As soon as Makao's husband started towards her the old woman stopped crying and in a very excited voice called out to him, 'I was just trying your tender heart . . . You were coming to help me first and now I will help your wife for you. (Mvungi, 69)

Only then does he see that Mwipenza is lying dead on the ground transfixed by a pole, killed evidently by the old woman's magic. The old woman smears a green fluid on Makao's wounds and she is miraculously made whole. The young couple turns to the ancient woman to ask how she overcame the killer:

The old doctor laughed and said, 'You two go along with your child.' (69)

The story is clearly not meant to be taken literally; the ancient witchdoctress is rather a figure of the matriarchy or the sororal principle which places the group above the individual and even the couple. She has something in common with the legendary anchoresses of the early Christian church, who emerged from their caves and huts only to perform prodigies.

Because of the nature of the human bond between suffering peasant and trusted sorceress, the good witch becomes endowed with great powers of healing: she is the forerunner, the mother, of the mesmeric healer, the hypnotist, and the (private) psychiatrist. In addition, because she is actually a combination of magician and empiricist, the sorceress acquires, by experimenting with drugs extracted from plants, a genuine knowledge of some powerful pharmacological agents. So advanced is her knowledge that, in 1527, Paracelsus, considered one of the greatest physicians of his time, burnt his official pharmacopoeia declaring that 'he had learned from the Sorceresses all that he knew'. (Sasz, quoted by Shuttle and Redgrove, 209)

Witch, healer, shaman, the older woman has another, immensely important function in pre-literate societies.

In those tribal communities where birth is aided, the assistant is most commonly *the woman's own mother*. In fact, mother and daughter may travel quite a distance to be together at this time. The second most common assistants at a tribal birth are women from the mother's family, her grandmother, her sisters and/or other female relatives from her clan ... In tribes that have made the transition from matrilineal clan to patriarchal family, the mother-in-law may assist ... (Goldsmith, 23–4)

Though mothers still need mothering, their mothers are no longer permitted to carry out this important function. Any man who claims to have sired the child, and some who do not even go so far, can assist a woman in childbirth. Any mother who demanded the right of entry to her daughter's labour room would be regarded as over-protective, interfering, even mischief-making. Mother-daughter relationships have decayed so far in our society that there is no reason to expect that a mother's presence would ease rather than exacerbate a daughter's anxiety. There is nothing that a mother knows about childbirth that could be of benefit to her labouring daughter, especially as she herself probably gave birth under anaesthetic. She certainly would not be allowed to perform her traditional duties of providing physical support at the mother's back, or massaging her abdomen, or keeping her clean and cool. The important change that would be felt, when the woman cradling her daughter between her thighs, supporting her back in her labour, urging her through her contractions, giving birth as it were by proxy to her own grandchild, sees her first grandchild emerge into the light, cannot happen so dramatically. Nowadays the mother's mother will probably not even be the first person to be telephoned or to learn of her changed status. It is hardly necessary to point out that the *father*'s mother would be as welcome in the birthplace as the wicked fairy at the christening of Snow White. We are not surprised to read that a high proportion of the women arraigned in the witch-hunts of the sixteenth and seventeenth centuries were midwives.

As patriarchal society evolved, the real power of women decayed. More and more they were obliged to make do with fantasy power, either to manipulate those with power over them, or to invent fantasy antidotes for real oppression, by casting spells or preparing potions. The realm in which these magical preparations worked was the imagination; a powerless person could be rendered powerful by an amulet or a philtre. He had only to wait for some misfortune to befall his oppressor to feel thoroughly avenged and give (dis)credit to the witch. The old woman who muttered the magic words or collected the moon-drenched herbs was not a cynical manipulator of the credulity of others; all too often she believed in her occult power herself and, as women have always done, shouldered the burden of communal guilt. The women who voluntarily accused themselves at witch-trials, however, represent only the tiniest proportion of women who strove for power over the imagination, most of whom were loved and revered as the tellers of tales.

In tutoring the imagination of the very young, the old wives romanticized and spiritualized a life that was in reality utterly monotonous and dreary. They filled the woods with yearning, sighing souls instead of wind currents and gossamer trails; they put out saucers of milk for the spirits of dead children that clung to the houses where they died young (so very, very many) and lo! in the morning the good sweet milk was gone and the hearth was swept clean and polished by their grateful hands. Grandmothers' fables made the world as thrilling a place as Steven Spielberg's fantasies do now, and did so in a fashion that stimulated the child's creative fantasy, rather than deadening it by repetitive overstimulation. Those who take Addison's view of their activities, and object that old wives' tales fill children with trepidation and make them timid, have misunderstood both how important it is that a child experience suspicion and how children love to be scared out of their wits.

It has often been pointed out that myths, rhymes, fairy tales and children's games shelter vestiges of the old religions. Out of northern myths and rites come Mother Goose and her nursery rhymes. A turn-of-the-century book-cover betrays the bird original of Mother Goose. From the letter 'M' of 'Mother' in the title hangs a pair of goose feet. Mother Goose herself is shown riding with her bird. The broomstick she rides is a whittled-down version of the sacred tree, the revered connection between sky and earth. She may not be as graceful as Aphrodite, but why should she be? She has fallen into a world turned away from nature, a world that in the sixteenth and seventeenth centuries . . . used fire and water to purge away all memory of her former position and of her very existence. (B. Johnson, 85)

What wiped out the domestic witch was the spread of literacy. Children have not needed any more to listen at grandmother's knee to fables of the rewards of good children and the deliciously

hideous punishments of naughty ones, since education was
compulsory and their imaginations given into the control of the
printed page. In all societies the illiterate elders begin to lose
authority once their children learn to read. When the pace of
social change is as dizzy as it has been since the end of the Second
World War, having been around longer is a positive disqualifica-
tion for knowing anything. A grey head is known to be stuffed
with obsolescent notions. The fact that university researchers are
now tramping the world looking for oral historians can be taken
as a sign that oral histories have become a matter for academics
and not for the communities who should be listening to them and
learning from them. We have lost all the art-forms of old women;
the lullaby vanished, leaving not one authentic strain behind; the
folk-song was collected when it was well cracked in the ring; the
fairy-tale was stolen, distorted, printed and discredited.

Tanya Luhrmann's recent definition holds that

Witchcraft is meant to be a revival, or re-emergence of an ancient
nature-religion, the most ancient of religions, in which the earth was
worshipped as a woman under different names and guises throughout
the inhabited world. She was Astarte, Inanna, Isis, Cerridwen – names
that ring echoes in archaeological texts. She was the Great Goddess
whose rites Frazer and Neumann – and Apuleius – recorded in rich
detail. Witches are people who read their books and try to create, for
themselves, the tone and feeling of an early humanity, worshipping a
nature they understand as vital, powerful and mysterious. They visit the
stone circles and pre-Christian sites and become amateur scholars of the
pagan traditions behind the Easter egg and the Yule log.

Above all witches try to connect with the world around them.
Witchcraft, they say, is about the tactile, intuitive understanding of the
turn of the seasons, the song of the birds; it is the awareness of all things
as holy . . . (45–6)

What is being described here is organized witchcraft, which is not
the witchcraft of every woman who hangs up a fatty bone for the
finches, who tries to be sure to greet the full moon face to face as a
mark of respect, who collects firewood on a waning moon and

sows seed on a waxing one, who says good morning to the
magpie and warns the bees of a birth or a death in the family.
Those of us who are gardeners do not need to train ourselves to be
aware of the seasons, intuitively or any other way, for the seasons
have us by the throat. One kind of witch gathers in pubs and
cellars to talk of Isis and Osiris; another kind of red-cheeked wild-
haired witch is to be found tramping along the hedgerows in the
wind and rain, followed possibly by her old dog or, even, her cat.

Real witches never had to learn their lore from Frazer,
Neumann and Apuleius; real witches were not people who read
books to find out what to do and when. Witchcraft is not a matter
of generalizations, if only because it has to be closely allied to the
spirit of place. Serious mistakes are made in herbal medicine
because people do not understand that a herb that grows in a
particular way in one place exercises a different function from the
same herb growing in different conditions, only a few miles away.
The proportions to be used and the methods of preparation must
reflect these differences. Certain combinations and decoctions can
be helpful in one environment and noxious in others. The meaning
of the winds, of dew, of moonshine is different on different sides
of the same hill. The books of witchlore that have tried to
systematize this vast body of knowledge and extract general
principles from it have produced meaningless prescriptions. The
kind of mistake they make can be illustrated from a modern
example. Researchers in Bangladesh were trying to extract the
active principle from an abortifacient used with great efficacy in a
particular area. None of their extracts seemed to have any em-
menagogic qualities at all. Eventually an old practitioner explained
that the women brewed the abortifacient potion in fermented rice
water in a copper vessel; the synergistic compound that resulted
from that procedure was too dangerous to be included in any
modern pharmacopoeia, but it certainly worked.

No witch these days would be allowed to hang out a shingle or
practise as a healer, except perhaps upon herself and her animals.
Yet in sophisticated Tuscany, people with intractable ailments still

go to the wise woman who is called by the modern version, *strega*, of her classic name *Strix*. She will charm warts away, charm straying love back again, prescribe a gentle wash for skin ailments or a posy of herbs to be fed to cows in the spring to clear their blood, and try a little conservative prediction now and then. She might instruct a young woman with cystitis to arise from her bed at first light and to go out, without urinating or breaking her fast, to find the young basal rosette of *Verbascum thapsiformis*, and, squatting low, to urinate upon it. In the only case I know of the cystitis was cured and never came back. I thought the walk with a full bladder was the most important part of the treatment; the patient was sure that an exhalation arose from the plant and entered her bladder. In the case of an old woman's cystitis the white witch prescribed a mild decoction of lime flowers and camomile to be drunk in quantity, the copious urine that resulted to be cast out where the evil humour would afflict slugs and snails instead of the patient. As an indirect assurance that the old lady would reverse the habit of a lifetime and drink enough water to dilute the acid urine that was irritating her bladder, this portentous to-do could hardly have been bettered.

Mostly, though, the white witch is limited to activities like those of Rosemary Dobson's grandmother, who like the classic *Strix* is half bird:

> My grandmother, living to be ninety, met
> Whatever chanced with kindness, held her head
> On one side like a sparrow's, had a bird's
> Bright eyes. At dinner used to set
> An extra place for strangers. This was done
> She said in Bendigo and Eaglehawk, it was
> A custom she observed. In her thin house
> That spoke aloud of every kind of weather
> She put out food for lizards, scattered crumbs
> For wrens beside the pepper-tree and saved
> The household water for geraniums.

'Amy Caroline'

The outdoor witches of England far outnumber the 30,000 or so who gather in subterranean gloom to burn incense and cast spells, and even the thousands more who dabble in the occult. When Maureen and Bridget Boland published their *Old Wives' Lore for Gardeners* in 1976, old wives rushed to buy it, and their children to buy it for them. Though, as the Boland sisters confessed, they were not old wives but old spinsters, their book contained 'the sort of lore their grandmothers passed down to them' which they wished to pass 'on to those who are not afraid of finding a certain amount of superstition mingled with good sense'.

In 1934 the great psychologist Helene Deutsch, then fifty years old, left Vienna and went to live in America. When it became clear that she and her family could never return to Vienna, they looked for a farm. After one false start they found a dilapidated property in New Hampshire. They renamed it 'Babayaga'.

What is the relationship of Babayaga to me, the would-be farm-wife immersed in her scientific and professional work? Babayaga is *me*, and the legend of this Polish witch leads directly back to my childhood. In Polish folklore, Babayaga is a good witch, who is especially kind to children; she is also a rustic witch, usually seen carrying on her back a load of wood, and sometimes children. Thus both my love for my grandchildren and my fantasies about being a countrywoman have fitted in very well with this figure; she is the prototype of the kind grandmother, even though her mode of transportation is a broom and her passageway the chimney. I told the children many stories about my role as a witch, and I think that Babayaga is to them, even today, associated with their real granny and beloved 'Gruhu'. (1973, 193)

On the next page Deutsch, who never mentions her own menopause, describes a period of conflict between her 'emotional preoccupations' and her 'intellectual self'.

I felt like the personification of a children's song my grandsons loved: A peculiar creature turns up in a chicken yard. She feels out of place and unwanted, and moves on to the goose yard. But there too she is greeted by protesting cackles. In despair she asks herself, 'Who am I? I am not a chicken. I am not a goose. I am a chirkendoose.' My grandsons enjoyed this song without knowing how much their grandmother identified with this strange animal. (194)

'Unconscious motives play an especially large role' in the apparently haphazard juxtaposition of themes in writing. The paragraph that follows this deals with Deutsch's pet hen, Jenny, and would have been followed by accounts of other woman-animal identifications if Deutsch had not been 'ashamed' of what the man who ran the farm for her (her superego) would 'think'. The solution is the identification with her land and her animals, the role that she finds in the *genius loci*, the white witch, Babayaga.

In December 1949 G. M. Carstairs went to live for a year in a village near Udaipur in Rajasthan. His next-door neighbours were Dhapu, a widow, her son, his wife and their baby. It was months before Carstairs discovered that Dhapu, a forceful woman with a foul temper and an inexhaustible vein of obscene abuse, was believed to be a *dakan* who had been blinding people and causing deaths and disease in the village for at least twenty years. The villagers believed that she had the power to know whenever her name was mentioned and would punish anyone who identified her. Carstairs tried to sympathize with the poor old woman, whom he saw as victimized by a suspicious community, but he was repelled by her vicious hostility towards her co-villagers, by her mendacity and because 'She seemed unable to accept my assurance that I did not believe that she was a witch and that I thought it unfair that she should be so regarded', (Carstairs, 1983, 21). Carstairs could not quite imagine that a woman would accept the role forced upon her, or that she would glory in her power over the imaginative life of the whole village.

Many of the confessional interrogatories, or penitentials, of the early Middle Ages include questions to be put by the priest regarding the practice of sorcery. This ranged from harmless foolishness like the placing of a fish between the labia to marinade, as it were, for a day or two before cooking it and serving it to a man whose affections one wanted to engage, to flying about at night and attending witches' sabbaths. Burchard's penitential, written at the beginning of the eleventh century, asked:

Have you believed what many women, turning back to Satan, believe and affirm to be true; as that you believe that on the silence of the quiet night . . . you are able, while still in your body, to go out through the closed doors, and travel through the spaces of the world, together with others who are similarly deceived; and that without weapons you kill people . . . and together cook and devour their flesh . . . if you have believed this, you shall do penance on bread and water for fifty days and likewise in each of the seven years following.

Clearly Burchard did not share the witches' delusion; the sin that was being confessed was not making a pact with Satan but pagan superstition. Though Burchard's punishment was harsh, it was enlightened compared to the summary vengeance wreaked on Dhapu. Six months after Carstairs left the village he learned that, as a result of the raving of a feverish woman who was thought to have been possessed by her, Dhapu, who had been beaten several times before, had been hit repeatedly about the face with an axe. The bones of her left forearm, flung up to protect herself, were smashed. As she sank unconscious to the ground, the feverish woman's ravings ceased. Three days later Dhapu the *dakan* died. Interestingly Carstairs was anxious that her murderers should not receive too harsh a sentence. In fact two of the killers got six months, of which they served a month, and the third eighteen months, of which he served a year. The woman involved got off scot-free. Meanwhile in the village 'the tension and mistrust seemed to have gone'. Dhapu's death, called 'tragic' by Carstairs, was entirely unregretted and unavenged, even by her son.

The priestly authorities of the Middle Ages were anxious to erect their own law in the place of mob law, so they punished, rather than the witches themselves, those who killed witches, by stoning, immersion, or flaying and burning them alive. Perhaps they understood that the witch functions by the consent and with the complicity of her community. As long as the people respect her occult power, they are failing to respect the visible power of church and state. Societies which make use of witches to exert control over the uncontrollable are the same societies that need to use extremes of brutality in eradicating them.

There would be no point in disembowelling a witch, and parading her intestines through her village, if she had not been a powerful individual. Witch-hood brings real power. The old woman whose very shadow can blight anything it falls upon need no longer play the meek, obliterated wife-mother. Her face is uncovered; her death-dealing eye looks out of her head, powerfully penetrating her environment, rather than being penetrated and mastered by it. The representatives of the ruling class have always been sceptical about such power and refused to capitulate to the popular superstition that needed to see witches magically routed by dismemberment or burning. The same lordly view that old women's power over others was merely a senile delusion on their part and crass credulity on the part of their clients was widely held until 1921 when Margaret Murray published *The Witch-Cult in Western Europe*, which argued that witches were adherents of an ancient pagan fertility cult. The argument held until 1969, when the anthropologist Lucy Mair pointed out that what witches have in common all over the world is that they are not defined by their adherence to religion but by their rejection of the prevailing moral and social order. In 1975 Norman Cohn demolished Murray's sources and exposed the ancient fertility religion as a fraud.

The element that remains underemphasized in modern discussions of witchcraft is the extent to which the assumption of a witch role represents a coherent protest against the marginalization of older women and a strategic alternative to it. Studies of spirit possession have been much more perceptive. In *Case Studies in Spirit Possession*, edited by V. Crapanzano and V. Garrison,

Twelve of the fifteen cases presented involve women, and the theme of female powerlessness, as well as the manner in which possession phenomena permit both temporary and long-term increases in women's power and control, is conspicuous in most of the histories. (xi–xii)

'Possession,' argues Crapanzano, 'is found most frequently among people of inferior, marginal, ambiguous or problematic status, especially women' (29). The anthropologists can see quite clearly that spirit possession forms part of a strategy on the part of powerless marginalized people seeking a central role in the life of their community. They agree generally that the strategy is unconsciously adopted, but conscious-unconscious is a continuum rather than a contrast. People in general, and uneducated people in particular, may and do know and not know at the same time. A woman of strong personality reacting against her increasing ir-relevance to the world of men and younger women may make a conscious decision to enter the realm of witchcraft, but thereafter certain consequences entail themselves and she may well be carried along upon a momentum that she herself has not generated. Every time an angry woman thinks of her persecutors and says to them in her heart, 'Just you wait. You'll be sorry,' she involves the age-long tradition of witching. When ill befalls them, as sooner or later it must, if her heart rejoices at their being brought low, she is affiliated for ever to the black art.

It makes sense that women, once released from their bondage to their fathers, husbands and sons after a lifetime of being told that they are unstable, unreliable, irrational creatures, should avenge themselves by making a principle out of instability and unreason, working through the superstition and credulity of beings weaker than themselves to positions of real power, well able to subvert duly constituted authority both religious and secular. It makes sense too that they should take as their allies in this strategy other defamed creatures for which society has no use, the owl and the bumble-bee of Daniel Defoe's famous parallel in *Appleby's Journal* (quoted by Nina Auerbach in *Woman and the Demon*).

Horrible! Frightful! Unsufferable! An OLD MAID! I had rather be metamorphosed into an *Humble Bee*, or a *Screech Owl*; the first, all the boys run after it to Buffet it with their Hats, then pull it a Pieces for a poor dram of Honey in its Tail; and the last, the Terror and Aversion of all Mankind, the fore-runner of Ill-luck, the foreboder of Diseases and Death. (110–11)

The witch's familiars are, like her, actually harmless, serviceable creatures, subjected to unreasonable abuse because they are considered unappealing and their real usefulness is unrecognized. In league with owls and toads, the old woman can both reject the world's devaluation of her and, by frightening her enemies, revenge herself against them. However, the male authority that the witch subverts by hobnobbing with creatures as unattractive and unnerving as herself may revenge itself with exemplary savagery.

With the exaltation of the natural that follows the triumph of empiricism all evidence of the supernatural or preternatural has to be seen as fraudulent at best, and most likely diabolical. To the convinced empiricist like Addison all invocation of magical power is subversion. The belief that women who have a special understanding of animals must be evil only grows up as distrust of animal nature deepens; that distrust is the product of male supremacist culture and there is no good reason why women should share it. Traditionally women have tended animals, especially small animals and birds. They have bred, fed, prepared and cooked them for their mutual masters' tables while those masters were acquiring the 'enlightened' rationalist education that would deliver the created world into their control.

In 1609, seventy-nine-year-old Maria de Zozaya was turned over to the Spanish Inquisition as a witch

... when the young priest of the town came home without a single hare after having been out hunting all day even he blamed Maria de Zozaya. In this case, however, she got no more than she deserved, for when the priest passed her house she would say: 'See that you catch plenty of hares, Father, so the neighbors can have jugged hare.' ... Maria de Zozaya confessed to the inquisitors that as soon as the priest had passed by she turned herself into a hare and ran ahead of him and his hounds the whole day long so that they returned home exhausted. This, she added, had occurred eight times during 1609. (Henningsen, 159)

Maria was to die in prison nine months later. It is but a short step from the old woman's imagining herself to be a hare outrunning the hounds until they died of exhaustion, to the huntsmen imagining that a particular hare is not a real hare but a witch transmogrified, as Wodrow records in his *Analecta* of one Elspey in 1698 (Black, 81). Fourteen years later Addison deplored the fact that

  If a hare makes an unexpected escape from hounds the huntsman curses Moll White ... I have known the master of a pack of hounds upon such an occasion send one of his servants to see if Moll White had been out that morning.

Though we can only guess at the justification or lack of it for suspecting Moll White of disrupting the hunt, we can see in the work of literate women of rank a similar attempt at subversion. The extraordinary Duchess of Newcastle wrote an extraordinary poem on 'The Hunting of the Hare' and published it herself in 1653. After a moving account of the hare's desperate attempts to outrun the hounds, she turns on man the hunter:

> Yet Man doth think himselfe so gentle, mild,
> When he of creatures is most cruell wild.
> And is so Proud, thinks only he shal live,
> That God a God-like Nature did him give.
> And that all Creatures for his sake alone,
> Was made for him, to Tyrannize upon.
>
> (Greer *et al.*, 170)

Lady Anne Finch, Countess of Winchilsea, loved to roam on a summer night, with none but owls and glow-worms for company.

> When nibbling sheep at large pursue their food,
> And unmolested kine rechew the cud;

When curlews cry beneath the village walls,
And to her straggling brood the partridge calls;
Their short-lived jubilee the creatures keep
Which but endures whilest tyrant man does sleep.

(Lonsdale, 23)

The Countess would have been astonished and displeased, perhaps if anyone had pointed out the similarity between her nocturnal carnival of the animals and a witches' sabbath. The Countess's ideals are nothing if not lofty, nevertheless as she announces her intention to gad about the fields all night she gives the slightest hint of a witch-like urge to eschew human intimacy and associate with members of the lower orders of creation.

. . . the free soul to a compos'dness charmed,
Finding the elements of rage disarmed,
O'er all below a solemn quiet grown,
Joys in th'inferior world and thinks it like her own.

In seeing herself and the other animals in 'A Nocturnal Reverie' as inhabitants of a twilit world unsuspected by the controller man, Anne Finch was lightly sketching in an important change in attitudes, which is an integral part of the gradual demystification of female power. Imaginative or spiritual affinity with the lower orders was not always considered evil. The Celtic princess Melangell, who is revered as a saint, fled into the wilds of Powys to live as an ascetic. A hare pursued by the Prince of Powys and his huntsmen dashed into the glade where she was praying and took refuge in her skirt. When the royal party rode up and the hare peered forth from Melangell's skirt the hounds fell back whining. When the master of the hunt lifted his horn and blew no sound came out. The prince was so impressed by this extraordinary circumstance, which he, less enlightened than the Spanish Inquisition or Joseph Addison, took to be evidence of great sanctity, that he granted the forest to Melangell. Ever thereafter hares congregated there and the people called them 'Melangell's lambs'.

This is only one of many stories of the early saints exercising power over and on behalf of animals. Both St Pharaildis and St Werburga are supposed to have restored a plucked and roasted goose to life and full plumage. St Milburga could command the birds of the air; St Bee was fed by sea-birds; St Thecla's feet were licked by the lions that should have killed her in the amphitheatre; St Ulphia commanded the frogs to be silent because they disturbed her sleep and the frogs in that locality are silent to this day; Blessed Viridiana had two snakes that fed from her plate; all kinds of animals ate out of the hand of St Colette; St Catherine of Vadstena was saved from a rapist by a stag (*Butler's Lives of the Saints*).

Radegund sent a dove to calm the raging tempest that threatened her servitors. Glodesind ensured the luck of a fisherman heading for her convent, by causing a large fish to jump voluntarily into his net. Aldegund kept a fish given to her community in a pond but it was threatened by crows when it accidentally beached itself. Happily a peaceable little lamb, most unnaturally, defended it with tooth and hoof until the nuns could come to the rescue. (McNamara, 46)

Some of the legends that associate saints with animals may represent survivals of older nature religion and goddess worship; the St Gertrude who is never pictured without mice running up and down her staff or playing on her distaff is thought to be a survival of Freya. St Walburga, the great healer, has her feastday on the witches' great festival, 1 May or Walpurgisnacht. As the animal world lost its sacredness and wonder faded into the daylight of rationalism, the women who had power over animals lost their prestige. As man asserted his superiority over the other animals and his right to use and abuse them as he pleased, he persecuted their protectors. Addison would have thought any woman praying in a glade a demented enthusiast. Less advanced thinkers would have suspected her of praying to the tree, or having sexual congress with the green man, now dethroned as a nature-god and a figure of Satan himself.

If we consider the stories of the female saints that are to be found in collections like the *Golden Legend* of Jacopus de Voragine, we cannot fail to be struck by the similarity of their supernatural powers to the proscribed activities of witches. There is hardly a female saint who does not have the gifts of prophecy and of reading hearts. Female saints come to people in dreams and appear to crowds in visions with less effort than it took a necromancer to conjure up a single imp. Magical virgins do not scruple to foretell dire punishments that will light upon their enemies, and the hagiographers gleefully recount the disasters that befell all who gainsaid them, whether they were blinded, or fell from a great height, or burst into flames or agonizing plague sores; the difference between a saint's prediction of divine vengeance and a witch's curse is to the victim merely academic. Virgin martyrs can be dropped into boiling lead or stuck with poniards to the hilt and feel as little as any witch with a bodkin driven into her witch-mark. Some saints, like St Christina the Astonishing, could fly; others, like St Mary of Egypt, could walk on water; still others could and did sail across the sea on a leaf. St Martha overpowered a dragon and led him about like a dog with her girdle as a leash. Most of these superwomen were young and virgin. The older woman in search of a role model will find little to emulate in their spectacular careers, in which far too much time was spent fighting off the lewd advances of earthly tyrants who revenged themselves by inflicting the most elaborate and ghastly mutilations and torments. The magical virgin's martyrdom is the precursor of the immolation of the witch; in the case of Joan of Arc, the two coalesced.

The mother of both the female saint and the witch is the sibyl. Representations of sibyls give us virtually the only examples of positive images of older women, whether they be Michelangelo's muscular examples in the lunettes of the Sistine Chapel or the musical versions by Orlandus Lassus. The name 'sibyl' is so ancient that no one knows its derivation. It is thought that sibyls are descendants of the traditional female seers of the Orient, who entered Greek religion through Judaic influence. Only fragments of the original Greek sibylline verses that were revered by the Romans as oracles can now be identified.

The Romans thought enough of these obscure Greek hexameters to scour the Mediterranean world for replacements after a fire had destroyed the originals in 83 BC ... Under the Empire, consultation of the Sibylline verses stored in the temple of Apollo on the Palatine was sporadic. Tiberius vetoed one attempt, but Nero consulted them after the great fire of AD 64. The last known consultation was made by Julian the Apostate in AD 363, and the books were destroyed by Stilicho in about 408. (McGinn, 9–10)

The eight books of Greek hexameters that were believed by the patristic authors, and by medieval and Renaissance writers, to be *Oracula Sibyllina* were in fact written between the mid-second century BC and about AD 300 and collected and edited by scholars in the late fifth and sixth centuries. The ten sibyls of Varro, namely the Persian, Libyan, Delphic, Cimmerian, Erythraean, Samian, Cumaean, Hellespontic, Phrygian and Tiburtine, became twelve to match the apostles, and were credited with foretelling the birth of Christ. They were supposed to have prophesied the outcome of the Trojan War to Agamemnon and to have led Aeneas through the underworld. Augustine numbered them among the few pre-Christians who would see Heaven. Thus transmogrified into precursors of Christianity, the ancient sibyls were much quoted and painted.

... the largely forgotten story of one of the more potent female images in Western Religious tradition. These prophetesses were able to make a remarkable transition from paganism to Christianity largely because they were seen not only as foretelling the gloomy message of coming doom and the fates of kings, but also because they were reckoned the peers of the Jewish prophets in their announcement of the good news of the Saviour's birth. Having made this adaptation from pagan prophetess to Christian seer, the Sibyl was not able to effect a similar transition to the modern world where the acids of historical criticism exposed the pious forgeries of the past. On the mythic level at least, the image of the Sibyl, the wise and beautiful old woman inspired by God, deserves our respect and consideration. (McGinn, 35)

If we are to be well, we must care for ourselves. We must not cast the old woman out, but become her more abundantly. If we embrace the idea of witchhood, and turn it into a positive, aggressive, self-defining self-concept, we can exploit the proliferation of aversion imagery to our own advantage. It is after all no shame or embarrassment to us to know that lager louts find our presence inhibiting. Perhaps we do spoil things for all the boys together propping up the bar in the local pub or littering our highways and by-ways with their cans or bashing and knifing each other at football matches. So much the better. Why not wear an invisible T-shirt that says 'A glance from my eye can make your beer turn rancid'? Some of the work being done with elderly female patients exhibiting the distorted behaviour associated with senile dementia has found that the old ladies screaming obscene abuse and deliberately soiling themselves have cause for bitter rebellion. Workers are at last considering the possibility that their bizarre behaviour is not evidence of brain decay but of frustrated protest which, if it can be verbalized and externalized, can be to some extent mollified. The expression of malevolence through the fantasy outlet of *maleficium* could be a kind of psychoprophylaxis for the corrosive resentment felt by disenfranchised old women who are denied the right to express any of the hositility and contempt that the younger generation assumes as its birthright. The stereotype of the snowy-haired granny beaming affectionately at her apple pie needs to be balanced by her dark side, with 'tangled black hair, long fingernails, pendulous breasts, flowing tongue between terrible fangs'. That, according to P. F. McKean, is what the Indonesian witch, Rangda, 'the mother who is also widow, the one who represents the beginning and end of fertility, or of life' (280), looks like.

Rangda does not creep; she dances. Mary Ellman tells us in *Thinking about Women* that 'the preternatural female is extinct, and none of her former manifestations carries conviction now'. Among the superfemales who have vanished from the earth she lists the 'domestic witch'.

Traditionally, magic was divided between men and women, exactly
as the professions and trades continue to be divided. Male magic was
intellectual, female magic was manual. The men pored over portentous
charts and symbols and were visited by high-ranking devils. The women
cackled and mixed vile broth in pots. This arrangement was felicitous:
the double standard rarely furnishes such lively parts to both performers.
But of course neither exciting approach survived later, and again separate,
commitments to science and industry. (141)

Thinking about Women is a book written with the lightest of
scalpel strokes. Ellman's half-serious distinction between male and
female magic is based upon a real historical distinction between
the black arts of necromancy and conjuration, with their elabora-
tion in satanism, all of which relied upon the cabbalistic texts, and
the traditional witching activities of illiterate women, who dealt in
divination, charms and healing. However, Ellman's view of
witchcraft itself, being based upon literary caricature, is libellous.

As long as illiteracy survives, witchcraft will survive. Until
traditional healers and birth-attendants have all been criminalized
and punished for competing with institutionalized medicine, the
domestic witch will survive. The western world had to burn its
witches out before the Addisons of the eighteenth century could
declare confidently that they had never existed. The rest of the
world still fears and respects the occult power of wise women. As
any health worker knows who has to deal with migrant workers
and their families, migrant women refuse to accept the explanations
of illness that doctors give them, refuse to carry out modern
treatments and struggle to take their sick children home so that the
evil influences responsible for their illness can be counteracted by
the necessary magic.

Ellman might have been surprised to find how many witches
are still in business even in Europe. Italian *streghe* still cast the beans
or the *cordella* and still collect porcupine spines for love philtres.
English fortune-tellers reading the tea-leaves, interviewees crossing
their fingers, women blowing on knotted string to cause impotence
in a straying lover, are all helpless people struggling to gain some

control over their destiny by magic. Girls sleeping with wedding-cake under their pillows are remembering old sympathetic magic from the same box of tricks as the mixing of a drop of menstrual blood in the beloved's food, or the murmuring of magic rhymes and looking in the mirror on midsummer night to see the shape of their husband-to-be. The experts in these non-religious rituals are of course the old women.

A first step on the road to witchhood is to say, 'You are wrong, my dear fellow. I am old. I am as old as the hills.'

> Witchcraft has not a pedigree
> 'Tis early as our Breath
> And mourners meet it going out
> The moment of our death –
> (Emily Dickinson)

Some ancient crones after all look good, very good. They are the white-bodied witches who tempt the ascetics in the patristic writings, the witches who turn into wrinkled hags during the act of love, as if age was a mark of satanism. Those people who deny to the fifty-year-old woman that she is old are the very people who find age shameful and obscene. They beg us to lie about it for their own comfort.

When Karen Blixen was preparing a speech on African women for the Danish Women's Association in 1937 she wrote:

All old women had the consolation of witchcraft; their relations with witchcraft were comparable to their relations with the art of seduction. One cannot understand how we, who will have nothing to do with witchcraft, can bear to grow old. (Thurman, 317)

Even those of us who look good know that the secret marks of age, the witch-marks, are there. The proliferation of moles and wens, the sags and wrinkles at knees and elbows, the pads on our knuckles, the spurs on our heels, the thinning of our hair, the bristles that sprout on our chins, all are easily hidden, but we know that they are there. If we were to be hauled off and stripped naked at our own witch-trial, they would be seen. So let us assume the witches' right and cackle in our turn. Let us as freely express our malice towards ageists as they towards us. Let us make caricatures of them as relentlessly belittling as their caricatures of us.

'Webs of Crones' have already been established by American women who have not been afraid to grow old (Walker). In 1986 the second number of *Women and Politics* was devoted to 'Women as Elders: Images, Visions and Issues'. Gert Beadle of the Kelowna Web of Crones contributed an article on 'The Nature of Crones':

It is in the nature of a Crone to lean to overview, for she is in a reflective period of her life and the big picture has her attention. She has walked in many moccasins not her own and has observed all that pinch and restrict the desire for freedom . . .' (xiii)

Why not walk in the aura of magic that gives to the small things of life their uniqueness and importance? Why not befriend a toad today?

> Witchcraft was hung, in History,
> But History and I
> Find all the Witchcraft that we need
> Around us, every Day –
>   (Emily Dickinson)

17

Serenity and Power

When Karen Blixen was forty-six she came out of Africa back to Denmark. Her coffee plantation in Kenya had gone broke; though it was auctioned off to pay the accumulated debts, the stockholders lost more than £150,000. Her unfaithful husband, whom she had forgiven for giving her syphilis, had insisted on a divorce which she had agreed to with reluctance. All her hopes of pregnancy had been dashed, and she had quarrelled with her lover who had been killed in a plane crash days later. She had attempted suicide at least once during this turbulent time. She was so thin and frail that her friends had suggested that she go to a clinic in Montreux; there she found out that her syphilis, which had been supposed cured, had become syphilis of the spine, *tabes dorsalis*. The course of the disease was well known; locomotor ataxia meant she would never again walk properly, anorexia meant that food would nauseate her, she would develop perforating stomach ulcers, and her face would soon take on a deadly pallor and be covered with a grid of tight wrinkles. Her greatest bereavement was the loss of Africa, which left her with a physical longing for the light, the sky and the bush that never faded. Crates of treasured possessions followed her to Denmark, but she did not open them for thirteen years.

Baroness Blixen's way of dealing with her intense physical and mental pain at this crisis time, a climacteric in every sense of the word, was to be reborn as Isak Dinesen. Isaac was the post-menopausal child of Abraham and Sarah, who said when he was born, 'God hath made me to laugh, so that all who hear will laugh

THE CHANGE

with me.' Dinesen was Blixen's maiden name. She herself called this time her fourth age, saying she began to write 'in great uncertainty about the whole undertaking, but, nevertheless, in the hands of both a powerful and happy spirit' (Thurman, 476).

In 1933 this new forty-eight-year-old writer produced *Seven Gothic Tales*. In the first of the tales, 'The Deluge at Norderney', a group of travellers, menaced by a flood tide, take refuge in a barn, where Malin Nat-da-Nog, like a *précieuse* of old, organizes them into a salon. For most of her life Malin has been a virginal spinster, until she begins to invent a rakish past for herself and voluntarily to confess to every kind of perversion and every lecherous excess. The night, which ends with the old noblewoman demanding a kiss of a young man, before placing the dripping hem of her skirt in his hand, for the water is rapidly rising round the barn, is a figure of woman's life. The old woman's heroic exercise of imagination on the brink of being overwhelmed is as clear a statement as Blixen ever made of the motivation of her own struggle. She is describing Malin Nat-da-Nog in this passage, but she might as well have been describing herself:

What changed her was what changes all women at fifty: the transfer from the active service of life – with a pension or the honors of war, as the case may be – to the mere passive state of a looker on. A weight fell away from her; she flew up to a higher perch and cackled a little. (Dinesen, 1934, 20)

The imagery of the caged bird is important in this collection; it recurs again and again at climactic moments in the stories. Women are seen as caged by their conditioning, by religion and convention; when they are older their grief and rage at their confinement are converted into passionate indignation when they see other creatures caged. In 'The Supper at Elsinore', one of the De Coninck sisters, 'spiritual courtesans' in their early fifties who conduct their own version of a salon, learns that she is soon to meet the ghost of her dead brother:

Her misery drove her up and down the avenues like a dry leaf before the wind – a distinguished lady in furred boots, in her own heart a great mad wing-clipped bird, fluttering in the winter sunset. (250)

In the story called 'The Monkey', the old Prioress actually changes bodies with her pet monkey. She is determined to procure a marriage between two of her younger kinsmen. The intended groom has a sudden glimpse of the kind of energy that older women can deploy:

Boris kissed her hand . . . and then all at once he got such a terrible impression of strength and cunning that it was as if he had touched an electric eel. Women, he thought, when they are old enough to have done with the business of being women, and can let loose their strength, must be the most powerful creatures in the whole world. (61)

The Prioress, of course, is caged by her religious vocation. As when she escapes she is merely a monkey her power must remain latent. Karen Blixen had every reason to believe that she had, as she said in a letter to Lady Daphne Finch Hatton, 'one foot in the grave', but once the first book of her fourth age was translated into Danish from the English in which she wrote it she was ready to write her masterpiece. *Out of Africa* is about the Africa she lost, and with it the love, hope, health and light that she would never know again; it is imbued with the elegiac feeling that is the reward for having been able to mourn and to let go. Hannah Arendt explains the importance of story-telling in Blixen's struggle to defy her dreadful illness:

Without repeating life in imagination you can never be fully alive, 'lack of imagination' prevents people from 'existing'. 'Be loyal to the story', as one of her story-tellers admonishes the young, means no less than Be loyal to life, don't create fiction but accept what life is giving you, show yourself worthy of whatever it may be by recollecting and pondering over it, thus repeating it in imagination; this is the way to remain alive. And to live in the sense of being fully alive had early been and remained to the end her only aim and desire. 'My life I will not let you go except you bless me, but then I will let you go.' The reward of story-telling is to be able to let go: 'When the story-teller is loyal ... to the story then, in the end, silence will speak.'

Karen Blixen exerted her old woman's power many times, enchanting several younger and stronger men into acting out her fantasies for years at a time. In these relationships, although she did not permit herself physical intimacy, she was as exacting as any lover. Using her emaciated appearance and her stark-white, fantastically wrinkled pixie face, with its huge, glittering, kohl-encircled eyes, she fascinated her prey and kept them subject to her whims by binding them fast with the yarns she spun. Racked by her cruel disease, Karen Blixen remains a virtuosa of the art of ageing.

There are not many women who took the art of ageing to such heights of refinement as Karen Blixen did. Possibly the greatest was Madame de Maintenon, who became 'Épouse du Roi' when she was forty-eight (see p. 377). Her explanation of the strange joy of old age, so unlike the mixture of unexamined conflicting emotions that afflict us when we are still battling with women's sexual and reproductive destiny, would have been perfectly understood by Karen Blixen, who conscientiously imitated what she imagined was the manner of the *grandes salonnières*: at the end of her life Madame de Maintenon described her feelings in these words:

I have no regret for the loss of my youth. I do not see anything that makes us happier than detachment and, because to achieve detachment it is necessary to have played one's part in the world, one burns one's youth in accumulating a small store of ecstasy and pain. Believe me, one is well content to find one's soul rich enough to be able to dispense with exaggerated feelings and vain agitations. What satisfaction to know that the drama is played out, and to enter into indifference.

People who are still being made miserable by the play of 'exaggerated feelings and vain agitations' persist in the irrational belief that their torment is what makes life worth living. In 1836 Anna Jameson wrote to her dear friend Ottilie von Goethe, devastated by an affair in her forties which resulted in the clandestine birth of an illegitimate third child, sixteen years after her second (legitimate) child:

Your life has been one of passion and suffering and intervals of *tranquillity* have been to you intervals of *ennui*. When the storm of sensation and emotion is over, you feel as if your heart were dead, but it is not so and I will prove it to you one day. (Erskine, 149)

The older woman, who can offer nothing but abiding affection and loyalty to her friend, has to endure many rejections. The very fact that she can be relied upon means that she will be forgotten in the storm of sexual relationships and must wait quietly and unreproachfully until she is required to comfort and console. Anna Jameson persevered in her friendship with Ottilie, which grew stronger and endured until her death in 1860.

Karen Blixen used to say, 'One must in this lower world love many things to know finally what one loves the best . . .' It is simply not true that the ageing heart forgets how to love or becomes incapable of love; indeed it seems as if, at least in the case of these women of great psychic energy, only after they had ceased to be beset by the egotisms and hostilities of sexual passion did they discover of what bottomless and tireless love their hearts were capable.

In 1862, Christina Rossetti, herself thirty-two, wrote a sonnet about the transformation of one woman, probably her mother, who would then have been in her late fifties. The woman's present condition is seen from the perspective of a younger woman, and is hardly encouraging, but the poet's conviction that a kind of spiritual grandeur resides in the winning of the struggle against negative emotions is genuine.

> Ten years ago it seemed impossible
>   That she should ever grow as calm as this,
>   With self-remembrance in her warmest kiss
> And dim, dried eyes like an exhausted well.

Slow-speaking when she has some fact to tell,
   Silent, with long unbroken silences,
   Centred in self yet not unpleased to please,
Gravely monotonous like a passing bell.
Mindful of drudging daily common things,
   Patient at pastime, patient at her work,
   Wearied perhaps but strenuous certainly.
   Sometimes I fancy we may one day see
Her head shoot forth seven stars from where they lurk
And her eyes lightnings and her shoulders wings.

(352)

Rossetti does not see in this monumental figure the calm of the Blessed Virgin, or any other passive saintly female figure; the figure she describes is that of a sexless Archangel.

Simone de Beauvoir rejected the characterization of old age as a time of calm, and even more the idea that ageing people should strive for a measure of detachment and tranquillity. She regarded the serene older woman as a perpetuation of the stereotype, a mere continuation of the submissiveness of the feminine woman, and no more authentic. De Beauvoir herself never abandoned the role of consort, although she had in reality very increasingly rare opportunities of playing it. She never looked to solitude and found it freedom, because she insisted to such a large extent on living through Jean-Paul Sartre. In cultures where women spend less of their time with men than with children and other women, the role of consort does not bulk so large. The ideal of a peaceful, contemplative third of one's life is more devoutly wished for by agricultural labouring women the world over than it could ever be in our cartoon-comic-strip world where all aunts babble, all old maids gnash their shaky teeth and grandmothers are black beetles equipped with death-dealing handbags and umbrellas.

In African village life the large, strong woman plays a very important role. In matrilocal societies, family life revolves about the senior female. Where outwork has taken fathers far away, their mothers must keep their wives and children safe. Older women play an important part in the struggle for the liberation of black Africa. The effects of slavery on the black family are such as to intensify its reliance upon the older woman. The Afro-American woman bears a strong family resemblance to her queenly African counterpart, even when she is forced to live in a menial condition: in *An Unfinished Woman*, Lillian Hellman describes her old nurse, Helen:

Other people always came in time, to like and admire her, although her first impression of them was not always pleasant. That enormous figure, the stern face, the few crisp words did not always seem welcoming, as she opened a door or offered a drink, but the greatest clod among them came to understand the instinctive good taste, the high-bred manners that once they flowered gave off so much true courtesy. And in the period of nobody grows older or fatter, your mummie looks like your girl, there may be a need in us for the large, strong woman, who takes us back to what most of us wanted and few of us ever had. (179)

Though aged writers do not often write about the greatest adventure of all, growing old, the subject seems to enthral and appal writers on the threshold of the ageing process, especially in the pre-menopause. This strengthens the impression of ageing as an external phenomenon, only identifiable from outside, by the young. There is a certain truth in this, for one's age is always the centre from which one looks forward and back, and one has no realization of the objective fact of one's age. Perhaps it is the young who need to define age, to push it off and away. I wonder if I am older or younger than the blue-tit I can see feasting off horse-chestnut flowers full of dew. He shall certainly die long before I do, so I guess I am younger after all. I look at women in Woolworths and I cannot tell if I am older or younger than many of them. Younger than the ones who smoke, older than the ones who don't drink, younger than the ones who are obese and older? No, younger than the ones who have less to do. Australians when they are annoyed by someone's behaviour often snap, 'Oh, be your age!' Though one cannot be anything else, one cannot consciously be one's age.

Vita Sackville-West was approaching forty when she wrote *All Passion Spent* for her sons, in order to give them some perspective on growing old. The account she gives of the last year in the life of the widow of a 'great man' is quietly and subtly subversive. Lady Slane, who had never lived independently in her life but had always quietly acceded to the wishes of others, did not like her children or grandchildren very much, was repelled by their graspingness and ambition, their noisiness and lack of sensitivity, and, rather than accept their rather grudging care, went to live in a house in Hampstead with her best friend, her French maid. There she made new friends of her own generation who understood her much better than her children, much better indeed than her husband. One of these is Mr Bucktrout, who owns the house she takes, principal apologist for their naughty life-style:

'The world, Lady Slane, is pitiably horrible. It is horrible because it is based upon competitive struggle – when I first went into business . . . I was fierce . . . When did I give up these principles? Well, I set a term on them; I determined that at sixty-five business, properly speaking, should know me no more. On my sixty-sixth [birthday] I woke a free man.' (120–23)

Though she makes a valiant attempt at entering the experience of an old woman, Vita Sackville-West was perhaps too young to get it quite right. Lady Slane's relationship with her old body seems topsy-turvy.

Her body had, in fact, become her companion, a constant resource and preoccupation; all the small squalors of the body, known only to oneself, insignificant in youth, easily dismissed, in old age became dominant and entered into the tyranny they had always threatened. Yet it was, rather than otherwise, an agreeable and interesting tyranny. (194)

Aches and pains are by no means 'insignificant in youth' but intolerable, unbearable. The young experience pain as an affront, and often as a source of anxiety, so that pain is complicated by a psychological dimension that makes it much worse. Part of the battle for pain relief is simply to remove attention from the pain, rather than to prevent the pain signal being sent. The young, outraged by their pain, refuse to ignore it, probe and pick at it; older people register it and forget it. Young people find certain squalors, flatulence for example, frightfully embarrassing. An old lady can accept the fact that she may occasionally belch or fart. Most of the aches and pains of eld cause no anxiety, being merely the creaking of an ageing frame. We acknowledge them, salute them like old friends, and learn gradually to accommodate them. They do not ask to be irritably rooted out, nor do they insist upon the taking of medicines to obliterate them. They can be ignored. It becomes a kind of contest with oneself to see how thoroughly one can forget the sore hip and the tender knucklebone. To begin to complain of a pain that must simply be endured is to give it the upper hand, is to suffer a small defeat, and simply to annoy the people, if there are any such, who care about one and grieve that they cannot help. One finds oneself marvelling at the seriousness with which younger people take minor ailments, the way they dramatize colds and exaggerate tummy upsets, and demand treatments of no known efficacy. They do not suspect that 'never mind' is actually a useful piece of advice.

Mr Bucktrout not only does not regret his own youth, he finds youth itself rather tiresome.

'I find that as one grows older one relies more and more on the society of one's contemporaries and shrinks from the society of the young. They are so tiring. So unsettling. I can scarcely, nowadays, endure the company of anybody under seventy. Young people compel one to look forward to a life full of effort. Old people permit one to look backward on a life whose effort is over and done with. That is reposeful. Repose, Lady Slane, is one of the most important things in life, yet how few people achieve it? The old have it imposed upon them. Either they are infirm or weary. But half of them still sigh for the energy which once was theirs. Such a mistake.' (98)

To the middle-aged woman, repose may seem a long way off. Repose is not torpor or oblivion, but the cessation of fever and fret, of snatch and grab. It has been said that the mark of a gentleman is that he never hurries; it is the paradox of ageing that to hurry is to waste time. If you wish to grasp the present, you must slow down and give the task in hand your full, wide-eyed attention. Christina Rossetti wrote of her mother:

> Her heart sat silent through the noise
> And concourse of the street;
> There was no hurry in her hands,
> No hurry in her feet.

It is difficult to learn not to hurry, especially when time seems to pass more and more rapidly as one grows older. The way to slow it down is of course to slow oneself down.

Mr Bucktrout reminded Lady Slane how choppy life is at twenty:

'. . . It is terrible to be twenty, Lady Slane. It is as bad as being faced with riding over the Grand National Course. One knows one will almost certainly fall into the Brook of Competition, and break one's leg over the Hedge of Disappointment, and stumble over the Wire of Intrigue, and quite certainly come to grief over the Obstacle of Love. When one is old, one can throw oneself down as a rider on the evening after the race, and think, Well, I shall never have to ride that course again.'

Lady Slane demurred.

'But you forget, Mr Bucktrout . . . when one was young, one enjoyed living dangerously – one desired it – one wasn't appalled.'

Vita Sackville-West had not learned her own lesson herself; still embroiled in slightly pointless *Sturm und Drang*, she imagined that the contemplative life of older people was a grisaille version of the multicolour of youth.

They were too old, all three of them, to feel keenly; to compete and circumvent and score . . . Those days were gone when feeling burst its bounds and poured hot from the foundry, when the heart seemed likely to split from complex and contradictory desires; now there was nothing left but a landscape in monochrome, the features identical but all the colours gone from them, and nothing but a gesture left in place of speech. (117)

The time when the landscape is monochrome is the time of obsession when unmanageable feeling colours all perception. The author has reversed her own image; when the molten matter issues from the foundry it casts on everything its lurid glow. Everything is ruddy and presents only a single glinting lit face to the observer. The lens, moreover, is distorted, for the self interposes between the observer and the thing seen. 'What about me?' it screams. 'Where do I fit in?' It is not possible to answer, 'But this is not about you.' When you are young, everything is about you. As you grow older, and are pushed to the margin, you begin to realize that everything is not about you, and that is the beginning of freedom. Elizabeth Jennings (born 1926) wrote for a collection published in 1972 as *Relationships* a poem called 'Let Things Alone':

> You have to learn it all over again,
> The words, the sound, almost the whole language
> Because this is a time when words must be strict and new
> Not concerning you,
> Or only indirectly,
> Concerning a pain
> Learnt as most people some time or other learn it
> With shock, then dark.
>
> The flowers will refer to themselves always
> But should not be loaded too much
> With meaning from happier days.
> They must remain themselves,
> Dear to the touch.
> The stars also
> Must go on shining without what I now know.
> And the sunset must simply glow.

(104)

423

While one is still the heroine of one's own tale one cannot understand, let alone accept, the rigour of this argument. In fact only by triumphing over self-consciousness can the feminine victim become the female hero.

As the ideal woman, the feminine type is the stepdaughter of masculine civilization, living the consequences of the cultural practices of sexualization and devaluation. Her estrangement from her real self is accommodation to a culture from which she is alienated. Her suffering is both a criticism of that culture and the price she has paid for a flight into dependent safety that 'protects' her from opposing conditions that oppress her. (Westkott, 199)

Marcia Westkott is here summarizing Karen Horney's theory of the function of psychotherapy, which is to deconstruct the feminine woman's distortion of herself to fit the conflicting demands and expectations of male supremacist culture. Whether we accept Horney's theory of conditioning or not, we cannot but be aware that the middle-aged woman no longer has the option of fulfilling the demands of patriarchal society. She can no longer play the obedient daughter, the pneumatic sex object or the madonna. Unless she consents to enter into the expensive, time-consuming and utterly futile business of denying that she has passed her sell-by date, she has sooner or later to register the fact that she has been junked by consumer culture. She is on her own; as menopause usually cures uterine dysfunction, it also cures the anguish of the feminine supermenial. Horney expected the younger woman to make the heroic pronouncements that are forced on the ageing woman:

First, I (and nobody else) am responsible for my life, for my growth as a human being, for the development of whatever talents I have. It is of no use to imagine that others keep me down. If they actually do, it is up to me to fight them.

Secondly, I (and nobody else) am responsible for what I think, feel, say, do, decide. It is weak to blame others and it makes me weaker. It is useless to blame others, because I (and nobody else) have to bear the consequences of my being and my doing. (Westkott, 200)

The woman ejected from feminine subjection by the consequences of her own ageing can no longer live through others, or justify her life by the sexual and domestic services that she renders. She must, being in free fall, take a long look at the whole landscape that surrounds her and decide how she is going to manage to live in it, no matter how chill the wind that buffets her ill-equipped person. At first she may cling to her old life, trying to claw back something of what she poured into it so unstintingly, but eventually, her grieving done, her outrage stilled, she must let go. Only if she lets go can she recover her lost potency. The younger woman needs her love objects too desperately to love them without hostility in an undestructive way. When the older woman releases or is forced to release her desperate stranglehold and feels herself dropping away, real love will bear her up.

Elizabeth Jennings explores her theme of letting things alone in a series of elegant and tough poems that speak directly to the woman who is turning back into herself, for example, the sonnet called 'Growing' from a 1975 collection called *Growing Points*:

> Not to be passive simply, never that.
> Watchful, yes, but wondering . . .
>
> (106)

The woman new-born after the climacteric can say to herself as Jennings does in 'Accepted' from the same collection:

> You are no longer young,
> Nor are you very old.
> There are homes where those belong.
> You know you do not fit
> When you observe the cold
> Stares of those who sit
>
> In bath-chairs or the park
> (A stick, then, at their side)
> Or find yourself in the dark
> And see the lovers who,

In love and in their stride,
Don't even notice you.

This is a time to begin
Your life. It could be new.
The sheer not fitting in
With the old who envy you
And the young who want to win,
Not knowing false from true,

Means you have liberty
Denied to their extremes.
At last now you can be
What the old cannot recall
And the young long for in dreams,
Yet still include them all.

(141)

In its beautifully spare diction, with no surface shimmer of effect and no display of technical virtuosity, this poem is the authentic utterance of the female survivor, not passive, never that, looking on and loving what she sees in a way more passionate because uneloquent. This voice is the idiom of 'disinterest', a word whose real meaning we have forgotten; her 'disinterest' means that the female hero values the life around her not because of any use she may make of it, but for itself. As Jennings said in 'Growing',

The poem leaves you and it sings. (106)

Jennings learnt this early, earlier than most of us who only open the eyes of the soul when we are forced to. From very early in her career her poems were not about her, nor was she displaying herself in them. In 1986 she wrote in the Preface to her own selection from her previously published collections:

When I re-read my past work I can see a development; to such an effect indeed, that some of them seem to be no longer any part of me. But of course once a poem is published it ceases to have much to do with oneself. Art is not self-expression while, for me, 'confessional poetry' is almost a contradiction in terms. (13)

426

Not all Jennings's later poems manifest the same serenity and power; indeed, any poem is the record of a struggle to achieve its own resolution between disparate and warring elements. Some of Jennings's poems adumbrate a worse bereavement than the one that prompted *Relationships*, as if the poet's detachment had been corroded by the deliberate assault of one who dispossessed her even more brutally than by dying, this time by lying.

The self-possessed woman walking in the golden light of her high detachment excites a certain kind of predator who longs to tumble her back into the darkness of need and hostility masquerading as real life. If she is taken unawares by this last encroachment on her integrity, the older woman can suffer even more bitterly than ever the younger woman writhed in the bonds of sexual passion. It may take her longer to realize the extent of her spiritual disease than it did when she was young, for the soul ages much as the body does, but the devastation is difficult to reverse. The recovery of serenity and power after such infection is painfully slow.

When she was in her early sixties Elizabeth Bishop wrote a deceptively simple poem called 'One Art' that makes a similar point to Jennings's 'Let Things Alone':

> The art of losing isn't hard to master;
> so many things seem filled with the intent
> to be lost that their loss is no disaster.
>
> Lose something every day. Accept the fluster
> Of lost door keys, the hour badly spent.
> The art of losing isn't hard to master.
>
> Then practise losing farther, losing faster;
> places and names, and where it was you meant
> to travel. None of these will bring disaster.

The point of the poem is, of course, that the art of losing *is* hard to master, and as for it not *bringing* disaster, we must conclude

427

with R. D. Laing that the 'disaster has already happened'. Every menopausal woman panics at her hopeless short-term memory, imagining that Alzheimer's is upon her, when in fact she always has never known where she put her keys. The problem is not the losing but the fear of losing; most of what we are afraid of losing is already gone and we have survived. Our illusions of omnipotence and perfectability were never anything but illusions. That is the dreadful thing that has already happened. Now we can relax and let things slip through our fingers.

Once we lose our sense of grievance everything, including physical pain, becomes easier to bear. As the inflammatory response in the body slows down, so does the inflammation of the mind. As we hoist in the fact that happiness is not something we are entitled to, nor even something we are programmed for, we begin to understand that there is no virtue in being miserable. We can then begin to strive for the heroism of real joy. As Dorothy L. Sayers reminded her readers in an essay called 'Strong Meat':

'Except ye become as little children', except you can wake on your fiftieth birthday with the same forward-looking excitement and interest in life that you enjoyed when you were five, 'ye cannot enter the kingdom of God'. One must not only die daily, but every day we must be born again. (15)

The lifting up of the heart is a strenuous business and we must work our way into it gradually. This is not a joy that comes from lack of awareness or refusal to contemplate the pain of the world. It comes rather from the recognition of the bitterness of the struggle, not just for ourselves, but for everyone, and the importance of survival. When silly death-wishes and juvenile self-destructiveness are at length driven out, the spiritual athlete can pile on the weights and smile genuinely in her own triumph over a nobler kind of pain than the pangs of self-pity that once beset her. George Eliot wrote in a letter in 1876, when she was fifty-seven:

Anyone who knows from experience what bodily infirmity is – how it spoils life even for those who have no other trouble – gets a little impatient of healthy complainants, strong enough for extra work and ignorant of indigestion. I at least should be inclined to scold the discontented young people, who tell me in one breath that they never have anything the matter with them, and that life is not worth having – if I did not remember my own young discontent. It is remarkable to me that I have entirely lost my personal melancholy. I often, of course, have melancholy thoughts about the destinies of my fellow-creatures, but I am never in that *mood* of sadness which used to be my frequent visitant even in the midst of external happiness. And this notwithstanding a very vivid sense that life is declining and death close at hand. (Haight, 1954–6)

The discontent of youth passes when you realize that the music you are hearing is not about you, but about itself. The important thing is not you listening to the music, but the self-realizing form of the music itself. Then you can begin to understand that beauty is not to be found in objects of desire but in those things that exist beyond desire, that cannot be subordinated to any use that human beings can make of them. Emily Dickinson may have been only thirty-four when she wrote the following poem, which was discovered and printed only after her death, but it describes with great fidelity the ageing woman's discovery of beauty.

> As imperceptibly as Grief
> The Summer lapsed away –
> Too imperceptible at last
> To seem like Perfidy –
> A Quietness distilled
> As Twilight long begun,
> Or Nature spending with herself
> Sequestered Afternoon –
> The Dusk grew earlier in –
> The Morning foreign shone –
> A courteous, yet harrowing Grace –
> As Guest, that would be gone –
> And thus, without a Wing

Or service of a Keel
Our Summer made her light escape
Into the Beautiful.

(642–3)

Only when a woman ceases the fretful struggle to *be* beautiful can she turn her gaze outward, find the beautiful and feed upon it. She can at last transcend the body that was what other people principally valued her for, and be set free both from their expectations and her own capitulation to them. It is quite impossible to explain to younger women that this new invisibility, like calm and indifference, is a desirable condition. At first even the changing woman herself protests against it; she may even take steps to reverse it, by wearing more revealing or garish clothes, but sooner or later she will be forced to accept it. Some of the evidence seems to show that women who have been short-changed by our education system, so that their minds are undeveloped and their imaginations unstimulated, never manage this transition but remain blind and embittered. When they are at the mercy of a mass culture that celebrates older women who 'still remain youthful', i.e. spend enormous sums of money in the attempt to fashion themselves into ghastly simulacra of youthful bodies, they have less chance than ever of surmounting the shock of invisibility. They are mocked by the endless succession of stories about middle-aged film-stars becoming engaged to be married, equipped like Jane Fonda and Cher with new silicone breasts to keep the new husbands entertained. Most middle-aged women are shrewd enough to notice that each new marriage of such celebrities breaks up rather sooner than the last. What is not so obvious is that often the husbands have to be paid off; marriage with an ageing box office property is a nice little earner. The shine in the wide eyes of the fifty-five-year-old Hollywood fiancée can also be seen as the white stare of desperation.

Most of us do not have the money that such self-delusion costs. We have to make use of other resources, spiritual resources. Even the woman whose mind and soul have been ignored by everyone, including herself, has within her the spiritual resources to make something of her new life, though she may have some difficulty in getting at them. If no one has ever cared what a woman thought she may have begun to doubt whether she did actually think. Under the pressure of brutalizing work in the home or out of it, she may have indeed stopped thinking; nothing deadens the soul more effectively than a dreary routine of thankless tasks. It may be necessary to break that routine quite violently to free the soul from the weight of petty cares. It may be necessary to disappear for a while, to go bush, in order to begin to reflect. Many of the tales of menopausal women's bad behaviour are simply descriptions of this process. There may be danger in taking time to be alone to reflect, and perhaps to grieve for times that can never return and, worse, bitterer, time that was wasted, but there is more danger in not taking it.

Religion is one of the easier ways that the ageing woman can unlock the door to her interior life. If she has been an unreflective Christian or Hindu or Muslim or Jew or Buddhist she may find it easiest to find her interior life by entering more deeply into the implications of her religion. Examples of the piety of older women are to be seen on all sides; what is not so easy to discern is the joy that entering into the intellectual edifices of the great religions can give, to those who have faith. Women who do not adhere to a particular creed will nevertheless find that in the last third of their lives they come to partake of the 'oceanic experience' as the grandeur and the pity of human life begin to become apparent to them. As one by one the Lilliputian strings that tie the soul down to self-interest and the short view begin to snap the soul rises higher and higher, until the last one snaps, and it floats free at last. That last string is probably the string of life itself, but you must not ask me to be more precise. My own gyves have only just begun to fall away — I cannot see so far.

There is nothing original in this view, that

> An aged man is but a paltry thing,
> A tattered coat upon a stick, unless
> Soul clap its hands and sing, and louder sing
> For every tatter in its mortal dress.
> (Yeats, 'Sailing to Byzantium')

Yeats was one who, in Seamus Heaney's phrase, did not whine at death (as Philip Larkin did) but withstood it. He knew that he had to gather all spirituality to confront the inevitablity of decay; when 'Sailing to Byzantium' was written his greatest poems were still to write.

Some may prefer a more prosaic formulation of the same idea, which does not invoke religious notions of the 'immortal soul' as a storehouse of grace. More acceptable terms for modern ears are 'self' for soul, and 'energy' for grace, as they are deployed in 'A Philosophy of Energy' by Stanley Jacobs, consultant to the London Borough of Southwark, Lewisham and the ILEA. Jacobs sees 'self' as the 'source of all energy', of 'infinite worth and value':

> And yet we still believe the most extraordinary things about ourselves
> – that we are unworthy and unlovable and unable to give love; that we
> are incomplete and inadequate, bad or mad; that we have been ir-
> reparably damaged by certain experiences of life – but self (soul) has
> always been and will forever be . . . (2)

Jacobs cites Camus, of all people, saying that 'in the midst of winter I finally learned that there was in me an invincible summer'.

When I first came to East Anglia, in 1964, I was twenty-five years old. I did not notice the huge skies. I had no time to stand and stare. I would have been surprised to learn that on a typical Mid-Anglia day, you can see on one side a great boil-up of cloud, black and lowering, trailing skirts of precipitation or flirting edges of blinding silver foam, and turned the other way the gaze may lose itself in a deep blue vault with chalky chunks of cloud floating in it, while at the zenith crinkled skeins of cirrus are shaken out by a high frigid air stream. Though I saw the obvious things – the green snouts of the crocuses poking through the snow, the red mist in the hedgerows as spring drew on, the flambeaux cast by the chestnuts – I was unaware of the titanic weather war being fought over my head. I could not feel immensity. I could not give in to wonder, because there in my mind's eye was I. Like all young people I was preoccupied with inventing myself. In order to survive I had to fashion a self and project it. A woman, any woman, has to fashion a self that will attract; in every situation, every encounter, she has to be self-conscious. She may be aware of the process that holds her captive, but she cannot escape it. Though I protested about it as a thirty-year-old feminist, I was still its victim and its beneficiary.

I walk the same paths now that I walked twenty-five years ago, but now I am not aware of the figure I am cutting. I neither expect nor hope to be noticed. I am hoping only to *take in* what is happening around me even on the bleakest winter day, the blood-warm glow of the upturned clods in the ploughland, the robin's greedy whistle, the glitter of the stubble against a dark sky. I want to be open to this, to be agog, spellbound. And to do that I have to shake myself free of footlingness. Lady Slane would have known what I mean:

> Certain Italian paintings depicted trees – poplar, willow, alder – each leaf separate, and sharp, and veined, against a green translucent sky. Of such a quality were the tiny things, the shapely leaves, of her present life: redeemed from insignificance by their juxtaposition with a luminous eternity.
>
> She felt exalted, she escaped from an obvious pettiness, from a finicking life, whenever she remembered that no adventure could now befall her except the supreme adventure for which all other adventures were but a preparation. (Sackville-West, 195–6)

You may say that the thrill of discovering such things is only important to Lady Slane and me because we feel nothing else. I would answer that I never knew such strong and durable joy before. Before I felt less on greater provocation; I lay in the arms of young men who loved me and felt less bliss than I do now. What I felt then was hope, fear, jealousy, desire, passion, a mixture of real pain, and real and fake pleasure, a mash of conflicting feelings, anything but this deep still joy. I needed my lovers too much to experience much joy in our travailed relationships. I was too much at their mercy to feel much in the way of tenderness; I can feel as much in a tiny compass now when I see a butterfly still damp and crinkled from the chrysalis taking a first flutter among the brambles. In her widowhood Willa Muir answered her own anguished cry, 'How shall I live without love?' in this wise.

> Where is my Love, my Dear?
> In my heart, in my head,
> Not here,
> Not in my bed.
>
> Where is my Love, my Dear?
> In my memory, in my mind,
> Not here,
> Not among humankind.
>
> Where is my Love, my Dear?
> In poems, in the air,
> Here, here,
> Nowhere and everywhere.

The feeling may well be elegiac. Though I do not make every third thought a thought about my death, I am aware of mortality as I never was before I was fifty. I do not squander my time now; I would never dream of bartering an hour of a spring morning to lie in bed. If I am sleepless I go out into the darkness to join the short-lived jubilee of the other creatures. As Mr Bucktrout said:

'Life is so transitory, Lady Slane, that one must grab it by the tail as it flies past. No good in thinking of yesterday or tomorrow. Yesterday is gone, and tomorrow problematical.' (Sackville-West, 126)

'What,' asked the men who were just now making me a new

434

driveway, 'what do you reckon is the best time of life?' They were boys from the black stuff, with a good deal of gypsy in their make-up, so I was less surprised by the question and less suspicious of it than I would have been in different circumstances.

'I reckon it were eighteen,' said the older of the two. 'I'm no good for anything now.'

'You might have been good for it then,' said the other, 'but London to a brick you couldn't get any.'

I found myself saying, 'The best time in life is always now, because it is the only time there is. You can't live regretting what's past, and you can't live anticipating the future. If you spend any amount of time doing either of those things you never live at all.' Such a commonplace cannot entirely explain my passion for being alive and my hunger to gather up each moment. The theme chimes over and over in Shakespeare's sonnets.

> In me thou see'st the glowing of such fire,
> That on the ashes of his youth doth lie,
> As the deathbed whereon it must expire,
> Consumed with that which it was nourished by.
> This thou perceivest, which makes thy love more strong,
> To love that well, which thou must leave ere long.
>
> (Sonnet 73)

If we continue to see our own age through the eyes of observers much younger, we will find it impossible to understand the peculiar satisfactions of being older. If we can conquer our own lack of interest in ourselves and our kind, and turn to older women's writing about being older women, we will find stated again and again the theme of joy. In 1741 when Mary Chandler, who had suffered all her life from a crooked spine, was fifty-four, she got her first proposal of marriage. This is how she answered it:

> At fifty-four, when hoary age has shed
> Its winter's snow, and whiten'd o'er my head,
> Love is a language foreign to my tongue:
> I could have learned it once, when I was young,

But now quite other things my wish employs:
Peace, liberty and sun, to gild my days . . .
I want no heaps of gold; I hate all dress,
And equipage. The cow provides my mess . . .
I'd rather walk alone my own slow pace,
Than drive with six, unless I choose the place.
Imprisoned in a coach, I should repine:
The chaise I hire, I drive and call it mine.
And, when I will, I ramble, or retire
To my own room, own bed, my garden, fire;
Take up my book, or trifle with my pen;
And, when I'm weary, lay them down again:
No questions asked; no master in the spleen –
I would not change my state to be a queen.

                                        (Lonsdale, 154)

Mary Chandler, who supported herself by working as a milliner, experienced her solitude as liberty. Women who have lived all their lives in houses filled with noisy other people, responding automatically to the demands of others, might find the sudden silence deafening and frightening, especially if it falls just when menopause is disrupting sleep patterns and mood control. Mary Chandler did not have to shift her focus radically to slide into old maidism, for she had always been alone. Nevertheless, her recipe, peace, liberty and sun, is not a bad one.

Besides liberty, the other important source of delight for the select band of older women who survived fifty years and wrote about it is friendship. For some, like the circle of wise and happy old ladies that surrounded Joanna Baillie and Hannah More, friendship signified society. For others a single relationship was important, as in what came to be called 'Boston marriages', in which two women pledged a life-long commitment to each other. The two women agreed to live together, two being able to live as cheaply as one, and to represent for each other emotional security and support in their intellectual or creative endeavours. Many such relationships, like that of Willa Cather and Edith Lewis, Sarah

Orne Jewett and Sally Fields, the Ladies of Llangollen and the women who called themselves 'Michael Field', began when the women were young. Some of them were clearly sexual liaisons, scarred with all the betrayals and infidelities that sexual relationships usually suffer. For some middle-aged women friendship flowered into deep sisterly attachment, less interesting to a modern mind but more durable and hardly less deep than the passionate attachments of younger women.

Charlotte Mary Yonge had a bad time in her mid-forties when severe headaches virtually crippled her. She was probably enduring a difficult pre-menopause at the same time that she had to bear the stress of her mother's long decline before she died of softening of the brain in 1868. Yonge was fifty when Gertrude Walker came to live with her and help her with her correspondence. The relationship was probably the happiest time of Charlotte's life; Gertrude, who was crippled, liked to call herself Char's wife. They were to remain together until Gertrude's death in 1897, nearly a quarter of a century later (Coleridge, 270–81).

Once we are past menopause we are all oddballs. We need feel no embarrassment about looking for relationships that do not follow the accepted paradigm. We may find the companionship that may have seemed to be lacking even when we were in the midst of family matters very close by, in a sister or brother we have not seen much of since we both lived in the same house, in a niece, a stepchild, or a home help. Stevie Smith lived with her maiden aunt, Margaret Annie Spear, in a house in Palmer's Green from the time she was three until her death, aged sixty-eight, in 1971. She instructed her biographers not to say

because I never married I know nothing of the emotions. When I am dead you must put them right. I loved my aunt. (Braybrooke)

That love, which was not easily come by, is celebrated in her poems:

> My spirit in confusion
> Long years I strove

437

But now I know that never
Nearer shall I move,
Than a friend's friend to friendship,
To love than a friend's love.

(1985, 186)

In the culture of coupledom where no love is worth the name that is not sanctified by genital congress, Stevie Smith's love for her lion-aunt is seen only as a kind of boarding-school substitute for real life. Stevie Smith was well aware of the intolerance that 'normal' or 'ordinary' people would unthinkingly feel about a life as oddly uneventful or 'unfulfilled' as hers, but she had no such feelings herself.

I love my Aunt. I love her. I love the life in the family, my familiar life, but I also like to go out and see how the other people get along, and especially I like to see how the married ladies get along, and I sit and listen and watch, and I see how much they think about their husbands even if they hate 'em like hell, there is this thought, this attention. (1979, 27)

Stevie Smith thought that happiness was 'to have a darling Aunt to come home to, that one admires, that is strong, happy, simple, shrewd, staunch, loving, upright and bossy . . .' (28) with 'lionish kind eyes' (30) or 'an eagle managing eye'. Her aunt was

the Begum Female Spider who has devoured her Suitors and who lives on and makes these crocodile-like pronouncements, and who is like a lion with a spanking tail who will have no nonsense. (38)

Stevie Smith's is not the paradigm of adult life that we have been taught to revere. There is nothing here of Márquez's making love 'like grown-ups'. The 'immaturity' of Stevie Smith's style is the expression of her rejection of the notion of female life that is considered normal, right and proper. She is forced to use the literary instrument shaped by centuries of male élitist culture, but she does so in a deliberately childish way, so that at the same time as she uses it, she subverts it. Her distorted prosody, and the

strange bluntness and simplicity of her vocabulary, enact and re-
enact her wry refusal to fit her emotions and her sexuality to the
contours of a man.

> Now I am old I tend my mother's sister
> The noble aunt who so long tended us,
> Faithful and True her name is. Tranquil.
> Also sardonic. And I tend the house.
>
> It is a house of female habitation
> A house expecting strength as it is strong
> A house of aristocratic mould that looks apart
> When tears fall. Counts despair
> Derisory. Yet it has kept us well. For all its faults,
> If they are faults, of sternness and reserve,
> It is a Being of Warmth, I think; at heart
> A house of mercy.

(1985, 411)

When you see that lumpy figure walking on the skyline with her
dog, just think, you can never know how happy she is. And as for
her, she does not feel the need to tell you. People who are really
happy do not concern themselves with convincing others of the
fact.

While the anophobes draw frightful caricatures of the untreated
menopausal woman, and the hormone replacers rend their gar-
ments and bemoan the tragedy of the cessation of ovulation,
women themselves remain silent. Let younger people anxiously
inquire, let researchers tie themselves in knots with definitions that
refuse to stick, the middle-aged woman is about her own business,
which is none of theirs. Let the Masters in Menopause congregate
in luxury hotels all over the world to deliver and to hearken to
papers on the latest astonishing discoveries about the decline of
grip strength in menopause or the number of stromal cells in the
fifty-year-old ovary, the woman herself is too busy to listen. She is
climbing her own mountain, in search of her own horizon, after
years of being absorbed in the struggles of others. The way is

hard, and she stumbles many times, but for once no one is scrambling after her, begging her to turn back. The air grows thin, and she may often feel dizzy. Sometimes the weariness spreads from her aching bones to her heart and brain, but she knows that when she has scrambled up this last sheer obstacle, she will see how to handle the rest of her long life. Some will climb swiftly, others will tack back and forth on the lower slopes, but few will give up. The truth is that fewer women come to grief at this obstacle than at any other in their tempestuous lives, though it is one of the stiffest challenges they ever face. Their behaviour may baffle those who have unthinkingly exploited them all their lives before, but it is important not to explain, not to apologize. The climacteric marks the end of apologizing. The chrysalis of conditioning has once for all to break and the female woman finally to emerge.

Works Cited

Abbott, D. (1981), *New Life for Old: Therapeutic Immunology*. London, Frederick Muller.

Aidoo, A. A. (1985), 'The Message'. In *Unwinding Threads: Writing by Women in Africa*, ed. C. H. Bruner. London, Heinemann.

Aksel, S., Scomberg, D., Tyrey, L., and Hammond, C. (1976), 'Vasomotor symptoms, serum estrogens and gonadatrophin levels in surgical menopause'. *American Journal of Obstetrics and Gynecology*, 126, pp. 165–9.

Allbutt, T. C., ed. (1896–9), *A System of Medicine by Many Writers*. London, Macmillan and Co.

Anderson, M. (1983), *The Menopause*. London, Faber & Faber.

Arendt, H. (1973), *Men in Dark Times*. Harmondsworth, Penguin.

Ashwell, S. (1844), *A Practical Treatise on the Diseases Peculiar to Women*. London, Samuel Highley.

Asso, D. (1983), *The Real Menstrual Cycle*. Chichester, Wiley.

Astruc, J. (1761), *Traité des maladies des femmes*. Paris, P. G. Cavelier.

Auerbach, N. (1982), *Woman and the Demon: The Life of a Victorian Myth*, Cambridge, MA, Harvard University Press.

Austen, J. (1978), *Emma*, ed. R. W. Chapman. Oxford, Oxford University Press.

Aylward, M. (1973), 'Plasma tryptophan levels and mental depression in post-menopausal subjects: Effects of oral piperazine-oestrone sulphate'. *International Research Communications System*, Vol. 1, p. 30.

Baekeland, F. (1970), 'Exercise deprivation, sleep and physical reactions'. *Archives of General Psychiatry*, 22, pp. 365–9.

Ballinger, C. B. (1975), 'Psychiatric morbidity and the menopause:

Screening of general population sample'. *British Medical Journal*, 3, pp. 344–6.

— (1976), 'Psychiatric morbidity and the menopause: Clinical features'. *British Medical Journal*, i, pp. 1183–5.

— (1977), 'Psychiatric morbidity and the menopause: Survey of a gynaecological outpatient clinic'. *British Journal of Psychiatry*, 131, pp. 83–9.

Banner, L. M. (1990), *The Meaning of Menopause: Aging and its Historical Context in the Twentieth Century*. Milwaukee, University of Wisconsin Center for Twentieth Century Studies.

Bardwick, J. M. (1980), 'The seasons of a woman's life', In *Women's Lives: New Theory, Research and Policy*, ed. D. G. McGuigan. Ann Arbor: University of Michigan Center for Continuing Education of Women.

Barlow, D. H., Brockie, J. A., and Rees, C. M. P. (1991), 'Study of general practitioners' consultations and menopausal problems'. *British Medical Journal*, No. 6771, Vol. 302, 2 February, pp. 274–6.

Barnett, R. C., and Baruch, G. K. (1978), 'Women in the middle years: A critique of research and theory'. *Psychology of Women Quarterly 3* (2), pp. 187–97.

— (1984), 'Mastery and pleasure: A two factor model of wellbeing of women in the middle years'. In *Social Power and Influence of Women*, eds. L. Stamm and C. D. Ryff. Epping, Bowker Publishing Co.

Barrett-Connor, E., Wingard, D., and Criqui, M., (1989), 'Post-menopausal estrogen use and heart disease factors in the 1890s'. *Journal of the American Medical Association*, 269, pp. 2095–100.

Bart, P. B. (1971), 'Depression in middle-aged women'. In *Woman in Sexist Society: Studies in Power and Powerlessness,* eds. V. Gornick and B. K. Moran. New York, Basic Books.

— and Grossman, M. (1978), 'Menopause'. In *The Woman Patient: Medical and Psychological Interfaces*, eds. M. Notman and C. Nadelson. New York, Plenum Press.

Beadle, Gert (1986), 'The nature of crones'. *Women and Politics*, 6, No. 2.

Bean, J. A., Leeper, J. D., Wallace, R. B., Sherman, B. M., and Treloar, A. E. (1979), 'Accuracy of recalled menstrual and reproductive history'. *American Journal of Epidemiology*.

Beard, R. J. ed. (1976), *The Menopause: A Guide to Current Research and Practice*. Baltimore, University Park Press.

Benedek, T. (1950), 'Climacterium: a developmental phase'. *Psychoanalytic Quarterly*, 19, pp. 1–27.

Beyene, Y. (1986), 'Cultural significance and physiological manifestations of the menopause: a biocultural analysis'. *Culture, Medicine and Psychiatry*, 10, pp. 47–71.

Billington, R. (1979), *A Woman's Age*. London, Hamish Hamilton.

Bishop, E. (1984), *The Complete Poems 1927–1979*. London, The Hogarth Press.

Black, G. F. (1938), *A Calendar of Witchcraft in Scotland 1510–1727*. New York, New York Public Library.

Blanch, L. (1954), *The Wilder Shores of Love*. London, John Murray.

Block, M. R., Davidson, J. L., Grambs, J. D., and Serock, K. E. (1978), *Uncharted Territory: Issues and Concerns of Women over 40*. University of Maryland, Center on Aging, Silverspring MD: Lifespan Research Associates.

Bodin J. (1587), *De la demonomanie des sorciers*. Paris, Jacques du Puys.

Bodnar, S., and Catterill, T.B. (1972), 'Amitriptyline in emotional states associated with the climacteric'. *Psychosomatics, 13*, pp. 117–19.

Boivin M. A. V., and Duges, A. (1834), *A Practical Treatise on Diseases of the Uterus and its Appendages* with notes by G. Heming. London, Sherwood, Gilbert & Piper.

Boland, M. and B. (1976), *Old Wives' Lore for Gardeners*. London, The Bodley Head.

Boorde, A. (1547), *The Breuiary of Helthe*. London, Wyllyam Myddleton.

Braybrooke, N. (1971), 'Poet Unafraid'. *Daily Telegraph*, 14 March, p. 11.

Bright, T. (1586), *A Treatise of Melancholie*. London, John Windet.

Brodin, G. (1950), *Agnus Castus: A Middle English Herbal*. Essays and Studies in English Language and Literature, Vol. 6.

Brody, S., Carlström, K., Lagrelius, A., Lunell, N.-O., and Mollerström, G. (1987), 'Adrenal steroids in post-menopausal women: relation to obesity and to bone mineral content'. *Maturitas*, Vol. 9, pp. 25–32.

Brooke, F. (1755), *The Old Maid*.

Brown, P. S. (1977), 'Female pills and the reputation of iron as an abortifacient'. *Medical History*, 21, pp. 292–9.

Browning, E. B. (1911), *The Poetical Works of Elizabeth Barrett Browning*. London, Oxford University Press.

Bucknill, J. C., and Tuke, D. H. (1858), *A Manual of Psychological Medicine* (facs. 1968), int. F. J. Braceland. New York, Hafner Publishing Co.

Burn, G. (1990), *Somebody's Husband, Somebody's Son: The Story of the Yorkshire Ripper*. London, Pan Books.

Burton, R. (1989), *The Anatomy of Melancholy*, ed. T. C. Faulkner, N. K. Kiessling and R. L. Blair. Oxford, Clarendon Press.

Butler's Lives of the Saints (1956), eds. H. J. Thurston and D. Attwater. London, Burns & Oates.

Caldwell, J. C., and Caldwell, P. (1977), 'The role of marital abstinence in determining fertility: a study of the Yoruba in Nigeria'. *Population Studies*, 31, pp. 193ff.

Campagnoli, C., Morra, G., Belforte, P. and L., and Tousijn, L. P. (1981), 'Climacteric symptoms according to body weight in women of different socioeconomic groups'. *Maturitas*, Vol. 3, pp. 279–87.

Campbell, S, ed. (1976), *The Management of the Menopause and Post-menopausal Years*. Lancaster, MTP Press.

— McQueen, J., Minardi, J. and Whitehead, M. I. (1978), 'The modifying effect of progestogen on the response of the post-menopausal endometrium to exogenous oestrogens'. *Postgraduate Medical Journal*, Vol. 54(2), pp. 59–64.

— and Whitehead, M. (1977), 'Oestrogen therapy and the menopause syndrome'. In *Clinics in Obstetrics and Gynaecology*, eds. R. B. Greenblatt and J. W. W. Studd, Vol. 4, No. 1. Philadelphia, Saunders.

Caplan, P. (1984), *Class and Gender in India: Women and their Organisations in a South Indian City*. London, Tavistock Publications.

Carstairs, G. M. (1983), *Death of a Witch: A Village in North India 1950–1981*. London, Hutchinson.

Chakravarti, S., Collins, W., Newton, J., Oram, D., and Studd, J. (1977), 'Endocrine changes and symptomology after oophorectomy in premenopausal women'. *British Journal of Obstetrics and Gynaecology*, 84, pp. 769–75.

Chandernagor, F. (c. 1981), *L'Allée du roi: souvenirs de Françoise d'Aubigny, marquise de Maintenon, épouse du roi de France*. Paris, Juillard.

Chari, S., Hopkinson, C. R. N., Daume, E., and Sturm, G. (1979), 'Purification of INHIBIN from human ovarian follicular fluid'. *Acta Endocrinologica*, 90, p. 197.

Clay, V. S. (1977), *Women, Menopause and Middle Age*. Pittsburgh, Know Inc.

Cohn, N. (1975), *Europe's Inner Demons: An Enquiry Inspired by the Great Witch-hunt*. London, Chatto, Heinemann for Sussex University Press.

Coleridge, C. (1903), *Charlotte Mary Yonge: Her Life and Letters*. London, Macmillan & Co.

Colette (1920), *Chéri*. Paris, Arthème Fayard et cie.

— (1926), *La Fin de Chéri*. Paris, Flammarion.

Colombey, G. (1968), *Correspondance authentique de Ninon de Lenclos*. Geneva.

Comfort, A. (1956), *The Biology of Senescence*. London, Routledge & Kegan Paul.

Cooper, W. (1987), *No Change: A Biological Revolution for Women*, London, Arrow Books.

Coppen, A., Bishop, M., Beard, R. J., *et al.* (1981), 'Hysterectomy, hormones and behaviour – a prospective study'. *Lancet*, i, p. 8212.

Crapanzano, V., and Garrison, V., eds. (1977), *Case Studies in Spirit Possession*. New York, London, Wiley.

Culpeper, N. (1826), *Culpeper's Complete Herbal and English Physician*. Manchester, Gleave & Son.

Cummings, S. R., Black, D. M., and Rubin, S. M. (1989), 'Lifetime risks of hip, Colles' or vertebral fracture and coronary heart disease among white postmenopausal women'. *Archives of Internal Medicine*, 149, pp. 2445–8.

The Cyclopaedia of Practical Medicine: Comprising Treatises on the Nature and Treatment of Diseases, Materia Medica and Therapeutics, Medical Jurisprudence . . . eds. J. Forbes, A. Tweedy and J. Conolly (1833–5). London, Sherwood, Gilbert & Piper.

D[oolittle], H. (1956), *Tribute to Freud*. New York, Pantheon.

David, K. (1980), 'Hidden powers: cultural and socio-economic accounts of Jaffna women'. In *The Powers of Tamil Women*, ed. S. S. Wadley. Syracuse NY, Maxwell School of Citizenship and Public Affairs, pp. 93–136.

Davis, D. L. (1986), 'The meaning of menopause in a Newfoundland fishing village'. *Culture, Medicine and Psychiatry*, 10, pp. 73–94.

Davis, M. (1957), *The Sexual Responsibility of Women*. London, Heinemann.

Davis, P. (1988), *Aromatherapy: An A–Z*. Saffron Walden, C. W. Daniel.

De Beauvoir, Simone (1962), *The Prime of Life*, trans. P. Green. London, André Deutsch and Weidenfeld & Nicolson.

— (1965), *Force of Circumstance*, trans, R. Howard. London, André Deutsch and Weidenfeld & Nicolson.

— (1977), *Old Age*, trans. Patrick O'Brien. Harmondsworth, Penguin.

— (1984), *The Second Sex*, trans. and ed. H. M. Parshley. Harmondsworth, Penguin.

Dege, K., and Gretzinger, J. (1982), 'Attitudes of families towards menopause'. In *Changing Perspectives on Menopause*, eds. A. Voda, M. Dinnerstein and S. O'Donnell. Austin, University of Texas Press.

Dement, W., Richardson, G., Prinz, P., Carskadon, M., Kripke, D., and Czeisler, C. (1986), 'Changes of sleep and wakefulness with age'. In *Handbook of the Biology of Aging*, 2nd edn, eds. C. E. Finch and E. L. Schneider. New York, Van Nostrand Reinhold, pp. 721–43.

Dennerstein, L. (1987), 'Depression in the menopause'. *Obstetric and Gynaecologic Clinics of North America*, pp. 33–48.

Des Longrois, J. (1781), *Conseils aux femmes de quarante ans*. Paris, Méquignon.

Deutsch, H. (1945), *The Psychology of Women*. New York, Grune & Stratton.

— (1973), *Confrontations with Myself: An Epilogue*. New York, Norton.

— (1984), 'The menopause'. *International Journal of Psycho-Analysis, 65* (1984), Pt I, pp. 55–62.

Dewees, W. P. (1833), *A Treatise on the Diseases of Females*. Philadelphia, Lea & Blanchard.

Dickinson, E. (1970), *The Complete Poems*, ed. T. H. Johnson. London, Faber & Faber.

Dickson, A., and Henriques, N. (1987), *Menopause: The Woman's View: A Change for the Better*. London, Grapevine.

Dinesen, I. (1934), *Seven Gothic Tales*, int. D. Caulfield. New York, Harrison Smith & Robert Haas.

— (1942), *Winter's Tales*. London, Putnam.

Dobson, R. (1965), *Cock Crow*. Sydney, Angus & Robertson.

Dominian, J. (1977), 'The role of psychiatry in the menopause'. *Clinics in Obstetrics and Gynaecology* 4 (1).

Donegan, J. (1986), *Hydropathic Highway to Health: Women and Water-cure in Ante-bellum America*. New York, Greenwood Press.

Donovan, J. C. (1951), 'The menopausal syndrome. A study of case histories'. *American Journal of Obstetrics and Gynaecology*, 62, pp. 1281–91.

Drake, E. F. (1902), *What Every Woman of Forty-five Ought to Know*. Philadelphia, Sylvanus Stall.

Dreifus, C. (1977), *Seizing Our Bodies*. New York, Vintage Books.

Du Toit, B. (1984), 'The cultural climacteric in cross-cultural perspective'. *The Climacteric in Perspective: Proceedings of the Fourth International Congress on the Menopause, Held at Lake Buena Vista, Florida, October 28–November 2, 1984*, eds. M. Notevolitz and P. A. Van Keep. Lancaster, MTP Press.

Dworkin, A. (1987), *Intercourse*. London, Secker & Warburg.

Ehrenreich, B., and English, D. (1973), *Witches, Midwives and Nurses*. Detroit, Black & Red.

Eisner, H., and Kelly, L. (1980), 'Attitude of women toward the menopause'. Paper presented at Gerontological Society Meeting, San Diego, California.

Eliot, G. (1895), *Adam Bede*. Edinburgh and London, Blackwood.

Ellman, M. (1968), *Thinking about Women*. London, Macmillan.

English, O. S., and Pearson, G. H. J. (1958), *Emotional Problems of Living: Avoiding the Neurotic Pattern*. London, George Allen & Unwin.

Erikson, E. (1951), *Child and Society*. New York, Imago.

Erskine, B. E. S. (1915), *Anna Jameson: Letters and Friendships*. London, T. Fisher Unwin.

Evans, B. (1988), *Life Change: A Guide to the Menopause, its Effects and Treatment*, 4th edn. London, Pan Books.

Exton-Smith, A. N. (1986), 'Mineral metabolism'. In *Handbook of the Biology of Aging*, 2nd edn, eds. C. E. Finch and E. L. Schneider. New York, Van Nostrand Reinhold, pp. 721–43.

Fairfax family, *Arcana Fairfaxiana Manuscripta* facs., int. G. Weddell. Newcastle-on-Tyne, Mawson, Swan & Morgan.

Fairfield, L. (1923), 'An Address on the Health of Professional Women'. *Lancet*, 3 July.

Fairhurst, E., and Lightup, R. (1980), 'Being menopausal: Women and medical treatment'. Paper presented to the medical sociology group of the British Sociological Association at the University of Warwick, 1980.

Fairlie, J., Nelson, J., and Popplestone, R. (1988), *Menopause – A Time for Positive Change*. London, Javelin Books.

Faithfull, T. (1968), *The Future of Women and Other Essays*. London, New Age Publishers.

Flamigni, C., and Givens, J. R., eds. (1982), *The Gonadatrophins: Basic Science and Clinical Aspects in Females*. London, Academic Press.

Fothergill, J. (1849), 'On the management proper at the cessation of the menses'. *Essays on Puerperal Fever and Other Diseases peculiar to Women*, ed. F. Churchill. London, Sydenham Society.

Fothergill, J. M. (1874), *The Maintenance of Health: A Medical Work for Lay Readers*. London, Smith, Elder & Co.

— (1885), *The Diseases of the Sedentary and Advanced Life: A Work for Medical and Lay Readers*. London, Baillière & Co.

Freud, S. (1987), *On Psychopathology, Inhibitions, Symptoms and Anxiety and Other Works*, Pelican Freud Library, Vol. 10. Harmondsworth, Penguin.

Fuchs, E. (1978), *The Second Season: Life, Love and Sex for Women in the Middle Years*. New York, Doubleday.

Furuhjelm, M. (1966), 'Urinary excretion of hormones during the climacteric'. *Acta Obstetrica Gynecologica*, 129, p. 557.

Galbraith, A. M. (1904), *The Four Epochs of a Woman's Life: A Study in Hygiene*. Philadelphia, W. B. Saunders & Co.

Gardanne, C. P. L. de (1816), *Avis aux femmes qui entrent dans l'âge critique*. Paris, Gabon.

— (1821), *De la Ménopause, ou de l'Age Critique des Femmes*. Paris, Méquignon-Marvis.

Gaskell, E. C. (1954), *Cranford*. London, J. M. Dent.

Gath, D., Cooper, P., and Day, A. (1982), 'Hysterectomy and psychiatric disorder: Levels of psychiatric morbidity before and after hysterectomy'. *British Journal of Psychiatry*, 140 (4), pp. 335–42.

Gayanake, I. (1987), 'Cessation of childbearing and the absence of contraception in Sri Lanka'. *Journal of Bio-social Science*, 19, pp. 65–71.

Geokas, M. C., and Haverback, B. J. (1969), 'The aging gastro-intestinal tract'. *American Journal of Surgery*, 117, pp. 881–92.

Gerard, J. (1985), *Gerard's herball: The Essence thereof Distill'd* by Marcus Woodward from the edition of Th. Johnson, 1636. London, Bracken Books.

Giele, J. Z. (1982), *Women in the Middle Years: Current Knowledge and Directions for Research and Policy*. New York, Wiley.

Gleason, R. B. (1870), *Talks to my Patients*. British Museum.

Goldsmith, J. (1984), *Childbirth Wisdom from the World's Oldest Societies*. New York, Congdon & Weed.

Goodale, Jane C. (1980), *Tiwi Wives. A Study of the Women of Melville Island, North Australia*. Seattle and London, University of Washington Press.

Goulin J., and Jourdain, A. L. B. (1771), *Le Médecin des Dames ou l'Art de les conserver en santé*. Paris, s. t.

Gowan, G., Warren, L. W., and Young, J. L. (1985), 'Medical perceptions of menopausal symptoms'. *Psychology of Women Quarterly*, 9 (1), pp. 3–14.

Greenblatt, R. (1974), *The Menopausal Syndrome*. New York, Medcom Press.

Greene, J. G. (1984), *The Social and Psychological Origins of the Climacteric Syndrome*. Aldershot, Gower.

— and Cooke, D. J. (1980), 'Life stress and symptoms at the climacteric'. *British Journal of Psychiatry*, 136, pp. 486–91.

Greer, G., Hastings, S., Medoff, J., and Sansone, M. (1989), *Kissing the Rod: An Anthology of Seventeenth Century Women's Verse*. London, Virago Press.

Guinan, M. E. (1987), 'Osteoporosis and estrogen replacement therapy – the jury is still out'. *Journal of the American Medical Women's Association*, 42 (3), pp. 92–3.

Haight, G. S. (1954–6), *The Eliot Letters*. London, Oxford University Press.

— (1969), *George Eliot: A Biography*. Oxford, Oxford University Press.

Halsband, R. (1960), *The Life of Lady Mary Wortley Montagu*. New York, Oxford University Press.

Hallström, T. (1979), 'Sexuality of women in middle age: the Göteborg study'. In *Fertility in Middle Age: Proceedings of the Eighth IPPF Biomedical Workshop*, eds. A. S. Parkes, M. A. Herbertson and J. Cole. *Journal of Biosocial Science*, Suppl. 6, London, Galton Foundation.

Hancock, E. (1985), 'Age or experience?' In 'The timing of women's psychosocial changes'. *Human Development*, 28, pp. 259–280.

Hanifi, M. J. (1978), 'The family in Afghanistan'. In *The Family in Asia*, eds. M. S. Das and P. D. Bardis. New Delhi, Vikas.

Hannon, L. F. (1972), *The Second Chance: The Life and Work of Dr Paul Niehans*. London, W. H. Allen.

Haspels, A. A., and Musaph, H., eds. (1979), *Psychosomatics in Peri-Menopause*. Lancaster, MTP Press.

Hausman P. B., and Weksler, M. E. (1986), 'Changes in the immune response with age'. *Handbook of the Biology of Aging*, 2nd edn., eds. C. E. Finch and E. L. Schneider. New York, Van Nostrand Reinhold, pp. 414–32.

Hayley, W. (1785), *A Philosophical, Historical and Moral Essay on Old Maids*.

Heller, J. (1974), *Something Happened*. London, Jonathan Cape.

Hellman, L. (1972), *An Unfinished Woman*. Harmondsworth, Penguin.

Henderson, B. E., Ross, R. K., and Lobo, R. A. (1988), 'Re-evaluating the role of progesterone therapy after the menopause'. *Fertility-Sterility*, 49 (Suppl.) 9s–13s.

Henderson, H. W. (1928), *Dianne de Poytiers*. London, Methuen.

Henningsen, G. (1980), *The Witches' Advocate: Basque Witchcraft and the Spanish Inquisition*. Reno, University of Nevada Press.

Herman, G. E. (1898), *Diseases of Women: A Clinical Guide to their Diagnosis and Treatment*. London, Cassell & Co.

— (1903) *Diseases of Women: A Clinical Guide to their Diagnosis and Treatment*, rev. edn. London, Cassell & Co.

— (1907) *Diseases of Women: A Clinical Guide to their Diagnosis and Treatment*, new and rev. edn. London, Cassell & Co.

— and Maxwell, R. D. (1913), *Diseases of Women: A Clinical Guide to their Diagnosis and Treatment*, London, Cassell & Co.

Hochman, S. (1972), *Earthworks: Poems 1960–1970*. London, Secker & Warburg.

Holte, A., and Mikkelsen, A. (1982), 'Menstrual coping style, social background and climacteric symptoms'. *Psychiatry and Social Science*, 2, pp. 41–5.

Horne, J. A., and Porter, J. M. (1975), 'Exercise and human sleep'. *Nature*, 256, pp. 573–5.

Horney, K. (1967), *Feminine Psychology*, ed. and int. H. Kelman. London, Routledge & Kegan Paul.

Hunter, D., Akande, O., Carr, P., and Stallworthy, J. (1973), 'The clinical and endocrinological effect of oestradiol implants at the time of hysterectomy and bilateral salpingo-oophorectomy'. *British Journal of Obstetrics and Gynaecology*, 80, pp. 827–33.

Hunter, M. (1990), 'Emotional well-being, sexual behaviour and hormone replacement therapy'. *Maturitas*, 12.

Hutton, J., Murray, M., Jacobs, H., and James, V. (1978), 'Relation between plasma oestrone and oestradiol and climacteric symptoms'. *Lancet*, i, pp. 678–81.

International Health Foundation (1969), *A Study of the Attitudes of Women in Belgium, France, Great Britain, Italy and West Germany*, Brussels, IHF.

— (1975), *The Mature Woman: A First Analysis of a Psychosocial Study of Chronological and Menstrual Aging*. Geneva, IHF.

— (1977), *La ménopause: étude effectuée en Belgique auprôs de 922 femmes entre 45 et 55 ans*. Geneva, IHF.

Jackson, S. H. (1798), *Cautions to Women Respecting the State of Pregnancy*. London, G. G. & J. Robson.

Jacobs, Stanley (1989), 'A Philosophy of Energy'. *Holistic Medicine*, 4 (2).

Jaszman, L., Van Lith, N., and Zaat, J. (1969a), 'The age at menopause in the Netherlands'. *International Journal of Fertility*, 14, pp. 106–17.

— (1969b), 'The peri-menopausal symptoms: the statistical analysis of a survey'. *Medical Gynaecology and Sociology*, 4, pp. 268–77.

Jebb, C. L. (1960), *With Dearest Love to All: The Life and Letters of Lady Jebb*, ed. M. R. Bobbitt. London, Faber & Faber.

Jennings, Elizabeth (1986), *Collected Poems*. London, Carcanet.

Johnson, B. (1988), *Lady of the Beasts: Ancient Images of the Goddess and Her Sacred Animals*. San Francisco, Harper & Row.

Johnson, M. L., ed. (1980), *Transitions in Middle and Later Life*. London, British Society of Gerontology.

Jones, J. (1985), *Labor of Love, Labor of Sorrow: Black Women, Work and the Family, from Slavery to the Present*. New York, Vintage.

Jorden, E. (1603), *A Briefe Discourse of a Disease called the Suffocation of the Mother*. London.

— (1631), *A Discourse of Naturall Bathes and Minerall Waters*. London.

Karacan, I., Rosenbloom, A. L., London, J. H., Salis, P. J., Thornby, J. I., and Williams, R. L. (1973), 'The effects of acute fasting on sleep and sleep growth hormone response'. *Psychosomatics*, 14, 33–7.

Kaufert, P. A. (1982), 'Anthropology and the menopause; the development of a theoretical framework'. *Maturitas*, 4, pp. 181–93.

—, and Tate, R. and Gilbert, P. (1986), 'Women, menopause and medicalisation'. *Culture, Medicine and Psychiatry*, 10, pp. 7–19.

— (1987), 'Defining menopausal status: the impact of longitudinal data'. *Maturitas*, 9, pp. 217–26.

Keep, P. A. van (1990), 'The history and rationale of hormone replacement therapy'. *Maturitas*, 12, pp. 163–70.

—, and Kellerhals, J. (1974), 'The impact of socio-cultural factors on symptom formation: some results of a study on ageing women in Switzerland'. *Psychotherapy and Psychosomatics*, 23, pp. 251–63.

—, Utian, W. H., and Vermeulen, A., eds. (1982), *The Controversial Climacteric: The workshop moderators' reports presented at the Third International Congress on the Menopause held in Ostend, Belgium, in June, 1981, under the auspices of the International Menopause Society*.

—, Serr, D. M., and Greenblatt, R., eds. (1979), *The Male and Female Climacteric*. Lancaster, MTP Press.

King, J. (1844), *Observations on Hydropathy*. London.

Kisch, E. H. (1926), *The Sexual Life of Woman in its Pathological and Hygienic Aspects*.

Kligman, A. M., Grove, G. L., and Balin, A. K. (1986) 'Aging of human skin'. In *Handbook of the Biology of Aging*, 2nd edn, eds. C. E. Finch and E. L. Schneider, New York, Van Nostrand Reinhold pp. 820–41.

Knopp, R. H. (1988), 'Cardiovascular effects of endogenous and exogenous sex hormones over a woman's lifetime'. *American Journal of Obstetrics and Gynaecology*, 158 (Suppl.), pp. 1630–43.

Koster, A. (1990), 'Hormone replacement therapy; use patterns in 51-year-old Danish women'. *Maturitas*, 12, pp. 345–56.

Kraepelin, E. (1896), *Psychiatrie; ein Lehrbuch für Studierende und Aertze*. Leipzig, Barth.

— (1904), *Lectures on Clinical Psychiatry*. London, Baillière & Co.

The Ladies Physical Directory (1727), London.

La Tour du Pin, Madame de (1969), *Memoirs of Madame de la Tour du Pin*, ed. and trans. Felice Harcourt. London.

Laurie, J. (1842), *Homeopathic Domestic Medicine*. London.

Lauritzen, C. (1973), 'The management of the pre-menopausal and the post-menopausal patient'. *Frontiers in Hormone Research*, 2, pp. 2–21.

— (1990), 'Clinical use of oestrogens and progestogens'. *Maturitas*, 12 (3).

Lessing, Doris (1973), *The Summer Before the Dark*. London, Jonathan Cape.

Levinson, D. J., Darrow, C. H., Klein, E. B., Levinson, M. H., and McKee, B. (1978), *Seasons of a Man's Life*. New York, Knopf.

Lock, M. (1985), 'Models and practice in medicine; menopause as syndrome or life transition'. In *Physicians of Western Medicine*, eds. R. A. Hahn and A. D. Gaines. Boston, D. Reidel.

— (1986), 'Ambiguities of aging: Japanese experience and perceptions of menopause'. *Culture, Medicine and Psychiatry*, 10, pp. 23–46.

Lonsdale, R., ed. (1989), *Eighteenth-Century Women Poets: An Oxford Anthology*, Oxford, Oxford University Press.

Lozman, H., Barlow, A. L., and Levitt, D. G. (1971), 'Piperazine oestrone sulphate and conjugated oestrogen equine in the treatment of the menopausal syndrome'. *Southern Medical Journal*, 64, pp. 1143–9.

Luhrmann, T. M. (1989), *Persuasions of the Witches' Craft: Ritual Magic and Witchcraft in Present Day England*. Oxford, Basil Blackwell.

Luria, G. and Tiger, V. (1976), *Everywoman*. New York, Random House.

McFayden, U. M., Oswald, I., and Lewis, S. A. (1973), 'Starvation and human slow wave sleep'. *Journal of Applied Physiology*, 35, pp. 391–4.

McGinn, B. (1985), '*Teste David cum Sibylla*: The significance of the Sibylline tradition in the Middle Ages'. In *Women of the Medieval World: Essays in Honor of John H. Mundy*, eds. J. Kirschner and S. F. Wemple. Oxford, Basil Blackwell.

McGrady, P. (1969), *The Youth Doctors*. London, Barker.

McGuigan, B. (1980), *Women's Lives: New Theory, Research, and Policy*.

Ann Arbor, Center for Continuing Education for Women, University of Michigan.

McKean, P. F. (1982), 'Rangda the witch'. In *Mother Worship: Themes and Variations*, ed. J. J. Preston. Chapel Hill, University of North Carolina Press.

Mackenzie, R. (1985), *Menopause: A Practical Self-help Guide for Women*. London, Sheldon Press, SPCK.

McKinley, S. M. (1987), 'Perimenopausal and postmenopausal use of exogenous oestrogen since 1981 in a general population'. 5th International Conference on the Menopause. Carnforth, Parthenon, p. 8246.

McNamara, J. K. (1985), *A New Song: Celibate Women in the First Three Christian Centuries*. New York, Harrington Park Press.

McPherson, M. (1981), 'Menopause as disease: the social construction of a metaphor'. *Advances in Nursing Science*, 3 (2), pp. 95–113.

Magne, E. (1926), *Ninon de L'Anclos*, trans. and ed. G. S. Stevenson. London, Arrowsmith.

Mankowitz, A. (1984), *Change of Life: A Psychological Study of Dreams and the Menopause*. Toronto, Inner City Books.

Márquez, Gabriel García (1988), *Love in the Time of Cholera*, trans. E. Grossmann. London, Jonathan Cape.

Mason, S. (1845), *The Philosophy of Female Health*. London, Hughes.

Masoro, E. J. (1986), 'Metabolism'. In *Handbook of the Biology of Aging*, 2nd edn, eds. C. E. Finch and E. L. Schneider. New York, Van Nostrand Reinhold.

Mathews, K. A., Meilahn, E., Kuller, L. H., *et al.* (1989), 'Menopause and risk factors for coronary heart disease'. *New England Journal of Medicine*, 308, pp. 862–8.

Maubery, J. (1724), *The Female Physician*. London, J. Holland.

Meigs, C. D. (1848), *Females and Their Diseases*. Philadelphia, Lea & Blanchard.

Menville de Ponsan, C. F. (1840), *De L'Age Critique chez les Femmes, des maladies qui peuvent survenir a cette époque de la vie, et les moyens de les combattre et les prevenir*. Paris, Baillière.

Michaëlis, K. (1912), *The Dangerous Age*, intr. Marcel Prévost. London, New York, John Lane.

Miles L. E., and Dement, W. C. (1980), 'Sleep and aging'. *Sleep*, 3, pp. 119–220.

Mishell, D. R. Jr, ed. (1987), *Menopause, Physiology and Management*. Chicago, MTP Press.

Montagu, M. W. (1967), *The Complete Letters of Lady Mary Wortley Montagu*, ed. R. Halsband. Oxford, Clarendon Press.

Moore, G. (1917), *Lewis Seymour and Some Women*. London, William, Heinemann.

Moreau de la Sarthe, J. L. (1803), *L'Histoire naturelle de la femme*. Paris, Dupart.

Morton, J. (1977), *Major Medicinal Plants: Botany, Culture and Uses*. Springfield, Ill., Charles C. Thomas.

Muir, W. (1969), *Laconics, Jingles and Other Verses*. London, Enitharmon Press.

Murdoch, Iris (1987), *Bruno's Dream*. Harmondsworth, Penguin.

Mulley, G., and Mitchell, J. (1976), 'Menopausal flushing: Does oestrogen therapy make sense?' *Lancet*, i, pp. 1397–9.

Murray, M. (1921), *The Witch-cult in Western Europe: A Study in Anthropology*. Oxford, Clarendon Press.

Mvungi, M. A. (1985), 'Mwipenza the Killer'. In *Unwinding Threads: Writing by Women in Africa*, ed. C. H. Bruner. London, Heinemann.

Nachtigall, L. E and L. B. (1990), 'Protecting older women from their growing risk of cardiac disease'. *Geriatrics*, 45 (5), pp. 24–34.

Nathanson, C. (1980), 'Social roles and health status among women: the significance of employment'. *Social Science and Medicine*, 14a, pp. 463–71.

Neugarten, B. L. (1968), *Middle Age and Aging*. Chicago, University of Chicago Press.

—, and Kraines, R. (1965), 'Menopausal symptoms in women of various ages'. *Psychosomatic Medicine*, 27, pp. 266–73.

Notevolitz, M., and Keep, P. A. van, eds. (1984), *The Climacteric in Perspective: Proceedings of the Fourth International Congress on the Menopause, Held at Lake Buena Vista, Florida, October 28–November 2, 1984*. Lancaster, MTP Press.

Parker, D. C., Rossman, L. G., and Vanderlaan, E. F. (1972), 'Persistence of human growth hormone release during sleep in fasted and nonisocalorically fed normal subjects'. *Metabolism*, 21, pp. 241–52.

Parkes, A. S., Herbertson, M. A., and Cole, J. (1979), *Fertility in Middle Age: Proceedings of the Eighth IPPF Biomedical Workshop Journal of Biosocial Science*, Suppl. 6. London, Galton Foundation.

Parry, B. M. (1980), 'Women's disorders'. *The Psychiatric Clinics of North America*, 12 (1).

Pastan, Linda (1978), *The Five Stages of Grief.* New York, W. W. Norton.

Pech[e]y, J. (1699), *A Plain and Short Treatise of an Apoplexy, Convulsions, Colick . . . and other Violent and Dangerous Diseases.* London.

Pettiti, D. B., Wingerd, J., Pellegrin, F., and Ramcharan, S. (1979), 'Risk of vascular disease in women. Smoking, oral contraceptives, non-contraceptive estrogens and other factors'. *Journal of the American Medical Association*, 242, pp. 1150–54.

Pincus, G., Romanoff, L. P., and Carlo, J. (1954), 'The excretion of urinary steroids by men and women of various ages'. *Journal of Gerontology*, p. 9.

Ploss, H. H., and Bartels, M. and P. (1935), *Woman: An Historical, Gynaecological and Anthropological Compendium*, ed. and trans. E. Dingwall. London, William Heinemann.

Polit, D., and Larocco, S. (1980), 'Social and psychological correlates of menopausal symptoms'. *Psychosomatic Medicine*, 42, pp. 335–45.

Powell, M. (1972), *The Treasure Upstairs.* London, Pan Books.

Procope, B. (1968), 'Studies on the urinary excretion, biological effects and origin of oestrogens in post-menopausal women'. *Acta Endocrinologica*, Suppl. 135:1.

Rees M. C. P., and Barlow, D. H. (1991), 'Quantitation of hormone replacement induced withdrawal bleeds'. *British Journal of Obstetrics and Gynaecology*, 98, p. 1067.

Reitz, R. (1979), *Menopause: A Positive Approach.* Hassocks, Harvester Press.

Riphagen, F. E., Fortney, J. A., and Koelb, S. (1988), 'Contraception in women over forty'. *Journal of Biosocial Science*, pp. 127–42.

Rosenthal, S. H. (1968), 'The involutional depressive syndrome'. *American Journal of Psychiatry*, 124, Suppl. 11, pp. 21–35.

Ross, M. S. F. and Brain, R. R. (1977), *An Introduction to Phytopharmacy.* Tunbridge Wells, Pitman Medical Publishing.

Ross, R. K., Paganini-Hill, A., Mack, T. M., Arthur, M., Henderson,

B. E. (1981), 'Menopause, oestrogen therapy and protection from death from Ischaemic Heart Disease', *Lancet*, 18 April (2).

Rossetti, C. (1908), *The Poetical Works of Christina Rossetti* with memoir and notes by W. Rossetti. London, Macmillan & Co.

Rossi, A. A. (1980), 'Lifespan theories and women's lives'. *Signs: Journal of Women in Society and Culture*, 6, pp. 4–32.

— (1986), 'Sex and gender in the aging society'. In *Our Aging Society . . . Paradox and Promise*, ed. A. Rossi. New York, W. W. Norton.

Roth, J. A., with the collaboration of Richard R. Hanson (1977), *Health Purifiers and Their Enemies: A Study of the Natural Health Movement in the United States with a Comparison to its Counterpart in Germany*. New York, Prodist; London, Croom Helm.

Rudolph-Touba, J. (1978), 'Marriage and the family in Iran'. In *The Family in Asia*, eds. M. S. Das and P. D. Bardis. New Delhi, Vikas.

Ruzicka, L. T., and Bhatia, S. (1982), 'Coital frequency and sexual abstinence in rural Bangladesh'. *Journal of Biosocial Science*, 14, pp. 397–420.

Sackville-West, V. (1931), *All Passion Spent*. London, L. & V. Woolf.

S[aucerotte], C. (1828), *Nouveaux conseils aux femmes sur l'âge prétendu critique*. Paris, Mme Auger-Méquignon.

Sayers, D. L. (1947), 'Strong Meat'. In *Creed or Chaos? and Other Essays in Popular Mythology*. London, Methuen & Co.

Sayers, J. (1991), *Mothering Psychoanalysis: Helene Deutsch, Karen Horney, Anna Freud, Melanie Klein*, London, Hamish Hamilton.

Schroeder, D., (1887), 'Oöphorectomy in neurotic affections'. *British Journal of Gynaecology*, 3, pp. 112–13.

Scot, R. (1585), *A Discoverie of Witchcraft*.

Seaman, B. (1969), *The Doctor's Case Against the Pill*. New York, P. H. Wyman.

— and Seaman, G., MD, (1977), *Women and the Crisis in Sex Hormones*. New York, Rawson Associates.

Selye, H., Strebel, R., and Mikulaj, L. (1963), 'A Progeria-like syndrome produced by Dihydrotachysterol and its prevention by Methyltestosterone and Ferric Dextran'. *Journal of the American Geriatrics Society*, Vol. 11 (i).

Severne, L. (1979), 'Psychosocial aspects of the menopause'. *Changing Perspectives on Menopause*, eds. A. Voda, M. Dinnerstein and S. O'Donnell. Austin, University of Texas Press.

Sévigné, Madame de (1927), *Letters of Madame de Sévigné to her Daughter and her Friends*, ed. Richard Aldington. London.

Sharma, V., and Saxena, M. (1981), 'Climacteric symptoms: A study in the Indian context'. *Maturitas*, 3, pp. 11–20.

Sheehy, G. (1976), *Passages: Predictable Crises of Adult Life*. New York, E. P. Dutton.

Sherman, B., Wallace, R. B., and Treloar, A. E. (1979), 'The menopausal transition: endocrinological and epidemiological considerations', *Fertility in Middle Age: Proceedings of the Eighth IPPF Biomedical Workshop*, eds. A. S. Parkes, M. A. Herbertson, and J. Cole. *Journal of Biosocial Science*, Suppl. 6, London, Galton Foundation.

Shock, N. W. (1986), 'Longitudinal Studies of Aging in Humans'. In *Handbook of the Biology of Aging*, 2nd edn, eds. C. E. Finch and E. L. Schneider. New York, Van Nostrand Reinhold, pp. 721–43.

Shreeve, C. M. (1987), *Overcoming the Menopause Naturally: How to Cope – without Artificial Hormones*. London, Arrow Books.

Shuttle, P., and Redgrove, P. (1986), *The Wise Wound: Myths, Realities and Meanings of Menstruation*. London, Grove Press.

Simms, H. S., and Stolman, A. (1937), 'Changes in human tissue electrolytes in senescence'. *Science*, No. 86, pp. 269–70; republished in *Aging*, ed. G. H. Emerson, Benchmark Papers in Human Physiology, 11. Stroudsburg Pa, Dowden, Hutchinson & Ross, 1977.

Smith, Stevie, (1979), *The Holiday*. London, Virago.

— (1985), *The Collected Poems of Stevie Smith*, Harmondsworth, Penguin Books.

Snaith M. L. and Ridley, B. (1948), 'Gynaecological psychiatry: a preliminary report on an experimental clinic'. *British Medical Journal*, ii, pp. 428–30.

Stamm, L. (1984), 'Differential power of women over the life course: a case study of age roles as an indicator of power'. In *Social Power and Influence of Women*, eds. L. Stamm and C. D. Ryff. Epping, Bowker.

Stevenson, G. S., trans and ed. (1925), *The Letters of Madame: The Correspondence of Elizabeth Charlotte of Bavaria, Princess Palatine, Duchess of Orleans*. London, Chapman & Dodd.

Stone, S., Mickal, A., Rye, P., and Phillip, H. (1975), 'Postmenopausal symptomatology, maturation index, and plasma estrogen levels'. *Obstetrics and Gynecology*, 45, pp. 625–7.

Stuart, M., ed. (1979), *The Encyclopedia of Herbs and Herbalism*. London, Orbis.

Studd, J. W. W., Chakravarti, S., and Oram, D. (1977), 'The climacteric'. *Clinics in Obstetrics and Gynaecology*, 4, 1, pp. 3–29.

Studd, J. W. W. and Thom, M. H. (1981), 'Oestrogens and endometrial cancer', *Progress in Obstetrics and Gynaecology*, ed. J. W. Studd. London, Churchill Livingstone.

— Paterson, M. E. L. and Wade-Evans, T. (1980), 'The prevention and treatment of endometrial pathology in post-menopausal women receiving exogenous oestrogens'. In *The Menopause and Post-menopause*, eds. N. and R. Paoletti and J. L. Ambrus. Lancaster, MTP Press.

Sturdee, D. W., and Brincat, M. (1988), 'The hot flush'. In *The Menopause*, eds. J. W. W. Studd and M. I. Whitehead, with a Foreword by R. M. Greenblatt. Oxford, Blackwell Scientific Publications.

Summers, M., ed. (1967), *The Works of Aphra Behn*, New York, Phaeton.

Sutherland, E. (1985), 'New Life at Kyerefaso'. In *Unwinding Threads: Writing by Women in Africa*, ed. C. H. Bruner. London, Heinemann.

Sydenham, T. (1701), *The Whole Works of that Excellent Practical Physician*, trans. J. Pechey. London, R. Wellington.

Tait, L. (1877), *Diseases of Women*. London, Williams & Norgate.

Thompson, B., Hart, S., and Durno, D. (1973), 'Menopausal age and symptomatology in general practice'. *Journal of Biosocial Science*, 5, pp. 71–82.

Thompson, S. G., Meade T. W., and Greenberg, G. (1989), 'The use of hormone therapy and the risk of stroke and myocardial infarction in women'. *Journal of Epidemiology and Community Health*, Vol. 43, No. 2.

Thurman, J. (1982), *Isak Dinesen – The Life of Karen Blixen*. Harmondsworth, Penguin.

Tiger, V. (1986), 'Woman of many summers: *The Summer Before the Dark*'. In *Critical Essays on Doris Lessing,* eds. V. Tiger and C. Sprague. Boston, G. K. Hall.

Tilt, E. J. (1857), *The Change of Life in Health and Disease*. London, John Churchill.

Tolstoy, S. A. (1929), *The Countess Tolstoy's Later Diary 1891–1897*. trans. and int. A. Werth. London, Victor Gollancz.

459

Treloar, A., Boyton, R. D., Benn, B. G., and Brown, B. W. (1967), 'Variation of the human menstrual cycle through reproductive life'. *International Journal of Fertility* 12, pp. 77–126.

Trimmer, E. (1967), *Rejuvenation: The History of an Idea*. London. Robert Hale.

Trye, M. (1675), *Medicatrix, or the Woman-Physician*. London, Henry Broome & John Leete.

Utian, W. (1978), *The Menopause Manual: A Woman's Guide to the Menopause*. Lancaster, MTP Press.

— (1980), *The Menopause in Modern Perspective*. New York, Appleton, Century, Crofts.

— (1987), 'The fate of the untreated menopause'. *Obstetric and Gynaecological Clinics of North America*, 14 (1), pp. 1–11.

— and Serr, D. (1976), 'The climacteric syndrome'. In *Consensus on Menopause Research*, eds P. A. Van Keep *et al.* Lancaster, MTP Press.

Van Look, P. F. A., Lothian, H., Hunter, W. M. *et al.* (1977), 'Hypothalmic–pituitary–ovarian function in perimenopausal women'. *Clinics in Endocrinology*.

Vermeulen, A. (1979), 'Decline in sexual activity in aging men: correlation with sex hormone levels and testicular changes'. *Journal of Biosocial Science*, Suppl. 6 (1979) p. 5.

— (1983), 'Androgen secretion after age 50 in both sexes'. *Hormone Research*.

— and Verdonck, L. (1979), 'Factors affecting sex hormone levels in postmenopausal women'. *Journal of Steroid Biochemistry*, 11, pp. 899–904.

Voda, A., Dinnerstein, M., and O'Donnell, S. (eds.). (1982), *Changing Perspectives on Menopause*. Austin, University of Texas Press.

Wahl, P., Walden, C., and Knopp, R. (1983), 'Effect of estrogen/progesterone potency on lipid lipoprotein cholesterol'. *New England Journal of Medicine*, 321, pp. 641–6.

Walker, B. G. (1985), *The Crone, Women of Age, Wisdom, and Power*. San Francisco, Harper & Row.

Wallace, R. B., Sherman, B. M., Bean J. A., Leeper, J. P., and Treloar, A. E. (1978), 'Menstrual cycle patterns and breast cancer risk factors'. *Cancer Research*, 38, pp. 4021–4.

Weideger, P. (1976), *Female Cycles: Menstruation and Menopause*. London, Women's Press.

Weissmann, M. M. (1979), 'The myth of involutional melancholia'. *Journal of the American Medical Association*, Vol. 242, pp. 742 ff.

Westcott, P. (1987), *Alternative Health Care for Women*. Wellingborough, Thorsons.

Westkott, Marcia (1986), *The Feminist Legacy of Karen Horney*. New Haven and London, Yale University Press.

Whitehead, M. I., Campbell, S., Dyer, G., Collins, W. P., Pryse-Davies, J., Ryder, T. A., Rodney, M. I., McQueen, J., and King, R. (1978), 'Progestogen modification of endometrial histology in menopausal women'. *British Medical Journal*, 2 (6152), pp. 1643–4.

—, McQueen, J., Minardi, J. and Campbell, S. (1978), 'Clinical considerations in the management of the menopausal endometrium'. *Postgraduate Medical Journal*, 54 (2), pp. 59–64.

—, Siddle, N. C., Lane, G., *et al.* (1987), 'The pharmacology of progestogens'. In *Menopause, Physiology and Management*, ed. D. R. Mishell, Jr. Chicago.

Wier, J. (1563), *De Praestigiis Daemonum*.

Wilbush, J. (1988), 'Climacteric disorders – historical perspectives'. In *The Menopause*, eds. J. W. W. Studd and M. I. Whitehead. Oxford, Blackwell Scientific Publications.

Williams, R., Karacan, I., and Hursch, C. (1974), *Electroencephalography EEG of Human Sleep: Clinical Applications*. London, Wiley.

Wilson, R. A. (1966), *Feminine Forever*. London, W. H. Allen.

Wiser, C. V. (1978), *Four Families of Karimpur*, Syracuse NY, Maxwell School of Citizenship and Public Affairs.

461

Index